THE POETRY OF BARUCH

SOCIETY OF BIBLICAL LITERATURE
SEPTUAGINT AND COGNATE STUDIES

Edited by
George W. E. Nickelsburg
and
Harry M. Orlinsky

Number 10

THE POETRY OF BARUCH: A RECONSTRUCTION AND ANALYSIS OF THE ORIGINAL HEBREW TEXT OF BARUCH 3:9–5:9

by
David G. Burke

THE POETRY OF BARUCH

A RECONSTRUCTION AND ANALYSIS
OF THE ORIGINAL HEBREW TEXT
OF BARUCH 3:9–5:9

by
David G. Burke

SCHOLARS PRESS

Published by

SCHOLARS PRESS
101 Salem Street
PO Box 2268
Chico, California 95927

THE POETRY OF BARUCH
A RECONSTRUCTION AND ANALYSIS
OF THE ORIGINAL HEBREW TEXT
OF BARUCH 3:9–5:9

by
David G. Burke

Library of Congress Cataloging in Publication Data

Burke, David G
The poetry of Baruch

(Septuagint and cognate studies series ISSN 0145-2754)
"Hebrew text of . . . Baruch . . . together with the Greek and/or Syriac text and an English translation."
Bibliography: p.
Includes index.
1. Bible. O. T. Apocrypha. Baruch–Criticism, Textual. 2. Bible. O. T. Apocrypha. Baruch–Criticism, interpretation, etc. I. Bible. O. T. Apocrypha. Baruch. III, 9–V, 9. Polyglot. 1980. II. Title. III. Series: Septuagint and cognate studies.
BS1775.2.B87 229'.5 80-10271
ISBN 0-89130-382-0 pbk.

Printed in the United States of America

To Dewayne and Lydia

With appreciation and thanks

TABLE OF CONTENTS

page

LIST OF ABBREVIATIONS

Abbreviations not appearing in this list can be found in the *SBL Member's Handbook* (1980) 83-97.

Text and Versions

BH	Biblical Hebrew
BHS	K. Elliger and W. Rudolph (eds.), *Biblia Hebraica Stuttgartensia*. Stuttgart: Deutsche Bibelstiftung, 1967-1977.
MH	Mishnaic Hebrew
Aram	Aramaic
MT	Masoretic Text
Niph	Niphal stem
Hiph	Hiphil stem
Hithp	Hithpael stem
Ethpe	Ethpeel stem
K	Kethib
Qr	Qere
LXX (G)	Septuagint Version
G^B	Codex Vaticanus, Uncial (HP, II)
G^Q	Codex Marchalianus, Uncial (HP, XII)
G^V	Codex Venetus, Uncial (HP, 23)
G^A	Codex Alexandrinus, Uncial (HP, III)
G^S	Codex Sinaiticus, Uncial (lacks Baruch)
O	Origenic (Hexaplaric) Recension (Minusc. 88 + Syh)
L	Lucianic Recension (Major group: Minusc. 22,36,48,51,96,231,311,763)
l	(Minor group: Minusc. 62,198,407,449)
L'	L + l
C	Catenae (Major group: Minusc. 87,91,490,567)
c	(Minor group: Minusc. 49,90,764)
C'	C + c
86'	Minusc. 86 + 710 (of the G^Q text family)
106'	Minusc. 106 + 410 (of the G^B text family)
Th	Theodotian
Aq	Aquilla
Sym	Symmachus

Joseph	Josephus
Tht	Theodoret
Didym	Didymus Caecus
Olymp	Olympiodorus
Hi	Hieronymus (Jerome)
Sy	Syriac translation for Bar and Ep Jer
Syh	Syrohexaplar translation (cf. O)
Sy^L	Lagarde edition of Sy
Sy^W	Walton edition of Sy (in London Polyglot)
La	Vetus Latina
La^C	Codex Cavensis, Latin
La^L	Codex Legionensis, Latin
La^S	Codex Vallicellianus, Latin
La^V	Vulgate
Bo	Bohairic translation
Sa	Sahidic translation
Fa	Fayumic translation
Copt	Coptic translation, Bo + Sa (+ Fa)
Eth	Ethiopic translation
Arm	Armenian translation
Ar	Arabic translation
NT	New Testament
OT	Old Testament
RSV	*Revised Standard Version: Apocrypha* (1952)
NEB	*New English Bible: Apocrypha* (1970)
JB	*The Jerusalem Bible* (1966)
frg	fragment
mg	margin
ms, mss	manuscript(s)
nom	nominative
gen	genitive
dat	dative
acc	accusative
voc	vocative
[ ]	lacuna or restoration in cited text
< >	editorial addition in cited text
> <	editorial deletion in cited text
>	becomes

( )	hypothetical reconstruction, or explanatory or clarificatory addition
::	contra

Publications

Boling	R. G. Boling. "Synonymous Parallelism in the Psalms." Ph.D. dissertation, Johns Hopkins University, 1959.
Harwell	R. R. Harwell. *The Principal Versions of Baruch.* New Haven, 1915.
HDB	James Hastings (ed.), *A Dictionary of the Bible.* Vols. 1-4. New York, 1905.
HNTT	R. H. Pfeiffer. *History of New Testament Times: with an Introduction to the Apocrypha* New York, 1949.
HP	R. Holmes and J. Parsons. *Vetus Testamentum Graecum cum variis lectionibus* (1798-1827).
HR	E. Hatch and H. A. Redpath. *A Concordance to the Septuagint.* Vols. 1, 2, and Suppls. Oxford, 1897-1906.
HSAT	*Die Heilige Schrift des alten Testaments*, Tübingen
Jackson	T. A. Jackson. "Words in Parallelism in Old Testament Poetry." Ph.D. dissertation, Johns Hopkins University, 1970.
Kahana	A. Kahana. *Hassefārîm Haḥîṣônîm.* Vol. 1. Tel Aviv, 1936-37.
Kneucker	J. J. Kneucker. *Das Buch Baruch.* Leipzig, 1879.
LAVTG	O. F. Fritzsche. *Libri Apocryphi Veteris Testamenti Graece.* Leipzig, 1871.
LVTAS	P. de Lagarde. *Libri Veteris Testamenti: Apocryphi Syriace.* Leipzig, 1861.
Mandelkern	S. Mandelkern. *Veteris Testamenti Concordantiae Hebraicae atque Chaldaicae.* Vols. 1, 2. Graz, 1955.
PS	R. Payne Smith. *Thesaurus Syriacus.* Tomes 1-4. Oxford, 1879-1897.
Rahlfs	A. Rahlfs (ed.), *Septuaginta.* Vols. 1, 2. 5th ed. Stuttgart, 1952.

ZÄS	*Zeitschrift für ägyptische Sprache und Altertumskunde*, Berlin
Ziegler	J. Ziegler (ed.), *Septuaginta, Vetus Testamentum Graecum Auctoritate Societatis Litterarum Gottingensis*, XV: *Ieremias, Baruch, Threni, Epistula Ieremiae*. Göttingen, 1957.

TRANSLITERATION OF HEBREW

Consonants	*Vowels*
ʼ = א	bāh = בָה, בָּה
b = ב, בּ	bô = בוֹ
g = ג, גּ	bû = בוּ
d = ד, דּ	bê = בֵי
h = ה	bè = בֶי
w = ו	bî = בִי
z = ז	bā = בָ
ḥ = ח	bō = בֹ
ṭ = ט	bū = בֻ
y = י	bē = בֵ
k = ך, כ, כּ	bī = בִ
l = ל	ba = בַ
m = ם, מ	bo = בָ
n = ן, נ	bu = בֻ
s = ס	be = בֶ
ʻ = ע	bi = בִ
p = ף, פ, פּ	b^a = בֲ
ṣ = ץ, צ	b^o = בֳ
q = ק	b^e = בֱ
r = ר	b^e = בְ
ś = שׂ	beh = בֶה
š = שׁ	$-^a$ḥ = חַ
t = ת, תּ	

TRANSLITERATION OF GREEK

a	= α	o	= ο
b	= β	p	= π
g	= γ	r	= ρ
d	= δ	rh	= ῥ
e	= ε	s	= σ, ς
z	= ζ	t	= τ
ē	= η	y	= υ
th	= ϑ	u	= υ (in diphthongs)
i	= ι	ph	= φ
k	= ϰ	ch	= χ
l	= λ	ps	= ψ
m	= μ	ō	= ω
n	= ν	h	= ‘
x	= ξ		

TRANSLITERATION OF SYRIAC

' =	ܐ	ʿ =	ܥ, ܥ
b =	ܒ	p =	ܦ
g =	ܓ	ṣ =	ܨ
d =	ܕ	q =	ܩ
h =	ܗ	r =	ܪ
w =	ܘ	s =	ܫ
z =	ܙ	t =	ܬ, ܬ
ḥ =	ܚ	a =	◌ܰ
ṭ =	ܛ	ā =	◌ܳ
y =	ܝ	e,ē =	◌ܶ
k =	ܟ, ܟ	i,ī =	◌ܺ
l =	ܠ, ܠ	u,ū =	◌ܽ
m =	ܡ, ܡ	-e =	*Murmelvokal*
n =	ܢ, ܢ	( ) =	*linea occultans*
s =	ܣ		

LIST OF TABLES

PREFACE

An interest in the poetic portion of the Apocryphal Book of Baruch, as well as a persistent curiosity about the nature and form of its original text, was first awakened for me while doing research for a seminar in Hebrew Poetry offered by Dr. Delbert R. Hillers at The Johns Hopkins University. Exploratory probes of the versional texts of Baruch indicated not only that the original language was Hebrew, but also that reconstruction would yield many commendable examples of classical Hebrew poetry. The following study, thus stimulated, represents the end product of a thoroughgoing inquiry into the long controverted question of the original text, form, and character of the Baruch poetry.

While the vast majority of biblical scholars now agree that the original language of Bar 3:9-5:9 was Hebrew, the only thoroughgoing attempt to demonstrate this by means of a reconstruction of the original Hebrew text was made over one hundred years ago in 1879. The advances made since then in biblical and apocryphal research, especially through the impact of Qumran, have so vastly improved our knowledge of the living Hebrew language and the diverse and prolific literary production within Judaism during the years 200 B.C.E.-100 C.E. as to leave such efforts seriously out of date.

Since there are still some contemporary scholars who demur with regard to the general consensus that Hebrew was the original language of the two poems, it is apparent that no past investigator has been able to present an altogether convincing case. Thus it soon became obvious to me that this matter was ripe for reexamination from the vantage point of our vastly improved perspective on the language and literary productivity of the so-called intertestamental period.

This study, then, has its focus in a systematic and scientific reconstruction of the original Hebrew text, the existence of which is shown to be supported by all the available evidence. Given the highly derivative character of the entire book of Baruch, most of the verses in the poetic sections are traceable back to source-texts in earlier canonical and noncanonical works.

In verse after verse phrases or even whole lines have been borrowed or adapted, often with only minor variations, and in a number of instances it is apparent that the borrowing was from the Hebrew text rather than the Greek. It is primarily this derivative nature that makes possible reconstruction of a no longer extant original text, a task that would be much more difficult in the case of an independent and highly original composition.

The reconstruction is facilitated by such factors as: (1) the many well-established and highly predictable lexical equivalencies that obtain between LXX and MT, (2) the direct borrowings from source-texts, (3) an abundance of parallels in various canonical, noncanonical, and Qumran works, and (4) the rather recent accumulation of data regarding Hebrew syntax and such salient features of classical Hebrew poetry as fixed pairing and parallelism.

Chapter I serves as an introduction both to the book of Baruch and this study itself. It surveys the range of scholarly opinion on the pivotal questions of authorship, original language, and date, and provides an introduction to the extant Versions of Baruch and a brief discussion of the thought of Baruch in its intertestamental context.

Chapters II and IV offer a reconstruction of the original Hebrew text of the Wisdom Poem and the Consolation Poem respectively. The detailed philological notes that follow the text sections in Chapters III and V assemble all the supportive evidence for the reconstruction.

Chapter VI conclusively verifies the existence of the Hebrew original by identifying and marshalling the examples of Hebraisms, mistranslations, and the like that appear in texts of the primary Versions. It also assembles the many significant examples of Hebrew poetic devices and features that appear in the reconstruction and offers a brief analysis of the metrical patterns that obtain.

The textual evidence collected in the concluding chapter, in addition to the various lines of textual and nontextual evidence adduced in the introductory chapter, overwhelmingly favors an original Hebrew text. The results of this reconstruction, combined with the other grounds favoring a Hebrew original, effectively represent the *coup de grâce* to the conception that the Baruch poetry was composed in Greek.

Translations, unless otherwise specified, are the author's. Citations and translations from the OT are based on *Biblia Hebraica Stuttgartensia* (1967-77). The Göttingen *Septuaginta* (Vol. 15; ed. J. Ziegler, 1957) has been used as the Greek text for Baruch (Chapters II and IV), and where this as yet incomplete work is available it has also served as the basis for other citations and translations from the Septuagint. For those biblical books not yet included in the Göttingen corpus, citations and translations are from A. Rahlfs, *Septuaginta* (5th ed., 1952). Paul de Lagarde's edition of the Syriac text of Baruch (1861) provides the text reproduced in Chapters II and IV, as well as the basis for citations and translations from that version. The eighth century codex Ambrosianus, as published by A. M. Ceriani (1861), is the basis for citations and translations from the Syro-hexaplar text.

For the fellowship support which made this work possible, and for the literary treasures of the Eisenhower Library that were always accessible to me, I am forever grateful to The Johns Hopkins University. I am also pleased to acknowledge my deep indebtedness to the faculty of the Department of Near Eastern Studies of The Johns Hopkins University, most particularly to Dr. Delbert R. Hillers for his invaluable suggestions and advice and constant encouragement. Finally, I express my thanks to my wife, Peggy, and to my children, Penny and Geoffrey, for their patience and love during the demanding time of research and writing.

CHAPTER I

INTRODUCTION

THE BOOK OF BARUCH

Synopsis

Introduction and Prayer of Confession (1:1-3:8)

Historical Introduction (1:1-14)

The title ascribes this book to Baruch, the friend and amanuensis of Jeremiah, in the fifth year after the fall of Jerusalem (apparently that of 587/6 B.C.E.). Baruch is said to have read this work to the exiled king, Jeconiah (Jehoiachin), and to the other exiles of 597 B.C.E. dwelling with him along the otherwise unknown river Sud[1] (1:1-4). The assembly, deeply stirred, wept, fasted, prayed, and even gathered a collection for Joachim, the high priest at Jerusalem (1:5-7). Baruch is reputed also to have sent along with this collection certain silver vessels that had been removed from the Jerusalem Temple by Nebuchadnezzar (1:8).

The request of the exiles was that their collection be used to underwrite the cultus in Jerusalem and that prayers be offered there for Nebuchadnezzar and Belshazzar[2] to the end that the forlorn captives might find favor with their captors (1:10-12). The people of Jerusalem are also implored to intercede for the exiles and to read Baruch's book annually as part of their confessional liturgy (1:13-14).

Confession of Sins (1:15-3:8)

1. The Confession of the Judean Remnant (1:15-2:10). God's own people, it is confessed, have sinned against his Law and disobeyed him (1:15-18; cf. Dan 9:7-10) ever since the Exodus from Egypt (1:19). Thus it is that the curse of Deuteronomy 28 has overcome them (1:20; cf. Dan 9:11). Disregarding prophetic warnings they persisted in following after other gods (1:21-22) and even after God brought disaster upon them (2:1-5) they have still steadfastly refused to listen to his voice or heed his orders (2:6-10).[3]

2. The Exiles' Confession and Prayer for Forgiveness (2:11-35). The exiles confess their willful disobedience and pray that the Lord, who has done mighty deeds in the past events of his people's history, would turn aside his wrath from the remnant in dispersion (2:11-13; cf. Dan 9:15) and hear their petition for his own sake--that all nations might observe his power and that some Israelites may be left alive to carry on his proper worship (2:14-18).[4] Although God has seen fit to exile his people in accord with his revelation to Moses (2:27-29; cf. Deut 28:62), the confidence is expressed that they will repent in the land of their exile (2:30-33) and will be returned home by God himself (2:34) who will then make with them an eternal covenant (2:35; cf. Jer 31:31, 32:40).

3. The Exiles' Prayer for Salvation (3:1-8). The exiles beseech God for mercy (3:1-3), noting that although they have now repented (3:4-7), they are still suffering for the sins of their fathers (3:8).

A Hymn in Praise of Wisdom (3:9-4:4)

The very wisdom of God is embodied in the instructive precepts of the Torah and must be heeded by Israel (3:9) if she is again to thrive. That Israel now languishes in exile (3:10-12) is attributed to her forsaking of the fountain of wisdom. The poet next notes very eloquently that none of the ancient rulers, nor the more recent successors to their thrones (3:15-21), nor the famous sages of Canaan and Edom, nor even the fabled giants of old (3:22-29), ever succeeded in finding Wisdom.

Indeed, reports the poet, only God, the omniscient Creator of all, has ever found Wisdom (3:29-36; cf. Job 28:12-27) and he has given her as a gift to his people Israel (3:37). So it is that she (i.e., Wisdom personified) is said to have dwelt among men (4:1). In fact, she is embodied in and identified with the Torah, obedience to which yields life (4:2).

Songs of Lament and Consolation Inspired in the main by Deutero-Isaiah (4:5-5:9)

Jerusalem laments her own desolation (4:5-20) and offers comfort to her exiled children (4:21-29)

The gist of Jerusalem's song is that the Eternal God has seen fit to exile his people because of their sins, but even though they have deeply grieved their "mother," Jerusalem, he will yet not completely destroy them (4:5-8). As a woman discoursing with her neighbors she addresses the nearby city-states, bemoaning her widowhood and the loss of her captive children (4:9-16). Then, addressing the exiles, she gives them assurance that even though she herself cannot come to their rescue, she will continue to mourn and pray in the sure confidence of their ultimate deliverance by the Eternal (4:17-20). She indicates that it will be soon, after the destruction of the oppressor has been achieved, that the Eternal will return her beloved exiles amidst much joy and gladness (4:21-26), and thus urges the exiles to seek after God most zealously (4:27-29).

Jerusalem is comforted (4:30-5:9)

Now Jerusalem is reminded that Babylon, the oppressor, will soon be devastated by the Eternal (4:30-35) and that the exiled children will subsequently return (4:36-37). She is urged to strip off all the accoutrements of mourning and garb herself in divine righteousness and glory, for she is to receive the new name, "peace of righteousness and glory of godliness" (5:1-4). In transparently Deutero-Isaianic rhetoric she is exhorted to get up and watch from the height the gathering of her children from the East and West (5:5) as they return under the glorious and marvelous aegis of the Eternal God (5:6-9).

Purpose

The book of Baruch combines several perspectives on the Exilic period and reflects upon certain features of that era for the purpose of further edifying a dispersed Judaism already well-acquainted with the history of the Exile. The readers addressed in this work knew well what was involved in the notorious

Babylonian Exile for it was still their lot to have to live with its aftereffects. They were also well aware that the realities of the return of 538 B.C.E. had not measured up either to the predictions of the prophets or the expectations of the people, and that the real gathering and return still awaited divine fulfillment. Thus the Exilic history, in general and in certain particulars, is the medium selected by the author or editor of the Baruch material to offer his fellow compatriots in dispersion a reasoned explanation for their plight as well as a perspective on the source and certitude of their eventual deliverance.

The literary device by which an author makes the protagonist or speaker in his composition a heroic figure from a past age is paralleled elsewhere in the Scriptures (e.g., Daniel, Esther, and Judith). The attempt in so doing to reset the historical stage for that figure so long after the actual events has, however, usually resulted in what are according to modern historiographical standards historical errors, inaccuracies, and inconsistencies. This is as true for Baruch (though only to a very limited extent since there are relatively few historical references in the work) as it is for such similar *ex post facto* works as Daniel and Esther.[5] But then the goal of the author, just as for the authors of Daniel and Esther, was not at all to represent a consistent and accurate chronicle of historical events in the modern sense of reporting history, but simply to edify and to interpret past events for the present generation.

Form, Content, and Style

Form

The first section (1:15-3:8) is a prose composition that may be categorized by *Gattung* as a national prayer of confession. Its primary source and prototype is the national prayer of confession in Daniel 9. Its text is a veritable patchwork of verses quoted, adapted, or inspired from earlier biblical works such as Daniel, Deuteronomy, Jeremiah, and others.

The second section or first poem (3:9-4:4) belongs to the genre of sapiential literature. It is a didactic poem composed in the form of a hymn, specifically a hymn in praise of divine

Wisdom. Its text is also highly derivative and draws on many source-texts, particularly Job 28 and 38. The metre of the poem is predominantly the typically didactic 3+3 (see Chapter VI for the metre of both poems).

The third section or second poem (4:5-5:9) is a collection of brief songs of lament and consolation, composed very consciously in the style of Second Isaiah and, textually, heavily dependent on that prior work. In traditional prophetic style sequences of short metrical units have been built up into a larger unit that is thematically developed around the tragedy of Israel's exilic disruption and the hope of its reunification.

Each individual unit in this third section is characteristically introduced in Isaianic fashion by an imperative plus a vocative. This feature, not incidentally, underscores the probability of Hebraic origin since such repetition of similar phrases is a common device in Hebrew poetics for indicating stanzaic divisions in verse. Scholars are not agreed on the precise delineation of these individual units, however, and while it is possible to isolate eleven such units introduced by an imperative plus a vocative, schemes involving eight,[6] seven,[7] or six[8] have also been proposed. The breakdown into units is as follows:

(1) 4:5-9a "Fear not, my people";
(2) 4:9b-13 "Listen, neighbors";
(3) 4:14-18 "Come, neighbors";
(4) 4:19-20 "Go, children";
(5) 4:21-24 "Fear not, children";
(6) 4:25-26 "Bear, children";
(7) 4:27-29 "Fear not, children";
(8) 4:30-35 "Fear not, Jerusalem";
(9) 4:36-37 "Look around, Jerusalem";
(10) 5:1-5:4 "Strip off, Jerusalem";
(11) 5:5-5:9 "Arise, Jerusalem."

The first seven units constitute the lament section of this poem in which Jerusalem is the speaker. With the exception of the fourth unit, which may preferably be treated as part of the third unit, all are of similar length. The last four constitute the consolation section in which Jerusalem is addressed with words of comfort. Here also the units are of approximately the same length.

The nine verses of chapter 5 were at one time thought to be originally independent of the preceding verses in chapter 4, as well as dependent on Psalms of Solomon 11. But the careful analysis of the two *Textformen* conducted by Wilhelm Pesch[9] has revealed that the verses of Baruch 5 are not only very intimately interrelated with those of Bar 4:5ff., but are as well clearly prior to the related verses of Psalms of Solomon 11.[10]

The introduction (1:1-14) is a manifestly unhistorical but edifying narrative intended to set the exilic backdrop and introduce the whole work as a liturgical reading.

Content

The Book of Baruch tells no tale but presents a series of exilic vignettes, the original contiguity of which is dubious. Indeed, the book gives every evidence of being an amalgam of originally independent works united by the (perhaps superimposed) overriding theme of the exilic disperson of Israel. The grounds for this conclusion are elaborated below[11] and need not be developed here.

For the sake of convenience, Baruch may be divided roughly into thirds, each clearly differentiated from the others (as noted above) by form and genre, and each manifesting signs of separate origins. The first, or prose, section consists mainly of a national prayer of confession freely, and sometimes verbally, borrowed from the great confessional prayer in Daniel 9 and expanded.[12]

The second section is a poetic homily didactically elaborating the theme of the "fountain of wisdom." The message in essence is that true Wisdom (i.e., the Torah) is so well concealed from the world that not even its greatest sages or wisest rulers ever really found her. However, God has beneficently bestowed her on Israel alone and it is her obligation to cherish more dearly and cling more closely to that most prized possession.

The third section, a chain of laments and consolation songs inspired largely by Second Isaiah, presents a personified "mother"

Jerusalem lamenting her dire straits and lost "offspring," and then being comforted with consoling words of hope for immanent deliverance.

Style

The imitative and highly derivative character of Baruch has led C. C. Torrey to label it "the last dying flame of typical Hebrew prophecy."[13] While the work in all its constituent parts may legitimately be characterized as a mosaic of borrowings from canonical Scriptures and is most often found openly imitating or adapting these earlier models, it is still not without its own measure of originality and skill. The first section, written in the style of a prose homily, displays a modicum of originality in its adapting of earlier scriptural models. Close scrutiny reveals numerous reminiscences of the style of Jeremiah in addition to the especially close (and at times literal) reflections of the Daniel 9 source-text.

The poetry, while equally derivative, is nonetheless from a technical and stylistic point of view well-conceived and constructed. Indeed, considerable technical skill has been exercised in both poems in weaving together a number of verses borrowed from or inspired by older sources into a harmonious and consistent thematic development. And, although each poem represents a genre entirely different from the other, the result is in each case a composition that is technically competent, consonant in form and style with the canons of Hebrew poetry, frequently eloquent and evocative of a genuine depth of emotion, and carefully representative of the genre.

Text and Versions

The Loss of the Original Hebrew Text

That a Hebrew original lay behind the first division of Baruch has long been agreed by scholars and evidence for such is cited throughout the handbooks.[14] The original language of the rest of Baruch has in contrast been the subject of considerable scholarly debate. However, in recent years most scholars have come to affirm the existence of a Hebrew original here as well.[15] The second and third divisions of Baruch (the two poems) are, as already noted, composed in the form of poetry. Significantly, this feature is not immediately apparent from the LXX and other Versions, but only becomes clear when the original Hebrew text is reconstituted. The LXX text, then, for the two poetic sections is at best an attempt in translation at a rhythmic prose style and in no way qualifies as poetry according to the canons of Greek prosody,[16] which were still very much in effect in Hellenistic times.

The Hebrew text of Baruch probably perished along with numerous other Semitic *Urtexte* near the close of the first century C.E. What can be known about it is thus dependent upon how much information may be gleaned from the LXX translation primarily, and from the Syriac, which also gives evidence of having had access to the Hebrew as well as the Greek text.

The closing centuries B.C.E. had witnessed a more or less continuous stream of writings of all varieties. The original language of a considerable number of these Apocryphal and Pseudepigraphical works was Semitic, usually Hebrew (or Aramaic), and their Greek translations were made by and for Greek-speaking Jews. It is certainly more than coincidence that so many of these Semitic originals were lost. Indeed, there is good reason to believe that they were at one time deliberately allowed to perish by official proscription.

Accompanying the disastrous events that beset the Jewish nation during and after the fall of Jerusalem in 70 C.E. was an abrupt and deliberate change in literary output. The wider varieties of popular Palestinian literature fell into disuse and literary productivity soon narrowed to what might be termed rabbinical literature. The introspective posture of early C.E. Judaism, focused as it was primarily on internal spirituality and matters of Torah, and aimed squarely at the securing of the true Jewish heritage from both syncretism and destruction, led quickly to the definitive categorization of the canonical Scriptures and the fervent conviction that no "outside books" should be perpetuated. Thus, so that none of the suddenly noncanonical "outside books" should benefit from even the appearance of equality with the approved Scriptures, they were proscribed. One can easily imagine the effect on the pious of such pronouncements as: "Whoever brings together in his house more than twenty-four books brings confusion" (*Midrash Qoheleth*, 12:12),[17] and "Among those who have no part in the world to come is he who reads in the outside books" (Rabbi Akiba, *Talmud Babli, Sanhedrin*, 100b).[18]

A comparison of the literary remains at Qumran (*terminus ad quem*, 68 C.E.)[19] with those of later vintage at Wadi Murabba'at (ca. 132-35 C.E.) reveals that the process of standardization with respect to text-type, script, and canon, yet unknown at Qumran where a certain amount of fluidity still characterized these matters, was thoroughly in effect little more than fifty years later. No more of these "outside books" were copied after the definitive fixing of the canon, and thus for such books as Baruch and numerous other Apocryphal and Pseudepigraphical works the original texts simply disappeared. That many did ultimately survive in Greek translations made well before the conscious elimination of the Semitic originals was due largely to preservation by Christians.

The Septuagint Translation (LXX)

The edition of the LXX used in the present study is the most recent, the Göttingen edition, currently being produced under the editorship of Joseph Ziegler.[20] This edition, like most other modern ones, is based on the assumption that a proto-LXX text is reconstitutable from critical use of the sources. While it claims to provide such a text, in general it relies on G^B as the best source. Accompanying this text is a thorough apparatus in which the sources are carefully grouped according to families (see below, p. 17). The LXX text reproduced below is thus, unless otherwise specified, that of the Göttingen edition.[21]

The text of LXX Baruch is preserved in four of the more than thirty LXX Uncial manuscripts:

G^A -- "codex Alexandrinus," London, British Museum, Royal 1D.vi, 5th century C.E. (in HP, III);

G^B -- "codex Vaticanus," Rome, Vatican Library, Vat. Gr. 1209, 4th century C.E. (in HP, II);

G^Q -- "codex Marchalianus," Rome, Vatican Library, Vat. Gr. 2125, 6th century C.E. (in HP, XII);

G^V -- "codex Venetus," Venice, Marciana Libr., Gr. 1, 8th century C.E. (in HP, 23, mistakenly classified as a Minuscule).

The text of LXX Baruch is not contained in G^S ("codex Sinaiticus") or G^C ("codex Ephraemi Syri rescriptus Parisiensis").

A total of thirty-four Minuscule manuscripts bear witness to the text of LXX Baruch:

22--London, British Museum, Royal 1B,ii, 11th-12th centuries C.E.;

26--Rome, Vatican Library, Vat. Gr. 556, 10th century C.E.;

36--Rome, Vatican Library, Vat. Gr. 347, 11th century C.E.;

46--Paris, Bibliothèque Nationale, Coislin Gr. 4, 13th-14th centuries C.E.;

48--Rome, Vatican Library, Vat. Gr. 1794, 10th-11th centuries C.E. (in HP, 238);

49--Florence, Biblioteca Laurenziana, Plutei xi,4, 11th century C.E.;

51--Florence, Biblioteca Laurenziana, Plutei x,8, 11th century C.E.;

62--Oxford, New Collection, 44, 11th century C.E.;

86--Rome, Vatican Library, Barber. Gr. 549, 9th-11th centuries C.E. (= "codex Barberinus");

87--Rome, Vatican Library, Chigi R., viii,54, 10th century C.E.;

88--Rome, Vatican Library, Chigi R., vii,45, 10th century C.E. (= "codex Chisianus");

90--Florence, Biblioteca Laurenziana, Plutei v,9, 11th century C.E.;

91--Rome, Vatican Library, Ottoboniani graeci 452, 11th century C.E.;

96--Copenhagen, Kongelige Bibliothek, Ny Kongelige Saml., 4th, No. 5, 11th century C.E.;

106--Ferrara, Biblioteca Comunale, 187 II, 14th century C.E.;

130--Vienna, Nationalbibliothek, Theol. gr. 23, 12th-13th century C.E. (in HP, 144);

198--Paris, Bibliothèque Nationale, Gr. 14, 9th century C.E. (includes only Bar 1:1-2:18);

231--Rome, Vatican Library, Vat. Gr. 1670, 10th-11th centuries C.E.;

233--Rome, Vatican Library, Vat. Gr. 2067, 10th century C.E.;

239--Bologna, Biblioteca Univ., 2603, dated at 1046 C.E.;

311--Moscow, ehem. Syn.-Bibl., Gr. 354, 12th century C.E.;

393--Grottaferrata, Basilian Monastery of Grottaf., A.γ. xv, 8th century C.E. (a palimpsest including the Baruch fragments, 1:13-2:3, 3:12-4:8);

407--Jerusalem, Patr. Bibl., Τάφου 2, 9th century C.E.;

410--Jerusalem, Patr. Bibl., Τάφου 36, 13th century C.E. (palimpsest);

449--Milan, Biblioteca Ambrosiana, D.96 sup. + E.3 inf., 10th-11th centuries C.E. (includes only Bar 1:1-4:35);

490--München, Staatsbibliothek, Gr. 472, 11th century C.E.;

534--Paris, Bibliothèque Nationale, Coislin. 18, 11th century C.E.;

538--Paris, Bibliothèque Nationale, Coislin. 191, 12th century C.E.;

544--Paris, Bibliothèque Nationale, Gr. 15, 11th century C.E.;

567--Paris, Bibliothèque Nationale, Gr. 158, 12th century C.E. (lacks Bar 5:1-9);

613--Patmos, Ἰωάννου τοῦ θεολόγου, 209, 13th century C.E. (includes only 1:1-4:24);

710--Sinai, Cod. gr. 5, 10th century C.E.;

763--Athos, Μονὴ βατοπαιδίου 514, 11th century C.E.;

764--Athos, Λαύρα 169, 13th-14th centuries C.E.[22]

Syriac Translations

Syh

Baruch is extant in two Syriac translations. The latest of these is the Syro-hexaplaric Version (Syh), a rendering into Syriac of the fifth column of Origen's Hexapla that incorporates even his critical symbols. According to the testimony of Gregory bar Hebraeus (13th century C.E.), this translation was made by Paul, the bishop of Tella in Mesopotamia, in 616-17 C.E. About a century after Monophysite dissatisfaction with the current Peshiṭta text had led to the slavishly literal Philoxenian Version, revision was begun anew in the monasteries of the Nitrian desert southwest of the Nile delta, and eventually the Monophysite patriarch, Athanasius of Antioch, commissioned Paul of Tella to bring this work to fruition in the form of a fresh translation.[23]

The most important Syh manuscript is the eighth century codex Ambrosianus, a copy only a century removed from the original translation. This codex, which probably represents the second volume of a once complete Syh manuscript, has been in Milan since the early seventeenth century, and an edition was produced there photolithographically by A. M. Ceriani in his *Monumenta Sacra et Profana* (Milan, 1861). The Syh text for Baruch appears in Tome I, fascicle 1, of that exhaustive collection. The script of Syh Baruch is the Serta or Jacobite script and the accompanying apparatus contains numerous notations to the text and, significantly, to the translations of Aquila, Symmachus, and Theodotian.

A curious feature of Syh Baruch is the appearance in the margin (at 1:17 and 2:3) of three notations to the effect that certain words are not found in the Hebrew. These notations have naturally been cited as proof of the existence of a Hebrew original, at least for this section of Baruch. Yet, since such notations would appear to contradict the superscription at the beginning of Syh Baruch stating that the whole book had been obelized (indicated as not extant in Hebrew) by Origen, other scholars have taken the marginal notes to refer rather to words not extant in the canonical source-texts from which the Baruch passages are quoted or borrowed.[24] This feature is thus ultimately inconclusive with regard to the existence of a Hebrew original, for by the time of Origen it may long since have fallen into obscurity.[25]

Sy

The other, earlier, Syriac Version representing Baruch is designated Sy by Ziegler. Although such scholars as A. M. Ceriani, Heinrich Ewald, and Emil Schürer[26] have identified this translation with the Peshiṭta, several factors militate against this identification. Like the Peshiṭta this translation gives evidence of access to the Hebrew original,[27] but it also manifestly has been subjected to revision in accord with the Lucianic recension of the LXX (late 3rd century C.E.).[28]

A number of the additions in Sy are Lucianic,[29] and the many doublets in its text can only reflect conflation of several text traditions.[30] Thus, while the numerous conflate readings, variants, and expansions of Sy, among other things, have led such scholars as Rost, Whitehouse, and Pfeiffer[31] to conclude that this translation was made on the basis of the Hebrew as well as the Greek text (*contra* Kneucker[32] and Harwell[33] who each contend that Sy had only a Greek *Vorlage*), they are not willing to identify this translation with the Peshiṭta.

In addition, it has traditionally been handed down that the Peshiṭta in its original scope did not include the Apocrypha, and that those deutero-canonical works were added from the Greek.[34] This tradition argues against identifying Sy Baruch with the Peshiṭta, but a significant exception to this pattern is the treatment of Sirach (for which the original Hebrew text has only rather recently been recovered). Sirach was translated into Syriac from the Hebrew and subsequently revised according to the Greek.[35] A similar pattern could easily be hypothesized for Baruch.

It is generally considered that the Peshiṭta itself was begun already in the first century C.E., with completion probably occurring sometime in the second century.[36] The Apocryphal corpus was apparently translated later, but it may be assumed from the testimony of Ephraem Syrus (306-373 C.E.) who specifically cites the book of Baruch, that Baruch had been rendered into Syriac by the fourth century.[37]

The Sy text, second only in importance to that of the LXX as a witness to the Hebrew original, was first published in the Paris and London (Walton) Polyglots (1645 and 1657, respectively).[38] Unfortunately, the basic Syriac text used for the *editio princeps*, the Codex syriaque b (in the Bibliothèque Nationale in Paris), was a very poor seventeenth century C.E. manuscript with little authority.[39] A considerable advance was achieved for Sy Baruch with the appearance in 1861 of Paul de Lagarde's edition of the Apocrypha in Syriac.[40] His Baruch text is based on ms 17105 in the British Museum and also gives the variants of the London Polyglot and other manuscripts.[41]

Sy Baruch has a number of passages in which the text deviates from the LXX tradition and indicates adherence to the original Hebrew. Several examples may be noted here: (1) Sy is considerably at variance with the LXX at 3:10-12, and its two tricola represent the original Hebrew more accurately than the awkward LXX text (see chapters 2 and 3, ad loc.); (2) at 3:11 Sy preserves the expected plural participle that is so integrally a part of the common Hebrew cliché, "those descending into Sheol," in sharp contrast to the freer, "those in Sheol," of the LXX and Syh; (3) Sy appears to preserve the fuller, more balanced original line at 3:21, and also has the correct "her way" in place of the secondary "their way" of the LXX; (4) the Sy *hā' ḥ^e^nan* "behold us," in 3:34, is the literal equivalent of the Hebrew *hinnēnû* which the LXX more approximately renders with *paresmen*; (5) at 4:7 Sy support for a construction with the finite verb vis-à-vis the participial construction of the LXX accords more closely with the quoted Hebrew source-text in Deuteronomy 32; and (7) at 4:32 Sy ("cities which enslaved your children") preserves the original sequence and parallelism in contrast to the LXX ("cities which your children served").[42]

Latin Translations

A number of Latin Bible manuscripts, all incomplete and ranging in scope from a few verses to passages to books, exhibit text-forms that constitute a pre-Jerome text. It remains a matter of dispute whether these extant fragmentary texts ultimately go back to an original or rather reflect a variety of versions of diverse origin. Regardless, they are customarily all lumped together under the convenient label, *Vetus Latina* (or Old Latin).

In the case of Baruch, the Latin text in the Vulgate derives from a time prior to Jerome. No fresh translation was made by Jerome for Wisdom, Sirach, 1 and 2 Maccabees, or Baruch. Instead he simply adopted the Old Latin translation current in the Roman Church.[43]

All the extant Latin translations go back to the Greek text[44] and thus can only represent a secondary witness to the original Hebrew text. Besides the text of Baruch preserved in the Vulgate (La^V)[45] there are several other Old Latin manuscripts that contain Baruch:

La^C -- "codex Cavensis," Cava, Badia 1(14); published by L. Mattei-Cerasoli, *Liber Baruch secondo il testo del Codici Biblico Cavense* (*Analecta Cavensia* 1), Cava, 1935 (9th century C.E.);

La^S -- "codex Vallicellianus," Rome, Biblioteca Vallicelliana, Ms. Orat. B. 7; published in parallel columns with La^V by P. Sabatier in *Bibliorum*

Sacrorum Latinae Versiones Antiquae, seu Vetus Italica et caetera (Paris, 1751), and even earlier by J. M. Caro (Rome, 1688);[46]

La^L -- "codex Legionensis," Léon (Spain), San Isidro, codex Gothicus Legionensis, dated to 960 C.E. The edition published by G. Hoberg, *Die älteste lateinische Übersetzung des Buches Baruch* (Freiburg, 1902), was based not on the original manuscript of the codex Gothicus Legionensis but rather on the cod. Vat. lat. 4859, a late copy of Legionensis dating from 1587 C.E.[47]

Coptic Translations

Various Coptic translations of canonical and deuterocanonical works were probably already extant by the end of the third century C.E.[48] These have survived in several dialect versions. The text of Baruch is preserved in two of these, the Bohairic and Sahidic. No portion of Baruch has yet appeared in the Fayumic (Fa) dialect. Kneucker considers the Coptic in general to reflect the text tradition of G^A,[49] but Ziegler more recently has identified the Coptic Versions with the G^B family.[50]

Bo

The Bohairic (Alexandrian) text for Baruch, which in the opinion of its editor goes back to a "sorgfältige Abschrift des gelehrten Kopten Herrn Kabis in Cairo,"[51] was edited and published by H. Brugsch as "Das Buch Baruch, Koptisch," in three installments in *Zeitschrift für ägyptische Sprache und Altertumskunde* during the years 1872-74.[52] Unknown to Brugsch, however, this same text had been published just two years earlier in Rome by a certain A. Bsciai as *Liber Baruch Prophetae* (Romae: typis S. congregationis de Propaganda fide, 1870).[53]

Sa

A number of published fragments of the Sahidic (Upper Egyptian) translation are listed by Ziegler.[54] The most recent and nearly complete text (not available to Ziegler) is that of the Papyrus Bodmer XXII, edited and published by Rodolphe Kasser in 1964.[55]

The Ethiopic Translation (Eth)

The earliest Ethiopic texts are very literal translations from the LXX dating from the fifth to the sixth centuries C.E., but known only from thirteenth century manuscripts.[56] The Ethiopic Version of Baruch is considerably briefer than its LXX *Vorlage*, with some passages abridged and others entirely lacking.[57] This Version was first edited and published (on the basis of six mss from Paris, London, and Berlin) by August Dillmann in the fifth volume of his *Biblia Veteris Testamenti Aethiopica* of 1894.[58] Ziegler characterizes the Ethiopic text for Baruch as being a freer rendering of the Greek than is the text for Jeremiah.[59] Kneucker again contends that Eth reflects in general the text tradition of G^A,[60] but Ziegler classifies it as belonging to the G^B text family.[61]

The Arabic Translation (Ar)

The Arabic translation from the Greek was first published in the Paris and London (Walton) Polyglots (the latter copied from the former). This Version, which in general faithfully represents its *Vorlage*, reveals a particularly close relationship to G^A and Minuscule 410.[62]

The Armenian Translation (Arm)

The translation of the Bible into Armenian reportedly began immediately after the invention of the Armenian alphabet in 406 C.E., and was completed before the end of the fifth century.[63] The first edition was that of Oskan, published in Amsterdam in 1666. An improvement, but an edition deemed no longer adequate for scholarly purposes, is the Zabrabian edition published in Venice in 1805.[64] The latter was used in Ziegler's collation. The translation from the Greek is generally literal. According to Kneucker it reflects G^A,[65] but Ziegler identifies it with the Hexaplaric text group.[66]

Text Families

The text groups or families for the LXX and Versional witnesses for the book of Baruch, according to the Göttingen LXX are the following:

(1) the B text group, witnessed by G^{B} (and G^{S} in the rest of the Jeremianic corpus), Minuscules 106-410 (= 106'), 130, 239, 538, and La, Copt, Eth, citations;

(2) the A text group, with Minuscules 106 and 410 in that order giving the most weighty support; also Ar;

(3) the Q text group, attested by G^{Q}, G^{V}, Minuscules 26, 46, 86, 534, 544, 613, 710; also Olymp;

(4) the Hexaplaric recension, represented by Minuscule 88 and the Syro-hexaplar (O), with support from Minuscule 233, G^{Qmg}, 86^{mg}, and also Arm, Hier;

(5) the Lucianic recension (L'), the chief witnesses (as in Ezekiel) being Minuscules 22, 36, 48, 51, 96, 231, 311, 763 (= L), with Minuscules 62, 198, 407, 449 (= l) representing a subsidiary group; also G^{Qmg}, 86^{mg}, Syh^{mg}, Sy, Tht;

(6) the Catena group (C'), for which a *Hauptgruppe* (C) is represented by Minuscules 87, 91, 490, 567, and an *Untergruppe* (c) by Minuscules 49, 90, 764.[67]

THE QUESTION OF AUTHORSHIP

The Historical Baruch and the Problem of his Alleged Authorship

The work as a whole purports to be the composition of the historical Baruch, the secretary and companion of Jeremiah, written while he was in exile in Babylon in approximately 582 B.C.E. This Baruch, the son of Neriah, appears prominently in the book of Jeremiah. He is remembered mostly as the amanuensis who committed to writing the prophecies of Jeremiah in about 605 B.C.E., and the spokesman who publically proclaimed their message of impending doom to the populace of Jerusalem.[68]

Little more is known about Baruch than that he went into hiding for a time along with Jeremiah under pressure of royal hostility, and that it was during this stay "underground" that the text of the Jeremianic compendium which King Jehoiakim had previously destroyed was rewritten and expanded (Jeremiah 36). Baruch is known to have survived two invasions of Jerusalem and two subsequent exilic processions to Babylon. However, when the Babylonian-appointed governor, Gedaliah, was assassinated, both Baruch and Jeremiah were taken forcibly to Egypt in the company of those fugitive rebels who had rejected Jeremiah's advice to stay put in Jerusalem (Jer 43:3-7). From this point on the record of Baruch's life is a *tabula rasa* and, significantly, contrary to later rabbinic traditions, there is not even a hint in the canonical Scriptures that he at any time went to Babylon.[69]

Notwithstanding the diversity of its constituent parts, the book as a whole appears on the surface to be a reasonably unified one. Closer scrutiny, however, suggests that such apparent unity is due rather to the expertise of an editor than to the intent of the author(s). There are numerous internal factors which combine powerfully to suggest that the three major sections here found joined together were in origin quite independent and distinct from one another. There are as well some very compelling reasons for believing that none of these three parts actually originated from the pen of the sixth century Baruch, the son of Neriah.

Thus it is that the scholars who have dealt with this work on any level tend in the main to regard it as a pseudepigraphic writing, compiled from diverse and obscure sources and subsequently ascribed to the renowned scribe of history. Pseudepigraphs, of course, flourished in the last several centuries B.C.E. and into the first several C.E., as fervent but obscure authors often sought to advance their works by capitalizing on the tested popularity of historical heroes. In this regard it is surely no accident that the two greatest scribes of history, Baruch and Ezra, figure prominently as the alleged authors of various Apocryphal or Pseudepigraphic works.

A Survey of Scholarly Opinion Regarding Authorship

The book of Baruch has now long been recognized to be a work fraught with historical inaccuracies, internal contradictions, and various literary problems (earmarks often of pseudonymic composition), and is considered by all but a very few scholars in modern times to have been the work actually of two, three, or even four different hands, linked together by an editor who may or may not have written one of the sections.

The only scholar in this century to advance the cause of Baruchian authorship of the entire work is the Roman Catholic scholar, Edmund Kalt.[70] In the nineteenth century and earlier this was typically the view of numerous Roman Catholic scholars, such as F. H. Reusch,[71] R. F. R. Bellarmine,[72] B. Welte,[73] and Johann M. A. Scholz.[74] The last Protestant critic to defend this position was apparently the eighteenth century British divine, G. Whiston.[75]

Several scholars, again of Roman Catholic persuasion, have contended that Baruch, the scribe of Jeremiah, was indeed the author of at least the first section of the work. Thus Johann Goettsberger[76] considers the second section (the Wisdom Poem) likely to have been a later interpolation into an authentic composition of the sixth century Baruch. In the judgment of Angelo Penna,[77] Paul Heinisch,[78] and Wenzel Stoderl[79] the first section is from the pen of the sixth century Baruch, but the two poems are thought to have originated independently from two unknown authors.[80]

The vast majority of scholars, for reasons which are outlined immediately below, consider the entire work to be a pseudepigraphic composite of the productivity of at least two distinct authors, neither of whom was Baruch. Thus Leonhard Bertholdt,[81] Eduard Reuss,[82] Otto F. Fritzsche,[83] Heinrich Ewald,[84] Adolf Hilgenfeld,[85] Herbert E. Ryle and Montague R. James,[86] Hermann L. Strack,[87] C. C. Torrey,[88] Carl H. Cornill,[89] Henry St. John Thackeray,[90] Otto Zöckler,[91] Ferdinand Hitzig,[92] and R. R. Harwell[93] have each recognized two essentially different units, namely, the prose section (1:1-3:8) and the poetic (3:9-5:9), and have affirmed independent authorship for each section. Other scholars have noted the same division but have stressed more energetically the additional differences between the two poems (3:9-4:4 and 4:5-5:9), and thus affirmed that the book of Baruch comprises the work of "two or more," "at least two," or "two or three" authors. Those holding this opinion are: Bruce M. Metzger,[94] R. H. Charles,[95] Henry S. Gehman,[96] Emil Schürer,[97] and Artur Weiser.[98]

Scholars who delineate the work of three distinct authors in this composite book of Baruch are: O. C. Whitehouse,[99] Bernard N. Wambacq,[100] W. J. Ferrar,[101] Johann Wilhelm Rothstein,[102] Wilhelm Pesch,[103] Otto Eissfeldt,[104] John L. McKenzie,[105] Robert H. Pfeiffer,[106] J. J. Kneucker,[107] Sidney S. Tedesche,[108] W. O. E. Oesterley,[109] and L. E. T. André.[110] Yet further, J. T. Marshall,[111] J. N. Birdsall,[112] and J. J. Battistone[113] agree in admitting the possibility of four different hands. A host of other scholars acknowledge the composite nature of the work but offer no specific opinion regarding the number of different hands involved in its evolution.[114] This cataloguing of scholarly opinion on the issue of authorship, while perhaps not exhaustive, is both thorough and representative enough to demonstrate the overwhelming scholarly inclination to treat the book of Baruch as a pseudepigraphic as well as composite work.[115]

Grounds for Assuming a Pseudepigraphic and Composite Origin

Historical Inaccuracies and Internal Inconsistencies

(1) As has been noted, there is not a shred of evidence that would credibly place Baruch in Babylon after any of the deportations from or captures of Jerusalem. Whether the "fifth year" (Bar 1:2) be understood as measured from the surrender of Jeconiah (598 B.C.E.) or the suppression of the revolt of Zedekiah (587 B.C.E.), it is in either case impossible for Baruch to have been in Babylon five years later since he is consistently found present with Jeremiah in Jerusalem after each deportation until carried off to Egypt following the assassination of Gedaliah in 582 B.C.E.

(2) A return of some sacred silver Temple vessels, alleged to have been made by Zedekiah (597-86 B.C.E.), is spoken of in connection with the sending of the letter (Bar 1:8) to Jerusalem, but the canonical historical books know only of a return of such sacred vessels under Cyrus (cf. Ezra 1:7-11).[116] Also, (3) a high-priest by the name of Joachim (Bar 1:7) is nowhere else known from the time of the historical Baruch but does appear about a century later (cf. Neh 12:10, 12, 26).[117]

(4) Probably the most serious historical flaw is the erroneous notion, indiscriminately borrowed along with much else from the book of Daniel, that the Babylonian crown prince, Belshazzar, was the son of Nebuchadnezzar (Bar 1:11-12; cf. Dan 5:2, 11, 18). In reality, Belshazzar was the son of the last Babylonian king, Nabonidus (555-38 B.C.E.).[118] (5) It is thus

reasonably contended that such indiscriminate telescoping of historical facts, along with other historical distortions, would simply be inconceivable from the pen of an author contemporary with the very times as was Baruch.

Further, two inconsistencies in the work as a whole argue against unity of authorship. (6) While the cultus appears to be intact in Bar 1:10, other parts of the work appear to lament the destruction of the Temple. If this had been a composition of Baruch written shortly after the deportation of Jeconiah the implications of a ruined Jerusalem would be open to suspicion, but if it had been composed shortly after the deportation of Zedekiah and the destruction of Jerusalem by Nebuchadnezzar then the implication that its cultus was still intact is suspect. This is a difficulty, though it must be admitted that historical facts and allusions throughout are very elusive and that the cultus could have been kept up covertly or within severe limitations.[119] (7) Whereas the tone of both poems is such that it conceives the Exile as being well-advanced and close to an end (cf. Bar 3:10, 4:21ff.), the date formula specifies only the fifth year. These facts are difficult to reconcile and suggest at the least the diverse origins of the work.[120]

Literary Problems

(1) It is widely agreed that the bulk of the first section is modeled on and derivative from the prayer of confession in Daniel 9 (ca. 165 B.C.E.). Thus, while it is quite possible that parts of Daniel (including this prayer) were written earlier and used literarily, it is scarcely possible that they could have been written so early as the sixth century B.C.E.[121]

(2) The highly derivative character of each section is now well-established. One of the few things each of the three parts does have in common is this pastiche method of stringing together passages borrowed or adapted from canonical sources. Such literary dependence on a wide variety of canonical books that ranges from Jeremiah and Isaiah to Deuteronomy, Job, Daniel and Sirach,[122] clearly precludes any early dating of this work. On this ground alone composition in the sixth century B.C.E. is ruled out. (3) Similarly, the derivative nature of this text,

culled and pieced together as it is from diverse canonical sources, suggests that the book was compiled not as a "prophecy" but to serve some liturgical institution, most probably the annual day of mourning over the desolation of Jerusalem, the ninth of Ab (cf. Jer 52:12f.).[123]

Some further literary problems militate particularly against unity of authorship. (4) The Wisdom Poem is strikingly different in tone from the other two parts, not to mention genre. It is silent on matters with which the other two are deeply concerned--repentance and forgiveness, exile and return. Only in its link verses (3:10-13), which may well be secondary, is there any such connection or even note of urgency.[124] By contrast this second section consists chiefly of reasoned statements rather than impassioned pleas, and its wisdom theme is rather narrowly concentrated in contrast to the other sections where the themes are more diffused.[125]

(5) It is the opinion of a number of scholars that the link verses of the Wisdom Poem (3:10-13) are a later interpolation added by an editor who sought to tie this originally unrelated poem to the other pieces by means of a common, contrived historical background--the Exile.[126] Similarly, the historical introduction (1:1-14) is considered by many to fit particularly badly with what follows.[127]

(6) It is significant that, while there are some obvious thematic similarities between the first and third sections of the book, there are also at least two very conspicuous differences (aside from the fact that the first is prose and the third poetry). (a) The first section displays an amenable attitude toward the Babylonian overlords, but the posture toward the same is markedly hostile in the third. (b) There is also a marked distinction between units in the use of divine names or of circumlocutions in lieu thereof. "The Eternal" is most characteristic of the final section, apparently as a circumlocution for the Tetragrammaton, but it is never found in either of the other two sections. In the first the Deity is usually styled "the Lord our God," and in the second simply "God."[128]

Other Problems

(1) There is also an argument from the point of view of canonicity; namely, why would the Palestinian canonical tradition have ignored this work had it been written by the historical Baruch? Despite the authority lent by the name of Baruch, the book never was admitted to the Hebrew canon nor long preserved in Hebrew. (2) Finally, a theological inconsistency must be mentioned. The identification of Wisdom with Torah is admittedly a post-exilic development and hardly to be expected in the time of the sixth century Baruch.[129]

In brief, the evidence strongly suggests (and the vast majority of scholars concur) that the three parts of the book arose independently, were subsequently united, and then ascribed pseudonymously to the popular and credible historical figure, Baruch.

THE QUESTION OF ORIGINAL LANGUAGE

A Survey of Scholarly Opinion

Since the oldest extant text of Baruch is in Greek, it is perhaps only natural that some scholars have maintained that Greek was the original language of the entire composition. Prominent among the relatively few (and mostly nineteenth century) scholars holding this view are: Theodor Nöldeke,[130] H. A. C. Hävernick,[131] Carl F. Keil,[132] Leonhard Bertholdt,[133] L. E. T. André,[134] Wilhelm Vatke,[135] and more recently, A. Lefèvre[136] and E. J. Goodspeed.[137]

Beginning with Otto F. Fritzsche,[138] Adolf Hilgenfeld,[139] Eduard Reuss,[140] and especially Emil Schürer,[141] who were subsequently followed by such scholars as Carl H. Cornill,[142] A. A. Bevan,[143] E. C. Bissell,[144] E. H. Gifford,[145] Crawford H. Toy,[146] M. R. James,[147] L. A. Iranyi,[148] H. T. Robins,[149] B. N. Wambacq,[150] and Rudolf Mayer,[151] the hypothesis has been advanced that the first section is a translation from an original Hebrew text, but that the two following poetic sections were originally composed in Greek.[152]

But again the majority of the scholars who have grappled with this problem have concluded that the original language of the work in its entirety was Hebrew.[153] Foremost among those defending a Hebrew original for the whole work is J. J. Kneucker. His monumental and exhaustive commentary on Baruch, *Das Buch Baruch* (1879), includes a careful attempt at reconstruction of the original Hebrew text (with extensive notes). This study, though now out of date in many respects and interpretively fanciful and unreliable, still remains the basic resource for entering into Baruch research.[154]

Kneucker, in taking this stand, was following the lead of his own mentor, Ferdinand Hitzig.[155] Other scholars concurring in this opinion are: Samuel Davidson,[156] Heinrich Ewald,[157] H. L. Strack,[158] Otto Zöckler,[159] H. Graetz,[160] F. H. Reusch,[161] Carl Steuernagel,[162] H. St. J. Thackeray,[163] R. H. Charles,[164] J. W. Rothstein,[165] C. C. Torrey,[166] R. R. Harwell,[167] Johann Goettsberger,[168] Marie-Joseph Lagrange,[169] Eduard König,[170] Aage Bentzen,[171] W. M. L. de Wette,[172] S. Tedesche,[173] Artur Weiser,[174] J. C. Dancy,[175] A. Fitzgerald,[176] Herbert G. May,[177] Wilhelm Pesch,[178] Otto Eissfeldt,[179] H. S. Gehman,[180] R. H. Pfeiffer,[181] John L. McKenzie,[182] J. N. Birdsall,[183] E. Kalt,[184] P. Heinisch,[185] W. O. E. Oesterley,[186] Curt Kuhl,[187] R. K. Harrison,[188] A. Kahana,[189] A. Penna,[190] and the editors of *The Jerusalem Bible*.[191]

Grounds for Assuming a Hebrew Original

From the above survey of scholarly opinion, it is obvious that all but a few who have dealt with this matter are agreed that the first (or prose) section had a Hebrew original. The evidence for this is abundant and is cited repeatedly in the handbooks and treatments mentioned above and thus need not be reassembled here.[192] With regard to the poetic sections, however, scholarly opinion favoring a Hebrew original, while nevertheless still substantial, has been offered with considerably more reserve or tentativeness. Only a few of the scholars favoring a Hebrew original for the poetry have presented specific evidence to back up this claim,[193] whereas most have been content simply to record their perception of a Hebraic cast or character to the poems.

But the poetic sections also reveal numerous Hebraisms,[194] reflections of Hebrew poetic and stylistic devices (most significantly the patterns of poetic parallelism, with the pairings frequently appearing in expected canonical sequence),[195] as well as various marks of Palestinian provenance (the Wisdom Poem, for example, contrasts sharply in tone and outlook with the Hellenistic Wisdom of Solomon).[196] It may also be mentioned in this regard that the evidence that the book was composed for and employed in liturgy scarcely betokens composition in Greek.[197]

The question, however, hinges chiefly on the nature of the poetry of these two sections. Schürer has characterized the LXX text of 3:9-5:9 as "fluent and rhetorical Greek" and "evidently a Greek original,"[198] and those who have followed him have simply accepted this speculative opinion as fact. Of all who have tackled the problem of the original language of the poetry apparently only R. R. Harwell has attempted to analyze the Greek text as poetry.[199] Unfortunately his findings appear to have been overlooked by most. From the point of view of the canons of Greek metrics, Bar 3:9-5:9 can in no way be construed as poetry; at best it could be labeled rhythmical prose, and as such is comparable to other LXX translations of originally Hebrew poetry.[200] It is only when the Hebrew original is reconstructed that Bar 3:9-5:9 may be recognized clearly and inescapably as poetry.[201]

While Schürer's contention that the Greek of Bar 3:9-5:9 is stylistically an improvement over that of 1:1-3:8 may be admitted, it is nevertheless little more than a subjective impression and hardly sufficient proof of a Greek original. Thus W. Pesch has remarked: "Schürer selbst bleibt uns die Beweise für diese 'offenbare Tatsache' schuldig . . . Das glattere Sprachgewand kann aber gut mit einem anderen Übersetzer erklärt werden, und schwierige Stellen, die vielmehr auf eine hebräische Vorlage schliessen lassen, gibt es auch im dritten Teile."[202]

J. J. Battistone, echoing the general tenor of Schürer's position, concludes that "the evidence . . . shows that the language and style of the material in Bar 1:1-3:8, in contrast to that of 3:9-5:9, has a strong Hebraic accent."[203] It must be asked, however, what is "Hebraic accent" in the former that is not in the latter? The so-called differences of language and style between these parts of the book are in fact the differences of Hebrew prose and poetry, not of different languages.

Further discussion of the evidence for the Hebrew original appears below throughout the philological notes and in the concluding chapter.

THE QUESTION OF THE DATE OF COMPOSITION

A Survey of Scholarly Opinion

The question of the date of this composite work, or of its originally independent subsections, is even more controverted than either that of authorship or original language. Scholars have dated the book or its constituent parts to widely diverse points along a time spectrum from the sixth century B.C.E. to the second C.E. For the sake of convenience (and at the risk of oversimplifying), the many scholarly opinions regarding the date of composition may be grouped roughly into fourteen categories according to the wording of the scholars' own statements.[204]

The majority of investigators prefer to locate the bulk of the Baruch material between 200-60 B.C.E. (roughly the Seleucid and Maccabean periods in Palestine). A sizeable minority would place the whole, or at least the poetry, in the first century C.E., particularly after 70 C.E. A few (for the most part representatives of the older, Roman Catholic position) contend for the Exilic or late Persian periods.[205] The following list delineates the fourteen time periods and indicates the individual scholars who support each (Roman numerals in parentheses represent the three major divisions of the book and the appearance of such after a scholar's name indicates that he dates only the sections mentioned to the period in question; the lack of a parenthetic insertion after a scholar's name indicates that he dates the entire work to the period in question).

(1) <u>The period of the Exile</u>: A. Penna (I, III),[206] F. H. Reusch,[207] P. Heinisch (I, III),[208] E. Kalt,[209] J. Goettsberger,[210] and W. Stoderl (I);[211]

(2) <u>The late Persian period</u>: H. Ewald (I),[212] E. H. Gifford (I),[213] E. C. Bissell (I),[214] M. R. James (I),[215] A. Penna (II),[216] P. Heinisch (II);[217]

(3) <u>ca. 320 B.C.E. (or shortly thereafter)</u>: J. T. Marshall (I),[218] H. Ewald (II, III),[219] S. Davidson,[220] E. Reuss (I);[221]

(4) The third century B.C.E.: C. C. Torrey (II, III);[222]

(5) The early second century B.C.E.: A. Gelin,[223] R. H. Charles,[224] H. St. J. Thackeray (I),[225] J. J. Battistone (II),[226] R. R. Harwell (II, III),[227] E. H. Gifford (II, III),[228] O. Plöger (I),[229] A. Lefèvre,[230] L. Rost (II),[231] A. Hilgenfeld (I),[232] H. T. Robins (I);[233]

(6) The Maccabean period: O. F. Fritzsche,[234] O. Zöckler,[235] C. F. Keil,[236] E. König,[237] R. H. Charles,[238] R. K. Harrison,[239] C. Kuhl (I),[240] H. S. Gehman (I),[241] B. N. Wambacq (I, II),[242] C. H. Toy (I, II),[243] R. H. Pfeiffer (I, II),[244] C. H. Cornill (I),[245] A. Weiser (I),[246] C. C. Torrey (final edition),[247] S. Tedesche (I),[248] L. Rost (I),[249] H. G. May (final edition);[250]

(7) Pre-100 B.C.E.: R. R. Harwell (I and final edition),[251] R. H. Pfeiffer (III),[252] C. Kuhl (II, III);[253]

(8) Second century B.C.E.-First century B.C.E.: J. L. McKenzie,[254] H. Strack,[255] *The Jerusalem Bible*;[256]

(9) The first century B.C.E.: H. S. Gehman (II, III),[257] J. J. Battistone (III),[258] C. H. Toy (III),[259] O. Plöger (II, III),[260] A. Bentzen (I),[261] S. Tedesche (II, III),[262] M.-J. Lagrange (III),[263] Georg Fohrer,[264] H. T. Robins (II);[265]

(10) ca. 60 B.C.E.: B. N. Wambacq (III and final edition),[266] L. A. Iranyi (final edition),[267] W. Pesch (III),[268] H. Graetz,[269] A. Weiser (II, III),[270] L. Rost (III),[271] A. Hilgenfeld (II, III);[272]

(11) First century B.C.E.-First century C.E.: B. M. Metzger,[273] O. Eissfeldt,[274] J. J. Battistone (I);[275]

(12) The early first century C.E.: J. J. Battistone (final edition),[276] A. Bentzen (II, III),[277] H. T. Robins (III);[278]

(13) 50-90 C.E.: G. R. Driver,[279] W. Vatke;[280]

(14) Post-70 C.E.: J. J. Kneucker,[281] F. Hitzig,[282] L. H. Brockington,[283] J. T. Marshall (II, III),[284] H. B. Swete,[285] H. St. J. Thackeray (II, III),[286] O. C. Whitehouse,[287] C. Steuernagel,[288] G. Volkmar,[289]

C. H. Cornill (II, III),[290] E. Schürer,[291] E. J. Goodspeed,[292] W. O. E. Oesterley,[293] L. E. T. André,[294] Ernst Haenchen,[295] M. R. James (II, III),[296] H. E. Ryle,[297] Ernst Sellin,[298] L. Rost (final edition).[299]

TABLE 1

NUMBER OF SCHOLARS DATING THE WHOLE OR INDIVIDUAL SECTIONS OF BARUCH TO A PARTICULAR TIME-PERIOD

	Time-period	Whole Book	Section I	Section II	Section III	Final Edition
(1)	Exile	4	2	. .	1	. .
(2)	Late Persian era	. .	4	1	. .	. .
(3)	ca. 320 B.C.E.	1	2	1	1	. .
(4)	3rd century B.C.E.	. .	. .	1	1	. .
(5)	Early 2nd century B.C.E.	3	4	4	2	. .
(6)	Maccabean period	6	9	3	. .	2
(7)	Pre-100 B.C.E.	. .	1	1	2	1
(8)	2nd century B.C.E.-1st B.C.E.	3	. .	. .	. .	. .
(9)	1st century B.C.E.	1	1	4	6	. .
(10)	ca. 60 B.C.E.	1	. .	2	4	3
(11)	1st century B.C.E.-1st C.E.	2	1	. .	. .	. .
(12)	Early 1st century C.E.	. .	. .	1	2	1
(13)	50-90 C.E.	2	. .	. .	. .	. .
(14)	Post-70 C.E.	12	. .	4	5	1

Grounds for Dating the Baruch Material in the Maccabean Period

As noted, the above survey reveals that the majority of scholars who have dealt at any depth with this problem of dating the whole or the component parts of the book of Baruch assign the work, or most of it, roughly to the time-period 200-60 B.C.E.

This general concensus is based on a number of points of evidence, the most salient of which are here outlined.

(1) The acknowledged historical errors, inaccuracies, and literary problems mentioned above, and especially the clear dependency of all the sections on various canonical books (e.g., Daniel, Deutero-Isaiah, and Job), effectively rule out the very early dates suggested.

(2) The Baruch material is characterized by a dearth of historical references or allusions, and what little may be discerned are all too vague and generalized to have had any possible reference to current or recent events. Indeed, one of the most prominent features of the work as a whole is its essential "datelessness," despite the fact that it consists of three different genres.[300]

(3) It is now widely recognized that the first section is highly dependent on the confessional prayer in Daniel 9.[301] The first section then may be assumed to have been written no earlier than 165 B.C.E.

(4) The second section has also been demonstrated to be dependent on such Wisdom passages as Job 28 and 38, Proverbs 28 and Sirach 24. This indicates an effective *terminus post quem* of ca. 180 B.C.E.[302]

(5) The concluding verses of the second section (4:2-4) present an appeal to the Jewish constituency to remain faithful to Torah. This suggests a time when loyalty to Torah was being strenuously tested, very possibly the early pre-Maccabean decades of the second century B.C.E.

(6) If the link verses of the Wisdom Poem (3:10-13) do actually represent a connective interpolation by a redactor,[303] this second section is virtually dateless. In any event, these link verses treat the Babylonian Exile, the only obvious historical allusion in the second section, as though its inception were an event of the remote past.

(7) With regard to the first as well as the second section it may be observed that the resurrection concept has not yet replaced the concept of Sheol (2:17; 3:11, 19). In the opinion of R. H. Charles,[304] this view of the dead points to the beginnings of the second century B.C.E.

(8) The third section is also dependent on various canonical works, frequently borrowing almost literally from Second and Third Isaiah. It must thus be dated later than these works.

(9) The last part of the third section, chapter 5, has long been known to have a very close relationship with Psalms of Solomon 11.[305] The question of priority has been debated for years, with scholars aligning themselves behind three different positions: (a) Baruch 5 has borrowed from Psalms of Solomon 11 and is thus later; (b) Psalms of Solomon 11 is derivative from and later than Baruch 5; (c) both are dependent on a common unpreserved source that was equally as dependent on Second and Third Isaiah as the two are individually.[306] Until rather recently, the position of Ryle and James[307] that Baruch 5 was secondary to Psalms of Solomon 11 held the fore. But it has now been demonstrated in a careful analysis of the two *Textformen* by Wilhelm Pesch[308] that the relationship of dependency is just the reverse--Psalms of Solomon 11 is actually secondary to Baruch 5. Thus, since the material in Baruch 5 is also closely interrelated with that of Baruch 4,[309] it may be assumed that this third section should be dated no later than ca. 60 B.C.E.

(10) Against the arguments of those who contend that such lament and consolation poems could only have been written in the wake of a major catastrophe (particularly, the destruction of Jerusalem by Titus), the pseudonymous Psalms of Solomon (ca. 60-40 B.C.E.) demonstrate that such consolation songs as those in Baruch are indeed appropriate to a time long before the catastrophic Roman destruction of Jerusalem.[310]

(11) Geographically the reflections of the Jewish dispersion in the third section encompass more than just the "East." Thus, references to "East and West" have been seized upon by those defenders of the post-70 C.E. dating scheme who envisage a broader, Roman-era dispersion. Nevertheless, these very reflections are found only in quotations borrowed from much older sources in Second and Third Isaiah where the dispersion is already depicted in terms of "East and West."[311]

(12) Similarly, the woes pronounced against "Babylon" cannot be pressed for dating support, for they merely repeat the older canonical prophecies (cf. 4:25, 32-35; Isa 34:14; 13:21ff.; Jer 50:39; and Isa 47:9, 11, 14).[312]

(13) Further, the tendency throughout the work to treat the nation as a unit is not supportive of the late dating schemes. R. H. Charles[313] has noted that the conception of the "wholeness" of the Jewish nation flourished during the Maccabean era, whereas the older, exilic concept of a divided or dispersed nation revived again in the first century C.E.

(14) The question of canonicity also comes into play. In the manuscripts of the LXX canon, Baruch has often been treated as a part of, or an appendix to, the book of Jeremiah.[314] That the translator of the second half of Jeremiah and especially the first part of Baruch were probably one and the same person is supported by the very close relationship that H. St. J. Thackeray[315] has demonstrated to have existed between the Greek texts of these two portions of Scripture. If then the whole Jeremianic corpus (Jeremiah + Lamentations, Baruch, Epistle of Jeremiah) is properly considered to have been included in the reference to the existence of the Greek Version of the Law, the Prophets, and the rest of the Books,[316] by the grandson of Ben Sirach in his prologue to the Wisdom of Sirach (132 B.C.E.), a *terminus ad quem* is provided for the translation of Baruch into the Greek. The close relationship of the Greek texts demonstrated by Thackeray[317] suggests that at least the first part of Baruch was already translated and being considered as a Jeremianic appendix. And even if all the Jeremianic materials were not intended in this reference, their subsequent incorporation could not have followed too much later.

Of course, Baruch was never incorporated into the Palestinian canon. This fact has been cited regularly by those who would date the work after 70 C.E. While this might suffice to explain its absence in the Hebrew Bible, it would then be impossible to explain how so late a work could have been included in the LXX canon. It is much more plausible to assume its considerably earlier Maccabean origins, subsequent incorporation into the LXX canon along with (and/or shortly after) Jeremiah, and then much later exclusion from the Palestinian canon, since in that provenance it lacked the sort of intimate identity with Jeremiah that marked its passage into the Greek tradition.[318]

(15) A few other observations militate particularly against the post-70 C.E. dating scheme. (a) In the third section of

Baruch it is not the destruction of Jerusalem that is lamented but the loss of her "children," and not rebuilding that is anticipated but the return of her "children."[319] (b) The conciliatory tenor of the historical introduction (generally acknowledged to have been the final redactorial phase) hardly fits the time of 70 C.E.+. It is almost impossible to conceive of any pious Jew in the years after 70 C.E. urging his compatriots to intercede for Vespasian and Titus, the historical figures assumed to be represented in this theory by the *Decknamen*, Nebuchadnezzar and Belshazzar. (c) In the first section all the references to the desolate state of Jerusalem found in the source-text (Dan 9:16, 17, 18) appear to have been deliberately omitted in the direct borrowings of Baruch, suggesting strongly that at the time of composition the city was not in ruins.[320]

Summary

In summary, the most persuasive evidence points to the Maccabean era as the time of origin. Unfortunately, it is at present not possible to be much more precise than ca. 180-100 B.C.E. for the composition and compilation of the several units. The Wisdom Poem is doubtless the earliest part and the historical introduction (1:1-14) the latest. It would appear in brief that the evolutionary process began with the linking of the poetic works for liturgical purposes. After the Prayer of Confession was then affixed as an introduction, so to speak, and the three parts linked at least superficially by the Exilic theme, a brief historical introduction was provided (to certify the liturgical character) by a final editor who was apparently not even aware that his conciliatory stance vis-à-vis foreign rulers contradicted attitudes expressed elsewhere in the composite work. The final product was then circulated pseudonymously under the name of the renowned Baruch, an indisputable eyewitness of "the" deportation of the sixth century B.C.E. and thereby presumably an expert on the subject.[321]

THE THOUGHT OF BARUCH

This collection of originally anonymous works known as Baruch preserves some valuable information about the religious life and thought of the Jewish diaspora, most particularly concerning the doctrine of God, of sin and retribution, and the themes of devotion to the Law and soteriological hope. That such themes do not appear uniformly throughout the three parts of Baruch may be attributed to the composite nature of the book itself. There are as well some common Apocryphal doctrinal themes (viz., Messianism, Angelology, and resurrection) that are most conspicuous by their absence from Baruch, a fact that in the main may be traced to the highly derivative and unoriginal character of the book.

Prominent Doctrines and Themes in Baruch

The Doctrine of God

Names and Titles of God

In the first section, God is consistently referred to as *Kyrios* "Lord" (e.g., *Kyrios*, *ho Kyrios*, *Kyrios theos hēmōn*, *Kyrios ho theos hēmōn*, *ho Kyrios theos hēmōn*, and *Kyrie pantokratōr ho theos Israēl*). In the second section, the Wisdom Poem, *Kyrios* does not appear. Here all references to the Deity are to *theos* or *ho theos*. A yet different situation emerges in the third section, the Consolation Poem. Here God is most frequently styled *ho aiōnios* "the Eternal." An elaboration of this in 4:22, *para tou aiōniou sōtēros hymōn*, corresponds precisely to the Isaianic "*YHWH* your Savior" (cf. Isa 49:26, 60:16). Also, the epithet *ho hagios* appears three times in the third section but never in the previous two.[322]

Attributes and Characteristics of God

Understandably, the first section places considerable emphasis on God's role as the *object of prayer and worship* (1:10, 11, 13, 14; 2:14, 32; 3:4-7). This theme is also found in the third section but to a much lesser extent (4:20-22, 27). God's *righteousness* (1:15; 2:6, 9, 18) and *mercy* (2:19, 27, 35; 3:2) are noticeably stressed in the first section, somewhat less in the third (5:2, 9; and 4:22, 27, 30; 5:9), and not appreciably at all in the second. The Deutero-Isaianic conception of God's mercy is apparent in the third part, especially in its preoccupation with comfort, cheer, and deliverance.

Among other attributes the *glory* of God is especially prominent in the third section (4:37; 5:1, 2, 3; cf. also 2:18). Mention of his *wisdom* (3:12-13, 35-37; 4:2) and *omniscience* (3:32f.) is limited exclusively to the second section. While all three parts reveal at least one reference to God's role as the *source of light*, this aspect of his nature receives the most attention in the second part (cf. 1:12; 3:14, 33; 4:2; 5:9). God is also characterized as *almighty*, or *absolute* in rule, at least once in each section (2:21ff.; 3:1; 3:24-25; 5:7-8).

Other aspects of the divine character brought out exclusively in the third section include God's *eternal* nature (4:8, 10, 14, 20, 22, 24, 35; 5:2), his capacity as *source and bringer of joy* (4:29, 36, 37; 5:9), and his intimate role as *name-giver* to his people (4:30; 5:4).

The Doctrine of Sin and Retribution

The themes of God's anger over sin (1:13; 2:13, 20; 4:6-7, 9-10, 25) and the resultant retribution (2:1, 4, 7; 4:14-15, 19, 29, 34-35) receive about equal attention in the first and third sections and next to none in the second (3:10-12). The older doctrine of retribution, the visitation of the sins of the fathers onto their descendants, is still operative in Baruch, but there is no espousal of the later corollary that ancestral righteousness is meritorious for one's descendants. The latter would, in fact, appear to be refuted in 2:19.[323]

The Theme of Devotion to the Law

In contrast to many post-biblical (especially apocalyptic) works evidencing a general lack of concern for matters of Torah, Baruch falls into place with such Apocryphal works as Sirach, Tobit, Judith, and First and Second Maccabees (as well as such pseudepigraphs and writings as Jubilees, Testaments of the Twelve Patriarchs, Fourth Maccabees, Second Baruch, and the Damascus Document) in giving deliberate and generous attention to the orthodox position of high veneration for the Torah.[324]

This theme is particularly strong in the second section where hypostatized Wisdom is conceived as embodied in Torah,

Israel's unique gift and privilege from God. The theme reflects the process of internalization that began to take shape already with the onset of Hellenism and the insistence that true wisdom may be found only in Israel's own prized and inalienable possession, the Torah.

The Theme of Salvation Hope

God's supreme role in the nation's soteriological hope as Deliverer, minimally set forth in the first section (2:34), is heavily stressed in the final section (4:18, 21, 23, 24, 29, 37; 5:6, 9). It is a fact of great significance that "salvation" in Baruch is still dealt with in the older thought patterns of "deliverance" from physical affliction and "return" to a new, but still terrestrial, life. Other-worldly aspects of salvation are not yet prominent.

The theme of salvation hope, so prominent in the third part is, as would be expected from the sources of that section, reflective of the soteriology of Second Isaiah. This is apparent throughout as the sub-themes of comfort, consolation, and joy are mingled with the stylized Isaianic motif of deliverance and return from exile.

Common Apocryphal Doctrines and Themes lacking in Baruch

The element of Messianism, so prominent in later post-biblical works (e.g., 2 Baruch), is absent from Baruch, as are apocalyptic and eschatological concepts in general. Also conspicuously missing is any trace of the Angelology (or Demonology) so common and well-developed in other Apocryphal works such as Tobit or Second Baruch[325] and at Qumran.

There is no sign as well of the doctrine of resurrection which is thematically often prominent in the later Apocryphal and Pseudepigraphical literature (e.g., 2 Baruch). Indeed, the conceptions of the netherworld set forth in 2:17; 3:11, 19 would appear to deny it. There is also no sign of the secrecy of "knowledge," or Hellenistic Gnosis, that does appear in numerous pseudepigraphs and in some of the Qumran writings.

While it is not the purpose of this section to defend the hypothesis of multiple authorship for the book, one can hardly avoid noticing that both the above-mentioned lexical and thematic evidence strongly indicate independent origins for the three parts. And even though the presence or absence of doctrinal themes is hardly a secure peg upon which to hang a dating scheme, it might at least be said that the particular motifs in evidence and those lacking would appear to lend significant support to the earlier, rather than later, Maccabean period.

Relationships to Qumran Doctrinal Themes

Several of the doctrinal themes prominent in Baruch are also prominent in the writings of the Qumran sectaries. God's righteousness and his absolute rule are essential features in both. Also, the thematic association of God with "light" throughout Baruch is matched in the Qumran literature (cf., e.g., the sect's own title, "The Sons of Light"). Other doctrines, particularly those of Angelology and resurrection and the future life, are in evidence at Qumran but noticeably lacking in Baruch.[326]

The Qumran Thanksgiving Hymns, or *Hôdāyôt*, so steeped in both the canonical Scriptures and the rules of the Manual of Discipline, exhibit the same compositional style as Baruch, namely, the pastiche framework of interwoven Biblical quotations, borrowings, or allusions. But, while revealing some of the same doctrinal motifs as Baruch, they nevertheless reflect others (as noted) which are not a part of the thought of Baruch. Most particularly, one may single out in this regard the Hellenistic conception of Gnosis or secret "knowledge" which is common in numerous apocalypses and clearly evident in the *Hôdāyôt*.[327]

THE SCOPE, METHOD, AND PURPOSE OF THE PRESENT STUDY

While the vast majority of biblical scholars agree that the original language of the poems attributed to Baruch was Hebrew, the only thoroughgoing attempt to demonstrate this by means of an actual reconstruction of the original Hebrew text was made in 1879. This was in the above-cited, systematic and laboriously detailed commentary on Baruch, *Das Buch Baruch*, by the

German pastor-scholar, J. J. Kneucker. This work, while still an invaluable initiator into Baruch studies in terms of its wealth of textual and philological detail, is nevertheless seriously flawed interpretatively by the author's most unscientific penchant to discover the most precise historical allusions in every obscure and general phrase. It has also simply become outdated in many respects, particularly through the impact that the enlightening documents from Qumran and the rapid advances of the past one hundred years in many areas of Biblical and Apocryphal research have had on the nature of the living Hebrew language and the diverse and prolific literary production within Judaism during the years 200 B.C.E.-100 C.E.

Since there are still a few modern scholars who demur with regard to the general consensus that Hebrew was the original language of the two poems, it is apparent that no past study of the problem has been able to present an altogether convincing case, short of recovery of the actual Hebrew autograph(s) or copies thereof. It has thus appeared to the present writer that this question was now ready to be reexamined from the vantage point of our vastly improved perspective on the language and literary production of the so-called intertestamental period.

Such an undertaking must then focus on a systematic and scientific reconstruction of the original Hebrew text, the existence of which is supported by all the available evidence. Thanks especially to the Qumran materials there is now an abundance of sources which demonstrate the fact that well after Hebrew had been supplanted as the vernacular of the Jewish populace it nevertheless continued in written use among the learned, and in relation to its indelible bond with the canonical Scriptures never wholly ceased to be a functional medium in liturgy. A vast and varied literary productivity in Hebrew is now well-documented for this period from which the Baruch material, by scholarly concensus, had its origin. Among many other things the Qumran material reveals the ongoing transmission processes with respect both to canonical and noncanonical Scriptures. One work in particular, the *Hôdāyôt*, offers a very close parallel to the Baruch poetry in terms of the manner of composition, each being a pastiche of Biblical borrowings.

Given the highly derivative character of the entire book of Baruch, most of the verses in the poetic sections can be traced back to sources in earlier canonical and noncanonical works. In verse after verse, phrases or even whole lines have been borrowed or adapted, often with only minor variations, and in a number of examples it can be seen that the borrowing was from the Hebrew Bible rather than the Greek.[328] It is this derivative nature of the work in particular that makes possible reconstruction of a nonexistent original text, a task that obviously would be extremely difficult in the case of an independent and highly original composition. Reconstruction is, of course, also facilitated by such factors as: (1) the existence of numerous well-established and highly predictable lexical equivalencies between the LXX and MT; (2) the availability of a wealth of parallels in various canonical and noncanonical (including Qumran) works, not to mention the actual source-texts quoted or adapted; (3) the significant accumulation of data in recent years regarding Hebrew grammar in general, syntax in particular, and such essential features of classical Hebrew poetry as fixed pairing and parallelism;[329] and (4) the ever-increasing body of information about contemporary Alexandrian Greek being derived from the various papyrological discoveries since the turn of the century.

Superficially, this project may give the appearance of being a mere exercise in solipsism, to reconstruct a no longer extant original text and contend for its prior existence on the basis of what that reveals. But such an appraisal hardly does justice to the full dimensions of this undertaking or of the variety of evidence in support of a Hebrew original. The textual evidence that appears in the following chapters (especially of Hebraisms and mistranslations in the Greek and Syriac texts, and of various Hebrew poetic devices), in addition to the various lines of textual and nontextual evidence adduced above in this introductory chapter, overwhelmingly favors an original Hebrew text. In effect, the results of the reconstruction, added to all the other grounds favoring a Hebrew original, represent the death knell for the conception that Bar 3:9-5:9 was composed in Greek.

It must therefore be carefully noted that in those passages where the Baruch material has been borrowed very directly and literally from older source-texts, or where the individual lexical items of a passage offer extremely regular equivalencies between the LXX and MT (i.e., where the wording of the Hebrew original may be considered certain), impressive examples of Hebrew poetry obtain. But it is not simply in such certain passages that reconstruction yields a high quality of poetry; that is, in general, the result throughout Bar 3:9-5:9. The familiar earmarks of Hebrew prosody, parallelism, repetition, and fixed pairs appearing in their expected canonical sequences, are in ample evidence in the highly certain passages and in those, for various reasons, of lesser certainty.

Obviously, in such an undertaking as this a certain amount of subjectivity is unavoidable, especially in those passages where the methodological criteria for reconstruction are least applicable. It is hoped, however, that such subjectivity has been kept to a minimum and that objectivity, and thus accuracy, prevail.

It will thus be the purpose of this study to (1) reconstitute as accurately as possible the original Hebrew text of the two poetic sections of Baruch by means of such methodological criteria as well-established LXX-MT equivalencies, quoted source-texts, numerous parallels from canonical, noncanonical, and Qumran works, and the various patterns and devices of Hebrew poetics; (2) provide detailed philological notes with the text, assembling therein all the supportive evidence for the reconstruction; and (3) conclusively establish the existence of the Hebrew original by identifying and marshalling the examples of Hebraisms and mistranslations in the texts of the primary Versions and of Hebrew poetic devices and metrical patterns in the reconstruction of the original text, as well as general reflections of Palestinian provenance.

NOTES TO CHAPTER I

[1]See J. Bewer, "The River Sud in the Book of Baruch," *JBL* 43 (1924) 226-27. This scholar contends that the LXX here misread the familiar Ahawa River as Sud (ΣΟΥΔ < ΕΟΥΑ).

[2]These two Babylonian rulers could hardly have ruled concurrently. Belshazzar was the crown prince under the final Babylonian king, Nabonidus (ca. 556-539 B.C.E.). Tradition has frequently confused the more obscure Nabonidus with his renowned predecessor, Nebuchadnezzar (ca. 605-562 B.C.E.).

[3]The function of 2:6-10 appears to have been introductory with respect to the two prayers that follow. It begins exactly as does the preceding section (1:15-2:5), and the essential distinction between these two parts may well be that the former confession was prepared for the use of the Jerusalem community while the latter was a confession of the exiles. See R. H. Pfeiffer, *A History of New Testament Times: with an Introduction to the Apocrypha* (New York: Harper and Brothers, 1949) 410 (hereafter: *HNTT*), and R. H. Charles, "Baruch," *Encyclopaedia Britannica*, 11th ed. (1910) III, 453.

[4]The appeal to the Deity's own self-interest is a familiar appeal found on the lips of many a pious lamenter throughout the literature of the Ancient Near East. Such suggestions that the Deity capitalize on an opportunity to enhance his reputation or take care lest he exhaust in his wrath his entire supply of devotees may be traced all the way back through the canonical Psalms to roots in the cuneiform literature of Mesopotamia. See, e.g., Ps 6:5-6, 30:9-10, 88:10ff.; and such works as W. G. Lambert, *Babylonian Wisdom Literature* (Oxford: Clarendon, 1960).

[5]See below, pp. 20-21.

[6]A. Fitzgerald ("Baruch," in *The Jerome Biblical Commentary*, eds. Raymond E. Brown, Joseph E. Fitzmyer, and Roland E. Murphy [Englewood Cliffs, NJ: Prentice-Hall, 1968] 618) isolates eight units: (1) 4:5-9a; (2) 4:9b-13; (3) 4:14-20; (4) 4:21-24; (5) 4:25-29; (6) 4:30-35; (7) 4:36-5:4; (8) 5:5-9.

[7]Henry St. John Thackeray ("Baruch," in *A New Commentary on Holy Scripture*, eds. Charles Gore, H. L. Goudge, and Alfred Guillaume [New York: Macmillan, 1929] 102-03) breaks it down into seven units: (1) 4:5-20; (2) 4:21-26; (3) 4:27-29; (4) 4:30-35; (5) 4:36-37; (6) 5:1-4; (7) 5:5-9.

[8]Leonhard Rost (*Einleitung in die alttestamentlichen Apokryphen und Pseudepigraphen einschliesslich der grossen Qumran-Handschriften* [Heidelberg: Quelle und Meyer, 1971] 52) and Artur Weiser (*The Old Testament: Its Formation and Development*, trans. from the 5th German ed. by Herbert Hartwell [New York: Association Press, 1966] 405-06) agree on six individual units: (1) 4:5-9a; (2) 4:9b-16; (3) 4:17-29; (4) 4:30-35; (5) 4:36-5:4; (6) 5:5-9.

[9]Wilhelm Pesch, "Die Abhängigkeit des 11 salomonischen Psalms vom letzten Kapital des Buches Baruch," *ZAW* 26 (1955) 251-63.

[10]See below, p. 30.

[11]See below, pp. 20-23.

[12]See, e.g., Emanuel Ṭov, *The Book of Baruch* (Missoula: Scholars Press, 1975) 1ff.

[13]C. C. Torrey, *The Apocryphal Literature* (New Haven: Yale University, 1945) 62.

[14]See below, pp. 23-26.

[15]Ibid.

[16]See below, pp. 25-26.

[17]This is quoted from Torrey, *The Apocryphal Literature*, 14-15.

[18]Ibid., 1.

[19]J. T. Milik, *Ten Years of Discovery in the Wilderness of Judea* (London: SCM, 1959) 54, and Albert Vincent, *Les Manuscrits Hébreux du Désert de Juda* (Paris: Librairie Arthème Fayard, 1955) 72.

[20]Joseph Ziegler, ed., *Septuaginta, Vetus Testamentum Graecum auctoritate Societatis Litterarum Gottingensis editum, XV: Ieremias, Baruch, Threni, Epistula Ieremiae* (Göttingen: Vandenhoeck und Ruprecht, 1957) (hereafter: Ziegler).

[21]Characterizations of the LXX text in general, and descriptions of its origin and history, abound in the many handbooks on the subject. An excellent introduction and bibliography may be found in the recent work of Sidney Jellicoe, *The Septuagint and Modern Study* (Oxford: Clarendon, 1968). For such matters as LXX translation techniques and evaluation of LXX Greek in the light of papyrological finds, one may initially consult the following: Jellicoe, *The Septuagint and Modern Study*, 314-18; Elias J. Bickerman, "The Septuagint as a Translation," *PAAJR* 28 (1959) 1-39; Adolf Deissmann, *The Philology of the Greek Bible* (London: Hodder and Stoughton, 1908) 60ff.; Ernst Würthwein, *The Text of the Old Testament*, trans. Peter R. Ackroyd (Oxford: Blackwell, 1957) 34-56; Suzanne Daniel, "Bible, Ancient Versions, Greek: The Septuagint," *Encyclopaedia Judaica* (1971) IV, cols. 851-56; and E. Ṭov, "Septuagint," *IDBSup* (1976) 807-11.

[22]See Ziegler, 7-10.

[23]Next to LXX Minuscule 88, Syh is the most significant representative of the Hexaplaric text. Because of the precision and reliability of its reproduction of its Greek *Vorlage*, it is frequently treated as a "Greek" manuscript.

[24]See Eberhard Nestle, "Septuagint," *HDB* IV, 450, and R. R. Harwell, *The Principal Versions of Baruch* (New Haven: Yale University, 1915) 52-53 (hereafter: Harwell).

[25]For further detail regarding Syh Baruch, and the Syh translation in general, see: O. C. Whitehouse, "1 Baruch," *APOT* I, 577-78; Ziegler, 27; Frederic G. Kenyon, *Our Bible and the Ancient Manuscripts* (New York: Harper and Brothers, 1958) 135; B. J. Roberts, *The Old Testament Text and Versions* (Cardiff: University of Wales, 1951) 227; and Jellicoe, *The Septuagint and Modern Study*, 125-27.

[26]See Whitehouse, "1 Baruch," 577.

[27]Ibid., 578-79. Concurring in this assessment are such scholars as L. Rost (*Einleitung*, 51) and R. H. Pfeiffer (*HNTT*, 423). See below, pp. 13-14 and n. 42.

[28]See Ziegler, 84-85.

[29]Ibid.

[30]In three instances (1:18, 2:19, and 4:26), Sy even has triplets; see Harwell (18-26) and Ziegler (29).

[31]See above, n. 27.

[32]J. J. Kneucker, *Das Buch Baruch: Geschichte und Kritik, Übersetzung und Erklärung auf Grund des wiederhergestellten hebräischen Urtextes* (Leipzig: F. A. Brockhaus, 1879) 163-73 (hereafter: Kneucker).

[33]Harwell, 10-28.

[34]Kenyon, *Our Bible*, 135.

[35]Ibid.

[36]Otto Eissfeldt, *The Old Testament, An Introduction: The History of the Formation of the Old Testament*, trans. Peter R. Ackroyd (New York/Evanston: Harper and Row, 1965) 699, and William Wright, *A Short History of Syriac Literature* (London: Adam and Charles Black, 1894) 3.

[37]Whitehouse, "1 Baruch," 577.

[38]Roberts, *The Old Testament Text*, 215.

[39]Ibid.

[40]Paul de Lagarde, *Libri Veteris Testamenti: Apocryphi Syriace* (Leipzig: F. A. Brockhaus, 1861) 93-104 (hereafter: *LVTAS*).

[41]Ibid., xiiiff.

[42]See Chapter V, n. 367, for further parallels. And see Chapter VI for a complete listing of data supporting Sy access to the Hebrew original. That the translator of Sy also had before him the Greek Version is clear from such passages as 4:20, where Sy employs a cognate loanword to render the Greek term, *stolē*; 3:30, where Sy with the LXX supports the problematic reading, "bring"; and 4:34, in which the Sy conflate reading is based on two LXX variants (*agalliama* and *agalmata*). In the opinion of Pfeiffer (*HNTT*, 423), such "merely confirms the view that the Syriac translator used the Greek text as well as the Hebrew." On the basis of the appearance in Sy of the term "helmet" for "diadem" in 5:2, and the phrase "by the tents" for "on the height" in 5:5, Whitehouse ("1 Baruch," 579) has suggested that the production of the Sy Version could plausibly be assumed to derive from a time in which a martial and anti-Roman fervor was waxing strong, viz., shortly after 132 C.E. With regard to the lengthy discussions of the Sy translation by both Kneucker (163-73) and Harwell (10-28), the admonition of Ziegler (28) for cautious and judicious application of their detail must be heeded.

[43]See Whitehouse, "1 Baruch," 579; Harwell, 29; and Ziegler, 20.

[44]Ziegler, 20.

[45]Ziegler uses the third (1929) Vulgate edition of Hetzenauer (p. 20). The present study has employed the more recent edition of Robert Weber, ed. (*Biblia Sacra: Iuxta Vulgatam Versionem*, Tome II [Stuttgart: Württembergische Bibelanstalt, 1969]).

[46]See Harwell, 29, and Ziegler, 21.

[47]See Ziegler, 21. The relationships between the two most important mss., La^V and La^S, and their Greek *Vorlagen* are treated by Kneucker (141-63) and by Harwell (29-46). In the opinion of the latter, La^S is not dependent on La^V as Kneucker surmised, but is of older derivation from a Greek text. Ziegler (22) recommends caution and a new study of the problem.

[48]"Bible, Ancient Versions: Egyptian (Coptic)," *Encyclopaedia Judaica* (1971) IV, col. 861.

[49]Kneucker, 184.

[50]Ziegler, 41-52.

[51]H. Brugsch, "Das Buch Baruch, koptisch.," *ZÄS* 10 (1872) 134; see also Ziegler, 22.

[52]H. Brugsch, "Das Buch Baruch, koptisch.," *ZÄS* 10 (1872) 134-36 (Bar 1,1-2,27); 11 (1873) 18-21 (Bar 2,28-4,37); 12 (1874) 46-49 (Bar 5 + Ep Jr).

[53]See Ziegler, 22-23.

[54]Ibid., 23.

[55]Rodolphe Kasser, ed., *Papyrus Bodmer XXII: Jérémie XL,3-LII,34; Lamentations; Epître de Jérémie; Baruch I,1-V,5; en sahidique* (Genève: Bibliotheca Bodmeriana, 1964). This edition has been used in the present study for citations from the Sahidic Version.

[56]"Bible, Ancient Versions: Ethiopic," *Encyclopaedia Judaica* (1971) IV, col. 860.

[57]The lacking verses are listed by Ziegler (36).

[58]August Dillmann, *Biblia Veteris Testamenti Aethiopici: Veteris Testamenti Aethiopici tomus quintus, quo continentur Libri apocryphi* (Berlin: A. Asher et Socios, 1894) 1-6.

[59]Ziegler, 36.

[60]Kneucker, 180.

[61]Ziegler, 41-52.

[62]See Ziegler, 37-38, and Kneucker, 178.

[63]See Michael E. Stone, "Bible, Ancient Versions: Armenian," *Encyclopaedia Judaica* (1971) IV, col. 861.

[64]Ibid., col. 862.

[65]Kneucker, 186.

[66]Ziegler, 67-79.

[67]Ibid., 41-98. The descriptions of these groupings by Ziegler include an examination of their respective character and a comparative study of their interrelationship and their bearing on the Hebrew text.

[68]See Josephus (*The Antiquities of the Jews*, trans. Ralph Marcus [LCL, VI; London: William Heinemann, 1937] X, ix, 1 [§158], pp. 246-47), who describes the scribe and companion of Jeremiah as one who "came of a very distinguished family and was exceptionally well instructed in his native tongue."

[69]The various rabbinical traditions about later events in Baruch's life are contradictory and unreliable for any real historical information. On the one hand, some represent Baruch as going from Egypt to Babylon, while others attest his death in Egypt. Though the predicted conquest of Egypt by Nebuchadnezzar (cf. Jer 43:10-13 and Ezek 29:17-20) never actually eventuated, Josephus (*Antiquities* X, ix, 7 [§§180-82] pp. 256-59) claims that it did and that it was followed by a deportation of the Jews who had taken refuge there. He does not specify which persons in particular were deported, but according to one legend (see B. Ratner, *Seder ʿolam Rabbah* [Wilna: Buchdruckerei v. W-we und Gebr. Romm., 1897] §26, p. 120), both

Jeremiah and Baruch were carried off at this time to Babylon. Another reports Baruch's traveling, after the death of Jeremiah in Egypt, to Babylon where he himself then died in the twelfth year after the destruction of Jerusalem (see E. H. Gifford, "Baruch," in *The Speaker's Commentary on the Holy Bible, The Apocrypha: with an Explanatory and Critical Commentary and Revision of the Translation*, ed. Henry Wace [London: John Murray, 1888] II, 243; and Kneucker, 2-3). The tradition generally accorded most credence is that reported by St. Jerome (*Commentariorum In Esaiam, Libri I-XI* [Corpus Christianorum, Series Latina, LXXIII, pars 2; Turnholti: Typographi Brepols Editores Pontificii, 1963] IX, ad. Ch. XXX:7, p. 386), namely, that both Jeremiah and Baruch died in Egypt, Jeremiah by stoning at the hands of fellow refugees who became enraged over his criticism of their apostasies (see Louis Ginzberg, "Jeremiah in Rabbinical Literature," *The Jewish Encyclopedia* [1904] VII, 102). This tradition of Baruch's demise is commonly regarded as the most trustworthy (see Kneucker, 2; Gifford, "Baruch," 243; et al.).

As if this were not confusion enough, there are yet further conflicting traditions. Absolutely at variance to any of the above is the tradition reported in 2 Apoc Bar (Syr), §10, 1-5, and Paralipomena Jeremiae III:10ff.; IV:5ff., that Jeremiah (!) went to Babylon while Baruch remained in the ruins of Jerusalem (see R. H. Charles, *The Apocalypse of Baruch: translated from the Syriac* [London: Adam and Charles Black, 1896] 13-14; idem, "II Baruch," *APOT* II, 485; J. Rendel Harris, *The Rest of the Words of Baruch: A Christian Apocalypse of the Year 136 A.D.* [London: C. J. Clay, 1889] 50ff.; Pfeiffer, *HNTT*, 414; and Edwin Cone Bissell, *The Apocrypha of the Old Testament*, Vol. XV in *A Commentary on the Holy Scriptures*, ed. John P. Lange [New York: Scribner's Sons, 1890] 414). There is additional legendary information concerning Baruch's alleged activity in Babylon. The tradition preserved in *Midrash Rabba* (at Ct 5:5) and in *The Babylonian Talmud* (*Megillah*, 16b) (see H. Freedman and Maurice Simon, eds., *Midrash Rabbah*, VI: *Song of Songs*, trans. Maurice Simon [London: Soncino, 1939] 5:5, pp. 235-36; and I. Epstein, ed., *The Babylonian Talmud, Seder Mo'ed*, pt. 2, vol. 8: *Megillah*, trans. Maurice Simon [London: Soncino, 1938] §16b, pp. 100-01) states that Baruch served there as the teacher of Ezra, and that at the time of Cyrus' edict Ezra chose to remain behind in Babylon to study Torah with his aged mentor rather than return to Jerusalem. See further, Pfeiffer (*HNTT*, 414); Kneucker (3), who notes that, according to such legends, Baruch would have been 168 at the time of his death; and Louis Ginzberg ("Baruch in Rabbinical Literature," *The Jewish Encyclopedia* [1902] II, 548-49).

Though a very few have attempted to defend such information as historically reliable (e.g., F. H. Reusch, *Erklärung des Buches Baruch* [Freiburg: Herder'sche Verlagshandlung, 1853] 22-23), it must be affirmed with Pfeiffer (*HNTT*, 414) that "It is idle to seek in such imaginary tales some confirmation for the hypothesis (which is supported by no evidence and is highly improbable) according to which Baruch was in Babylonia in 582." Such traditions as these simply cannot supply verifiable historical data, and are thus for all practical purposes useless for this final period of Baruch's life.

It should be stressed that the silence of the canonical Scriptures (which know only of a journey to Egypt) on this matter of Baruch's alleged presence in Babylon is most significant. For if Baruch had ever really shared in the life of the Babylonian *Gôlāh* it would only be reasonable to expect that that fact would surely have been stated by Jeremiah or Ezekiel (see W. O. E. Oesterley, *An Introduction to the Books of the Apocrypha* [London: S.P.C.K., 1953] 259). It is a likely hypothesis that the tradition which places Baruch in Babylon resulted from a misunderstanding of Jer 51:59, where the dispatching of Baruch's brother, Seriah, with a message to Babylon may well have given substance to the notion that Baruch himself had gone there. See Bissell, *The Apocrypha*, 414. J. W. Rothstein ("Das Buch Baruch," in *Die Apokryphen und Pseudepigraphen des alten Testaments*, ed. E. Kautzsch [Tübingen: J. C. B. Mohr, 1900] I, 213) has noted in this regard that in the Syriac text (Sy) Baruch is said to have sent his missive *l^ebābel* "to Babylon."

It is, of course, possible that Baruch could have gone to Babylon after Jeremiah's death (thus Wenzel Stoderl, *Zur Echtheitsfrage von Baruch 1-3,8* [Münster in Westf.: Druck der Aschendorffschen Buchdruckerei, 1922] 16-17), but it would have been impossible for him to have been there at the time given in Bar 1:2 (see below, p. 20). Otto F. Fritzsche (*Kurzgefasstes exegetisches Handbuch zu den Apokryphen des Alten Testaments* [Leipzig: Weidmanns, 1851] B. I, 170) suggests a chronological error here, but is not successful in thereby defending a journey of Baruch to Babylon.

[70]Edmund Kalt, *Das Buch Baruch* (*HSAT* VII, 3/4; Bonn: Peter Hanstein, 1932) 1-2, 5ff.

[71]Reusch, *Erklärung des Buches Baruch*, 21-22.

[72]This information is derived from Pfeiffer (*HNTT*, 412).

[73]This information is derived from Samuel Davidson (*An Introduction to the Old Testament* [Covent Garden/Edinburgh: Williams and Norgate, 1863] III, 428) and Carl F. Keil (*Lehrbuch der historisch-kritischen Einleitung in die kanonischen und apokryphischen Schriften des Alten Testaments*, 3rd ed. [Frankfurt: Heyder und Zimmer, 1873] 751).

[74]Ibid.

[75]This information is derived from Pfeiffer (*HNTT*, 412) and Davidson (*An Introduction*, 428).

[76]Johann Goettsberger, *Einleitung in das Alte Testament* (Freiburg im Breisgau: Herder, 1928) 307-10.

[77]Angelo Penna, *Baruch* (*La Sacra Bibbia* 11; Torino/Rome: Marietti Editori, 1952) 8-14.

[78]Paul Heinisch, "Zur Entstehung des Buches Baruch," *TGl* 20 (1928) 696ff.

[79]Stoderl, *Zur Echtheitsfrage*, 3.

[80]Heinisch ("Zur Entstehung des Buches Baruch," 708) would in fact identify the third section more precisely as the product of a disciple of Second Isaiah.

[81]Leonhard Bertholdt, *Historischkritische Einleitung in sämmtliche kanonische und apokryphische Schriften des Alten und Neuen Testaments* (Erlangen: J. J. Palm, 1819) IV, 1762-66.

[82]Eduard Reuss, *Das Alte Testament*, Band VI: *Religions- und Moralphilosophie der Hebräer* (Braunschweig: C. A. Schwetschke, 1894) 426-27; and idem, *Die Geschichte der Heiligen Schriften, Alten Testaments* (Braunschweig: C. A. Schwetschke, 1881) 633-34.

[83]Fritzsche, *Kurzgefasstes Handbuch* I, 173.

[84]Heinrich Ewald, *Die Propheten des Alten Bundes*, Band III: *Die Jüngsten Propheten des Alten Bundes mit den Büchern Barukh und Daniel*, 2nd ed. (Göttingen: Vandenhoeck und Ruprecht, 1868) 252, 268-69; and idem, *Die Geschichte des Volkes Israel* (Göttingen: In der Dieterischen Buchhandlung, 1864) IV, 266ff.

[85]Adolf Hilgenfeld, "Das Buch Baruch, *ZWT* 5 (1862) 199-204; idem, "Das Buch Baruch und seine neueste Bearbeitung," *ZWT* 22 (1879) 437-54; and idem, "Baruch," *ZWT* 23 (1880) 412-22.

[86]Herbert E. Ryle and Montague R. James, *Psalmoi Solomontos: Psalms of the Pharisees commonly called the Psalms of Solomon* (Cambridge: The University Press, 1891) lxviii.

[87]Hermann L. Strack, *Einleitung in das Alte Testament einschliesslich Apokryphen und Pseudepigraphen mit eingehender Angabe der Literatur*, 4th ed., rev. (München: C. H. Beck, 1895) §70, p. 161.

[88]Torrey, *The Apocryphal Literature*, 59-60.

[89]Carl H. Cornill, *Einleitung in das Alte Testament mit Einschluss der Apokryphen und Pseudepigraphen*, 4th ed., rev. (Freiburg/Leipzig: J. C. B. Mohr, 1896) 272-73.

[90]Henry St. John Thackeray, *The Septuagint and Jewish Worship*, 2nd ed. (London: The British Academy 1923) 86; and idem, "Baruch," 103.

[91]Otto Zöckler, *Die Apokryphen des Alten Testaments* (*Kurzgefasstes Kommentar zu den Heiligen Schriften*, Series A, Abt. 9; München: C. H. Beck, 1891) 239-40.

[92]Ferdinand Hitzig, "Zur Kritik der apokryphischen Bücher des Alten Testaments: (3) einige Bemerkungen über das Buch Baruch," *ZWT* 3 (1860) 262-73.

[93]Harwell, 63-64.

[94]Bruce M. Metzger, *An Introduction to the Apocrypha* (New York: Oxford University, 1957) 89.

[95]Charles, "Baruch," 453, and idem, *Religious Developments Between the Old and New Testaments* (New York: Henry Holt, n.d.) 215-16.

[96]Henry S. Gehman,""Apocrypha," *The New Westminster Dictionary of the Bible* (Philadelphia: Westminster, 1970) 52.

[97]Emil Schürer, "Apocrypha," *The New Schaff-Herzog Encyclopedia of Religious Knowledge* (1908) I, 219, and idem, *A History of the Jewish People*, II/iii, 189.

[98]Weiser, *The Old Testament*, 406.

[99]Whitehouse, "1 Baruch," 570-71, 574-75.

[100]B. N. Wambacq, "L'unité du livre de Baruch," *Bib* 47 (1966) 574-76.

[101]W. J. Ferrar, *The Uncanonical Jewish Books: A Short Introduction to the Apocrypha and the Jewish Writings* (London: S.P.C.K., 1918) 38.

[102]Rothstein, "Das Buch Baruch," 213-15.

[103]Pesch, "Die Abhängigkeit des 11 Salomonischen Psalms," 253.

[104]Eissfeldt, *The Old Testament*, 593-94.

[105]John L. McKenzie, "Baruch," *Dictionary of the Bible* (Milwaukee: Bruce Publishing, 1965) 82.

[106]Pfeiffer, *HNTT*, 413.

[107]Kneucker, 13-20, 37-61.

[108]Sidney S. Tedesche, "Book of Baruch," *IDB* (1962) I, 362.

[109]W. O. E. Oesterley, *The Jews and Judaism During the Greek Period* (London: S.P.C.K., 1941) 52; idem, *The Books of the Apocrypha: Their Origin, Teaching and Contents* (New York/ Chicago: Fleming H. Revell, 1914) 495ff.; and idem, *An Introduction*, 262-63.

[110]L. E. T. André, *Les Apocryphes de L'Ancien Testament* (Florence: Osvald Paggi, 1903) 255-57, 259-60.

[111]J. T. Marshall, "Book of Baruch," *HDB* I, 251.

[112]J. N. Birdsall, "Apocrypha," *The New Bible Dictionary*, eds. J. D. Douglas et al. (London: Inter-varsity Fellowship, 1962) 46.

[113] J. J. Battistone, "An Examination of the Literary and Theological Background of the Wisdom Passage in the Book of Baruch," Ph.D. dissertation, Duke University (1968) 2-46 (esp. 13-14, 32-34, 44-46).

[114] See Eduard König, *Einleitung in das Alte Testament* (Bonn: Eduard Weber, 1893) §103, pp. 485-86; Crawford H. Toy, "Book of Baruch," *The Jewish Encyclopedia* (1902) II, 556-57; Keil, *Lehrbuch der historisch-kritischen Einleitung*, 751-52; H. Graetz, "Abfassungszeit und Bedeutung des Buches Baruch," *MGWJ* 36 (1887) 385-401; Bissell, *The Apocrypha*, 413-18; Carl Steuernagel, *Lehrbuch der Einleitung in das Alte Testament mit einem Anhang über die Apokryphen und Pseudepigraphen* (Tübingen: J. C. B. Mohr, 1912) 790; Henry Barclay Swete, *An Introduction to the Old Testament in Greek*, 2nd ed., rev. by R. R. Ottley (Cambridge: The University Press, 1914) 275; Gifford, "Baruch," 242-47, 250; A. A. Bevan, "Book of Baruch," *Encyclopaedia Biblica* (1889) I, col. 493; Otto Plöger, "Baruchschriften," *RGG*[3] (1957) I, cols. 900-01; Albert Gelin, *Jérémie, Les Lamentations, Le Livre de Baruch* (*La Sainte Bible* XX, 2nd rev. ed.; Paris: Le éditions du Cerf, 1959) 284-86; Aage Bentzen, *Introduction to the Old Testament* (Copenhagen: G. E. C. Gad, 1949) II, 231-33; Fitzgerald, "Baruch," 615; Rost, *Einleitung*, 52; Curt Kuhl, *Die Entstehung des Alten Testaments*, 2nd rev. ed. (Sammlung Dalp, Band 26; Bern/München: Francke, 1960) 321; L. A. Iranyi, "Book of Baruch," *New Catholic Encyclopedia* (1967) II, 138; J. C. Dancy, "Baruch," *The Cambridge Bible Commentary: The Shorter Books of the Apocrypha*, eds. Peter R. Ackroyd et al. (Cambridge: The University Press, 1972) 169, 172; Michael E. Stone, "Book of Baruch," *Encyclopaedia Judaica* (1971) IV, cols. 272-73; Herbert G. May, "(Introductory Notes to) Baruch," *The Oxford Annotated Apocrypha: The Apocrypha of the Old Testament, RSV*, ed. Bruce M. Metzger (New York: Oxford University, 1965) 198; E. J. Goodspeed, *The Story of the Apocrypha* (Chicago: University of Chicago, 1939) 103; R. K. Harrison, *An Introduction to the Old Testament* (Grand Rapids: William B. Eerdmans, 1969) 1239; and H. T. Robins, "The Complexity of the Book of Baruch," *International Journal of the Apocrypha* 20 (January, 1910) 4-7.

[115] A few other scholars, while rejecting the possibility that the historical Baruch could have authored the work, have rejected as well the idea of compositeness and have endeavored to defend a unity of authorship. Such include: Davidson, *An Introduction*, 426, 428; Wilhelm Vatke, *Historisch-kritische Einleitung in das Alte Testament* (Bonn: Emil Strauss, 1886) 753; and A. Lefèvre, "Baruch," *Introduction à la Bible*, eds. A. Robert and A. Feuillet (Tournai: Desclée, 1959) I, 733-34, 737.

[116] See Rost, *Einleitung*, 52, and Pfeiffer, *HNTT*, 414.

[117] See Pfeiffer, *HNTT*, 414 n. 8.

[118] Ibid., 414. These two Babylonian kings were apparently widely confused after their time, as, for example, in the popular legend of Nebuchadnezzar's madness (cf. Daniel 4). See

further David Noel Freedman, "The Prayer of Nabonidus," *BASOR* 145 (1957) 31-32, and Rudolf Meyer, "Das Qumrānfragment 'Gebet des Nabonid,'" *TLZ* 85 (1960) cols. 831-34.

[119]See Bissell, *The Apocrypha*, 414; Torrey, *The Apocryphal Literature*, 60; and Pfeiffer, *HNTT*, 414.

[120]See Torrey, *The Apocryphal Literature*, 61.

[121]See Battistone ("An Examination," 48-73) for a recent evaluation of the relationship between these two prayers. Only a small minority of scholars hold that the Daniel material is dependent on Baruch. See Kneucker (31) for further references to the earlier Protestant scholars holding such a view. Most recently, Stoderl (*Zur Echtheitsfrage*, 5-9) has maintained this stance. Kalt (*Das Buch Baruch*, 4) tends to follow him in this.

[122]All canonical and extra-canonical source-texts are identified throughout the philological notes attached to the reconstruction of the text (Chapters III and V).

[123]For evidence of actual liturgical use, sketchy though it may be, see Thackeray, "Baruch," 102-05; Schürer, *A History of the Jewish People*, II/iii, 193; Bissell, *The Apocrypha*, 417; Pesch, "Die Abhängigkeit des 11 Salomonischen Psalms," passim; and Oesterley, *The Books of the Apocrypha*, 500ff.

[124]See Wambacq, "L'unité du livre de Baruch," 575-76.

[125]See Dancy, "Baruch," 169-70.

[126]See André, *Les Apocryphes*, 260f.; Wambacq, "L'unité du livre de Baruch," 574-76; and Battistone, "An Examination," 26-27.

[127]See Marshall, "Book of Baruch," 252, and Dancy, "Baruch," 171.

[128]See the philological notes below, ad loc. A convenient summary of the use of divine names and titles in Baruch may be found in Gifford ("Baruch," 253).

[129]See further Battistone, "An Examination," 205.

[130]Theodor Nöldeke, *Die alttestamentliche Literatur in einer Reihe von Aufsätzen dargestellt* (Leipzig: Quandt und Händel, 1868) 214, n.

[131]H. A. C. Hävernick, *De libro Baruchi, commentatio critica* (Königsberg: Boruss, 1843) 3ff.

[132]Keil, *Lehrbuch*, 753-54.

[133]Bertholdt, *Historischkritische Einleitung*, 1762-66.

[134]André, *Les Apocryphes*, 253-54.

[135] Vatke, *Historisch-kritische Einleitung*, 753.

[136] Lefèvre, "Baruch," 738, 733f.

[137] Goodspeed, *The Story of the Apocrypha*, 100. The names of a few other seventeenth and eighteenth century scholars who have affirmed the originality of the Greek text may be found listed in Kneucker (20-21).

[138] Fritzsche, *Kurzgefasstes Handbuch*, 171-72.

[139] Hilgenfeld, "Das Buch Baruch," 199ff. See also Schürer, *A History of the Jewish People* II/iii, 191.

[140] Reuss, *Das Alte Testament* VI, 426-27, and idem, *Die Geschichte der Heiligen Schriften*, 633-34.

[141] Schürer, *A History of the Jewish People* II/iii, 190-91. This position is perhaps best epitomized in Schürer's statement (190): "The style and mode of expression widely differ, being in the first half Hebraistic, and in the second fluent and rhetorical Greek."

[142] Cornill, *Einleitung*, 272-73.

[143] Bevan, "Book of Baruch," col. 493.

[144] Bissell, *The Apocrypha*, 413-18.

[145] Gifford, "Baruch," 248-50.

[146] Toy, "Book of Baruch," 556.

[147] M. R. James, "Apocrypha," *Encyclopaedia Biblica* (1889) I, col. 252. See also Ryle and James, *Psalmoi Solomontos*, lxxvii.

[148] Iranyi, "Book of Baruch," 138.

[149] Robins, "The Complexity of the Book of Baruch," 4-7.

[150] Wambacq, "L'unité du livre de Baruch," 575. Wambacq considers all but the Prayer of Confession to have been composed in Greek, allowing for the possibility that the Wisdom Poem may have had a Hebrew original.

[151] Rudolf Mayer, *Einleitung in das Alte Testament* (München: Max Hueber, 1967) 239.

[152] Battistone ("An Examination," 6-14, 94) appears to favor this position but is ultimately noncommittal. A slightly variant position is maintained by Rost (*Einleitung*, 51) and Whitehouse ("1 Baruch," 571-73). This view holds that the first two sections (1:1-4:4) were originally composed in Hebrew but the third section in Greek. This view is also mentioned by Stone

("Book of Baruch," cols. 272-73), but without indication of his own commitment. Gelin (*La Sainte Bible* XX, 285) holds a Hebrew original for the first two sections (1:1-4:4) but offers no comment with regard to the last section. Yet different is the position taken by Marshall ("Book of Baruch," 252-53). He contends that the original languages of the three major units of Baruch were the following: (1) Hebrew (Prayer of Confession); (2) Aramaic (Wisdom Poem); and (3) Greek (Consolation Poem). In this contention he is followed by Swete (*An Introduction*, 275). Plöger ("Baruchschriften," col. 901) suggests that the prose section (1:1-3:8) was composed in Hebrew or Aramaic but has no comment on the two poems. Also see Ṭov, *The Book of Baruch*, 7.

[153] This group thus includes as strange bedfellows, so to speak, both those who have contended for the authenticity of authorship by the sixth-century Baruch and those who find no possibility of such.

[154] Seven years after the appearance of Kneucker's book, another attempt at reconstruction was ventured by a scholar named Herbst. His work (*Das apokryphische Buch Baruch, aus dem Griechischen ins Hebräische übertragen* (*Programm Hildesheim*, 287; 1886, pp. 1-10) has not been accessible to the present writer.

[155] Ferdinand Hitzig, *ZWT* 3 (1860) 262-73. This information is derived from Kneucker (20-29) and Charles (*Religious Developments*, 216).

[156] Davidson, *An Introduction*, 426-27.

[157] Ewald, *Die Jüngsten Propheten*, 256.

[158] Strack, *Einleitung*, §70, p. 161.

[159] Zöckler, *Die Apokryphen*, 239.

[160] Graetz, "Abfassungszeit," 387-93.

[161] Reusch, *Erklärung*, 21-22.

[162] Steuernagel, *Lehrbuch der Einleitung*, 791.

[163] Thackeray, "Baruch," 103.

[164] Charles, *Religious Developments*, 217. See also the general editor's note in R. H. Charles, ed., *APOT* I, 573-74.

[165] Rothstein, "Das Buch Baruch," 213, 215.

[166] Torrey, *The Apocryphal Literature*, 62.

[167] Harwell, 52-56.

[168] Goettsberger, *Einleitung*, 307-08.

[169] Marie-Joseph Lagrange, *Le Judaïsme avant Jésus-Christ* (Paris: J. Gabaldi et fils, 1931) 157.

[170]König, *Einleitung*, 405.

[171]Bentzen, *Introduction* II, 232.

[172]W. M. L. de Wette, *Lehrbuch der Historisch-kritischen Einleitung in die Bibel Alten und Neuen Testaments* (Berlin: Georg Reimer, 1869) §391, p. 602.

[173]Tedesche, "Book of Baruch," 362-63.

[174]Weiser, *The Old Testament*, 406.

[175]Dancy, "Baruch," 172. This affirmation, however, is not made without some reservations.

[176]Fitzgerald, "Baruch," 614. This scholar has some reservations with regard to the third section but leans toward a Hebrew original.

[177]May, *The Oxford Annotated Apocrypha*, 198.

[178]Pesch, "Die Abhängigkeit des 11 Salomonischen Psalms," 255-56.

[179]Eissfeldt, *The Old Testament*, 593.

[180]Gehman, *The New Westminster Dictionary of the Bible*, 52.

[181]Pfeiffer, *HNTT*, 417, 419-21, 422-23.

[182]McKenzie, *Dictionary of the Bible*, 82.

[183]Birdsall, "Apocrypha," 46.

[184]Kalt, *Das Buch Baruch*, 6-7.

[185]Heinisch, "Zur Entstehung des Buches Baruch," 697-98.

[186]Oesterley, *An Introduction*, 266. This represents the latest position of this scholar on the subject. In his much earlier work (*The Books of the Apocrypha* [1914] 504-06), he tended to follow J. T. Marshall in assuming the three main units to have been composed respectively in Hebrew, Aramaic, and Greek.

[187]Kuhl, *Die Entstehung*, 322. Reservations are expressed here with regard to the two poetic sections.

[188]Harrison, *An Introduction to the Old Testament*, 1239.

[189]A. Kahana, *Hassefārîm Hahîṣônîm* (Tel Aviv: Masada, 1936-37) I, 356ff (hereafter: Kahana).

[190]Penna, *Baruch*, 15.

[191]"Introduction to the Prophets: Baruch," *The Jerusalem Bible*, eds. Alexander Jones, et al. (Garden City: Doubleday,

1966) 1128. This list, while thorough, is not absolutely exhaustive. It may be supplemented with regard to the very early nineteenth and eighteenth century scholars by recourse to such surveys as may be found in Davidson (*An Introduction*, 426) (where, for example, the names of thirteen additional older scholars subscribing to a Hebrew original may be found) and Kneucker (20-28).

[192] See especially the summaries in Pfeiffer, *HNTT*, 416-17; Kneucker, 20-28; Battistone, "An Examination," 6-14; Graetz, "Abfassungszeit," 387ff.; Gifford, "Baruch," 248-50; Bissell, *The Apocrypha*, 416-17; and Charles, "Baruch," 453-54. It is of some significance that in the margin of the Syro-Hexaplar text three words in the first section are obelized as lacking in the Hebrew *Urtext* (1:17; 2:3). Eberhard Nestle ("Septuagint," 450) has suggested that in the light of the prefatory statement at the beginning of Syh Baruch to the effect that the whole work had been obelized by Origen, these marginal notes may refer not to the text of Baruch, but rather to the canonical source-texts being quoted in Baruch. Davidson (*An Introduction*, 427) has also observed that the text of LXX Baruch begins with *kai* (1:1). Such a syntactical construction, while awkward in Greek, in the form of the Hebrew equivalent, *waw*, is common and natural in BH as "*waw* consecutive." Here, however, *waw* would seem to be introducing a pericope.

[193] Some of the more conspicuous efforts are those of Kneucker, 24-26, et passim; Pfeiffer, *HNTT*, 420-23; Charles, editor's note in *APOT* I, 573-74; Harwell, 54-55; and Torrey, *The Apocryphal Literature*, 62.

[194] See below, Chapter VI, pp. 299-310.

[195] See below, Chapter VI, pp. 310-20.

[196] See Pfeiffer, *HNTT*, 419-20, 422-23. The following features in particular may be noted: (1) geographic orientation in 3:22-23 toward Palestinian and closely proximate states and peoples (Phoenicia, Arabia, Ishmaelites, and Midianites); (2) the tradition of ancient giants, indigenous to Canaan, in 3:26; (3) the imagery of the peculiarly Canaanite thunderstorm phenomenon in 3:33; (4) the mention of Jerusalem (4:7, 8, 30, 36; 5:1) and Zion (4:9, 14, 24), each bespeaking Palestinian orientation; (5) the reference in 4:9 to the nearby city-states as the "neighbors of Zion," indicating the same geographic orientation; and (6) the allusion in 5:8 to the woods and fragrant trees which collectively constitute the most notable physical feature of the Canaan/Lebanon area.

[197] In the first place the work, according to the historical introduction (1:14), is expressly intended for liturgical use on particular occasions, viz., on the festivals and the days of solemn assembly. Thackeray ("Baruch," 103) suggests the possibility that such a provision for dual usage may disguise the fact that a brief writing designed for reading on a single annual festival was later expanded for adaptation to serial usage during a particular season in the Jewish calendar.

In the second place the compilation of this work for the benefit of a liturgical institution is bespoken, according to Pesch by "der epigonenhafte Mangel an Originalität und die äusserst häufigen Zitate" ("Die Abhängigkeit des 11 Salomonischen Psalms," 254). Scholars are agreed that the institution reflected here was the 9th/10th of Ab, the annual day of mourning over the destruction of Jerusalem (Jer 52:12f.). It is the (perhaps overly!) ingenious theory of Thackeray ("Baruch," 104) that the very structure of the book of Baruch is arranged as a pericope coordinated to the themes of the Ab seasonal cycle.

Despite the remark of Jerome to the effect that in his day the Jews neither read nor even possessed the book of Baruch (*Prologue to the translation of Jeremiah, apud Hebraeos nec legitur nec habetur*), there is some credible evidence that Baruch was being used at the time of Jerome in Jewish worship in the Upper Syrian diaspora. According to the late fourth century (C.E.) *Apostolic Constitutions*, XX, the following is reported: *kai gar kai nyn dekatē tou mēnos Gorpiaiou synathroizomenoi tous thrēnous 'Ieremiou ana ginōskousin . . . kai ton Barouch*, "For even now on the tenth of the month Gorpiaeus they [the Jews] assemble and read the Lamentations of Jeremiah . . . and Baruch." See Schürer, *A History of the Jewish People* II/iii, 193, and Thackeray, "Baruch," 105. These two scholars have concluded that the dates, 10th of Gorpiaeus and 10th of Ab, are probably the same, noting that Josephus and others have dated the destruction to the 10th of Ab. In addition, the Syrian Christian, Ephrem Syrus, in a Palm Sunday sermon attributed to him refers to a Jewish fast in which the worshipers are represented as chanting parts of the book of Baruch (4:9ff.) at that very time. With respect to Christian use the text of the Syro-Hexaplar is provided with indicators for beginning and ending appointed lessons (Thackeray, "Baruch," 106). See also Oesterley (*The Books of the Apocrypha*, 500ff.) for additional comments on the liturgical character of the book of Baruch.

[198] Schürer, *A History of the Jewish People* II/iii, 190-91.

[199] Harwell, 56.

[200] Ibid. Harwell asks rhetorically: "What do these scholars mean by the use of the words 'poems,' 'odes'?," and gives his own rejoinder: "Certainly they do not mean to assert that any part of Baruch is written in the form of Greek poetry which is based on a regular succession of long and short syllables, for that would be meaningless. Why then do they speak of poetry at all? It is because this section, though not metrical in the Greek, exists in a certain measured form which makes itself felt even in a Greek translation. There is an unbroken series of short sentences which betray their origin. And the fact that there are two poems, each in a different meter, is presumptive evidence that they were originally written in Hebrew."

The present writer's own scrutiny of these poems from the point of view of Greek metrics has discerned no metrical patterns, and several colleagues have concurred in the judgment that the Greek text may be considered at the most only rhythmical prose. It is the opinion of Thackeray that with the exception of two books, Wisdom and Proverbs, the books of the Greek

Old Testament do not exhibit signs of attempts at translation into metrical Greek. See Thackeray, "The Poetry of the Greek Book of Proverbs," *JTS* 13 (1912) 44-66. Thackeray's methods of scansion with respect to LXX Proverbs are open to criticism, however, and are in fact taken up critically by Gillis Gerleman in "Studies in the Septuagint: Proverbs," (*Lund University Års-skrift*, N.F., Avd. 1, 52, 3 [Lund: C. W. K. Gleerup, 1956] 15-17). Gerleman nevertheless does agree with Thackeray's conclusion that LXX Proverbs does exhibit some examples of hexameter endings (the so-called *versus paroemiaci*), characteristic of the "proverb verse" par excellence from classical Greek times.

Unfortunately, this matter of LXX metrics has never benefitted from a thoroughgoing investigation. Thus, little more can be said at present than to acknowledge that there apparently was a conscious attempt by the translator of Proverbs to include stylistic devices of the Greek poetic tradition (Gerleman, "Studies in the Septuagint: Proverbs," 1-63, has pointed out several others besides metrical structuring), and at the same time admit that the Baruch poetry gives no evidence of any metrical structure.

[201] Harwell (56) observes: "A retranslation of the text into Hebrew has certain limitations, yet that it is possible to translate this Greek at all into Hebrew measures without doing violence to the thought expressed, is convincing evidence that the Greek is not original. That any author would write out an original composition in Greek prose, even if the ideas were drawn from the Old Testament, so that it would fall into two Hebrew poems, each of which sustained an appropriate measure throughout, is scarcely within the realm of possibility." Although Harwell's point is well-taken, it should be pointed out that his analysis of the metre of the two poems as consisting respectively of absolutely consistent and invariable 3 + 3 and 3 + 2 measures is altogether too inflexible and artificial to be credible. His partial reconstruction must thus be used with great caution.

[202] Pesch, "Die Abhängigkeit des 11 Salomonischen Psalms," 255-56.

[203] Battistone, "An Examination," 14.

[204] See Table 1, p. 28.

[205] Ibid.

[206] Penna, *Baruch*, 10-14.

[207] This information is derived from Marshall ("Book of Baruch," 252).

[208] Heinisch, "Zur Entstehung des Buches Baruch," 696ff. According to Heinisch, the first section is authentically from the pen of Baruch, while the third section, the product of a disciple of Second Isaiah, was composed during the Exile (p. 704). He places the second section later in the Persian period, ca. 480-350 B.C.E. (p. 710). See also Penna, *Baruch*, 10.

[209]Kalt, *Das Buch Baruch*, 1-5.

[210]Goettsberger, *Einleitung*, 308-10.

[211]Stoderl, *Zur Echtheitsfrage*, 3ff.

[212]Ewald, *Die Jüngsten Propheten*, 252, and idem, *Die Geschichte des Volkes Israel* IV, 266.

[213]Gifford, "Baruch," 250-51.

[214]Bissell, *The Apocrypha*, 417.

[215]James, "Apocrypha," col. 252.

[216]Penna, *Baruch*, 10-14.

[217]Heinisch, "Zur Entstehung des Buches Baruch," 710.

[218]Marshall, "Book of Baruch," 253.

[219]Ewald, *Die Jüngsten Propheten*, 268-69.

[220]Davidson, *An Introduction*, 428.

[221]Reuss, *Das Alte Testament* VI, 426.

[222]Torrey, *The Apocryphal Literature*, 64.

[223]Gelin, *La Sainte Bible* XX, 284-85. This scholar excepts the historical introduction, however, as a slightly later Maccabean product.

[224]Charles, *Religious Developments*, 217.

[225]Thackeray, "Baruch," 105.

[226]Battistone, "An Examination," 91.

[227]Harwell, 66.

[228]Gifford, "Baruch," 250-51.

[229]Plöger, "Baruchschriften," col. 901.

[230]Lefèvre, "Baruch," 735-37.

[231]Rost, *Einleitung*, 52.

[232]Hilgenfeld, "Das Buch Baruch und seine neueste Bearbeitung," 437-54.

[233]Robins, "The Complexity of the Book of Baruch," 4-7.

[234]Fritzsche, *Kurzgefasstes Handbuch*, 173.

[235]Zöckler, *Die Apokryphen*, 240-41.

[236]Keil, *Lehrbuch*, 753f.

[237]König, *Einleitung*, 485.

[238]Charles, "Baruch," 454. In this article for the authoritative 11th edition of the *Encyclopaedia Britannica* (1910), Charles favors the Maccabean era, but in another (undated) work, *Religious Developments Between the Testaments*, he preferred a slightly earlier designation. See n. 224 above.

[239]Harrison, *An Introduction to the Old Testament*, 1240.

[240]Kuhl, *Die Entstehung*, 322.

[241]Gehman, *The New Westminster Dictionary of the Bible*, 52.

[242]Wambacq, "L'unité du livre de Baruch," 574-76.

[243]Toy, "Book of Baruch," 556-57.

[244]Pfeiffer, *HNTT*, 416, 419.

[245]Cornill, *Einleitung*, 273-74.

[246]Weiser, *The Old Testament*, 406.

[247]Torrey, *The Apocryphal Literature*, 62.

[248]Tedesche, "Book of Baruch," 363.

[249]Rost, *Einleitung*, 52.

[250]May, *The Oxford Annotated Apocrypha*, 198.

[251]Harwell, 66.

[252]Pfeiffer, *HNTT*, 421.

[253]Kuhl, *Die Entstehung*, 322.

[254]McKenzie, *Dictionary of the Bible*, 82.

[255]Strack, *Einleitung*, §70, p. 161.

[256]"Introduction to the Prophets: Baruch," *The Jerusalem Bible*, 1128.

[257]Gehman, *The New Westminster Dictionary of the Bible*, 52.

[258]Battistone, "An Examination," 93.

[259]Toy, "Book of Baruch," 557.

[260]Plöger, "Baruchschriften," col. 901.

[261]Bentzen, *Introduction* II, 232.

[262] Tedesche, "Book of Baruch," 363.

[263] Lagrange, *Le Judaïsme avant Jésus-Christ*, 157.

[264] Georg Fohrer, "Baruch," *Calwer Bibellexicon* (Stuttgart: Calwer, 1959) 127.

[265] Robins, "The Complexity of the Book of Baruch," 4-7.

[266] Wambacq, "L'unité du livre de Baruch," 574-76.

[267] Iranyi, "Book of Baruch," 139. This scholar generally follows the conclusions of Wambacq.

[268] Pesch, "Die Abhängigkeit des 11 Salomonischen Psalms," 251-63. The composition of the third section of Baruch is here found to have been prior to ca. 60 B.C.E. by virtue of the demonstrated dependency of Psalms of Solomon 11 (ca. 60-40 B.C.E.) on the third section of Baruch.

[269] Graetz, "Abfassungszeit," 395-97, 400-01.

[270] Weiser, *The Old Testament*, 406. The poetry is here attributed to the second half of the first century B.C.E.

[271] Rost, *Einleitung*, 52.

[272] Hilgenfeld, "Das Buch Baruch und seine neueste Bearbeitung," 437-54; see also Pesch, "Die Abhängigkeit des 11 Salomonischen Psalms," 255.

[273] Metzger, *An Introduction to the Apocrypha*, 89.

[274] Eissfeldt, *The Old Testament*, 593.

[275] Battistone, "An Examination," 88.

[276] Ibid., 100.

[277] Bentzen, *Introduction* II, 232.

[278] Robins, "The Complexity of the Book of Baruch," 4-7.

[279] G. R. Driver, *The Judean Scrolls* (New York: Schocken, 1965) 452.

[280] Vatke, *Historisch-kritische Einleitung*, 753.

[281] Kneucker, 32-61.

[282] Hitzig, "Zur Kritik der apokryphischen Bücher," 262ff.

[283] L. H. Brockington, *A Critical Introduction to the Apocrypha* (London: G. Duckworth, 1961) 11.

[284] Marshall, "Book of Baruch," 253.

[285] Swete, *An Introduction*, 275. The final edition at least is here considered to be post-70 C.E.

[286] Thackeray, "Baruch," 105.

[287] Whitehouse, "1 Baruch," 575-76.

[288] Steuernagel, *Lehrbuch der Einleitung*, 790-91.

[289] This information is derived from Pfeiffer (*HNTT*, 422).

[290] Cornill, *Einleitung*, 273-74.

[291] Schürer, *A History of the Jewish People* II/iii, 192; and idem, "Apocrypha," 219.

[292] Goodspeed, *The Story of the Apocrypha*, 100.

[293] Oesterley, *The Books of the Apocrypha*, 500, 504-06; idem, *The Jews and Judaism*, 52; and idem, *An Introduction*, 263ff.

[294] André, *Les Apocryphes*, 257-59.

[295] Ernst Haenchen, "Das Buch Baruch," in *Gott und Mensch* (Tübingen: J. C. B. Mohr, 1965) 299-334.

[296] James, "Apocrypha," col. 252.

[297] H. E. Ryle, *The Canon of the Old Testament* (London: Macmillan, 1892) 137. See also Ryle and James, *Psalmoi Solomontos*, lxxvii.

[298] Ernst Sellin, *Introduction to the Old Testament*, trans. W. Montgomery (New York: George H. Doran, 1923) 245.

[299] Rost, *Einleitung*, 52.

[300] See Dancy, "Baruch," 169.

[301] The relationship between these two prayers of confession has recently undergone a thorough analysis in Battistone ("An Examination," 48-73); see also Pfeiffer, *HNTT*, 415.

[302] See Rost, *Einleitung*, 52; Battistone, "An Examination," 91; and Pfeiffer, *HNTT*, 418-19.

[303] As a step in the process of uniting the independent sections of Baruch, these introductory verses to the second section may plausibly be construed as an interpolated connector. See Pfeiffer, *HNTT*, 418; Wambacq, "L'unité du livre de Baruch," 574-76; André, *Les Apocryphes*, 260f.; Battistone, "An Examination," 26, 90; et al.

[304] Charles, "Baruch," 454.

[305] This was first observed by P. E. E. Geiger in *Der Psalter Salomos* (Augsburg: J. Wolff, 1871) 137.

[306]Most recently Battistone ("An Examination," 74-85) discusses this question in detail with respect to these three basic positions and the respective alignment behind them of various scholars.

[307]Ryle and James, *Psalmoi Solomontos*, lxxii-lxxvii.

[308]Pesch, "Abhängigkeit des 11 Salomonischen Psalms," 251-63.

[309]Ibid., 257-58.

[310]Ibid., 254. M.-J. Lagrange (*Le Judaïsme avant Jésus-Christ*, 157 n. 40) had noted earlier that a textual comparison of Bar 5:1-9 and Pss Sol 11:2-7 reveals that the latter manifests an obvious expansion of the supernatural wonders, a more refined parallelism, a more obvious ordering of the material, and avoidance of repetition vis-à-vis the former. And now the detailed study of Pesch has demonstrated that the passage in Psalms of Solomon 11 constitutes a streamlining (with some refinements and expansions) of the often rambling and repetitious passage in Baruch 5.

[311]See Heinisch, "Zur Entstehung des Buches Baruch," 701.

[312]See Torrey, *The Apocryphal Literature*, 62.

[313]Charles, "Baruch," 454.

[314]Many of the early church fathers (e.g., Tertullian, Iraenaeus, Athanasius, Clement, et al.) made citations from Baruch which they attributed, however, to the prophet Jeremiah. See Schürer, *A History of the Jewish People* II/iii, 93-94; Bissell, *The Apocrypha*, 411; Davidson, *An Introduction*, 430-31; and Battistone, "An Examination," 95-96. The most complete assemblage of patristic citations of Baruch may be found in Reusch (*Erklärung*, 1-22, 268ff.).

[315]H. St. J. Thackeray, "The Greek Translators of Jeremiah," *JTS* 4 (1902-03) 245-66. See also Ṭov, *The Book of Baruch*, 1.

[316]See Swete, *Introduction to the Old Testament in Greek*, 24.

[317]See Thackeray, "Baruch," 103, 105; and Marshall, "Book of Baruch," 252.

[318]See above, n. 315.

[319]Battistone, "An Examination," 92-93.

[320]See Marshall, "Book of Baruch," 252; and B. N. Wambacq, "Les prières de Baruch (1,15-2,19) et de Daniel (9,5-19)," *Biblica* 40 (1959) 468-75. The reference in Bar 2:26 to the desolate state of the Temple is often considered an interpolation (see Charles, "Baruch," 454).

[321] B. N. Wambacq is one of very few scholars who have attempted in any detail to ascertain the various steps involved in this compilation process. His slightly different theory, while objectionable in certain details, is nonetheless plausible and merits attention. He maintains that the author of the third section was the redactor of the entire work, and that in about 63 B.C.E. that author composed his consolation poem (in Greek). This author/redactor is then conceived to have added a penitential prayer (section 1) that was current at that time (because it supposedly deplores the deportation of Pompey), adopting the existent Greek translation. Then by means of a small linking interpolation (3:10-13) he is assumed to have inserted between these a didactic Wisdom poem (perhaps, like the prayer, based on a Hebrew original), and prefaced the whole with an introduction (composed in Greek), 1:1-14. See Wambacq, "L'unité du livre de Baruch," 576.

C. C. Torrey (*The Apocryphal Literature*, 60) briefly theorizes that the anonymous pictures of Israel in exile (the two poems) suggested to some creative mind a book of Baruch and that the prayer section was then written to "introduce" this "typical prophecy in metrical form" (i.e., anonymous poems were credited to Baruch and then provided with an introduction). J. J. Battistone ("An Examination," 88-100) sketchily approaches an analysis of the compilation process and suggests approximate dates for the various sections of the book as follows: (1) the Wisdom Poem, second century B.C.E.; (2) the Consolation Poem, first century B.C.E.; (3) the Prayer of Confession, historical introduction, and final editing, first century B.C.E.-first century C.E. (with the final editing occurring at some point early in the first century C.E.). Leonhard Rost (*Einleitung*, 52-53) suggests that the independent parts of the book could well have derived from the second or first centuries B.C.E., but that they were not coordinated together until after 70 C.E. H. St. J. Thackeray ("Baruch," 103) envisages a yet different process--that the prayer of confession (of Maccabean vintage) was the "book" sent by the exiles to Jerusalem and that an editor later added the two poems (late first century C.E.) incorporating the older work into a larger scheme.

J. J. Kneucker (*Das Buch Baruch*, 32ff., 61ff., et passim) goes far afield by pressing overly hard on supposed historical allusions. He assumes composite authorship, for the most part well after 70 C.E., but considers the Baruch material to have originated among Pharisaic members of the Jewish diaspora in Rome (despite the prominence of Jerusalem and the general Palestinian orientation of the work as a whole). Kneucker champions Hebrew as the original language of the composition despite the incongruity that that presents for a supposed Roman origin. His theory of Roman origin is grounded on a series of alleged historical allusions involving that city. But they are in reality extremely fanciful and forced interpretations which succeed only in wringing the most ingenious specifics out of the most vague and general texts. Two examples of such will suffice to illustrate this implausible scheme: (1) Bar 3:16-17 is interpreted as a reference to the dedication of the Roman Colosseum by Titus, where "abgerichtete Vögel kämpften" (p. 49); and (2) even more extravagantly the three great catastrophes of the time of Titus are found reflected in Bar 4:34-35--the eruption of Vesuvius, and the fire and the plague in Rome (p. 53).

[322]The evidence of the names and titles of God in use in the various sections of Baruch is conveniently assembled in an appendix in Gifford ("Baruch," 253).

[323]See Whitehouse, "1 Baruch," 581; and Oesterley, *The Jews and Judaism*, 165-72.

[324]See Oesterley, *The Jews and Judaism*, 59-63.

[325]The lone reference to demons in Bar 4:35 is uninstructive. It is a borrowing from the older canonical source in Isaiah 34 and reflects simply the old superstition about demons inhabiting ruined tells. It thus cannot be considered reflective of contemporary thought as can, for example, the references to demons in Tobit.

[326]See A. Dupont-Sommer, *The Essene Writings from Qumran*, trans. Geza Vermes (Cleveland/New York: World, 1962) 51-52.

[327]Ibid., 200.

[328]See below, Chapter VI, pp. 299-308.

[329]See initially such works as: Francis I. Andersen, "Studies in Hebrew Syntax," Ph.D. dissertation, Johns Hopkins University (1960) 2 vols.; Robert G. Boling, "'Synonymous' Parallelism in the Psalms," Ph.D. dissertation, Johns Hopkins University (1959); Thomas A. Jackson, "Words in Parallelism in Old Testament Poetry," Ph.D. dissertation, Johns Hopkins University (1970); David Noel Freedman, Prolegomenon to G. Buchanan Gray, *The Forms of Hebrew Poetry: Considered with Special Reference to the Criticism and Interpretation of the Old Testament* (1915; reprinted, New York: Ktav, 1972) vii-lvi; Stanley Gevirtz, *Patterns in the Early Poetry of Israel* (Studies in Ancient Oriental Civilization 32; Chicago: University of Chicago, 1963); Sigmund Mowinckel, *The Psalms in Israel's Worship*, trans. from the Norwegian by D. R. Ap-Thomas (1962; reprinted, New York/Nashville: Abingdon, 1967) II, 261-66; T. H. Robinson, *The Poetry of the Old Testament* (London: Gerald Duckworth, 1960); Arlis J. Ehlen, "The Poetic Structure of a Hodayah from Qumran: An Analysis of Grammatical, Semantic, and Auditory Correspondence in 1QH 3:19-36," Ph.D. dissertation, Harvard University (1970); Delbert R. Hillers, *Lamentations* (AB 7A; Garden City: Doubleday, 1972) xxx-xxxvii; and Ronald J. Williams, *Hebrew Syntax: An Outline* (Toronto: University of Toronto, 1967).

CHAPTER II

A RECONSTRUCTION OF THE HEBREW TEXT OF THE WISDOM POEM OF BARUCH (3:9-4:4), TOGETHER WITH THE GREEK AND/OR SYRIAC TEXT AND AN ENGLISH TRANSLATION

3:9

שְׁמַע יִשְׂרָאֵל חֻקּוֹת הַחַיִּים   "Ακουε, Ισραηλ, ἐντολὰς ζωῆς,

"Hear, O Israel, the commandments of life

הַאֲזִינוּ לָדַעַת בִּינָה   ἐνωτίσασθε γνῶναι φρόνησιν.

Pay attention, that you may gain insight!

3:10-12

לָמָּה זֶּה יִשְׂרָאֵל   ܡܢܐ ܐܝܣܪܝܠ[a]

Why is it, O Israel,

כִּי בְּאֶרֶץ-אוֹיֵב בָּלִיתָ   ܥܬܩܬ ܒܐܪܥܐ ܕܒܥܠܕܒܒܐ ܟܠܗ

That you grow old in enemy territory,

וּבְאֶרֶץ נָכְרִיָּה נִטְמֵאתָ[b]   ܘܒܐܪܥܐ ܢܘܟܪܝܬܐ ܐܬܛܡܐܬ

And are defiled[c] in a foreign land?

עִם מֵתִים נֶחְשַׁבְתָּ   ܥܡ ܡܝܬܐ ܐܬܚܫܒܬ[d]

With the dead you are counted,

וְעִם יוֹרְדֵי שְׁאוֹל[e]   ܘܥܡ ܢܚܬܝ ܫܝܘܠ

And with those going down to Sheol,

---

[a]For discussion of the relative merits of the LXX and Sy texts for vss. 10-12, see Chapter III, ad loc.

[b]Or Hithpael, הִטַּמֵּאתָ.

[c]Or the reflexive, "defile yourself."

[d]Cf. Syh, ܐܬܚܫܒܬ.

[e]Or perhaps בּוֹר.

עָזַבְתָּ מְקוֹר חָכְמָה ܫܒܩܬ ܡܒܘܥܐ ܕܚܟܡܬܐ

ἐγκατέλιπες τὴν πηγὴν τῆς σοφίας.

For you have abandoned the source of wisdom.

3:13

לוּ הָלַכְתָּ בְּדֶרֶךְ אֱלֹהִים — τῇ ὁδῷ τοῦ θεοῦ ἐι ἐπορεύθης,

If you had walked in the way of God,

יָשַׁבְתָּ בְּשָׁלוֹם עַד-עוֹלָם — κατῴκεις ἂν ἐν εἰρήνῃ τὸν αἰῶνα.

You would have lived in peace forever.

3:14

לְמַד אֵי-זֶה מְקוֹם בִּינָה — μάθε ποῦ ἐστι φρόνησις,

Learn where there is understanding,

אַיֵּה גְּבוּרָה אַיֵּה תְּבוּנָה — ποῦ ἐστιν ἰσχύς, ποῦ ἐστι σύνεσις

Where there is strength, where there is intelligence,

לָדַעַת יַחַד אַיֵּה אוֹרֶךְ-יָמִים וְחַיִּים — τοῦ γνῶναι ἅμα, ποῦ ἐστι μακροβίωσις καὶ ζωή,

That you may at the same time perceive where there is length of days and life,

אַיֵּה אוֹר עֵינַיִם וְשָׁלוֹם — ποῦ ἐστι φῶς ὀφθαλμῶν καὶ εἰρήνη.

Where there is light for the eyes and peace.

3:15

מִי מָצָא מְקוֹמָהּ — τίς εὗρε τὸν τόπον αὐτῆς,

Who has found her place,

וּמִי בָא אֶל-אוֹצְרוֹתֶיהָ — καὶ τίς εἰσῆλθεν εἰς τοὺς θησαυροὺς αὐτῆς;

And who has entered her treasure-houses?

3:16-18

אַיֵּה מוֹשְׁלֵי הָעַמִּים	ποῦ εἰσιν οἱ ἄρχοντες τῶν ἐθνῶν

Where are the leaders of the nations,

וְרוֹדֵי בְחַיְתוֹ אֶרֶץ	καὶ οἱ κυριεύοντες τῶν θηρίων τῶν ἐπὶ τῆς γῆς,

And those who had dominion over the wild animals,

מְשַׂחֲקֵי בְצִפּוֹר שָׁמַיִם	οἱ ἐν τοῖς ὀρνέοις τοῦ οὐρανοῦ ἐμπαίζοντες

Those who made sport with the birds of the air;

וְאוֹצְרֵי כֶסֶף וְזָהָב	καὶ τὸ ἀργύριον θησαυρίζοντες καὶ τὸ χρυσίον,

And those who hoarded up silver and gold,

בּוֹ בָטְחוּ אֲנָשִׁים	ᾧ ἐπεποίθεισαν ἄνθρωποι,

In which men have trusted,

וְאֵין קֵצֶה לְקִנְיָנָם	καὶ οὐκ ἔστι τέλος τῆς κτήσεως αὐτῶν,

And there was no end to their acquisition;

חוֹרְשֵׁי כֶסֶף[f] וְדֹאֲגִים	οἱ τὸ ἀργύριον τεκταίνοντες καὶ μεριμνῶντες,

Those who schemed for silver and were anxious,

וְאֵין חֵקֶר לְמַעֲשֵׂיהֶם	καὶ οὐκ ἔστιν ἐξεύρεσις τῶν ἔργων αὐτῶν;

And whose deeds were beyond discovery?

3:19

אָבְדוּ וְיָרְדוּ שְׁאוֹל[g]	ἠφανίσθησαν καὶ εἰς ᾄδου κατέβησαν,

They have vanished and gone down to Sheol,

---

[f]Another possibility is perhaps, חָרָשֵׁי הַכֶּסֶף.

[g]Or perhaps, שְׁאוֹלָה.

וַאֲחֵרִים קָמוּ[h] תַּחְתָּם καὶ ἄλλοι ἀντανέστησαν ἀντ' αὐτῶν.

And others have arisen in their place.

3:20-21

קְטַנִּים[i] רָאוּ אוֹר νεώτεροι εἶδον φῶς

More recent generations have seen the light of day,

וְיָשְׁבוּ[j] עַל הָאָרֶץ[k] καὶ κατῴκησαν ἐπὶ τῆς γῆς,

And have inhabited the earth;

וְדֶרֶךְ בִּינָה לֹא-יָדְעוּ ὁδὸν δὲ ἐπιστήμης οὐκ ἔγνωσαν

But they did not learn the way of knowledge,

וְלֹא הֵבִינוּ נְתִיבוֹתֶיהָ οὐδὲ συνῆκαν τρίβους αὐτῆς

Nor discover her paths,

וְלֹא הֶחֱזִיקוּ-בָהּ בְּנֵיהֶם οὐδὲ ἀντελάβοντο αὐτῆς· οἱ υἱοὶ αὐτῶν

And their sons did not lay hold of her;

מִדַּרְכָּהּ רָחֲקוּ וְסָרוּ[l] [illegible]

ἀπὸ τῆς ὁδοῦ αὐτῶν πόῤῥω ἐγενήθησαν.

From her way they have strayed far and rebelled.

3:22

לֹא נִשְׁמְעָה בִּכְנַעַן οὐδὲ ἠκούσθη ἐν Χανααν

She has not been heard of in Canaan,

---

[h]Or perhaps, עָמְדוּ.

[i]Perhaps אַחֲרוֹנִים or צְעִירִים.

[j]Or perhaps the imperfect consecutive, וַיֵּשְׁבוּ.

[k]Or בָּאָרֶץ.

[l]Or perhaps the imperfect consecutive, וַיָּסוּרוּ. Forms from other verbal roots are also possibilities: וּמָרוּ (מָרָה), וּמָרְדוּ (מָרַד).

וְלֹא נִרְאֲתָה בְתֵימָן	οὐδὲ ὤφθη ἐν Θαιμαν,

Nor seen in Teman.

3:23

בְּנֵי-הָגָר הוֹרְשֵׁי-בִינָה[m] בָּאָרֶץ	οὔτε υἱοὶ Αγαρ οἱ ἐκζητοῦντες τὴν σύνεσιν ἐπὶ τῆς γῆς,

Not even the sons of Hagar,
who search after understanding on earth,

רוֹכְלֵי מְדָן וְתֵימָא	οἱ ἔμποροι τῆς Μερραν καὶ Θαιμαν

The traders of Medan and Tema,

וְהַמּוֹשְׁלִים וְשׁוֹחֲרֵי[n] בִינָה[m]	καὶ οἱ μυθολόγοι καὶ οἱ ἐκζητηταὶ τῆς συνέσεως,

Nor the tale-spinners and seekers of understanding,

דֶּרֶךְ חָכְמָה לֹא-יָדְעוּ	ὁδὸν δὲ σοφίας οὐκ ἔγνωσαν

Have known the way of wisdom

וְלֹא זָכְרוּ נְתִיבוֹתֶיהָ	οὐδὲ ἐμνήσθησαν τὰς τρίβους αὐτῆς.

Or remembered her paths.

3:24

[o]יִשְׂרָאֵל מַה-גָּדוֹל בֵּית-אֱלֹהִים[p]	ὦ Ισραηλ, ὡς μέγας ὁ οἶκος τοῦ θεοῦ

O Israel, how great is the house of God,

וְרָם מְקוֹם קִנְיָנוֹ	καὶ ἐπιμήκης ὁ τόπος τῆς κτήσεως αὐτοῦ

And vast his domain!

---

[m]Perhaps תְּבוּנָה or שֵׂכֶל.

[n]Perhaps דוֹרְשֵׁי or מְבַקְשֵׁי.

[o]Or הוֹי יִשְׂרָאֵל.

[p]Or אֵל.

3:25

גָּדוֹל הוּא וְאֵין-קֵץ   μέγας καὶ οὐκ ἔχει τελευτήν,

It is great and boundless;

גָּבוֹהַּ וְאֵין מִדָּה[q]   ὑψηλὸς καὶ ἀμέτρητος

It is high and immeasurable.

3:26

שָׁם יֻלְּדוּ[r] הַנְּפִילִים   ἐκεῖ ἐγεννήθησαν οἱ γίγαντες

There were born the giants,

אַנְשֵׁי הַשֵּׁם   οἱ ὀνομαστοὶ

Men of renown,

אֲשֶׁר מֵעוֹלָם   οἱ ἀπ' ἀρχῆς, γενόμενοι
אַנְשֵׁי-מִדּוֹת   εὐμεγέθεις

Who in ancient times were immense in stature,

מְלֻמְּדֵי מִלְחָמָה   ἐπιστάμενοι πόλεμον.

Skilled in battle.

3:27

לֹא-בְאֵלֶּה בָּחַר אֱלֹהִים   οὐ τούτους ἐξελέξατο ὁ θεὸς

God did not choose these people,

וְדֶרֶךְ-בִּינָה לֹא-נָתַן לָהֶם   οὐδὲ ὁδὸν ἐπιστήμης
ἔδωκεν αὐτοῖς·

Nor give them the way of knowledge.

---

[q]Or perhaps וּרְחַב יָדַיִם.

[r]The LXX variant, ἐγενήθησαν, suggests the Hebrew הָיוּ. See Chapter III, ad loc.

3:28

וְאָבְדוּ בִּבְלִי-דַעַת   καὶ ἀπώλοντο παρὰ τὸ μὴ ἔχειν φρόνησιν,

So they perished for lack of sense,

אָבְדוּ בְּאִוַּלְתָּם   ἀπώλοντο διὰ τὴν ἀβουλίαν αὐτῶν.

They came to an end through their own folly.

3:29

מִי-עָלָה שָׁמַיִם וּלְקָחָהּ[s]   τίς ἀνέβη εἰς τὸν οὐρανὸν καὶ ἔλαβεν αὐτὴν

Who has ascended the heavens and taken her,

וּמִנִּי שְׁחָקִים הוֹרִידָהּ   καὶ κατεβίβασεν αὐτὴν ἐκ τῶν νεφελῶν;

And brought her down from the clouds?

3:30

מִי-עָבַר אֶל-עֵבֶר הַיָּם וּמְצָאָהּ[t]   τίς διέβη πέραν τῆς θαλάσσης καὶ εὗρεν αὐτὴν

Who has crossed the ocean and found her,

וְקָנָהּ[t] בְּחָרוּץ נִבְחָר   καὶ οἴσει αὐτὴν χρυσίου ἐκλεκτοῦ;

And purchased her with fine gold?

3:31

אֵין יוֹדֵעַ דַּרְכָּהּ   οὐκ ἔστιν ὁ γινώσκων τὴν ὁδὸν αὐτῆς

No one knows her way,

וְאֵין מֵבִין נְתִיבָתָהּ   οὐδὲ ὁ ἐνθυμούμενος τὴν τρίβον αὐτῆς·

No one recognizes her path.

---

[s] Or perhaps the imperfect consecutive, וַיִּקָּחֶהָ.

[t] Or the imperfect consecutives, וַיִּמְצָאֶהָ, וַיִּקְנֶהָ. See Chapter III, ad loc.

3:32

רוֹאֶה-כוֹל הוּא יְדָעָהּ	ἀλλὰ ὁ εἰδὼς τὰ πάντα γινώσκει αὐτήν,

Only the One who perceives all things knows her,

הוּא חֲקָרָהּ בִּתְבוּנָתוֹ	ἐξεῦρεν αὐτὴν τῇ συνέσει αὐτοῦ·

He has discovered her with his intelligence.

הַמֵּכִין אֶרֶץ עַד-עוֹלָם	ὁ κατασκευάσας τὴν γῆν εἰς τὸν αἰῶνα χρόνον,

The One who established the earth for all time

מִלְאָהּ הוֹלְכֵי עַל-אַרְבַּע[u]	ἐνέπλησεν αὐτὴν κτηνῶν τετραπόδων·

Filled it with quadrupeds;

3:33

הַמְשַׁלֵּחַ אוֹר וְיֵלֵךְ	ὁ ἀποστέλλων τὸ φῶς, καὶ πορεύεται,

The One who sends forth the light,[v] and it goes,

יִקְרָאֵהוּ וְיִשְׁמַע-אֵלָיו בִּרְעָדָה[w]	ἐκάλεσεν αὐτό, καὶ ὑπήκουσεν αὐτῷ τρόμῳ

Who calls it and it obeys him with trembling

3:34

וְהַכּוֹכָבִים בְּמִשְׁמְרוֹתָם יָאִירוּ וְיִרַנֵּנוּ[x]	οἱ δὲ ἀστέρες ἔλαμψαν ἐν ταῖς φυλακαῖς αὐτῶν καὶ εὐφράνθησαν,

--The stars at their watchposts shine joyfully,

יִקְרָא לָהֶם וְיֹאמְרוּ הִנֵּנוּ	ἐκάλεσεν αὐτούς, καὶ εἶπαν πάρεσμεν,

When he calls them they respond, "Here we are!"

---

[u]Or perhaps בְּהֵמָה.

[v]I.e., lightning.

[w]See Chapter III, ad loc., for a possible restoration from Sy.

וְאִירוּ בְשָׂשׂוֹן ἔλαμψαν μετ᾽ εὐφροσύνης
לִפְנֵי עוֹשֵׂיהֶם τῷ ποιήσαντι αὐτούς.

They shine gladly for their creator--

3:35

הוּא אֱלֹהֵינוּ וְאֵין מִבַּלְעָדָיו[y] οὗτος ὁ θεὸς ἡμῶν,

ܗܢܘ ܐܠܗܢ [ܘܠܝܬ ܐܚܪܢܐ ܠܒܪ ܡܢܗ]

This One is our God, and there is no other;

אַחֵר לֹא יֵחָשֵׁב זוּלָתוֹ ܘܠܐ ܢܬܚܫܒ ܐܚܪܢܐ ܠܒܪ ܡܢܗ

οὐ λογισθήσεται ἕτερος πρὸς αὐτόν.

No other can be considered besides him.

3:36

(הוּא) חָקַר כָּל־דֶּרֶךְ בִּינָה (οὗτος) ἐξεῦρε
πᾶσαν ὁδὸν ἐπιστήμης

He has found out the whole way of knowledge,

וּנְתָנָהּ לְיַעֲקֹב עַבְדּוֹ καὶ ἔδωκεν αὐτὴν
Ιακωβ τῷ παιδὶ αὐτοῦ

And he has granted her to Jacob his servant,

וּלְיִשְׂרָאֵל יְדִידוֹ καὶ Ισραηλ τῷ
ἠγαπημένῳ ὑπ᾽ αὐτοῦ·

And to Israel his well-beloved.

3:37

אַחֲרֵי־זֶה[z] μετὰ τοῦτο ἐπὶ
עַל הָאָרֶץ נִרְאָתָה τῆς γῆς ὤφθη

Thereupon, she appeared on earth

---

[x]Perhaps וְשָׂשׂוּ or וְיִשְׂמְחוּ. See Chapter III ad loc.

[y]Or עוֹד. For discussion of the Sy text and the reconstruction of this colon, see Chapter III, ad loc.

[z]Or אַחֲרֵי־זֹאת; perhaps אָז.

וּבְתוֹךְ אֲנָשִׁים הִתְהַלָּכָה	καὶ ἐν τοῖς ἀνθρώποις συνανεστράφη.

And lived among men.

4:1

זֶה-סֵפֶר מִצְוֹת הָאֱלֹהִים	αὕτη ἡ βίβλος τῶν προσταγμάτων τοῦ θεοῦ

This is the book of the commandments of God,

וְהַתּוֹרָה הָעוֹמֶדֶת לְעוֹלָם	καὶ ὁ νόμος ὁ ὑπάρχων εἰς τὸν αἰῶνα·

The law that stands forever.

כָּל-מַחֲזִיקֶיהָ לְחַיִּים	πάντες οἱ κρατοῦντες αὐτὴν εἰς ζωήν,

All who hold fast to her will live,

וְעוֹזְבֶיהָ יָמוּתוּ	οἱ δὲ καταλείποντες αὐτὴν ἀποθανοῦνται.

But those who abandon her will die.

4:2

שׁוּבָה יַעֲקֹב וְהַחֲזֶק-בָּהּ	ἐπιστρέφου, Ιακωβ, καὶ ἐπιλαβοῦ αὐτῆς,

Return, Jacob, and hold fast to her;

הִתְהַלֵּךְ לְנָגְהָהּ לִפְנֵי-אוֹרָהּ	διόδευσον πρὸς τὴν λάμψιν κατέναντι τοῦ φωτὸς αὐτῆς.

Set your course toward her radiance
in the presence of her light!

4:3

אַל-תִּתֵּן לְאַחֵר כְּבוֹדֵךְ	μὴ δῷς ἑτέρῳ τὴν δόξαν σου

Do not give your glory to another,

וְטוֹבָתְךָ[aa] לְגוֹי[bb] נָכְרִי	καὶ τὰ συμφέροντά σοι ἔθνει ἀλλοτρίῳ

Nor your good fortune to a foreign people.

4:4

אַשְׁרֵינוּ יִשְׂרָאֵל	μακάριοί ἐσμεν, Ισραηλ,

Happy are we, O Israel,

[cc] כִּי-הַטּוֹב בְּעֵינֵי-אֱלֹהִים	ὅτι τὰ ἀρεστὰ τῷ θεῷ

For what is pleasing to God

לָנוּ נוֹדָע	ἡμῖν γνωστά ἐστιν.

Is known to us.

[aa]Perhaps וְיִתְרוֹנְךָ or וְקַרְנְךָ.

[bb]Or לְעָם.

[cc]Or אֵל. Possible alternatives for this expression are הַיָּשָׁר בְּעֵינֵי-, הַטּוֹב לֵאלֹהִים, and טוֹב אֱלֹהִים. See Chapter III, ad loc.

CHAPTER III

PHILOLOGICAL NOTES ON THE RECONSTRUCTED HEBREW TEXT OF THE WISDOM POEM OF BARUCH, 3:9-4:4

3:9

šᵉmaʿ yiśrāʾēl = *akoue Israēl*

The source for this familiar expression is clearly Deut 6:4 where the same equivalency appears; cf. also 4 Ezra 9:30. For the parallel pairing, *šᵉmaʿ* (A) // *haʾᵃzînû* (B), cf. Isa 1:2, *šimʿû šāmayim wᵉhaʾᵃzînî ʾereṣ*; 1:10; 42:23; Prov 4:1; Job 33:1; Sir 30:27; Gen 4:23; Num 23:18; et al. This sequence of the verb *šāmaʿ* as A-word to the B-word *heʾᵉzîn* is very regular in the poetic parallelism of BH and can be considered normal.[1] Also, the equivalency between *heʾᵉzîn* and *enotizomai* is consistent in the LXX.[2]

Prima facie the disagreement in number of the two imperatives in this parallel seems to constitute a discrepancy since both have *yiśrāʾēl*[3] as referent. *Haʾᵃzînû* is used in Isa 1:10 with a singular referent, *ʿam*, which (as Israel in our passage) may be construed as collective and thus, in effect, plural. In Isa 1:2 (quoted above), the singular imperative, *haʾᵃzînî*, has a singular referent, *ʾereṣ*. The combination of two imperatives, one singular and the other plural, applied to the same collective referent, may appear odd but it is not impossible for BH. Indeed, this very mixed pattern is also consistently preserved in the Versions (cf. LXX, La^V, Sy, and Syh).

ḥuqqôt haḥayyîm = *entolai zoēs*

The same phrase is in Ezek 33:15--*bᵉḥuqqôt haḥayyîm*. While it is true that *entolē* is by far more frequently employed in the LXX to render *miṣwāh*,[4] it is nevertheless used for *ḥōq* in Deut 16:12 and for *ḥuqqāh* in Deut 28:5, 1 Kgs 11:38, and Ezek 18:21. The combination *miṣwôt haḥayyîm* does not occur in BH but the above reconstruction does verbatim in Ezek 33:15. The LXX renders Ezek 33:15 with *prostagmasin zōēs*, using its more usual equivalent for *ḥōq/ḥuqqāh*.[5] Sy and Syh agree in offering the plural of *puqdānā'* "commandment," a term also used in translating such passages as Ezek 16:27; 37:24; Ps 50:16; 119:8, 54; et al., where the Hebrew text has *ḥōq/ḥuqqāh*. But on the other hand, this Syriac term is used, as are the interchangeable Greek synonyms, *entolē* and *prostagma*, with less than complete translational consistency. It also appears commonly as the equivalent of *miṣwāh*, as, for example, in Lev 4:2 and Ps 111:1.

For the combination *šᵉmaʿ ḥuqqôt*, cf. Deut 4:1, *šᵉmaʿ 'el-haḥuqqîm*; and Deut 4:6, *yišmᵉʿûn 'et kol-haḥuqqîm*. In the light of the above evidence, our reconstruction seems certain and Ezek 33:15 appears to have been the direct source.

lādaʿat bînāh = gnōnai phronēsin

The closest parallel here is in Prov 4:1 where *lādaʿat bînāh = gnōnai ennoian*. This Greek term, *ennoia* "insight," is used also in Prov 23:4 to render *bînāh* although it is more frequently the LXX equivalent for *mᵉzimmāh* "discretion," one of many roughly synonymous terms for "understanding" in the Hebrew Wisdom vocabulary. From this point on throughout the poem we will encounter a group of four practically synonymous Greek terms for "understanding": *synesis* (3:14, 23, 32), *phronēsis* (3:9, 14, 28), *sophia* (3:12, 23), and *epistēmē* (3:20, 27, 36). These correspond elsewhere in the LXX to a similar group of Hebrew counterparts: *ḥokmāh*, *bînāh*, *tᵉbûnāh*, *śekel*, and *daʿat*. With the exception of a fairly regular association of *ḥokmāh* and *sophia*, there is no perceptible pattern to the equivalencies involved. Each of the Greek terms may be, and is, used for each of the Hebrew.[6] Semantic particularities have thus become obscured since the convergence of the Greek and Hebrew terms is so thoroughgoing.

Our recovery of the particular equivalents must then in each case be qualified and determined solely on the merits of the available parallels, there being no assistance forthcoming from any predictable patterns of equivalency in these cases. The patterns of equivalency that have emerged in our reconstruction (with regard to these particular terms) must necessarily be considered more in the realm of probability than of certainty because of the inevitable subjectivity required for the weighing of the usual jumble of parallels. Nonetheless, it is perhaps instructive to observe that in one LXX Codex, G^A, great care has apparently been taken to hold to the principle of consistent translation of a Hebrew term by a Greek one,[7] so that in G^A the following are regular correspondencies: *synesis* = *bînāh*, *epistēmē* = *śekel*, *sophia* = *ḥokmāh*, and *phronēsis* = *t*ᵉ*bûnāh*. But whether or not our results agree will not be of any significance due to the pronounced lack of consistency in the other LXX Codices and elsewhere.

For the equivalence of *phronēsis* and *bînāh*, cf. Prov 1:2, 7:4, 8:14, 16:16, 24:25. In the second colon, Sy offers an expanded, and probably conflate, reading: *sūkālāh w*ᵉ*ḥekm*ᵉ*tā'*, "understanding and wisdom."[8]

3:10-12

The text of Sy in these three verses is at substantial variance with that of LXX. Its two tricola appear to represent the original Hebrew more accurately in this case than does that of LXX. The LXX text for this section allows at best for the reconstruction of an awkward Hebrew text beset with an illogical internal arrangement, improbable syntax, and metrical imbalance. Thus for the reconstruction of this section the superior text of Sy has been followed. For purposes of comparison, the Greek text and the reconstructed Hebrew text that it yields are given here.

(10) *ti estin Israēl,*
*mah-l*ᵉ*kā yiśrā'ēl*
"Why is it, Israel,

ti hoti en gē tōn echthrōn ei,
*kî hāyîtā b*ᵉ*'ereṣ 'ôyēb*
That you are in enemy territory,

epalaiōthēs en gē allotria,
*bālîtā b*ᵉ*'ereṣ nokriyyāh*
That you grow old in a foreign land,

(11) *synemianthēs tois nekrois,*
niṭmē'tā bammētîm
That you are defiled with the dead,

proselogisthēs meta tōn eis hadou;
neḥšabtā 'im-yôr^{e}dê-š^{e}'ôl
Counted among those in Sheol?

(12) *egkatelipes tēn pēgēn tēs sophias.*
'āzabtā m^{e}qôr ḥokmāh
You have abandoned the source of wisdom."

lāmmāh-zzeh = *mānaw* (Sy)

The Sy *mānaw* "why is it?" and the Syh *l^{e}mānā'* "why?" support *lāmmāh-zzeh* as the probable Hebrew equivalent.[9] The LXX reading, *ti estin* . . . >*ti*< *hoti*, "Why is it . . . >why< that," would appear rather to support the Hebrew construction, *mah-l^{e}kā* . . . *kî*.[10] Cf. Isa 22:1, *mah-lāk* . . . *kî* = *ti* . . . *hoti*; Ps 114:5, *mah-l^{e}kā* . . . *kî* = *ti esti* . . . *hoti*; and Exod 16:7. In these passages the interrogative and conjunction do double duty for the succeeding colon (although LXX repeats *hoti*).[11]

bālîtā = *epalaiōthēs* (LXX) = *b^{e}layt* (Sy)

In the LXX *palaioō* "become old" is used five times for *'ātaq* (all in Job), once for *yāšēn*, and never at all for *zāqēn* or *śîb*. It is most frequently used for the Qal or Piel stems of *bālāh* "grow old, wear out." Whereas the comparatively much later Syh employs the verb *'^{e}teq* "become antiquated," Sy has the cognate *b^{e}lā'*. In BH, *bālāh* is used of clothing and shoes,[12] heaven and earth,[13] and people.[14]

It is at this point that the superior internal arrangement in Sy becomes especially apparent. Its placement of the verb *b^{e}lā'* within vs. 10b yields much more plausible Hebrew and much better sense. Further, the Sy parallelism between "grow old in enemy territory" and "be defiled in a foreign land" is sound both poetically and conceptually.

However, in the LXX the apparent displacement of the verb *palaioō* from the second to the third colon of vs. 10 has resulted in the concomitant shift of the following verb, *symmiainō* "be defiled with," into the first colon of vs. 11, yielding there the conceptually questionable "being defiled with the dead" standing in dubious parallelism with "counted among those in Sheol" in vs. 11b. The LXX-derived parallelism in vs. 10b-c between "are in enemy territory" and "grow old in a foreign land" is weak, and it is quite possible that the copula in vs. 10b is an editorial facilitation added after the intern-nal cohesion of this section had been disrupted in the LXX. However that may be, *bālāh* appears certain as the original Hebrew.[15]

*b*ᵉ*'ereṣ 'ôyēb = en gē tōn echthrōn* (LXX) = *d*ᵉ*b(')ar'ā' dab'eld*ᵉ*bābē'* (Sy)

These equivalencies are extremely regular and do not necessitate comment.[16]

*b*ᵉ*'ereṣ nokriyyāh = en gē allotria* (LXX) = *b(')ar'ā' nukr*ᵉ*yātā'* (Sy and Syh)

These equivalencies also exhibit a high degree of constancy[17] (cf. Exod 2:22 and 18:3). The above reconstruction from the LXX text as an interrogative clause followed by two (four?) consecu-tive clauses for which the *kî* of the first consecutive clause serves double duty is paralleled in Ps 114:5.[18]

niṭmē'tā = synemianthēs (LXX) = *'etṭanapt* (Sy)

The Greek verb *symmiainō* is a hapax legomenon in the LXX. It occurs only here in the passive sense of "being defiled with." Its root, *miainō*, is consistently employed in the LXX to render the Hebrew root *ṭāmē'* "be unclean, defiled." In the original Hebrew of our passage the stem was probably the common Niphal as reconstructed, or perhaps the reflexive Hithpael, *hiṭṭammē'tā*.[19] The Sy verb, *ṭ*ᵉ*nep* "defile, profane," expresses the same passive meaning through its Ethpaal stem, "be defiled, polluted." A Hebrew cognate to this Syriac verb occurs as a hapax legomenon in BH with the meaning "soil" or "defile" in Ct 5:3. Syh attains the same meaning, "be defiled," through its use of the Ethpaal stem of *ṭûš* "besmear" (in Pael, "defile, pollute"). Following Sy (and not LXX), this verb must properly be taken with vs. 10c.

neḥšabtā = proselogisthēs (LXX) = *'etḥᵉšebt* (Syh)

Proslogizomai "reckon, count" is quite rare in the LXX, appearing only six times. In four of those six, the Hebrew equivalent is determinable and in each case it proves to be the verb *ḥāšab* "count, reckon." Twice the correspondence is with the Niphal stem which offers precisely the passive sense that is required by the Greek and Syriac equivalents.[20] In addition, this conclusion is amply corroborated by the Syh reading of the cognate *ḥᵉšab* in the Ethpeel stem.

Intriguingly, Sy has in place of the expected *ḥᵉšab* a different verbal root, *ḥᵉbaš* "confine, imprison." This, however, must certainly represent a mere scribal error involving the simple interchange of two consonants rather than a genuine variant.[21]

'im-yôrᵉdê-šᵉ'ôl = eis hadou (LXX) = *'am nāḥᵉtay šᵉyūl* (Sy)
= *'am hānun dᵉbašyūl* (Syh)

A parallel in Ps 88:5 is so close that *bôr* "Pit" must be considered a possibility for the Hebrew original: *neḥšabtî 'im-yôrᵉdê-bôr = proselogisthēn meta tōn katabainontōn eis lakkon*. The parallelism in such passages as Ps 28:1, 30:4 and 143:7 indicates clearly that the literal expression, "those who go down to the Pit," means simply "those in the Pit." The "Pit" is a common designation in BH for Sheol or the netherworld.[22]

More likely, however, is *yôrēd šᵉ'ôl* as in Job 7:9. Other verbal forms of *yārad* are also found in combination with *šᵉ'ôl* elsewhere.[23] This data, together with the appearance of the cognate *šᵉyūl* in both Sy and Syh, strongly supports *šᵉ'ôl*. Also, the LXX is more likely to have used *hadēs* for *šᵉ'ôl* than for the more general *bôr*. Sy, standing much closer in time to the original autograph than Syh, not only reads *šᵉyūl* but also preserves the plural participle that the LXX, and in consequence Syh, omits (cf. as well LXX Minuscule 22 and La^V: *cum descendentibus in infernum*).

'āzabtā = egkatelipes

The Greek verb *egkataleipō* "abandon" is consistently used in the LXX to render Hebrew *'āzab*[24] as is the Syriac *šᵉbaq* in the Syriac translations.[25]

mᵉqôr ḥokmāh = pēgēn tēs sophias

An exact parallel may be found in Hebrew in Prov 18:4. The LXX there has "fountain of life" perhaps because of the influence of the much more frequent Hebrew figure, *mᵉqôr ḥayyîm* (*mᵉqôr ḥokmāh* occurs only in Prov 18:4), or because it possibly reflects a different Hebrew text tradition.[26] This uncertainty is evident in the conflate text of La^{S}, *vitae et sapientiae*, but the bulk of the textual evidence supports *ḥokmāh* (cf. La^{V}, *fontem sapientiae*). A further extra-biblical parallel that is semantically if not lexically exact occurs twice in the Qumran *Ḥōdāyôt*: *mqwr d't* in 1QH 2:18 and 12:29 (cf. also the extra-biblical *1 Enoch* 96:6 and 4 Ezra 14:47).[27]

3:13

lû . . . yāšabtā = ei . . . katōkeis an

For this construction, cf. Judg 13:23, *lû ḥāpēṣ YHWH . . . lō' lāqaḥ*.[28] Although there is some amount of interchange between *lû* and *'im* in BH, *lû* is properly used in cases where the condition is to be represented as either not fulfilled in the past (as here) or as not capable of being fulfilled in the present or future. On the other hand, *'im* is properly used if the condition be regarded as already fulfilled or together with its consequence be thought of as possibly (or probably) occurring in the future.

derek 'ᵉlōhîm = tē hodō tou theou

Numerous parallels are available for this phrase; cf. especially Ps 81:14, 119:3; Isa 42:24; Deut 5:33f.; Judg 2:22; Jer 5:4, 5; Job 23:11; Ps 86:11; Gen 18:19; Josh 22:5; 1 Kgs 2:3, 3:14; and Isa 2:3. In Isa 59:8, God's way is the *derek šālôm* and in Bar 4:12, *tôrat 'ᵉlōhîm*.

'ad-'ôlām = (eis) ton aiōna (chronon)

Although G^B does not include *chronon*, it is supported by G^A, G^Q, many LXX minuscules, Sy, Syh, Arm, Arab, Copt, et al.[29] In both Isa 34:17 and 9:6, the LXX translates *'ad-'ôlām* by *eis ton aiōna chronon* and this Greek phrase is paralleled exactly in Bar 3:32 (cf. Exod 14:13, Isa 34:10). Another possibility would perhaps be *lᵉ'ôlām* (cf. Bar 4:1; 5:1, 4). For its use in combination with *tēšēb*, cf. Ps 102:13, *lᵉ'ôlām tēšēb*; 125:1; Joel 4:20; Lam 5:19; Isa 14:20; Ps 29:10. More remote possibilities are *lāneṣaḥ* (cf. Isa 13:20, 34:10; Bar 4:35) or *'ad-neṣaḥ* (cf. Ps 49:20, Job 34:36).

bᵉšālôm = en eirēnē

For this concept, cf. Ps 4:9 and 1 Kgs 5:5.

3:14

lᵉmad 'ê-zeh mᵉqôm bînāh = mathe pou esti phronēsis

The source-text here is Job 28:12, 20, *'ê-zeh mᵉqôm bînāh*, "Where is the place of understanding?" The LXX equivalent for *bînāh* is in the first instance *epistēmēs*, and in the second, *syneseōs*.

gᵉbûrāh . . . tᵉbûnāh = ischys . . . synesis

While *synesis* is used with some frequency in the LXX for at least five Hebrew synonyms for "understanding,"[30] its most common equivalents are *bînāh* and *tᵉbûnāh*. Close parallels suggest that in this case the equivalency is with *tᵉbûnāh*; cf., e.g., Ps 147:5, *wᵉrab-kōᵃḥ litbûnātô 'ên mispār = megalē hē ischys autou kai tēs synesis autou ouk estin arithmos*; and Sir 14:20 where *ḥokmāh* (A) // *tᵉbûnāh* (B) = *sophia* (A) // *synesis* (B).

Also, despite the more frequent and normal correspondence that exists between *ischys* and *kōᵃḥ* "might" in the LXX, support for *gᵉbûrāh* "strength" appears in some close parallels; cf., e.g., Prov 8:14, *'ᵃnî bînāh lî gᵉbûrāh = emē phronēsis emē de ischys*; and Isa 63:15, *'ayyēh qin'ātᵉkā ûgᵉbûrōtekā = pou estin ho zēlos sou kai hē ischys sou*. For the entire phrase, cf.

Dan(Th) 2:20, *dî ḥokm^{e}tāʾ ûg^{e}bûr^{e}tāʾ dî-lēh hîʾ = hē synesis kai hē ischys autou esti*; and Job 12:13, *ʿimmô ḥokmāh ûg^{e}bûrāh lô ʿēṣāh ût^{e}bûnāh = parʾ autō sophia kai dynamis, autō boulē kai synesis*.

yaḥad = hama

There is slight support for the omission of *hama* in LXX Minuscules 22, 48, 51, 91, 96, 231, 763 and Bo. An alternate possibility is *yaḥdāw*.

ʾôrek-yāmîm = makrobiōsis

The noun, *makrobiōsis* "longevity of life," is a hapax legomenon in the LXX. The Hebrew concept, *ʾôrek yāmîm*, is usually there represented by *makroēmereusis* (Sir 1:12, 20; 30:22), *makrotēs hēmerōn* (Ps 21:5, 23:6, 91:16), or *mēkos biou* (Prov 3:2, 16:17). Job 12:12 offers a helpful parallel: *bîšîšîm ḥokmāh w^{e}ʾōrek yāmîm t^{e}bûnāh* (LXX, *pollō biō*), "Wisdom is with the aged, and understanding in length of days."[31] The same idea is expressed by *rb ymym* in 1QH 17:15.

ʾôr ʿênayim = phōs ophthalmōn

This is synonymous with the several terms for "happiness"; cf. Ps 38:11, Tob 10:5, and Bar 1:14.

3:15

māṣāʾ . . . bāʾ = heure . . . eisēlthen

The equivalencies here represented, *māṣāʾ = heuriskō* and *bôʾ = eiserchomai*, are both frequent and normal in the LXX.[32]

ʾôṣ^{e}rôtèhā = tous thēsaurous autēs

The Hebrew term *ʾôṣār* "storehouse, treasure" is an important item in the Wisdom lexical stock. It is often found in combination with the verb *bôʾ* as in Job 38:22, *h^{a}bāʾtā ʾel-ʾōṣ^{e}rôt šeleg*, and elsewhere.[33] The conception that Wisdom is difficult to locate is paralleled in Eccl 3:11, Sir 1:3 and 20:30. Sy is here expanded with the conflate reading: *l(ʾ)awṣ^{e}rāh walbēt gazzāh*, "into her stores and treasure-house."

3:16-18

môšelê hā'ammîm = hoi archontes tōn ethnōn

This expression has BH parallels in Ps 105:20, *mōšēl 'ammîm;* Isa 28:14; and 2 Chr 23:20. Possible alternatives are *môšelê haggôyīm* (cf. Ps 22:29, 2 Chr 20:6) or *śārê hā'ām* (cf. Ezek 11:1, 2 Chr 24:23, Neh 11:1). The latter is, however, applied during post-exilic times only to the leaders or officials of the Jewish community. Statistically, the Greek terms, *archōn* and *ethnos*, are most frequently used in the LXX as equivalents for *śar* and *gôy* respectively.[34] Sy reads *šallîṭē' de'ālemē'*, "rulers of the ages." Doubtless a mere scribal error inadvertently transformed *'a(m)mē'* "peoples" into *'ālemē'* "ages."

werôdê beḥaytô 'ereṣ = hoi kyrieuontes tōn thēriōn tōn epi tēs gēs

The archaic form, *ḥaytô*, is found in the so-called "elevated prose" of the source-text for this phrase--Gen 1:24, *ḥaytô 'ereṣ*. There it is the equivalent of *ḥayyat hā'āreṣ* in Gen 1:25. This form is found also in the following poetic passages: Ps 79:2; 50:10; 104:11, 20; Isa 56:9; and Zeph 2:14.[35]

In the light of Gen 1:24-28 our Hebrew verb is most probably *rādāh*. The LXX renders *rādāh* with *kyrieuō* also in Isa 14:2; cf. as well Sir 17:4, *katakyrieuein thēriōn*, and Wis 9:2. Syh offers a curious explanatory gloss: *ḥaywāt šennā'*, literally "beasts of tooth" (i.e., carnivores). The Greek term, *thērion*, actually refers specifically to wild game that is hunted.[36] Other biblical allusions to the proverbial dominion of Nebuchadnezzar over the wild beasts and fowl may be compared in Jer 27:6, Dan 2:38, and Jdt 11:7.

meśaḥaqê beṣippôr šāmayim = hoi en tois orneois tou ouranou empaizontes

The source for this expression is Job 40:29, *hatśaḥeq-bô kaṣṣippôr wetiqšerennû lena'arôtêkā*, "will you make sport with him [Leviathan] like a bird, or put him on a leash for your maidens?" This combination, *ṣippôr šāmayim*, occurs also in Job 40:20, Ps 104:26 and 8:9. In the light of these passages and especially its close association with the verb *šāḥaq* in Job 40, *ṣippôr šāmayim* is much more likely as the Hebrew original than the statistically more numerous *ʿôp haššāmayim*.[37]

ʾôṣᵉrê . . . bô bāṭᵉḥû = thēsaurizontes . . . hō epepoitheisan

The first equivalency, *ʾāṣar = thēsaurizō*, is normal. The same participle is illustrated in Amos 3:10.[38] For the equation of *bāṭaḥ* with the second perfect tense of *peithō* "trust," cf. Prov 14:16, 28:26; Ps 49:7; Job 6:20; et al.

wᵉʾên qēṣeh lᵉqinyānām = kai ouk esti telos tēs ktēseōs autōn

In the previous clause the LXX translator correctly employed past tense, but for this common Hebrew verbless idiom he appears inadvertently to have used the present tense (*esti*). In a similar context of acquiring and storing silver and gold, cf. Isa 2:7, *ʾên qēṣeh lᵉ- = ouk ēn arithmos*. Other significant parallels include: Nah 2:10; 3:3, 9; Eccl 12:12; Isa 9:6; Job 22:5; Eccl 4:5. For "acquiring," cf. Prov 4:7, *bᵉkol qinyānᵉkā qᵉnēh bînāh*; Lev 22:10; Ps 105:21. Both Sy and Syh use the cognate term, *qenyānāʾ* "acquiring, acquisition."

ḥôrᵉšê kesep = hoi to argyrion tektainontes

This is a notorious crux. On the one hand, the Hebrew noun *ḥārāš* "artificer, craftsman, smith" would seem to be the natural and logical reading in relation to the *kesep* which follows (i.e., "silversmith"). In support is La[V]: *qui argentum fabricant*. Kneucker[39] thus interprets the phrase as referring to silversmiths who cast idols and whose work was of such superior craftsmanship as to be unfathomable. This would mean in context that it was not just the powerful and rich who vanished, but also these skilled craftsmen whose products were so unsearchable in quality.

Yet on the other hand, the more metaphorical sense of the root *ḥāraš* "devise, scheme" is suggested by the fact that the Greek equivalent, *tektainō*, is never used in the LXX with respect to materials, but rather to denote a moral working in the sense of "contrive" or "devise" how to get something. *Ḥāraš* appears frequently in Proverbs, always translated in the LXX by *tektainō*, and always in the sense of devising or scheming evil (Prov 3:29; 6:14, 18; 12:20; 14:22) or even good (14:22). It is worth noting that in the LXX this Prov 14:22 passage also has within its following context *merimnōnti* "being careful, circumspect." Other significant parallels are 1 Sam 23:9 (where the Hiphil stem is used in the sense "fabricate evil"), Ps 124:3, Ezek 21:36, Sir 11:32, and 27:22. None of the above lends support to the interpretation of working in silver.[40]

Further, the Greek equivalent, *tektainō*, is used by the classical authors only in the middle voice with the meaning "build" or "frame."[41] This clearly does not correspond to the root sense of the Hebrew *ḥāraš* which is "carve, engrave, or artifice." Also, *kesep* "silver" is often used in an extended sense to mean simply "money."

The reading in Sy, *qānîn* "those who acquire," is also supportive of the metaphorical interpretation. Syh, however, employs the verb *ḥ^{e}šal* which clearly admits only the material interpretation since it is used with respect to metal-working in the sense of "forge, cast, or craft." But the lateness of Syh vis-à-vis Sy diminishes its weight.

There is little likelihood that Hebrew *qānāh* would have stood in the original autograph, for *tektainō* is used by the LXX to render only *ḥāraš* (7 times), *ḥārāš* (once), and *šît* (once).[42] Many translations (e.g., Kneucker, Whitehouse, Kautzsch, JB, and Kahana)[43] have followed the "silversmiths" interpretation that assumes a Hebrew original, *ḥārāšê hakkesep*. Others (e.g., RSV, NEB, Fritzsche, Bissell, Reuss, and Gifford)[44] have pursued the alternative, assuming as the original Hebrew, *ḥôr^{e}šê kesep*. Although the above evidence is perhaps at best inconclusive, the latter would appear to represent the more plausible and best supported reading--"those who scheme for silver."

w^{e}dō'^{a}gîm = kai merimnōntes

The LXX uses this verb seven times to render six different Hebrew roots. It appears for Hebrew *dā'ag* in Ps 38:19, *'ed'ag mēḥaṭṭā'tî*, "I am anxious about my sins." The plural participle, *dō'^{a}gîm*, is found in Jer 42:16. Sy offers *wašqîlîn ṣeptā'*, "and who are burdened with anxiety."

'ên ḥēqer = ouk estin exeuresis

This expression has close parallels in the Wisdom literature. The one in Job 5:9 (= 9:10) is especially significant: *'ōśeh gᵉdōlôt wᵉ'ên ḥēqer niplā'ōt 'ad-'ên mispār*, "who does great things that are beyond searching, wonderful things that are innumerable." Others are: Prov 25:3, *wᵉlēb mᵉlākîm 'ên ḥēqer*; Ps 145:3, *ligᵉdūllātô 'ên ḥēqer*; and Job 36:26, *mispār šānāw lō' ḥēqer*. Sy here reads *menyānā'* "numbering, counting" instead of "searching out." Though this reading may well be inferior, it is at least consistent with Wisdom conventions as is evident in the above examples.

<u>3:19</u>

'ābᵉdû wᵉyārᵉdû = ēphanisthēsan, kai . . . katebēsan

BH uses this frequentative perfect consecutive[45] construction for past actions repeatedly brought to a conclusion in the past following an equivalent tense representing actions which have continued or been repeated in the past. The Greek verb *aphanizō* represents twenty-three different Hebrew roots in the LXX.[46] This verb properly has the sense of "vanish" or "disappear and be heard of no longer."[47] The original Hebrew verb was probably *'ābad* "perish" (cf. Esth 3:13, 9:24; Job 4:9; Ps 1:6, 2:12).[48] Sy reads *'ethabbalw* which in this context means "they were destroyed" (i.e., "they perished").

šᵉ'ôl = eis hadou

For the combination with *yārad* "descend," cf. above Bar 3:11; Ps 55:16, *yērᵉdû šᵉ'ôl*; Ezek 32:27, *yārᵉdû šᵉ'ôl*; Job 7:9, *yōrēd šᵉ'ôl*; Isa 14:11, *hûrad šᵉ'ôl*; Isa 14:15; Job 17:16. For *šᵉ'ôl* with *he locale*, cf. Gen 37:35; 42:38; 44:29, 31; Num 26:30; Ezek 31:17.

qāmû taḥtām = alloi antanestēsan ant' autōn

This is a familiar idiom in BH. Several examples will suffice to illustrate this: Num 32:14, *wᵉhinnēh qamtem taḥat 'ᵃbōtêkem*, "and behold, you have risen up in place of your fathers"; and 1 Kgs 8:20, *wā'āqūm taḥat dāwid 'ābî*, "and I have risen up in place of David my father." The Hebrew root *ʿāmad* "stand" is also a possibility here. It is used in the causative with *taḥat* to express the very same idea in Job 34:24, *yārōᵃʿ kabbîrîm lō'-ḥēqer wayyaʿᵃmēd 'ᵃḥērîm taḥtām*, "he shatters the mighty without investigation, and others he sets in their place."[49]

3:20-21

qᵉṭannîm = neōteroi

The comparative degree of the Greek adjective *neos* "young" is expressed by *neōteros* "younger, newer." In the LXX it normally represents the Hebrew adjective *qāṭōn/qāṭān* "small, young" (24 times in all). Less frequently (12 times) it represents *ṣāʿîr* "little, young." Thus *qᵉṭannîm* "younger ones" and the similar meaning *ṣᵉʿîrîm* are both distinct possibilities for the original Hebrew here.

A further possibility is perhaps *'aḥᵃrônîm* "those that come after," even though this Hebrew substantive is never represented by *neos/neōteros* in the LXX. This is the reading proposed by both Kneucker[50] and Kahana,[51] but the only real parallels for the meaning "next generation(s)" are with the idiom *dôr 'aḥᵃrônîm*. This, however, is consistently rendered in the LXX by *genea hetera* "another generation," and never by *neōteros*.[52] Lacking any direct parallels, the best choice for reconstruction appears to be *qᵉṭannîm*.

rā'û 'ôr = eidon phōs

"To see the light" is metaphorical for "to be born" or "to live." Parallels in MT may be found in Job 3:16, 33:30; Eccl 6:5, 11:7; Ps 49:20, 56:14, and 36:10. The use of the negative with this idiom, as in Job 3:16 and Ps 49:20, yields the opposite meaning.

wᵉyāšᵉbû ʿal hā'āreṣ = katōkēsan epi tēs gēs

This verbal equivalence is both frequent and regular in the LXX.[53] Ezek 37:25 offers a close parallel: *wᵉyāšᵉbû ʿal-hā'āreṣ*. The imperfect consecutive construction, *wayyēšᵉbû*, could also be considered a possibility if it could be somehow determined that our author was biblicizing at this point. Other possibilities for the prepositional phrase are *bāʾāreṣ* (cf. Gen 34:21, 1 Chr 5:23) and *ʿal-ʾadmātāh* (cf. Ezek 36:17, 39:26).[54]

wᵉderek bînāh lōʾ yādᵉʿû = hodon de epistēmēs ouk egnōsan

The "way of knowledge" is also found in Prov 9:6, *wᵉʾišrû bᵉderek bînāh* (cf. also Bar 3:27, 36; Job 28:12). While the precise phrase, *derek bînāh*, does not appear in BH as the object of the verb *yādaʿ*, there are parallels for "knowing the way": Isa 59:8, *derek šālôm lōʾ yādāʿû*; Jer 5:4-5, *lōʾ yādᵉʿû derek YHWH*; and Ps 95:10, *lōʾ yādᵉʿû dᵉrākāy*.

hēbînû nᵉtîbôtèhā = oude synēkan tribous autēs

This is paralleled in Job 38:20, *wᵉkî tābîn nᵉtîbôt bêtô*, and with the verb *yādaʿ* in Ps 142:4 and Job 28:7. The parallel pairing, *derek* (A) // *nᵉtîbāh* (B), is very regular in BH.[55] Likewise, the sequence, *yādaʿ* (A) // *bîn* (B), is normal in BH.[56]

middarkāh rāḥᵃqû = apo tēs hodou autōn/autēs porrhō egenēthēsan

The variant, *autēs*, is supported by Sy, LXX Minuscules 26 and 239, and Arm. With this reading the referent of the Hebrew suffix is thus Wisdom herself (i.e., "from her way") and not the ancestors. For the verbal equivalency, cf. Prov 19:7; Job 30:10; Ps 22:12, 20; 35:22; 38:22; and 71:12.

wᵉsārû = wamradw (Sy)

This reading, restorable from Sy, yields a better balanced colon. For parallels, cf. Dan 9:5, Ps 14:3, Deut 11:16, Exod 32:8, *sārû . . . min-hadderek*. The Hebrew verb *mārāh* "rebel" is also a possibility.[57] The Hebrew cognate *mārad* "rebel" is not common in the biblical Wisdom literature, but the phrase, *mōrᵉdê ʾôr*, does occur in Job 24:13 where the parallel cola contain both *derek* and *nᵉtîbôt*.

bᵉnêhem = hoi huioi autōn

This is generally taken as the subject of the second colon of the final bicolon in this section, following the internal arrangement of G^B and that of many of the Versions.[58] However, G^A, La, and Ar would indicate a reading with *hoi huioi autōn* serving as the subject of the verb in the first colon: *oude antelabonto autēs hoi huioi autōn*, "But their sons did not lay hold of her."[59]

3:22

The geographic designation, Canaan, has reference to the area of the great Phoenician port cities long renowned for their culture, wealth, and wisdom. Allusions to this reputation for wisdom in BH may be found in Zech 9:2, where among certain cities claimed as possessions of *YHWH* are listed "Tyre and Sidon, though they are very wise," and in Ezek 28:4, where it is said of Tyre: "by your wisdom and understanding [*ḥokmāh ûtᵉbûnāh*] you have gotten wealth for yourself."

Teman, meaning literally "the south," represents roughly the Edomite region.[60] Its association with wisdom in BH may be observed most clearly in Jer 49:7, "Concerning Edom. Thus says *YHWH* Sabaoth: 'Is wisdom no more in Teman?'" Other allusions to Temanite wisdom are in Obad 8-9, "Will I not in that day, says *YHWH*, destroy the wise men out of Edom, and understanding out of Mount Esau? And your mighty men shall be dismayed, O Teman," and Job 2:11, "Eliphaz the Temanite." For the equation of *ōphthē* "be seen" with the Niphal stem of *rā'āh*, cf. Judg 5:8, Exod 13:7, 34:3, Deut 16:4, and Bar 3:37 below. The pairing, *šāma'* (A) // *rā'āh* (B), appears in the same sequence in Isa 6:9, but the reverse is found in Ps 115:5-6.

3:23

bᵉnê-hāgār dôrᵉšê bînāh = *huioi Agar hoi ekzētountes tēn synesin*

The *bᵉnê-hāgār* are the Ishmaelites.[61] The normal Hebrew equivalent for *ekzēteō* "search out" is *dāraš* "seek out, consult,"[62] just as *zēteō* "seek" is normal in the LXX for Hebrew *biqqēš* "seek."[63] In Eccl 1:13, Qoheleth sets his heart *lidrôš wᵉlatûr baḥokmāh* = *tou ekzētēsai . . . en tē sophia*, "to seek out and examine wisdom." In addition to its basic sense of "seek," *dāraš* is used in BH with such frequent nuances as "consulting" (*YHWH* in Ps 34:11, and *'ᵉlōhîm* in Ps 69:33) and "studying" (the divine ordinances in Ps 119:94, 155, and wisdom in Eccl 1:13). This verb, so nuanced, is also prominent in the Qumran literature.[64] The reconstruction of *dāraš* as part of the original Hebrew would thus in this light appear to be a certainty.

But there are complications. In the LXX text the same combination of verbal root and noun, *ekzēteo* and *synesis*, appears twice in this same verse. Sy follows suit with *bā'în sûkālā'* in both instances, but Syh employs variation: a participle (*bā'în*) from one verbal root for the first occurrence, a noun (*bāṣûyā'*) derived from another for the second occurrence, plus two different nouns derived from the same verbal root (*sᵉkal*) as equivalents of *synesis*. La^V uses the same verb (*exquiro*) in both instances, but has two different nouns (*prudentia* and *intelligentia*). This constitutes at least slight support for the plausible assumption that the original Hebrew would likely have displayed here its common predilection for synonymous pairing rather than mere repetition of the same terms. Thus two different Hebrew verbs have been reconstructed, but it remains quite possible that the normal equivalent, *dāraš*, may originally have stood in both places.[65]

The same noun has been reconstructed in both instances primarily because it is likely that this element of the combination was originally the same. It is, of course, equally possible that different nouns stood in the original Hebrew, the most common equivalents for *synesis* being *bînāh*, *tᵉbûnāh*, and *śēkel*.[66]

A good case can also be made for *biqqēš* for at least one of the verbal occurrences, even though its normal equivalence is with *zēteō*. Especially significant is the fact that it appears frequently in parallel with *dāraš*. In three instances it is the B-word to *dāraš* (Ezek 34:6, Ps 24:6, Judg 6:29) and in three it is the A-word (Zeph 1:6, Ps 38:13, 1QS 5:11). Also, *biqqēš* is often used in BH for "seeking wisdom or knowledge." In Prov 14:6 and Eccl 7:25 its object is *ḥokmāh*, and in both cases the LXX equivalent is *sophia*. In Prov 15:14 and 18:15 its object is *da'at*, but the LXX equivalents are none of our usual synonyms for "knowledge." In Dan 8:15 appears the very close parallel *wā'ᵃbaqšāh bînāh = kai ezētoun synesis* (cf. 1QHf 18:3, *wmbqšy bynh*). These last parallels are supportive of *bînāh* as the original Hebrew noun, but *zēteō* would probably be expected in the LXX if *biqqēš* were indeed in the original Hebrew verse.

Although there is no precedent in the LXX for such an equivalency, *šāḥar*(II) "search diligently" also has much in its favor.[67] This is the very verb used in Prov 1:28 where hypostatized Wisdom (*ḥokmôt* in Prov 1:20) declares: *yᵉšaḥᵃrūnᵉnî wᵉlō' yimṣā'ūnᵉnî*, "They will seek me diligently, but will not find me." The use of its Qal participle is illustrated in Prov 11:27, *šōḥēr ṭôb*.[68] The significant parallel, *dāraš* (A) // *šāḥar* (B), occurs in Ps 78:34. While this then is the particular pairing that has been reconstructed here, it hardly needs saying that this solution is at best tentative and that *biqqēš* remains clearly a strong possibility.

The equivalent of *synesis* here in Bar 3:23 is not likely to be *ḥokmāh* since that term appears in this same verse for *sophia* (Sy and Syh have the cognate *ḥekmᵉtā'*). In the light of parallels for "seeking knowledge" *bînāh* appears most probable, but from the point of view of frequency of equivalence other synonyms, as suggested above, are also possible.

Regrettably, the reconstruction of this particular verse necessitates altogether too much subjectivity. If anything is clear it is that the options must remain open and that this particular reconstruction is at best tentative.

Kneucker[69] has an entirely different idea: that either the LXX translator misread *šōḥᵃrê tᵉbûnāh* for *sōḥᵃrê tᵉbû'āh*, "who trade commodities (in the land)," or that a scribal confusion of one consonant in each word had already occurred in the Hebrew. This assumption yields what he considers a more acceptable parallelism. But the whole argument rests on the undemonstrable premise that the Hebrew equivalent of *ekzēteō* was in the first occurrence *šāḥar* rather than *dāraš*.[70] It is indeed an ingenious proposal, but too much so. For the point of the entire verse, and the parallelism of this tricolon, is the lack of wisdom on the part of these Edomite traders despite their reputation for it. To read the first two cola of the tricolon as "The sons of Hagar who traded merchandise in the land, the traders of Medan and Tema" would be to obfuscate or lose entirely the real parallel that exists between the first and third cola in the theme of wisdom. The second colon actually only elaborates or identifies (or perhaps glosses?) the first.

bāʾāreṣ = epi tēs gēs

This phrase is treated as a gloss by Whitehouse[71] in an apparent attempt to improve the metre. But, it may be noted that in Bar 3:37 the same phrase clearly has the more general sense, "upon the earth."[72] Admittedly, the metre of verse 23a is difficult, but it does permit analysis as a tricolon, 3(4)/3/3, as in the above reconstruction.[73]

mᵉdān wᵉtêmāʾ = Merran kai Thaiman

Merran is undoubtedly corrupt even though there is no known variant. The most plausible conjecture is orthographic confusion. The common Hebrew *d/r* confusion probably accounts for the LXX orthography of this geographic placename, originally the Medan/Midian of Gen 25:2, 37:36, 1 Chr 1:32, Isa 60:6, et al. The reading in Sy, *mûrat*, represents the biblical toponym, Marah, as it does in Exod 15:23. Syh approximates the LXX reading: *mēʾrān*.

Tema[74] is probably to be read in place of the more general term, Teman ("south"), since it is a specifically geographic and gentilic name in BH, indeed a name still preserved in the modern Northwest Arabian town, Teima. It is significant that the LXX uses *Thaiman* consistently for both Teman and Tema. On the other hand, since Teman is used in general for the region of Edom, it could perhaps have a claim to originality here.

hammôšᵉlîm = hoi mythologoi

The *mythologoi* are the ancient "balladeers," "storytellers," "myth-makers," "reciters of fables," or the like. This term is a hapax legomenon in the LXX but it undoubtedly reflects the *māšāl*, the Hebrew version of the common Near Eastern convention of expressing thoughts through parables, riddles, stories, myths and fables. Num 21:27 is illustrative: *'al-kēn yō'm^e rû hammōš^e lîm*, "therefore the storytellers say. . . ."[75]

zāk^e rû = emnēsthēsan

Sy, instead of the expected verb form of the cognate *d^e kar* "remember," here offers *'adrekw*. This is obviously an Aphel perfect form of the verb *d^e rek* "tread," which in the Aphel has the sense "come upon," "attain," or "find." The meaning is thus: "They did not find its paths." However, this reading is hardly a real variant, but rather the result of a metathesis within the word that occurred during the course of the intra-Syriac transmission of the text: *'dkrw* > *'drkw*.

3:24

yiśrā'ēl = ō Israēl

The LXX employs the particle *ō* to add emotion to simple vocative address or to express such lamenting Hebrew interjections as *hôy*, *'ôy*, *hāh*, et al. The first is more probable since the tenor of the address here is hardly lamenting. If a Hebrew particle be deemed likely the most probable of such would be *hôy*, as in Ezek 34:2 where in LXX *ō* is combined with *Israēl*.

bêt-'^e lōhîm = ho oikos tou theou

In BH this expression consistently denotes a building or place where God has granted his presence. Here it can scarcely have such a meaning, but rather the far wider sense that *oikos theou* has in the writings of Philo, "the whole created universe."[76] Perhaps a similar conception is being expressed here by the two clauses together; namely, that heaven is "the house of God" and earth "the place of his possession."[77]

3:25

For the equivalency, *'ên-qēṣ = ouk echei teleutēn*, see verse 17 above.

gābôᵃh wᵉʾên middāh = *hypsēlos kai ametrētos*

The absolute use of *gābôᵃh* "high" may also be found in Job 41:26, where God is said to see *kol-gābōᵃh*, and in Ezek 21:31. Elsewhere in BH it appears over twenty-five times as an adjective modifying mountains, hills, towers, gates, trees, and the like. Apart from *bāmāh* "high place," a highly specialized and contextually limited term in BH,[78] *gābôᵃh* is the most common Hebrew equivalent for *hypsēlos*.[79]

The LXX uses *ametrētos* "immeasurable" in Isa 22:18 to render *rᵉḥab yādayim* "spacious." However, in other passages where this Hebrew idiom occurs, the LXX consistently translates it with the adjective *platys* "broad, spacious."[80] Both Sy and Syh use terms derived from the root *mᵉšaḥ*(II) "measure." In the light of the above, and of the parallel with *ʾên-qēṣ*, the expected Hebrew wording would be *ʾên middāh* "no measure," even though there are admittedly no exact parallels. The idiom, *rᵉḥab yādayim*, is, of course, also possible. The parallelism of this bicolon is, at any rate, striking, with the assonant pair, *gādôl* // *gābôᵃh*, beginning the halves of the bicolon and the subsequent pairing of the two negative phrases concluding them.

3:26

šām yullᵉdû hannᵉpîlîm = *ekei egennēthēsan hoi gigantes*

This verse is manifestly dependent on Gen 6:4. At first sight there appears to be a discrepancy with regard to the verb of this clause. On the basis of the source from which this is borrowed, Gen 6:4, one would perhaps expect the verb *hāyû*, "there were the giants." And indeed there is considerable support in the LXX and Versions (G^{A}, G^{Q}, O-Syh, $La^{C,L,S,V}$, et al.)[81] for the reading, *egenēthēsan* "they were."[82] However, more significantly, the reading *egennēthēsan* "they were born" is supported by both the primary Greek witness, G^{B}, and the primary Semitic witness, Sy (*ʾetîledw*). Since *gennaō* "beget, bear" in the LXX almost exclusively corresponds to one or another of the stems of Hebrew *yālad* "beget, bear,"[83] this evidence amply substantiates the above reconstruction of the Qal passive verb form from *yālad*.[84] It is also noteworthy that *gi(g)nomai* is not the Greek verb in Gen 6:4, but rather *eimi*.[85] This then strongly indicates that the LXX variant in Bar 3:26, *egenēthēsan*, is indeed secondary, very probably resulting from a haplography.

All commentators are agreed that this verse is a borrowing from Gen 6:4, a verse whose context is a story about the antediluvian Nephilim: "It was then that the Nephilim appeared on earth--as well as later--after the divine beings had united with human daughters. Those were the heroes of old, men of renown."[86] The borrowing is clear when the two texts are compared, except that *hāyāh* is not properly an equivalent for *gennaō*.

It is contended here that the author of Baruch was more creative and eclectic than wooden in his literary borrowing, and that the real borrowing that occurred here was from the latter part of Gen 6:4 where *yālad* appears (as well as the other borrowed part of this bicolon, *'anšê haššēm*). In the LXX of Bar 3:26, the verb is passive (*egennēthēsan*), so it is surely not insignificant that *yālad* does appear as a Qal passive in the first line of the Genesis story (Gen 6:1): *ûbᵉnôt yullᵉdû lāhem*.

It would seem then that the author drew directly on the Genesis passage, not in rigid verbatim but with his usual careful reworking. His method of procedure appears to have been the following: appropriation of the verbal idea not of the first part of Gen 6:4 but of the latter part, namely, the fact that the Nephilim or renowned heroes of old *were born* (*yullᵉdû*) in these ancient times, and then borrowing the idiom "men of renown" from the end of that verse. Subsequently, he appears to have utilized the borrowed expression, "from of old," to introduce the parallel bicolon in Bar 3:26 which, apart from this, contains new information about the Nephilim not found in Gen 6:4.

These "giants" of Gen 6:4 are also the point of reference in Wis 14:6, Sir 16:7, 3 Macc 2:4, *1 Enoch* 7, CD 2:19. Indeed, this story from Genesis 6 exercised considerable influence in the later Jewish writings.

'anšê haššēm = hoi onomastoi

This idiom, as noted, has also been appropriated from Gen 6:4 where the LXX reads, *hoi anthrōpoi hoi onomastoi*. Further examples in BH may be found in Num 16:2, 1 Chr 5:24 and 12:30. The currency of this idiom at Qumran may be determined from such passages as 1QM 2:6, 3:3 and 1QSa 2:11, 13.[87]

'ᵃšer mē'ôlām 'anšê middôt mᵉlummᵉdê milḥāmāh = ap' archēs genomenoi eumegetheis, epistamenoi polemōn

The phrase *'ᵃšer mē'ôlām* is also derived from Gen 6:4, but the remainder of this colon has parallels elsewhere. For *'anšê middôt*, cf. Isa 45:14, Num 13:32, 1 Chr 11:23, and 20:6. The root *lāmad* "learn" is used in BH several times in passive forms combined with *milḥāmāh* "war" to express the idea of men "trained or instructed in warfare"; for example, 1 Chr 5:18, *lᵉmûdê milḥāmāh = dedidagmenoi polemon*; Ct 3:8, *mᵉlummᵉdê milḥāmāh = dedidagmenoi polemon*; Isa 2:4, 2 Sam 22:35 (= Ps 18:35), 1 Macc 4:7, 6:30. This concept is also prevalent, as might be expected, in the Qumran "War Scroll":[88] 1QM 6:11, *mlwmdy mlḥmh*; 14:6; 6:13; 2:7; 9:5; and 4QMᵃ 4, *llmd mlḥ[mh]*.[89]

The LXX here in Bar 3:26, however, has *epistamenoi polemon*, a common enough idiom in Greek for the meaning "skilled or well-versed in warfare."[90] It is a problem that out of more than fifty occurrences of this verb in the LXX it is used in all but five for some form of the Qal stem of *yāda'* "know," and that in none of the exceptions is it ever used to render the root *lāmad*. Indeed, the Qal participle of *yāda'* is used frequently in BH to express the same idea--"knowing or skilled"--although never in combination with *milḥāmāh*.[91]

In view of the absolute consistency of *lāmad* in the Hebrew idiom of "training for warfare" in the numerous examples that obtain from BH and Qumran, and despite the lack of precedent for the equation of *epistamai* and *lāmad* in the LXX, the original Hebrew must certainly have been *mᵉlummᵉdê milḥāmāh*.

3:27

lō' b^e'ēlleh bāḥar '^{e}lōhîm = ou toutous exelexato ho theos

The verbal equivalency is normal.[92] This colon has been reconstructed with the negative emphasis on the object of the verb standing in first position following the arrangement of LXX and Sy (*lā' h^{e}wā' l^{e}hālēn g^{e}bā' 'allāhā'*).[93] Other close parallels in BH suggest the possibility of a different sequence for this clause; cf. 1 Sam 16:10, *lō'-bāḥar YHWH bā'ēlleh*; 16:8, *gam-bāzeh lō'-bāḥar YHWH*; 16:9; and Deut 7:7.

w^{e}derek bînāh lō' nātan lāhem = oude hodon epistēmēs edōken autois

Some positive expressions with *nātan* are illuminating: Eccl 2:26, *nātan ḥokmāh w^{e}da'at w^{e}śimḥāh*; Job 38:36, *'ô mî-nātan laśśekwî bînāh*; 1 Chr 22:12, *'ak yitten-l^{e}kā YHWH śēkel ûbînāh*; and some negative ones: Job 1:22, *w^{e}lō'-nātan tiplāh lē'lōhîm*; Jer 16:13, *lō'-'ettēn lākem ḥ^{a}nînāh*; and Job 39:17. It seems most probable that the verb here is active (as in LXX, Sy, and Syh) with God as the subject, and with the negative modifying the verbal action rather than especially stressing the indirect object as Kahana's passive reconstruction[94] presumes.

The phrase *derek bînāh* is the same here as in verse 20 above for both LXX and Syh. Sy, however, once again offers a variant, *'ûr^{e}ḥā' d^{e}ḥekm^{e}tā'*, "the path of *wisdom*."[95]

3:28

w^e'āb^{e}dû . . . 'āb^{e}dû = kai apōlonto . . . apōlonto

Although *apollyō* "perish" (in middle voice) is used in the LXX to render thirty-eight different Hebrew verbs, many of these equivalencies occur only once and it is by far most frequently utilized for the Hebrew verb *'ābad*.[96] This repetition of the same verb is very consistent in the Versions as comparison of the major witnesses, LXX, Sy, Syh, and La^V, will reveal. Examples of such verbal repetition may be seen in Ps 22:5, *b^{e}kā bāṭ^{e}ḥû '^{a}bōtênû bāṭ^{e}ḥû watt^{e}pall^{e}ṭēmô*, and Gen 1:27, *wayyibrā' . . . bārā'*.[97]

biblî-da'at = para to mē echein phronēsin

This common idiom is also found in Deut 4:42, 19:4; Josh 20:3, 5; Job 35:16; 36:12; a similar expression with *min-* (*mibbᵉlî-da'at*) occurs in Isa 5:13 and Hos 4:6. For the equation of *da'at* and *phronēsis*, cf. Prov 24:5. Other references in the apocryphal and pseudepigraphical literature to this perishing of the ante-diluvian giants in the flood may be found in Wis 14:6, 3 Macc 2:4, Sir 16:7, *1 Enoch* 6-11, *2 Apoc. Bar.* 56:12-15.

bᵉ'iwwaltām = dia tēn aboulian autōn

In Prov 14:17, *'iwwelet* "thoughtlessness, folly" is translated by *aboulia* "thoughtlessness," and in Prov 14:18, *'iwwelet* stands antithetically parallel to *da'at*.

3:29

mî 'ālāh šāmayim ûlᵉqāḥāh = tis anebē eis ton ouranon kai elaben autēn

The primary source for this verse and the next is manifestly Deut 30:12-13. In this verse the correspondence is especially close with Deut 30:12, *mî ya'ᵃleh lānû haššāmaymāh wᵉyiqqāḥeh lānû*, and also Prov 30:4, *mî 'ālāh šāmayim wayyērad*.[98] The closeness of the latter parallel suggests that, even though the *waw* consecutive construction was by this time passé in Hebrew literature, *wayyiqqāḥehā* might be expected here if the author was quoting instead of (as it appears) adapting.[99]

ûminnî šᵉḥāqîm hôrîdāh = kai katebibasen autēn ek tōn nephelōn

The longer poetic variant of *min* "from" is reconstructed here *metri causa*.[100] Another possibility for this colon would perhaps be that of the imperfect consecutive in first position (*wayyôrîdehā*), but again such usage in this later period is improbable. The *šᵉḥāqîm* are the highest light clouds. In poetry this term appears consistently as the B-word parallel to *šāmayim* "skies," as in Deut 33:26; Jer 51:9; Prov 8:27-28; Ps 36:6; 57:10; 108:5; Isa 45:8; Job 35:5; 38:37.[101]

3:30

'ābar 'el-'ēber hayyām = diebē peran tēs thalassēs

The source-text here is, as noted, Deut 30:13, *mî ya'ᵃbor-lānû 'el-'ēber hayyām* (cf. also Jer 25:22, Prov 28:14).

ûmᵉṣā'āh = kai heuren autēn

Deut 30:13 has *wᵉyiqqāḥehā*, an imperfect verb standing in simple consecution in relation to the preceding imperfect verb, but for "finding wisdom" parallels may be found in Prov 3:13, *māṣā' ḥokmāh*; 8:9-10, *lᵉmōṣᵉ'ê da'at* (followed by *lāqaḥ* in vs. 10); 28:12, 20; Job 17:10; 32:13; 1 Chr 20:2; Gen 16:7.

wᵉqānāh = kai oisei autēn

In the LXX, *pherō* (here in the future tense) has the meaning "fetch, bring, bear." The Aphel imperfect of *'etā'* appears in Sy and Syh, likewise meaning "bring." Two problems are apparent: (1) that this fourth verb in this series of four parallel cola should suddenly be future in tense vis-à-vis the past tense of the preceding, and (2) that wisdom is here said to be "brought" for money when the usual (and logical) idiom is "bought."[102]

The first could perhaps be solved by the assumption that the Hebrew was in this case a converted imperfect. The odds, however, do not favor such a supposition for this late period. Since the poet has in this section drawn material from several sources and in the process switched from future to past tense in his adaptation of the main source (Deut 30:12-13) in particular, it must be emphasized at this point that it is simply not possible to determine whether he was following the then prevalent style of simple consecution of verbal clauses, so manifestly a fixture in MH,[103] or was instead consciously biblicizing with the older BH *waw* consecutive construction.[104] Thus, although the *waw* consecutive construction would not likely have been an alternative for literary composition in Hebrew at the time of these poems' origin, nevertheless their pronounced character as pastiches of biblical allusions and borrowings (akin in this regard to the *Hôdāyôt*), suggests that the possibility at least of the use of *waw* consecutives must be granted.

The second problem diminishes if, in the light of very significant parallels in Proverbs, the Hebrew verb be reconstructed as *qānāh* "acquire, buy" instead of "bring." The parallels are the following: Prov 4:5 (and 7), *qᵉnēh ḥokmāh qᵉnēh bînāh*; Prov 16:16, *qᵉnōh-ḥokmāh ṭôb mēḥārûṣ ûqᵉnôt bînāh nibḥār mikkāsep*; Prov 17:16, *liqnôt ḥokmāh*; and Prov 18:15, *yiqneh-da'at*. It is, however, difficult to explain how the Versions in consequence have consistently represented the sense of "bring."[105] Against the idea that the verb "bring" derives from the Deut 30:12-13 source-text is the fact that the second colon of Bar 3:30 (just as the second colon of 3:29) does not have its source in Deut 30:12-13. In addition, while the verbal form, *wᵉyiqqāḥehā* (commonly translated in context, "who will cross over the sea for us *and bring it* to us"), does appear in Deut 30:13, the LXX does not translate it there with *pherō* "bring." Thus, while it seems clear from the parallels that what one does with money with respect to wisdom is "buy" (*qānāh*), the Versional consensus on "bring" may possibly be related to the presence of a form of the verb *lāqaḥ* in the Deut 30:12-13 source and the relatively high potential for visual confusion that would obtain between a form of *lāqaḥ* and such forms of *qānāh* as *wᵉqānāh* or *wayyiqnehā*.

bᵉḥārûṣ nibḥār = chrysiou eklektou

Close parallels may be found in Prov 15:16 (quoted above); Prov 8:10, *qᵉḥû mûsārî wᵉ'al-kesep wᵉda'at mēḥārûṣ nibḥār*; Prov 8:19; Wis 7:7-10; Sir 51:28; and Job 28:15-19. Sy here expands: "Who has crossed the ends and extremities of the sea, found her, and brought her up as of choice gold?"

3:31

'ên mēbîn nᵉtîbātāh = oude ho enthymoumenos tēn tribon autēs

In the light of the common parallelism between *yāda'* "know" and *bîn* "understand, discern," the Hiphil participle of *bîn* has been reconstructed in this second colon as B-word to *yāda'*. Close parallels include Job 38:20, *wᵉkî tābîn nᵉtîbôt bêtô*; Dan 1:4, *wᵉyōdᵉ'ê da'at ûmᵉbînê maddā'*; and Neh 10:29, *kōl yôdēaʿ* <û>*mēbîn*.[106]

3:32

This verse begins a section describing God's creative activity as extending over all his works, confirming the fact that he knows fully the way of wisdom, for indeed he can only have done all this by wisdom. The development of this thought in Baruch is highly dependent on Job 28:23ff.

rô'ēh-kôl hû' yᵉdāʿāh = ho eidōs ta panta ginōskei autēn

The Greek verb *eidō* has a dual meaning. Its basic sense is "see," but it also means "know," as here the participle of the perfect tense is used in the sense that what one has seen one knows. It is indeed this sense of "knowing" that is most commonly employed in Greek. The Hebrew verb *rā'āh* manifests a similar, though not nearly so marked, character. While it too fundamentally means "see," it frequently connotes various nuances that fall somewhere between "seeing" and "knowing," and is used with some frequency in parallel with, or as a synonym for, *yādaʿ*. An example is Eccl 8:16 where *gnōnai // idein = ladaʿat // lir'ôt*, and in which *lir'ôt* has the sense, "to perceive." Other passages where "perceive" is the meaning of *rā'āh* and *eidō* is its LXX equivalent are Isa 5:19, 26:10, and Num 11:15. In addition, *rā'āh* has the sense "consider" in such passages as Deut 11:2, 33:9, and Isa 6:9 (in each of which it also stands in parallel with *yādaʿ*). It is perhaps best nuanced "observe" in Job 11:11 and 1 Sam 6:9 (again in parallel with *yādaʿ*), and "experience" in Ps 16:10, 89:48, and Eccl 5:18. A very close parallel obtains in Job 28:24, *taḥat kol-haššāmayim yir'eh*, "He sees [perceives?] everything under all the heavens." One may also compare 11QPs^{a} XXVIII, 7-8 (Ps 151:4), *hkwl r'h 'lwh hkwl hw' šmʿ*, "Everything has God seen, everything has he heard."[107]

The translation, "perceives," has been chosen here because it balances between, and conveys something of, the sense of both verbs of cognition. While there is no exact parallel for *rô'ēh-kol* (*or eidōs ta panta*) elsewhere, there are the very close parallels in Job 28:24 and 11QPs^{a} and a significant semantic one involving *ḥāzāh* and *blepō*, each meaning "see," that suggests the possible existence of an appellation, "the One who *sees* all." This is in Sir 15:18, where *blepōn ta panta* = *wḥwzh kl* (cf. also Sir 17:19 and 23:19-20).

The *alla* "but" of the LXX text does not necessarily represent a Hebrew particle. While it does at times serve to render *kî* (e.g., Prov 23:17) or *w*^{e} (e.g., Prov 27:4), it is also often supplied by the LXX for the sense where the Hebrew employed no particle (e.g., Prov 20:22 and 25:5).

hû' ḥ^{a}*qārāh bitbûnātô* = *exeuren autēn tē synesei autou*

The Greek verb *exeuriskō* "find out, discover" does not occur in the LXX in any books, canonical or apocryphal, for which there is an extant Hebrew *Vorlage*. It is found only in Bar 3:32, 3:36 and 2 Macc 7:23. But since the related noun *exeuresis* does appear as the equivalent of *ḥēqer* in Isa 40:28 (and elsewhere only in Bar 3:18), it would seem that the Hebrew verb *ḥāqar* "search, explore, ascertain" can confidently be assumed here. In a very close parallel in Job 28:27, it is said concerning Wisdom, *h*^{e}*kînāh w*^{e}*gam-ḥ*^{a}*qārāh*, "He [God] established it and searched it out" (cf. Ps 44:22 and 139:1).

For *bitbûnātô* there are relevant parallels in Prov 3:19, *YHWH b*^{e}*ḥokmāh yāsad-'āreṣ kônēn šāmayim bitbûnāh*, and Jer 10:12, *'ōśēh 'ereṣ b*^{e}*kōḥô mēkîn tēbēl b*^{e}*ḥokmātô ûbitbûnātô nāṭāh šāmayim* (cf. also Bar 3:14, 23).

hammēkîn 'ereṣ = *ho kataskeuasas tēn gēn*

There are a number of parallels available for this expression: especially the two passages cited immediately above (Prov 3:19 and Jer 10:12), Jer 33:2, *YHWH 'ōśāh 'ereṣ yôṣēr 'ôtāh lah*^{a}*kînāh*, and Ps 119:90, *kônantā 'ereṣ watta'*^{a}*mōd*.[108]

'ad-'ôlām = *eis ton aiōna chronon*

For this idiom of continuous existence or unending time, cf. verse 13 above, Ps 48:9, *'*^{e}*lōhîm y*^{e}*kōn*^{e}*neh 'ad-'ôlām*, and the lexica.

hôl^{e}*kê 'al-'arba'* = *ktēnōn tetrapodōn*

The literal meaning of this Greek phrase is "animals, quadrupeds." The fact that the LXX here uses both these synonymous words in combination, whereas *tetrapous* is otherwise employed regularly in the LXX to translate *bᵉhēmāh* alone (cf. Gen 1:24-26, Prov 12:10, Sir 7:22), suggests that the Hebrew original was more substantial than merely *bᵉhēmāh*. It thus seems likely that it would have been the above reconstructed idiom, found elsewhere in Lev 11:20, 21, 27, 42, and meaning literally "those which go about on all fours." Of course, *bᵉhēmāh* must remain a possibility for reconstruction, but the metre here may perhaps be considered best balanced only with the above lengthier phrase.[109]

3:33

hammᵉšalleᵃḥ 'ôr wᵉyēlak = *ho apostellōn to phōs, kai poreuetai*

This expression is paralleled in Job 38:35, alluding to the lightning flashes' ready obedience to God, *hatšallāḥ bᵉrāqîm wᵉyēlēkû wᵉyō'mᵉrû lᵉkā hinnēnû*. For *šālaḥ*, cf. Ps 104:10.

This has been interpreted by some as a reference to the sun,[110] following Job 31:26 which is the only place in the LXX where *'ôr* is translated by *hēlion* "sun." There is, however, more substantial support for taking this as a reference to the lightning. Indeed, *'ôr* is used for lightning in Job 36:30, 32; 37:3, 11, 15. This plus Job 38:35 (quoted above) and the aspect of "quaking" or "trembling" (*rᵉ'ādāh*) at the end of the Baruch verse strongly suggest not only that the reference is to lightning but also that these Job passages are in fact the source of the idea expressed here. Also significant in its coupling of lightning with what follows in Bar 3:34 is *1 Enoch* 43:1, "And I saw other lightnings and the stars of heaven, and I saw how he called them all by their names and they hearkened unto him."[111] This same calling by name is found in Bar 3:34, Ps 147:4, Isa 40:26, Num 12:5 and *1 Enoch* 69:21. Further, the use of *poreuomai* for Hebrew *hālak* is extremely regular in the LXX.[112]

wᵉyišma' 'ēlāyw bir'ādāh = *kai hypēkousen autō tromō*

The Hebrew idiom *šāma' 'el-* "obey" is well illustrated in Gen 28:7, *wayyišma' ya'ᵃqōb 'el-'ābîw* (cf. Gen 39:10). That *tromos* here means something more concrete and vivid than "fear" is made clear by the Syriac equivalents in Sy and Syh. Sy offers *bartîtā'* "with quaking," using a term (*r^e^tîtā'*) that is sometimes used in the plural for the violent shocks of earthquakes, while Syh has *b^e^rā'^e^lā'* "with reeling." In Ps 2:11, *tromos* translates *r^e^'ādāh* "quaking, trembling" which there stands in parallel with *yir'āh* "fear." The same equivalency is found in Job 4:14, where the parallel is with *paḥad* "dread" (cf. also Ps 48:7, Isa 33:14).

Sy reveals a fuller ending to this verse than is evident elsewhere: *wa'nāy(hy)* ['*ar'ā'*] *bartîtā'*, "and [the earth] answered him with trembling." Whitehouse has suggested that this "might appear to indicate a lost line."[113] A major difficulty is the fact that the word "earth" is found only in the *Walton Polyglot* edition of the Sy text, and not in that of Lagarde or others,[114] which could well indicate that it is an explanatory gloss or merely another example of the expansionary tendency of the Sy text. It is, however, intriguing to speculate that if this Sy reading could somehow be confirmed as genuine, a rather clumsily balanced 3+3 bicolon could be obviated in favor of a well-balanced 3+3+3 tricolon:

(33) *hamm^e^šallē^a^ḥ 'ôr w^e^yēlak*
"The One who sends forth the light and it goes,

yiqrā'ēhû w^e^yišma' 'ēlāyw
Summons it and it obeys him,

w^e^ta'^a^nēhû [hā'āreṣ] bir'ādāh
And [the earth] answers him with trembling."

<u>3:34</u>

b^e^mišm^e^rôtām = en tais phylakais autōn

This use of a military metaphor in which the stars as the host of the heavens keep the night watches may be compared with Sir 43:10, Ps 136:9, 1QS 10:1ff., Hab 2:1, and Isa 21:8.

yā'îrû = elampsan

The Greek verb *lampō* "shine" appears only ten times in the LXX and in only four of those is there a Hebrew counterpart:

ṣāḥaḥ "be dazzling" in Lam 4:7, *zāhar* "enlighten, instruct" in Dan 12:3, *nāgah* "shine" in Isa 9:1, and the noun *nōgah* "brightness" in Prov 4:18. While the first two are unlikely prospects for this context, support for *nāgah* may be found in Joel 2:10, 4:15, and the MH and Aramaic *nôgah/nôgᵉhā'* "Venus."[115] But even though the equation *lampō* = *'ôr*(Hiphil) does not occur in the LXX, by comparison with such passages as Gen 1:15, 17, Ps 139:12, Isa 60:19, and Exod 13:21, in which the causative stem of this Hebrew verb specifies the giving off of light, this seems the most likely reconstruction.[116]

wîrannᵉnû = euphranthēsan

The Greek verb *euphrainō* is used quite regularly in the LXX for Hebrew *śāmaḥ*, but in Deutero-Isaiah, the major biblical source for this poem, it is very frequently used for *rānan* "rejoice."[117] Indeed, Isa 44:23 and 49:13 in particular feature a cosmological context. Most significantly, there is only one passage in BH which specifically portrays the stars as "rejoicing"--Job 38:7, *bᵉron-yaḥad kôkᵉbê bōqer*. This passage, in which the verb is *rānan*, would thus appear to be a primary source here.

In Trito-Isaiah *euphrainō* is often the equivalent of *śîś* "rejoice" (cf. Isa 61:10, 62:5, 65:18).[118] Any of these verbs is theoretically possible, but in the light of the one clear parallel, *rānan* must be deemed the most probable.

hinnēnû = paresmen

The LXX employs *pareimi* "be present, near" to approximate the Hebrew quasi-verbal *hinnēh* + suffix. This is exemplified in the response of the lightning flashes in Job 38:35, *hinnēnû*. Syh, adhering closely to the LXX, has *qarrîbînan* "we are nigh,"[119] but Sy, reading *hā' ḥᵉnan* "behold us," leaves little doubt about the originality of *hinnēnû* in the Hebrew, not to mention its value in confirming Hebrew as the language of the *Vorlage*.[120]

yiqrā' lāhem = ekalesen autous

Other passages dealing with stars such as Isa 40:26, *lᵉkullām bᵉšēm yiqrā'*, Ps 147:4, and Job 38:7, suggest that the sense here is "he calls them (by name?)."[121]

yā'îrû bᵉśāśôn lipnê 'ôśêhem = elampsan met' euphrosynēs tō poiēsanti autous

The common equivalency between *poieō* and *'āśāh* in the LXX is well illustrated in such passages as Isa 22:11, 42:5 and Ps 111:10. For the equivalency between *śāśôn* and *euphrosynē*, cf. below, 4:11.

<u>3:35</u>

This verse as it stands in the LXX will not allow reconstruction of a balanced metre. The overbalance of the second member is clear even in the usual English translation:

> This is our God,
> no other can be compared to him.

Sy contains an additional phrase in the first colon, but its authority is dubious and it is bracketed in the Lagarde edition (Sy^L) as a gloss. If this were included, it would serve well to balance the verse: *hānāw 'allāhā' [wᵉlayt (')ḥᵉrîn lᵉbar mennēh] / wᵉlā' netḥᵉšab (')ḥᵉrîn lᵉbar mennēh*, "This is God [and there is no other besides him], / and no other can be counted besides him." The enduring problem, however, is the matter of determining what authority (if any) this phrase possesses. Is it perhaps a phrase original to the text, but subsequently lost by homoioteleuton (the last three of the four words are the same as those at the end of the second colon)? Or is it rather a gloss by a copyist who felt the imbalance?

There are numerous parallels in the poetry of Second Isaiah, especially chapters 42-48, which would suggest that this may indeed reflect what originally lay in the Hebrew text. Similarity with the following passages is obvious enough, but it becomes even more heightened in the light of the Sy reading: Isa 45:5, *'ᵃnî YHWH wᵉ'ên 'ôd zûlātî 'ên 'ᵉlōhîm*; Isa 45:21, *hᵃlō' 'ᵃnî YHWH wᵉ'ên-'ôd 'ᵉlōhîm mibbal'āday 'ēl-ṣaddîq ûmôšîᵃ' 'ên zûlātî*; Isa 46:9, *kî 'ānōkî 'ēl wᵉ'ên 'ôd 'ᵉlōhîm wᵉ'epes kāmônî*; Isa 43:10-11; 44:6; 45:14, 18, 22; Ps 18:32, *kî mî 'ᵉlôᵃh mibbal'ᵃdê YHWH ûmî ṣûr zûlātî 'ᵉlōhênû*; and 2 Sam 7:22 (prose) . . . . *YHWH kî-'ên kāmôkā wᵉ'ên 'ᵉlōhîm zûlātekā*.[122]

It is significant that in the few places in BH where *mibbal'ᵃdê* and *zûlāh* are in parallel (Isa 45:21 and Ps 18:32) the former is consistently the A-word and the latter the B-word. This fact alone casts considerable doubt on the proposal of Kahana, *hû' 'ᵉlōhênû* [*wᵉ'ên zûlātô*] / *'aḥēr lō' yēḥāšēb mibbal'ādāyw*, in the opposite sequence of the attested parallelism of this pair.[123] The reading, *wᵉ'ên mibbal'ādāyw*, has been adopted here for the first parallel colon in the light of the previous observation, but judging by the other parallels noted a case could also be made for reconstructing *wᵉ'ên 'ôd*.

yēḥāšēb = logisthēsetai

That *ḥāšab* is the Hebrew verb here is beyond question. With only a few exceptions, *logizomai* is always used in the LXX for *ḥāšab*. Further, both Sy and Syh employ the cognate *ḥᵉšab*.

3:36

(hû') ḥāqar = (houtos) exeure

The presence of the demonstrative emphatically beginning the clause in Sy, La^V, Eth, and Ar (as well as other minor witnesses),[124] suggests that this element was perhaps lost from the beginning of the verse in the LXX by virtue of its similarity to the final word of the previous verse, *auton*. Similar use of *hû'* in BH may be seen in such passages as Gen 3:15, Ps 48:15, Isa 36:7, et al. For the verbal equivalency, cf. above, verse 32.

kol-derek = pasan hodon

Parallels for "the whole way" may be found in Prov 3:6, 31; 4:26; Ps 91:11; 119:168; 139:3; 145:17; Job 28:23ff.; cf. above, verses 20, 27, for the "way of knowledge."

lᵉya'ᵃqōb 'abdô = Iakōb tō paidi autou

The Greek noun *pais*, meaning primarily "lad, boy, child" (cf. Latin *puer*), can also be used to mean "servant, slave." In one instance (Judg 19:19), the LXX uses *pais* to translate *'ebed* "servant, slave." *Ya'ᵃqōb* and *'ebed* are associated elsewhere in Isa 44:1, 2; 45:4; Jer 30:10; and Gen 32:19.

ûlᵉyiśrā'ēl yᵉdîdô = kai Israēl tō ēgapēmenō hyp' autou

While there is no exact parallel to support this reading, the equivalency *yādîd = ēgapēmenos* does occur three times in the LXX: Deut 33:12, Isa 5:1, and Jer 11:15. The first is applied to Benjamin while the latter two are figurative of the people of Jerusalem and Judah. In the LXX of Deut 32:15, *Iakōb* is paired with *ēgapēmenos*. Sy has here *ḥabbîbeh* "his beloved."

The sequence *ya'ᵃqōb* (A) // *yiśrā'ēl* (B), conforms to the attested canonical sequence for the parallelism of these two frequently paired names.[125] This verse has been understood here to have been a tricolon of which the final colon was apocopated by the ellipsis of a verbal element comparable to that of the other two cola.

3:37

'aḥᵃrê-zeh = meta touto

This Greek idiom, consisting of the preposition plus the accusative of time, literally means "after this" or "thereupon." Syh follows the LXX closely with *bātar hāde'* "after this, afterward," but Sy presents a reading, *wᵉmen bātar hālēn*, "and after these things," which corresponds much more closely to the widely attested LXX variant, *kai meta tauta*,[126] especially with its conjunction and plural demonstrative. Kahana has proposed the reconstruction of *'āz* "then, at that time," but there are no examples of such an equivalency in the LXX.[127]

A more probable reconstruction that is metrically, and indeed semantically, preferable is *'aḥᵃrê-zeh(zō't)* "after that, thereupon." The following may be compared: Ezra 9:10, *'aḥᵃrê-zō't = meta touto*; Sir 47:1, *'ḥryw = meta touto*; 1 Macc 3:55, *kai meta touto*; and Job 42:16. The same compounding of Syriac prepositions, *men + bātar*, is found in Josh 23:1 as the equivalent of the Hebrew *min + 'aḥarê* in the expression, "and a long time after." Not in combination with *men*, Syriac *bātar* is also used for Hebrew *'aḥarê* in Joel 2:14.

nir'ātāh = ōphthē

Parallels for "appeared" may be found in Gen 12:7, 1 Sam 3:21, and elsewhere.

hithallākāh = synanestraphē

This Greek verb appears elsewhere in the LXX only in Gen 30:8, where it has quite another sense (as the equivalent of the Niphal stem of *pātal* "wrestle, twist"), and Sir 41:5, where it seems to have the meaning "go about in" (i.e., "dwell"). The root verb *anastrephō* has the meaning "turn around, turn upside down." It is often used in a more extended sense, "turning oneself about in a place" (i.e., to "tarry" or "dwell" there), as in the phrase *gaian anastrephomai*, "to go and dwell in a land." Here the *syn-* prefix simply adds the dimension of "together with" to the basic sense of "dwell" or "go about" (i.e., "live"). In both Prov 20:7 and Ezek 19:6, *anastrephō* is the verb used to render the Hithpael stem of *hālak*, "walk about, live, dwell" (cf. Eccl 4:15).

That this is indeed the sense of the LXX here can be observed from the slavishly close Syh reading, *'akḥedā' 'ethappak*, "he lived together with," even though it specifies 3ms for the Ethpaal perfect verb instead of 3fs (thus intending God himself as the subject, rather than Wisdom, according to the common Christian incarnational interpretation of this passage).[128] The Syriac (*'ayk + ḥedā'*>) *'akḥedā'* "at the same time, together with" is that language's equivalent for the Greek prefix *syn-* "together with." The Syh verb *hepak* also has the root meaning "overturn, turn about," and in the Ethpaal stem (+ *be*) it has the sense "go about, be occupied, live in." Sy has a similar reading: *'ethappak bêt*, "he went about, lived among."

It is not necessary at all to delete this verse with Kneucker[129] as a Christian gloss, for the subject of the action (though the gender is not apparent in the Greek) clearly must have been hypostatized Wisdom herself. There was ample precedent before Baruch for the conception of Wisdom dwelling with men on earth; for example, Prov 8:31, 22; Sir 24:3ff.; Wis 9:10; 4 Macc 1:16-17.[130]

4:1

zeh-sēper miṣwôt . . . wᵉhattôrāh = hautē hē biblos tōn prostagmatōn . . . kai ho nomos

Kneucker,[131] following ample biblical parallels for *sēper tôrat 'ᵉlōhîm*,[132] has reconstructed *zeh-sēper tôrat 'ᵉlōhîm*. Granting that there are parallels for this phrase, the above reconstruction nevertheless appears more probable in the light of the following data. The Greek noun *prostagmatōn* is inescapably plural, as is *puqdānaw(hy)* in both Sy and Syh, and no textual variants mitigate this fact. The Hebrew noun *tôrāh*, common enough in the plural (as "laws" or "teachings"), is still more frequently singular (often denoting the Deuteronomistic law code). In the Wisdom literature and elsewhere in BH (except Esther), it almost invariably has as its LXX equivalent *nomos* "law, norm."[133]

Further, the plural of *miṣwāh*, often in the context of or connoting legal codification ("commandments"), is rendered in the LXX by the plural of *prostagma* in such passages as Exod 20:6, Lev 26:14-15, Deut 5:10, and Dan 9:4-5 (though admittedly the more normal equivalencies are *prostagma* = *ḥôq* and *entolē* = *miṣwāh*). Finally, from the viewpoint of the conventions of BH parallelism, the evidence[134] indicates that where these two words are paired in BH poetry, the sequence *miṣwāh* (A) // *tôrāh* (B), occurs three times (Prov 6:20, 23; 7:2), and the reverse only once (Prov 3:1). The above reconstruction has thus been deemed the most probable.

hā'ômedet = hyparchōn

The Greek participle is masculine in gender, corresponding to the masculine noun *nomos*, but the Hebrew participle must be feminine since *tôrāh* is feminine. Significant parallels are:

Eccl 1:4, *l^{e}'ôlām 'ōmādet*; Ps 19:10, *'ômedet lā'ad*; Ps 33:11, *l^{e}'ôlām ta'^{a}mōd*; Ps 148:6, *wayya'^{a}mîdēm lā'ad l^{e}'ôlām*. Both Sy and Syh here employ the particle of existence to express "that which exists forever."[135]

kol-maḥ^{a}zîqèhā // 'ôz^{e}bèhā = pantes hoi kratountes autēn // hoi kataleipontes

A comparable pairing, also referring to Wisdom, may be found in Prov 4:13, *haḥ^{a}zēq bammûsār 'al-terep niṣṣ^{e}rehā kî-hî' ḥayyèkā*, where the Hiphil stem of *rāpāh* "let go, abandon" functions as the equivalent of *'āzab* "abandon." The same parallelism between "hold fast" and "(not) abandon" is found in Job 27:6, *b^{e}ṣidqātî heḥ^{e}zaqtî w^{e}lō' 'arpeh*. Also instructive are the following parallels: Prov 3:18, *'ēṣ-ḥayyîm hî' lammaḥ^{a}zîqîm bāh* (of Wisdom); 4:2, *tôrātî 'al-ta'^{a}zōbû*; 10:17, *'ôzēb tôkaḥat*; 15:10, *l^{e}'ôzēb 'ōraḥ*; and Bar 3:12, *'āzabtā m^{e}qôr ḥokmāh*.[136]

l^{e}ḥayyîm // yāmûtû = eis zōēn // apothanountai

Of particular relevance here are Prov 11:19, *kēn-ṣ^{e}dāqāh l^{e}ḥayyîm ûm^{e}raddēp rā'āh l^{e}môtô* (Versions, *lāmût*); Prov 8:35-36, *kî mōṣ^{e}'î māṣā' (Q) ḥayyîm wayyāpeq rāṣôn miyYHWH / w^{e}ḥōt^{e}'î ḥōmēs napšô kol-m^{e}śan'ay 'āh^{a}bû māwet*; Prov 19:16; 14:27; 10:16; 19:23; 18:21; Sir 11:14; and Deut 30:15.

4:2

šûbāh = epistrephou

This imperative (often plus a vocative) appears in such similar passages as Hos 14:2, *šûbāh yiśrā'ēl 'ad YHWH '^{e}lōhèkā = epistraphēti, Israēl, pros Kyrion ton theon sou*; 14:3, *šûbāh 'el-YHWH*; Jer 3:12, 14, *šûbāh m^{e}šûbāh yiśrā'ēl*; and Isa 44:22, *šûbāh 'ēlay kî-g^{e}'altîkā* (the antecedent here addressed is Jacob // Israel in 44:21).[137]

hithallēk . . . lipnê = diodeuson . . . katenanti

Even though the Greek verb *diodeuō* "journey through" represents the Hebrew verb *'ābar* "pass through" in ten of its twelve LXX occurrences with Hebrew equivalents,[138] and the

Hithpael stem of *hālak* "walk about, set a course, live" only once (Gen 13:17), the latter is nevertheless the likely equivalent here. This is so because on the one hand in every example of the equivalency with *ʿābar* the literal sense, "travel through," is expressed (almost exclusively with reference to ruined cities or desolated lands that have been rendered impassable), but on the other the Baruch context demands the metaphorical sense. The use of the reflexive stem of *hālak* is in fact quite prominent in BH as a figure for "living,"[139] and is much more apt here. This same Hithpael imperative appears in Gen 17:1 (also combined with *lipnê*) with the sense, "walk [i.e., "live"] blameless before me."

This combination of the Hithpael stem of *hālak* plus *lipnê* (usually plus *YHWH* or Elohim) constitutes a common Hebrew formula, "walk before" or "live in the presence of," that is idiomatic of a person's relationship with God.[140]

l^e^noghāh = pros tēn lampsin [*autēs*]

The feminine suffix referring to Wisdom (or Torah?)[141] is most probably to be restored.[142] Support for *autēs* appears in LXX minuscule 239, La^V, the Old Latin codices La^C and La^S, and Sy (though Sy is here expanded and the words differently combined). The loss of this element can be readily accounted for on either the Hebrew or Greek level by the assumption of a haplography. The Hebrew suffix (*h*) would have been preceded by that very same consonant, a rather rare conjuncture that would make the suffix especially susceptible to loss. The Greek pronoun likewise could easily have been lost because of the close proximity of the same pronoun at the end of the verse.

The Greek *lampsis* "shining" is a hapax legomenon in the LXX.[143] That the Hebrew original would have been *nōgah* is suggested by such passages as Prov 4:18, *k^e^ʾôr nōgah = homoiōs phōti lampousin*; Isa 62:1; 60:3; Ezek 10:4; Hab 3:4; and Bar 4:24.[144]

The choice here is thus to treat verse 2b as a unit (following Sy) with unsuffixed *nōgah* in construct with *ʾôrāḥ* or as a combination of two phrases (following LXX) with suffixed *nōgah*. The latter has been followed.[145]

4:3

'al-tittēn lᵉ'aḥēr kᵉbōdekā = mē dōs heterō tēn doxan sou

The source of this expression lies in Deutero-Isaiah, especially 42:8 (= 48:11), *'ᵃnî YHWH hû' šᵉmî ûkᵉbôdî lᵉ'aḥēr lō'-'ettēn*. As *YHWH* does not relinquish any of his glory, neither should his people. The Greek noun *doxa* "glory" appears regularly in the LXX for Hebrew *kābôd* "glory," most pronouncedly in Proverbs, Ecclesiastes, and Psalms.[146]

wᵉṭôbātᵉkā = kai ta sympheronta soi

The present participle of the Greek verb *sympherō* "be useful, be advantageous" is commonly used substantively to mean "advantage, expediency, welfare." It is not common in the LXX, but in four of the six occurrences that have Hebrew equivalents it is used to translate Hebrew *ṭôbāh/ṭôb* "good" (or, as frequently, in a more extended sense, "prosperity, weal, good fortune").[147] In Deut 23:7, one of the passages in which this equivalency occurs, this term is specifically applied on a national level as here and used in the extended sense of "prosperity": *lō'-tidrōš šᵉlōmām wᵉṭōbātām kol-yāmèkā lᵉ'ôlām* (cf. 2 Macc 4:5, *sympheron koinē*, "the public welfare," and Ps 65:12).

Both Kneucker[148] and Kahana[149] have reconstructed *yitrôn* "advantage, profit" as the original Hebrew term. In BH this word appears only in Ecclesiastes[150] where it quite consistently denotes the personal sort of advantage that accrues to the wise man. But it is not used with a corporate referent, much less a national one. A further drawback is that such an equivalency never occurs in the LXX.

The very close parallel in Sir 49:5[151] suggests yet another possibility: *qeren* "horn," frequently employed in BH in an extended sense to mean "fortune, prestige, power," or the like.[152] This may be applied to an individual (1 Sam 2:1, 10; Ps 89:25) or to a nation (Ps 89:18), and yet this also would assume an equivalency unknown in the LXX.

Thus *ṭobāh* has been reconstructed in the light of precedent for such an equivalency and the evidence of semantic correspondence, but the other options must nevertheless be seriously considered. Deut 4:6-8 suggests that Israel's "glory" and "fortune" par excellence were Torah, already identified here in Baruch with Wisdom.

l^e gôy nokrî = ethnei allotriō

Two passages vie here for consideration as the source-text: Exod 21:8, *l^e'am nokrî = ethnei de allotriō* (in the context of a legal proscription against selling slaves to foreigners),[153] and Sir 49:5, *wytnw qrnm l'ḥr wkbwdm lgwy nkry*[154] = *edōkan gar to keras autōn heterois, kai tēn doxan autōn ethnei allotriō,* "For they gave their 'horn' to others, and their glory to a foreign nation."

This latter corresponds so closely to the Baruch passage in its entirety that, if not the original source, it must surely derive from a common source. The supposition that *gôy* is the Hebrew original finds further confirmation in the evidence of the LXX equivalencies: *ethnos* is used in the LXX with great frequency and regularity as the equivalent for *gôy*,[155] and *allotrios* likewise is normal for forms of the Hebrew root *nkr*, especially *nokrî*.[156] A contemporary, nonbiblical parallel is found in CD 14:15, *lgwy nkr.*

Sy again has an apparently conflate text: "Do not give to others your glory and your honor, nor whatever is good and advantageous to you to a strange people."

<u>4:4</u>

'ašrênû yiśrā'ēl = makarioi esmen, Israēl

The likely source here is Deut 33:29, *'ašrèkā yiśrā'ēl.*[157]

lānû nôdā' = hēmin gnōsta estin

This phrase is paralleled in Isa 19:21, *nôdā' l^e-*; Prov 31:23; and Eccl 6:10.

kî haṭṭôb b^e'ênê-'^elōhîm = hoti ta aresta[158]

The Greek verbal adjective generally has the sense of a passive participle, and thus here, as elsewhere in the LXX, *aresta*[159] denotes "things that are pleasing or acceptable."

Both Sy and Syh employ the familiar participial adjective, *šappîr*, in the same sense--"fair" (i.e., "pleasing"). Where *arestos* is used in the LXX it is most typically in rendering the formulaic *haṭṭôb/hayyāšār b*^{e}*'ênê-* as, for example, in Deut 6:18, *w*^{e}*'āśîtā hayyāšār w*^{e}*haṭṭôb b*^{e}*'ênê YHWH*, or Isa 38:3, *w*^{e}*haṭṭôb b*^{e}*'ênêkā 'āśîtî*.[160]

A significant parallel appears in Tob 4:21,[161] *kai poiēsēs to areston enōpion autou*, "and do that which is pleasing in his [God's] sight." This is markedly Hebraic and evocative of the standard Deuteronomistic formula.[162]

Relevant parallels also occur in Sir 48:22, the Hebrew text of which is available in an incomplete, yet nonetheless useful, state of preservation, *epoiēse gar ezekias to areston Kyriō* = [*ky 'śh yḥz*]*qyhw 't hṭw*[*b*], "[For Heze]kiah [did] what was pleas[ing],"[163] and Wis 9:18, *kai ta aresta sou edidachthēsan anthropoi*, "and men were taught the things that are pleasing to you [God]."[164]

There are also some less direct parallels which nevertheless strongly suggest that what Israel knows that makes her so happy is indeed "the things that are pleasing to God" rather than "the good things of God":[165] Ps 119:1-2, Prov 3:32, Ps 94:12, 103:7, and Deut 29:28.[166]

The most convenient reconstruction (perhaps too much so) for metre and balance would be *kî haṭṭôb lē'lōhîm*, as first proposed by Whitehouse.[167] It would accord more closely to the equivalent constructions in the Syriac[168] and LXX in that all are lacking here the common element, "in the sight of" (Hebrew *b*^{e}*'ênê-*), which is quite consistent in the usual formulation. But it is a problem that there is really only one BH parallel for this construction: Deut 23:17, *baṭṭôb lô*, "where it pleases him best."

Another possibility for reconstruction is that proposed by Kahana,[169] involving a different interpretation of the text: *kî ṭûb '*^{e}*lōhîm*, "for the goodness of God (is known to us)." This yields the interpretation that Israel is happy because the people now know or experience the goodness of God. The Syriac texts do not admit of such an interpretation, nor does the LXX text as it stands in both the Rahlfs and Ziegler editions,[170] *tō theō*, "to God." But although the LXX variant, *tou theou*, "of God," does not enjoy wide support (only G^B and Tht), the fact that it is the reading of the weighty Codex Vaticanus indicates that the support for such a reading as "the pleasing things of God" is not altogether insignificant.

Support for such an interpretation may also be found in biblical parallels such as: Ps 145:7, *zēker rab-ṭûbᵉkā yabbîʿû*, "they will pour out the fame of your abundant goodness"; Ps 65:5, *niśbᵉʿāh bᵉṭûb bêtekā*, "we will be satisfied with the goodness of your house"; Ps 31:20; Exod 33:19; Ps 27:13; 25:7; Hos 3:5. In Jer 31:12, 14, it is the *ṭûb YHWH* with which the people are said to be satisfied.[171]

NOTES TO CHAPTER III

[1]See Thomas A. Jackson, "Words in Parallelism in Old Testament Poetry," Ph.D. dissertation, Johns Hopkins (1970) 106-08. The parallel pairing, *šmʿ* (Qal) // *ʾzn* (Hiph), occurs eleven times in BH. The reverse sequence occurs only once (Deut 32:1). In the Psalms, this sequence is never reversed. See Robert G. Boling, "'Synonymous' Parallelism in the Psalms," Ph.D. dissertation, Johns Hopkins (1959) 35, or "'Synonymous' Parallelism in the Psalms," *JSS* 5 (1960) 241. In relation to all the words with which *šmʿ* is paired in parallel in BH it is most commonly the A-word, especially in the Psalms where the ratio is 22:8.

[2]Edwin Hatch and Henry A. Redpath, *A Concordance to the Septuagint* (Oxford: Clarendon, 1897) I, 482 (hereafter cited as HR).

[3]Harwell (56) omits *yiśrāʾēl* as a supposed gloss in order to accommodate this verse to the absolutely invariable 3 + 3 metre that he seeks to find throughout the entire poem. This is all very dubious.

[4]Note that Kahana (358) renders it *miṣwôt ḥaḥayyîm*. Since this standard and frequently reprinted edition of the Jewish Apocrypha and Pseudepigrapha will often be compared in the course of this study, it should be clear at the outset that this work was not intended by its editor to be an attempt exactly at reconstruction of the original Hebrew but rather a "translation" from the available Versions (primarily the LXX) into understandable Hebrew. This explains a number of readings that are dubious as reconstructions and several examples of modern Hebraisms.

[5]Lev 26:15 illustrates these two synonyms in their usual equivalencies: *beḥuqqôtay . . . kol-miṣwōtay = ta prostagmata mou . . . pasas tas entolas mou*. See also S. H. Blank, "The Septuagint Renderings of Old Testament Terms for Law," *HUCA* VII (1930) 259-83.

[6]See HR, ad loc.

[7]See Hans Conzelmann, "*syniemi, synesis*," *TWNT* VII, 888 n. 18.

[8]O. C. Whitehouse ("1 Baruch," 588) suggests that the Sy reading may represent an attempt to balance the metre: "The fuller expression in S maintains a more equable and rhythmic parallelism." Conflation is a more likely explanation.

[9]Cf. Gen 18:13, 25:32, 32:30(29), 33:15; Exod 2:20, 5:22, 17:3; Jer 6:20, 20:18; Amos 5:18; et al.

[10]Although it does appear in G^B, the second interrogative, *ti*, is most probably to be omitted with G^A and G^Q. It also has no support in Sy.

[11]Cf. further Judg 18:23, Gen 20:9, Num 16:11, 2 Kgs 8:13, Ps 8:5, Job 21:15, Isa 3:15, et al.

[12]Deut 8:4, 29:4; Neh 9:21.

[13]Ps 102:27, Isa 51:6.

[14]Ps 32:3, Lam 3:4, Gen 18:12, Ps 49:15, Job 13:28, Isa 50:9.

[15]Harwell (54) has suggested that *bālāh* in Baruch would have had the connotation "be afflicted." He interprets this as clear evidence of an original Hebrew composition for Baruch in that *bālāh* in late BH and in MH came to be used as a synonym for *ʿānāh* III "be afflicted," and that had the LXX translator been aware of this, his translation would have reflected this nuance in such a context as that of our passage. In 1 Chr 17:9 *bālāh* is used instead of the original *ʿānāh* III of the earlier source text (2 Sam 7:10), and the Aramaic cognate, *b^elāʾ*, does reveal in Dan 7:25 a similar sense of "wearing out someone by continual harassment."

[16]See HR I, 240-55, 589-91.

[17]Ibid., 57.

[18]See also E. Kautzsch, ed., *Gesenius' Hebrew Grammar*[28], 2nd Eng. ed. rev. and trans. by A. E. Cowley (Oxford: Clarendon, 1910; reprinted, 1960) §107u, pp. 318-19 (hereafter cited as *GKC*).

[19]The MH Nithpaʿel **niṭṭammēʾtā* could also be considered a possibility. See M. H. Segal, *A Grammar of Mishnaic Hebrew* (Oxford: Clarendon, 1927) 64-67.

[20]See HR II, 1218.

[21]There is here a remote possibility of a real variant, but such depends too much on supposition to be very credible. Support for the conception of being "confined with the dead" could perhaps be adduced from BH (and 1QH) but only with the undemonstrable proviso that the root *ḥpš* in Ps 88:5-6 (*bammētîm ḥopšî*) be interpreted as a biform of *ḥbš* "bind, confine" (resulting from the otherwise attested interchange of voiced and unvoiced labials), thus having the meaning "confined" rather than the traditional "free." Similarly in two passages in 1QH which exhibit contexts comparable to that of Bar 3:10-12 (8:28-29, [ ]*mh ʿly kywrdy šʾwl wʿm / mtym yḥpś rwḥy*, "[ ] over me, as those who descend to Sheol. / My spirit is concealed with the dead"; and 10:33-34, *wnhmty ʿd thwm tbwʾ / wbḥdry šʾwl tḥpś yḥd*, "My groaning goes down to the Abyss / and is concealed even in the chambers of Sheol"), there is the remote possibility that the root *ḥpś* "seek, be concealed (in passive)" might instead have been *ḥpš* used as a biform of *ḥbš*, yielding the sense of "confined with the dead" or "confined in the chambers of Sheol." Needless to say, this is all too hypothetical to be considered

anything more than speculation. At any rate, either of the Syriac alternatives, "counted" or "confined," is preferable to the improbable LXX combination, "defiled with the dead." Nevertheless, the Sy reading is still most easily explained by metathesis.

[22]Cf. further Ezek 26:20; 31:14, 16; 32:24, 25, 29, 30; Isa 14:19; 38:18; and 14:15.

[23]Ps 55:16; Ezek 32:27; Isa 14:11, 15; 2:6; Num 16:30, 33; Gen 42:38; 44:29, 31. Cf. also Bar 3:19 below.

[24]Only rarely is it used for *nāṭaš*: Deut 32:15, Isa 16:8, 32:14.

[25]See Robert Payne Smith, *Thesaurus Syriacus* IV (Oxford: Clarendon, 1897) 4036 (hereafter: PS).

[26]Cf. Jer 2:13; 17:13, *ʿāzᵉbû mᵉqôr mayim-ḥayyîm.*

[27]Kahana (358) has conjectured a supposed lost parallel in verse 12 in an attempt to circumvent the difficulty of this section: *ʿāzabtā mᵉqôr ḥokmāh // [nāṭaštā maʿyan bînāh]*. The pairing of *ḥokmāh* (A) // *bînāh* (B) is well-established in BH (cf., e.g., Prov 4:5, 7; Isa 29:14; Dan 1:20), and so is that of *māqôr* (A) // *maʿyān* (B) (cf., e.g., Hos 13:15). But the sequence, *ʿāzab* (A) // *nāṭaš* (B) (cf. Jer 12:7), is not as common as the reverse (cf. Isa 32:14, Ps 27:9, 94:14). Regardless of whatever merits such may have, there is no textual support in any of the Versions for such a restoration.

[28]Cf. the similar construction with *waw* consecutive in Isa 48:18, *lûʾ hiqšabtā . . . wayhî*. Cf. also Judg 8:19, and see *GKC*, §151e, §159 l, m, x, y, z.

[29]See Ziegler, 460.

[30]The wide range of equivalencies for *synesis*, for example, merely in the book of Sirach, amply illustrates the abovementioned thorough convergence that prevails generally in the LXX with respect to the Greek and Hebrew lexical stock for "understanding."

[31]Cf. also Ps 21:5, 23:6, 91:6, 93:5; Deut 30:20; Lam 5:20; Prov 3:2, 16; 4:10; 9:11.

[32]See HR I, 410-13 and 576-79.

[33]Dan 1:2, Neh 13:12, Ps 135:7, Mal 3:10, Jer 38:11. For the combination with *māśāʾ*, cf. Isa 39:2, Sir 6:14, 40:18. Cf. in general Prov 2:4, 3:14, 8:21, 10:2, 15:16, 21:20; Wis 7:14; Job 28:12, 20, 23.

[34]See HR I, 166-69 and 368-73. The combination, *śārê haggôyim*, is theoretically possible as well, but it does not occur in BH nor in the Qumran literature.

[35]Cf. also *GKC*, §90o, and BDB, 312.

[36]Note that in this light *The New English Bible: Apocrypha* (Oxford: Oxford University, 1970) translates this and the following colon: "Where are those who have hunted wild beasts or the birds of the air for sport?" (255).

[37]See BDB (733), which cites thirty-eight examples, and Solomon Mandelkern, *Veteris Testamenti Concordantiae Hebraicae atque Chaldaicae* (Graz: Akademische Druck und Verlagsanstalt, 1955) II, 834.

[38]Cf. Isa 39:6 = 2 Kgs 20:17, Ezek 28:4, Prov 11:28, Job 6:20, Ps 49:7, Eccl 5:9.

[39]Kneucker, 286ff.

[40]These LXX passages are collected and discussed in Gifford, "Baruch" (277).

[41]The use of the active voice, *tektainō*, instead of the more usual middle, *tektainomai*, is a late phenomenon in Greek. In classical Greek, the verb is properly used in the middle voice and has the meaning, "do carpenter work, frame, join," as in Homer (*Iliad*, 5.62) and Aristophanes (*Lysistrata*, 674). Plato, indeed, takes special pains to distinguish this as "joiners'" work as clearly opposed to "smiths'" work in *Laws* (viii, 846, D, E): *to de tōn allōn dēmiourgōn poiein chrē kata tade . . . mēdeis chalkeuōn hama tektainesthō, mēd' au tektainomenos chalkeuontōn allōn epimeleisthō mallon ē tēs autou technēs*, "Moreover, for craftsmen we ought to make regulations in this wise . . . No man who is a smith shall act as a joiner, nor shall a joiner supervise others at smith-work, instead of his own craft." Cf. Plato, *Laws*, trans. R. G. Bury (LCL, II; London: William Heinemann, 1926) viii, 846, D, E, pp. 182-85. The metaphorical sense, "devise, contrive (by craft or cunning)," is also in evidence among the classical authors; cf., e.g., Aristophanes, *Acharnenses*, 660; Plato, *Sophistes*, 224d; and *Timaeus*, 91a.

[42]See Whitehouse, "1 Baruch," 588-89; and HR II, 1342.

[43]See Kneucker, 286 et seq., "die Silberschmiede"; Whitehouse, "1 Baruch," 588, "they that wrought in silver"; Rothstein, "Das Buch Baruch," 220, "die das Silber schmiedten"; *The Jerusalem Bible* (Garden City: Doubleday, 1966) 1356, "those who displayed such artistry in silver"; and Kahana, 359.

[44]See *The Apocrypha of the Old Testament, Revised Standard Version* (New York: Thomas Nelson and Sons, 1957) 175, "those who scheme to get silver"; NEB, 255, "those who scheme to get silver"; Fritzsche, *Kurzgefasstes Handbuch* I, 190, "*tektainein* ist nicht schmieden . . . sondern bildlich"; Bissell, *The Apocrypha*, 426, "The language is figurative [for 'they sought wealth']"; Reuss, *Das alte Testament*, 432; and Gifford, "Baruch," 277.

[45] See *GKC*, §112d, e, h.

[46] See HR I, 181-82.

[47] See H. G. Liddell and Robert Scott, *A Greek-English Lexicon*, 9th ed. rev. and augmented by H. S. Jones (Oxford: Clarendon, 1940) 286 (hereafter: LSJ).

[48] See Whitehouse, "1 Baruch," 571-72.

[49] Cf. also Eccl 4:15, Job 36:20, Dan 12:5.

[50] Kneucker, 291.

[51] Kahana, 359.

[52] Cf., e.g., Deut 29:21; Ps 48:14; 78:4, 6; 102:19.

[53] See HR II, 751-55; also cf. Bar 3:13, 4:35.

[54] Cf. Kahana, 359, *wayyēšᵉbû bā'āreṣ*.

[55] Cf. Isa 42:16, Prov 3:17, Hos 2:8, Ps 119:105, Lam 3:9 (also chiastic).

[56] Cf. Ps 82:5, Isa 44:18, Prov 1:2, 14:7-8, Ps 73:16-17, Dan 1:4. For the much less frequent reverse sequence, cf. Prov 28:2 and Job 28:23. For a complete statistical documentation supporting this as the normal sequence for this pairing, cf. Boling (41-42, 56) and Jackson (38, 56).

[57] Cf. Ps 105:28, Isa 1:20, Lam 1:20, Sir 16:7.

[58] E.g., Sy, Syh, and Eth.

[59] Cf. La^{V}, *neque filii eorum susceperunt eam*. This passage (Bar 3:20-21) has been held suspect by some. Kahana (359) has conjectured two additional parallel cola to be restored:

(20) *'aḥᵃrônîm rā'û 'ôr*
"More recent generations have seen the light,

wayyēšᵉbû bā'āreṣ
And have inhabited the earth;

[*mᵉqôm haḥokmāh lō' rā'û*]
[They did not perceive the place of wisdom,]

wᵉderek bînāh lō' yādā'û
And they did not learn the way of knowledge;

lō' hēbînû nᵉtîbôtèhā
Nor did they discover her paths,

[*ûma'gᵉlôtèhā lō' yādā'û*]
[Or know her by-ways.]

(21) *wᵉlō' heḥᵉzîqû bāh bᵉnêhem*
And their sons did not lay hold of her;

middarkāh rāḥᵃqû wayyāsûrû
From her way they have strayed and rebelled."

This results in a series of four nicely balanced (3+3) bicola. For the first conjectured restoration, cf. Bar 3:14-15 and note that Sy preserves an apparently conflate *wadḥekmᵉtā'*. For the second, cf. Prov 5:6, 4:11, 5:21. Each of these involve *ma'gᵉlôt* as the B-word for *derek* or *'ōraḥ*. But in Isa 59:8 it is the B-word in relation to *derek* and yet still precedes the C-word, *nᵉtîbôt*. Apart from the lack of textual support these conjectural restorations appear quite dubious from the point of view of the conventions of Hebrew parallelism, especially with respect to pairing and sequence. As the text stands, the pairings, *yāda'* (A) // *bîn* (B) and *derek* (A) // *nᵉtîbôt* (B), both common pairings in BH, appear precisely in the normal and expected sequence. But if the conjectured restorations be followed, *yāda'* would then become a B-word to both *bîn* and *rā'āh*. As noted above, the sequence *bîn* (A) // *yāda'* (B) does occur, but it is abnormal compared to the greater frequency of the reverse sequence. The sequence *yāda'* (A) // *rā'āh* (B), is also of greater frequency than the reverse. Further, a sequence in which *derek* would occur as a B-word to *māqôm* has no precedent in BH and seems far less probable than the common pair already standing in normal sequence in the text. Cf. Job 24:13 and the discussion above.

60 See Roland de Vaux, "Téman, ville ou région d'Edom," *RB* 76 (1969) 379-85. The conclusion of this scholar is that we search in vain for any village by this name and that the name always has reference to a region. See further R. H. Pfeiffer, "Edomitic Wisdom," *ZAW* 3 (1926) 13-14.

61 Cf. Gen 16:15, 25:12, 37:25, Ps 83:7, 1 Chr 5:20, 27:31. Cf. also the *bᵉnê-qedem* in 1 Kgs 5:10.

62 See HR I, 430-31.

63 Ibid., 597-98.

64 See K. G. Kuhn, *Konkordanz zu den Qumrantexten* (Göttingen: Vandenhoeck & Ruprecht, 1960) 52-53, and cf., e.g., 1QS 1:1, *ldrwš 'l*; 6:6, *dwrš btwrh*; CD 6:7 and 7:18, *dwrš htwrh*.

65 Or, in the light of other parallels for "seeking wisdom," *biqqēš* is also a possibility for one (or both?) of the occurrences of *ekzēteō*; cf. below.

66 See above, verse 14, and HR II, 1314. The LXX and Sy readings may ultimately have resulted from harmonization of the verbs due to the influence of the noun equality, for the Versions as a whole evidence slightly more variety with the verbs than with the nouns.

67 Cf. the Akkadian cognate, *saḫāru* "turn toward." See W. von Soden (*Akkadisches Handwörterbuch* 11 [Wiesbaden: Otto Harrassowitz, 1972] 1006 n. 6) for the meaning "to seek" (especially of seeking a god).

68 It stands here as the A-word in parallel with the comparable Qal participle of *dāraš*. In Hos 5:15, *šāḥar* is the B-word in relation to *biqqēš*. It is also used frequently for "seeking God." Cf. Job 7:21, 24:5, Prov 8:17, Isa 26:9, Ps 63:2.

[69]Kneucker, 355, 293ff.

[70]This he contends despite the fact that in the only instance of their pairing in BH *dāraš* is the A-word vis-à-vis *šāḥar*, and (as noted) *ekzēteō* is never used in the LXX to represent *šāḥar*. Kahana (359) has apparently followed Kneucker in this assumption of a pairing, *šāḥar* (A) // *dāraš* (B).

[71]Whitehouse, "1 Baruch," 589.

[72]Cf. also verse 20, above.

[73]Much less plausibly, verse 23a might be analyzed as two bicola, but such would be contingent on there having been an additional word in the original Hebrew. One possibility is that the *oute* of the LXX text (commonly used in linking negative clauses) might perhaps indicate the presence of *wᵉlō'* in the Hebrew *Vorlage*. But *oute* is more likely functioning here in its customary manner as a Greek syntactical requirement for expressing a continuing negative force which the Hebrew is not required to indicate textually, nor is likely to in this case since the verb and negative for which verse 23a is the subject follows directly in verse 23b. Even less probable is the supposition that, in comparison to Lam 4:21, a geographic place-name has been lost after *bᵉ'ereṣ*. The MT reading in Lam 4:21 is *bᵉ'ereṣ 'ûṣ* for which the LXX has only *epi tēs gēs*.

[74]Cf. Gen 25:15, 1 Chr 1:30, Isa 21:14, Jer 25:23, Job 6:19.

[75]Cf. also Ezek 17:2; 18:2, 3; Ps 49:5; 78:2.

[76]See, e.g., Philo, *De Aeternitate Mundi*, trans. F. H. Colson (LCL, IX; Cambridge: Harvard University, 1941) §112, pp. 262-63, *theion de ti <dia to> megethos ho kosmos kai oikos theōn aisthētōn apodedeiktai*, "while the world is divine in its vastness and has been shown to be the dwelling-place of visible deities"; idem, *De Cherubim*, trans. F. H. Colson and G. H. Whitaker (LCL, II; London: William Heinemann, 1929) §52, pp. 40-41, *en oikō theou*; and idem, *De Opificio Mundi*, trans. F. H. Colson and G. H. Whitaker (LCL, I; London: William Heinemann, 1929) §21, pp. 22-23, where the heavens are "the most holy house" of divine beings.

[77]The term "house" has often been too literally interpreted here and as a result overly much has been made of this verse to support a post-70 C.E. date for the composition itself. Josephus (*The Jewish War*, trans. H. St. J. Thackeray [LCL, III; London: William Heinemann, 1928] V, 458, pp. 342-43) duly reports the desperate retort of the beleaguered Jewish defenders of Jerusalem to the taunts of Titus, and within this hollow boast is the following line: *kai naon ameinō toutou tō theō ton kosmon einai*, "and that the world was a better temple for God than this one." In a translator's footnote, Thackeray thence directs the reader to Bar 3:24 and observes that "writing after the tragedy of A.D. 70 the author of that work says in effect 'The house of God is not the ruined Temple but the broad universe.'"

[78]See the discussion below, 5:5, 7 (pp. 248, 253, 294).

[79]See HR II, 1419-20.

[80]Cf. Judg 18:10, Gen 34:21, Isa 33:21, Neh 7:4, 1 Chr 4:40.

[81]See Ziegler, 461.

[82]The Greek verb *gi(g)nomai* "be, become" in this first Aorist passive form (*egenēthēsan*) differs from the comparable form of *gennaō* "beget" (*egennēthēsan*) by only one letter. Note also that *gi(g)nomai* is sometimes used in the sense of "be born, come into being" with respect to persons. See LSJ, 349.

[83]See HR I, 237-38.

[84]Note that Kahana (359), in accord with the LXX variant, has retroverted *hāyû*, apparently in the light of Gen 6:4. The form *yulledû* is now generally recognized as a Qal passive rather than a Pu'al form. The Pi'el stem of *yld* appears to be specialized in BH in the sense of "act as a midwife."

[85]Gen 6:4 begins *hann*e*pīlîm hāyû bā'āreṣ* = *hoi de gigantes ēsan epi tēs gēs*.

[86]E. A. Speiser, *Genesis* (AB 1; Garden City: Doubleday, 1964) 44.

[87]See Yigael Yadin, *The Scroll of the War of the Sons of Light against the Sons of Darkness*, trans. B. and C. Rabin (Oxford: Oxford University, 1962) 265, 269, and D. Barthelemy and J. T. Milik, *Discoveries in the Judean Desert*, I: *Qumran Cave 1* (Oxford: Clarendon, 1955) 108, pls. 22-24.

[88]See Yadin, *The Scroll of the War*, 287-88, 327, 289, 299, 265.

[89]See Claus-Hunno Hunzinger, "Fragmente einer älteren Fassung des Buches Milḥamā aus Höhle 4 von Qumrān," *ZAW* 69 (1957) 135. For further background on *m*e*lumm*e*dê milḥāmāh*, see Jonas C. Greenfield, "Ugaritic *mdl* and Its Cognates," *Bib* 45 (1964) 527-34.

[90]The present participle of *epistamai* "know how, know surely, be well-versed" may also function as an adjective to mean "knowing, skillful, expert."

[91]Cf., e.g., Gen 25:27, *yōdēa' ṣayid* "skilled in hunting"; Isa 29:11-12, *yōdēa' sēper* "skilled in writing"; Amos 5:16, *yôd*e*'ê nehî* "skilled in mourning" (i.e., "professional mourners"), 1 Kgs 9:27, *yōd*e*'ê hayyām* "skilled mariners"; 1 Sam 16:16, 18, *yōdēa' naggēn* "skilled in playing"; and 1 Kgs 5:20; 2 Chr 2:6, 7, 13.

[92]See HR I, 435.

[93]See Kneucker, 302.

[94]Kahana (359) employs a passive verb form in this colon, *lō' lāhem nittān*, "not to them was it given." But the verb in the LXX is an Aorist active indicative form, *edōken*, and in both Syriac texts it is the simple Peal perfect of *y^ehab* "give" that is used. Also, in none of these texts is any negative stress placed on the indirect object.

[95]Cf. Sy at verse 20, *w(')ûr^ehā' d^esukālā' w^eḥekm^etā'*, and also at verse 28, *ḥekm^etā' w^esukālā'*.

[96]Cf. Bar 3:19, 4:25, and see HR I, 136-38.

[97]Kahana (359) renders the second *apōlonto* in verse 28 with Hebrew *sāpû*, apparently in the light of Amos 3:15, *w^e'ab^edû bāttîm haššēn w^esāpû bāttîm rabbîm*. This is despite the fact that *apollyō*, used in the LXX to translate thirty-eight different Hebrew verbs, is never used for *sûp* "come to an end." Further, the witness of the Versions is consistently against this.

[98]Cf. also *1 Enoch* 93:12, 42:1, 4 Ezra 4:8, Sir 24:3-6, and the general idea of Wis 9:4.

[99]See the discussion of this problem below at verse 30.

[100]Cf. Judg 5:14, Isa 46:3, Ps 44:11, 68:32, and Job passim.

[101]Cf. further Ps 89:7, 38; Job 36:28; 37:18, 21; Prov 3:20; Ps 68:35; 77:18; 78:23.

[102]Cf. Proverbs passim.

[103]This stylistic feature had been developing already in the lastest books of BH and was ultimately fulfilled in MH, but at Qumran it was still to some extent in transition. In the more archaizing and biblicizing *Hôdāyôt*, for example, the BH *waw* consecutives are found in use, but in the other Qumran lit-literary works they are extremely rare.

[104]See Joseph Reider, "The Dead Sea Scrolls," *JQR* 41 (1950) 67-68; Driver, *The Judean Scrolls*, 437; and Segal, *A Grammar of Mishnaic Hebrew*, 51.

[105]For an attempt, see Kneucker, 304. HR II, 1426-28, lists twenty-eight different Hebrew words which are rendered by *pherō* in the LXX. The most frequent equivalency is with the Hiphil stem of *bô'* "bring." Fairly common equivalencies, but far less so than the above, are with the verbs *nāśā'* and *'ālāh*. Equivalencies occurring in each case once only are with *yārad*, *lāqaḥ*, *'ābar*, and *'āśāh*. In no LXX passage does *pherō* ever represent Hebrew *qānāh*.

[106]This pairing is discussed above at verses 20-21 and in n. 55. Cf. further Ps 142:4, Isa 42:16, Prov 17:24, Job 28:7, 13, 20-28. The Hithpolel stem, "show oneself perceptive" or "consider diligently," is perhaps also a possibility here. Cf. also Job 37:14, Isa 43:18, 1:3, et al.

[107]J. A. Sanders, *The Psalms Scroll of Qumran Cave 11* (11QPs^a) (DJD, IV; Oxford: Clarendon, 1965) 55-56. Cf. Ps 33: 13-15.

[108]Cf. also Isa 45:18, Ps 24:2, 48:9, 65:7, 74:16.

[109]Kahana (359) suggests in a footnote another possibility, *bhmwt b'lwt 'rb' rglym*, but such is unprecedented in BH and with such the metre alone would make the colon unwieldy and this proposal unlikely.

[110]See Kneucker, 306.

[111]R. H. Charles, *The Book of Enoch*, 2nd ed. (Oxford: Clarendon, 1912) 82, and idem, "The Book of Enoch," *APOT* II, 213. See further, idem, *The Ethiopic Version of the Book of Enoch* (*Anecdota Oxoniensia*, XI; Oxford: Clarendon, 1906) 84.

[112]See HR II, 1189-94. Cf. also Bar 3:13; 4:13, 26.

[113]Whitehouse, "1 Baruch," 590.

[114]See *LVTAS*, 98, xiv.

[115]See Marcus Jastrow, *A Dictionary of the Targumim, the Talmud Babli and Yerushalmi, and the Midrashic Literature* (1903; reprinted, New York/Berlin: Choreb, 1926) II, 883.

[116]Cf. also Jer 31:35.

[117]Cf. Isa 42:11, 44:23, 49:13, 52:8, 54:1, and also 26:19, 24:14, 16:10, 12:6, and Jer 38:12.

[118]Cf. also Deut 28:63, Isa 35:1, Ps 148:3.

[119]That is, literally, "we are near ones" (*qarrîbîn ḥ^{e}nan* > *qarrîbînan*). Cf. Theodor Nöldeke, *Compendious Syriac Grammar*, 2nd rev. German ed. trans. James A. Crichton (London: Williams and Norgate, 1904) §64, p. 45.

[120]Cf. Jdt 9:6, *idou paresmen*; Isa 6:8; 1 Sam 22:12.

[121]Cf. also Num 12:5, *1 Enoch* 43:1, 69:21, Bar 3:33.

[122]Cf. further Isa 42:8, 48:11, Exod 34:14 for similar constructions with *'aḥēr*, and also Hos 13:4, 1 Sam 21:10, Ruth 4:4, Isa 26:13, 64:3.

[123]Kahana, 359.

[124]See Ziegler, 462; cf. Sy, *hānāw*; La^V, *hic*; Eth, *we'etū*; Ar, *hū'a*.

[125]See Jackson, 63, 66, and cf. Num 23:7, and passim; Deut 33:10; Ps 147:19; 14:7 and passim; Isa 9:8; 40:27 and passim; Mic 3:8; Sir 24:8, 10.

[126]Cf. Syh, Eth, Ar, several LXX Minuscules, numerous Greek and Latin fathers, et al. For a full citation of these authorities, cf. Ziegler, 462.

[127]Kahana, 359. For the combination, *'āz* + perfect verb, cf., e.g., Josh 10:33, Exod 4:26, Gen 4:26, in none of which is *'āz* ever rendered by *meta touto* in the LXX.

[128]See Kneucker (310-12) who considers this entire verse a Christian gloss. An early example of the sort of incarnational interpretation of this passage that became common among the Greek and Latin fathers may be seen in the quotation of this passage by the third century African bishop, Commodian, in his *Carmen Apologeticum* (371-72): *Hieremias ait. Hic Deus est noster aequalis, / Post haec et in terris visus est conversatus humanis*; see Commodian, *Carmen Apologeticum* (*Corpus Scriptorum Ecclesiasticorum Latinorum*, XV; Vindobonae: C. Geroldi Filium Bibliopolam Academiae, 1887) 371-72, p. 139. This may be compared with the La^{V} text of Bar 3:36-38, *hic Deus noster . . . post haec in terris visus est et cum hominibus conversatus est.* See also Whitehouse,("1 Baruch," §10, pp. 580-81) and note that other Versions (notably Sy, Copt, Ar) feature God as the subject here.

[129]Kneucker, 310-12.

[130]For the identification of Wisdom with Torah, cf. Bar 4:1, Sir 24:23, and see G. F. Moore, *Judaism in the First Centuries of the Christian Era* (Cambridge: Harvard University, 1927) I, 263-70; H. Ringgren, *Word and Wisdom: Studies in the Hypostatization of Divine Qualities and Functions in the Ancient Near East* (Lund: H. Ohlsson, 1947) 114-15, 139-41; and Battistone, "An Examination," 189-95.

[131]Kneucker, 313.

[132]E.g., Deut 28:61, 29:20, 30:10, Josh 24:26, Lev 26:46, and 2 Kgs 22:11.

[133]Note Josh 24:26 where the singular *tôrat* is the equivalent of the plural *nomōn* in the LXX. See also Blank, "The Septuagint Renderings," 275ff.

[134]This is assembled in Jackson (77).

[135]Cf. Ezek 22:14 with this and what follows in 4:1b.

[136]Cf. also Job 2:3, 9; Prov 2:13; 27:10.

[137]Cf. Ps 126:4, 6:5, 90:13; 2 Sam 15:27; Num 10:36, 2 Chr 6:24.

[138]See HR I, 336, and cf. Gen 12:6, Jer 2:6, 9:11, 50:13, Ezek 5:14, 14:15, 36:34, Zeph 3:6, Zech 7:14, Ps 89:41.

[139]See BDB, 236a.

[140]Ibid. Cf. particularly Ps 56:14, 116:9, and also Isa 38:3 = 2 Kgs 20:3, 1 Sam 12:2, 2:35, Gen 17:1, 24:40, 48:15.

[141]Cf. Prov 6:23, Isa 51:4, Ps 119:105, Wis 18:4.

[142]Cf. Joel 2:10, 4:15.

[143]See HR II, 853, and LSJ, 1028.

[144]See below, 4:24, for further discussion.

[145]Sy here appears to be expanded, constituting a tricolon:

Return and incline yourself, Jacob,
Hold fast and walk in her path
Toward the brightness of her light,

but it cannot be entirely dismissed thereby because of its noticeable similarities to such biblical passages as Isa 60:3, Prov 3:18, 4:13, et al.

[146]See HR I, 341-43. Cf. also Bar 4:24, 37; 5:1, 2, 4, 6, 7, 9. Cf. also expressions in BH with *hôd* "splendor, majesty" as, e.g., in Num 27:20, Ps 21:6, Dan 11:21, 1 Chr 29:25. Pfeiffer (*HNTT*, 419) sees in this verse an indirect warning against the lures of Hellenistic philosophy.

[147]See HR II, 1306; BDB, 375; and cf. Deut 23:7, Jer 26:14, Sir 30:18, 37:28.

[148]Kneucker, 316.

[149]Kahana, 359.

[150]Eccl 1:3, 2:13, 5:15, 7:12, 10:10-11.

[151]See the discussion immediately below for the citation of this passage.

[152]This is especially common in the phrase, "raise the fortunes/horn of." Cf. 1 Sam 2:1, 10; Lam 2:17; Ps 75:11; 89:18, 25; 92:9; 112:9.

[153]Cf. Deut 28:32, *lᵉʻam ʼaḥēr* (in a context of military capture).

[154]Rudolf Smend, *Die Weisheit des Jesus Sirach* (Berlin: Georg Reimer, 1906) 57. See also Francesco Vattioni, *Ecclesiastico: Testo ebraico con apparato critico e versioni greca, latina e siriaca* (Naples: Istituto Orientale di Napoli, 1968) 267 (*wytn qrnm lʼḥwr wkbwdm lgwy nbl nkry*).

[155]See HR I, 368-73; cf. also Bar 4:6, 15.

[156]See HR I, 57.

[157] Cf. also Ps 33:12; 112:1, 119:1, 2; 144:15; Isa 56:2; Prov 29:18; Deut 33:29; Eccl 10:17; and Ps 128:2, *'ašrèkā wᵉṭôb lāk*, "You will be happy and it will be well with you." Note again the expanded Sy reading: "Happy are we, happy are you, Israel."

[158] Other possibilities for the original Hebrew discussed below are: (1) *kî hayyāšār bᵉ'ênê-'ᵉlōhîm*; (2) *kî haṭṭôb lē'lōhîm*; and (3) *kî ṭûb 'ᵉlōhîm*.

[159] This is the verbal adjective of *areskō* "please" (neuter, plural, accusative). See also LSJ (238) and Hjalmar Frisk, *Griechisches Etymologisches Wörterbuch* (Heidelberg: Carl Winter, 1960) I, 1, p. 136.

[160] Cf. as well 1 Kgs 15:11 and passim; Deut 12:8, 13:19, 21:9, Gen 16:6, Exod 15:26, Lev 10:19.

[161] This idiomatic expression is repeated in slightly varied form in 3:6 and 4:3 as well (cf. also 14:7).

[162] Interestingly, in the medieval (12th century) Fagius translation of Tobit into Hebrew (from the text of G^B), *to areston* is translated by *hayyāšār*. See D. C. Simpson, "Tobit," *APOT* I, 213.

[163] Smend, *Die Weisheit*, 56; and Vattioni, *Ecclesiastico*, 265. Cf. also Sir 48:16, *yš mhm 'šw ywšr*, "some did what was pleasing" (Vattioni, *Ecclesiastico*, 263).

[164] Significantly, this verse ends: "and were saved by wisdom."

[165] For the latter interpretation, see Kahana (360) and the discussion immediately below.

[166] Cf. also Jdt 3:2, 8:17, 12:14, Ps 25:4-9, Deut 30:9.

[167] Whitehouse, "1 Baruch," 591.

[168] Cf. Sy, *dᵉšappîr l(')allāhān*, and Syh, *dᵉšāpᵉrān l(')allāhā'*.

[169] Kahana, 360.

[170] Alfred Rahlfs, *Septuaginta*, 5th ed. (Stuttgart: Privilegierte Württembergische Bibelanstalt, 1952) II, 753, and Ziegler, 462.

[171] Cf. further Ps 89:16 for the combination of *'asrê* and *yāda'*, and for the general sense Ps 34:9, 144:15, 3:13, 8:32-35, and Isa 56:2-5. The least probable solution would be *rᵉṣôn 'ᵉlōhîm*, though cf. Neh 9:24, 37; Ezra 10:11; Ps 40:9; 103:21, and 143:10.

CHAPTER IV

A RECONSTRUCTION OF THE HEBREW TEXT OF THE CONSOLATION POEM OF BARUCH (4:5-5:9), TOGETHER WITH THE GREEK AND/OR SYRIAC TEXT AND AN ENGLISH TRANSLATION

4:5

אַל-תִּירָא עַמִּי   θαρσεῖτε, λαός μου,

"Fear not,[a] my people,

זֵכֶר יִשְׂרָאֵל   μνημόσυνον Ισραηλ.

Memorial[b] of Israel!

4:6

(כִּי) נִמְכַּרְתֶּם לַגּוֹיִם   ἐπράθητε τοῖς ἔθνεσιν

ܡܛܠ ܕܐܙܕܒܢܬܘܢ ܠܥܡܡܐ

(For) it was not for destruction

לֹא לְהַשְׁמִיד   οὐκ εἰς ἀπώλειαν,

ܠܐ ܗܘܐ ܠܐܒܕܢܐ

That you were sold to the nations,

וְיַעַן[c] הַכְעִיסְכֶם[d]   διὰ δὲ τὸ παροργίσαι
אֶת-אֱלֹהִים   ὑμᾶς τὸν θεὸν

But you were delivered up to the enemy

הָסְגַּרְתֶּם לַצָּרִים   παρεδόθητε τοῖς ὑπεναντίοις

Because you vexed God to anger;

---

[a]LXX: "Be confident!"

[b]Torrey, (*The Apocryphal Literature*, 62 n. 59) suggests that the Greek translator perhaps falsely read *zikrôn* for *zikrû*, "remember!" See below, Chapter V, ad loc.

[c]Perhaps וְיַעַן כִּי or כִּי יַעַן. See below, Chapter V, ad loc.

[d]Or perhaps הִכְעַסְתֶּם.

4:7

כִּי הִקְנֵאתֶם (אֱלוֹהַּ) [e] παρωξύνατε γὰρ τὸν
עֹשֵׂיכֶם ποιήσαντα ὑμᾶς

For you provoked the One who made you

זְבַחְתֶּם לַשֵּׁדִים θύσαντες δαιμονίοις
לֹא-אֱלוֹהַּ καὶ οὐ θεῷ.

By sacrificing to demons--non-divinities![f]

4:8

וַתִּשְׁכְּחוּ (אֵל) [g] ἐπελάθεσθε δὲ τὸν τροφεύσαντα
מְחוֹלֶלְכֶם אֵל-[h] עוֹלָם ὑμᾶς θεὸν αἰώνιον,

And you forgot the eternal God who nurtured you;

אַף-הֶעֱצַבְתֶּם ἐλυπήσατε δὲ καὶ τὴν
יוֹלַדְתְּכֶם יְרוּשָׁלַם ἐκθρέψασαν ὑμᾶς Ιερουσαλημ·

You even grieved Jerusalem who reared you.

4:9

כִּי רָאֲתָה אַף-אֵל εἶδε γὰρ τὴν ἐπελθοῦσαν
הַבָּא עֲלֵיכֶם [i] ὑμῖν ὀργὴν παρὰ τοῦ θεοῦ

For she saw the wrath of God that came upon you,

וַתֹּאמֶר שִׁמְעוּ אֵלַי [j] שְׁכֵנֵי καὶ εἶπεν ᾿Ακούσατε, αἱ
צִיּוֹן πάροικοι Σιων,

ܘܐܡܪܬ ܫܡܥܘܢܝ ܫܒܒܬܗ ܕܨܗܝܘܢ

And she said: 'Listen to me, neighbors of Zion;

---

[e]This is perhaps to be included; cf. Deut 32:15, Isa 44:2, and 51:13. Also see below, Chapter V, ad loc.

[f]Or perhaps "demonic non-divinities." See below, Chapter V, ad loc.

[g]This is perhaps to be included; cf. Deut 32:18b. See below, Chapter V, ad loc. The verb form may be וּשְׁכַחְתֶּם.

[h]Or -אֱלֹהֵי.

[i]Or perhaps כִּי רָאֲתָה הָאַף הַבָּא עֲלֵיכֶם מֵאֵת אֵל הַיּוֹם.

[j]This is perhaps to be omitted with the major LXX Uncials. The verb form in this colon may be וְאָמְרָה. It is difficult to determine whether or not *waw*-consecutives were used.

הֵבִיא אֱלֹהִים עָלַי אֵבֶל גָּדוֹל	ἐπήγαγέ μοι ὁ θεὸς πένθος μέγα·

God has brought great mourning upon me!

4:10

כִּי רָאִיתִי שְׁבִי בָּנַי וּבְנוֹתַי	εἶδον γὰρ τὴν αἰχμαλωσίαν τῶν υἱῶν μου καὶ θυγατέρων,

For I saw the captivity of my sons and daughters,

אֲשֶׁר הֵבִיא עֲלֵיהֶם יהוה[k]	ἣν ἐπήγαγεν αὐτοῖς ὁ αἰώνιος·

Which the Eternal[l] brought upon them;

4:11

כִּי בְשָׂשׂוֹן גִּדַּלְתִּים	ἔθρεψα γὰρ αὐτοὺς μετ' εὐφροσύνης,

Indeed, I had reared them with joy,

וּבִבְכִי וְאֵבֶל שִׁלַּחְתִּים	ἐξαπέστειλα δὲ μετὰ κλαυθμοῦ καὶ πένθους.

But I let them go with weeping and mourning.

4:12

אִישׁ אַל-יִשְׂמַח לִי	μηδεὶς ἐπιχαιρέτω μοι

ܠܐ ܐܢܫ [illegible]

Let no one rejoice over me,

הָאַלְמָנָה וַעֲזוּבַת הָרַבִּים	τῇ χήρᾳ καὶ καταλειφθείσῃ ὑπὸ πολλῶν.

ܐܪܡܠܬܐ ܘܫܒܝܩܬܐ ܡܢ ܟܢܫܐ

Widowed and forsaken of populace;[m]

---

[k]Perhaps אֵל עוֹלָם; see below, Chapter V, ad loc.

[l]LXX (Hebrew = *YHWH*).

[m]Or "many"; see below, Chapter V, ad loc.

עַל-חַטֹּאת בָּנַי נְשַׁמּוֹתִי	ἠρημώθην διὰ τὰς ἁμαρτίας τῶν τέκνων μου,

[illegible]

I am destitute because of the sins of my children.

4:12d-13a

יַעַן מִתּוֹרַת-אֱלֹהִים סָרוּ	διότι ἐξέκλιναν ἐκ νόμου θεοῦ

Because they swerved away from the law of God,

וּמִשְׁפָּטָיו[n] לֹא-יָדָעוּ	καὶ δικαιώματα αὐτοῦ οὐκ ἔγνωσαν

And took no regard of his rulings;

4:13

בְּדַרְכֵי מִצְוֹת אֱלֹהִים לֹא הָלָכוּ	οὐδὲ ἐπορεύθησαν ὁδοῖς ἐντολῶν θεοῦ

They did not walk in the ways of God's commandments,

וּנְתִיבוֹת מוּסַר צִדְקָתוֹ לֹא דָרָכוּ	οὐδὲ τρίβους παιδείας ἐν δικαιοσύνῃ αὐτοῦ ἐπέβησαν.

Nor tread the paths of the instruction of his righteousness.

4:14

בֹּואוּ[o] שְׁכֵנֵי צִיּוֹן	ἐλθάτωσαν αἱ πάροικοι Σιων,

[illegible]

Come, neighbors of Zion!

זִכְרוּ שְׁבִי בָנַי וּבְנוֹתַי	καὶ μνήσθητε τὴν αἰχμαλωσίαν τῶν υἱων μου καὶ θυγατέρων,

Remember the captivity of my sons and daughters,

---

[n]Or perhaps וְחֻקָּיו/וְחֻקּוֹתָיו; see below, Chapter V, ad loc.

[o]Another imperative, הִתְבּוֹנְנוּ, is perhaps restorable from the Sy text ("make up your minds!"). Note the metrical imbalance between the members of the tricolon and see Sy and Chapter V, ad loc. The difference in persons in the Greek imperatives

אֲשֶׁר הֵבִיא עֲלֵיהֶם יהוה   ἣν ἐπήγαγεν αὐτοῖς ὁ αἰώνιος·

Which the Eternal brought upon them!

4:15

כִּי נָשָׂא עֲלֵיהֶם גּוֹי מֵרָחוֹק   ἐπήγαγε γὰρ ἐπ᾽ αὐτοὺς ἔθνος μακρόθεν

For he brought against them a distant nation,

גּוֹי עַז-פָּנִים וְעִמְקֵי שָׂפָה   ἔθνος ἀναιδὲς καὶ ἀλλόγλωσσον,

An insolent nation, of unintelligible language,

פְּנֵי זָקֵן לֹא נָשָׂאוּ   οἳ οὐκ ᾐσχύνθησαν πρεσβύτην

Which had no respect for the elderly,

וְנַעַר לֹא חָנָנוּ   οὐδὲ παιδίον ἠλέησαν

Nor any mercy for youths.

4:16

וְהוֹלִיכוּ[p] אֶת-יְדִידֵי הָאַלְמָנָה   καὶ ἀπήγαγον τοὺς ἀγαπητοὺς τῆς χήρας

They carried off the beloved sons of the widow,

וְאֶת-הַיְחִידָה הֶחֱרִיבוּ[q] מִבָּנוֹת   καὶ ἀπὸ τῶν θυγατέρων τὴν μόνην ἠρήμωσαν.

And stripped the lonely woman of daughters.

4:17-18

וַאֲנִי מָה-אוּכַל לְעָזְרְכֶם   ἐγὼ δὲ τί δυνατὴ βοηθῆσαι ὑμῖν;

As for me, how shall I be able to help you?

---

may also be noted here. The imperative mood in Greek, unlike Semitic, may be used in the third person as well as the more common second. Both imperatives in vs. 14 of Sy are second person masculine plural.

[p]Or perhaps the imperfect consecutive, וַיּוֹלִיכוּ.

[q]Or הֵשַׁמּוּ.

כִּי-הַמֵּבִיא הָרָעָה עֲלֵיכֶם   ὁ γὰρ ἐπαγαγὼν τὰ κακὰ [ὑμῖν][r]

ܗܘ ܓܝܪ ܕܐܝܬܝ ܥܠܝܟܘܢ ܒܝܫܬܐ

For the One who brought this evil upon you

[s]יַצִּיל אֶתְכֶם מִיַּד-אוֹיְבֵיכֶם   ἐξελεῖται ὑμᾶς ἐκ χειρὸς ἐχθρῶν ὑμῶν.

ܗܘ ܢܦܪܘܩ ܠܟܘܢ ܡܢ ܐܝܕܝ̈ ܒܥܠܕܒܒܝ̈ܟܘܢ

Will deliver you from the hand of your enemies.

4:19

לְכוּ בָנִים[t] לְכוּ   βαδίζετε, τέκνα, βαδίζετε,

Go, children, go,

כִּי-אֲנִי חָרְבָּה[u] נִשְׁאַרְתִּי   ἐγὼ γὰρ κατελείφθην ἔρημος·

For I have been left desolate!

4:20

בִּגְדֵי שָׁלוֹם פָּשַׁטְתִּי   ἐξεδυσάμην τὴν στολὴν τῆς εἰρήνης,

I have stripped off the garments of peace,

וְשַׂק תַּחֲנוּנַי[v] לָבַשְׁתִּי   ἐνεδυσάμην δὲ σάκκον τῆς δεήσεώς μου,

And have donned the sackcloth of my supplication;

בְּיָמַי אֶקְרָא אֶל-יהוה   κεκράξομαι πρὸς τὸν αἰώνιον ἐν ταῖς ἡμέραις μου.

In all my days I will cry out to the Eternal!

---

[r]Read with G^A, L', Sy, and La^V.

[s]A pleonastic הוּא perhaps precedes the verb. See Chapter V, ad loc, and Sy.

[t]Sy has *b^e nay* "my children," as also in vss. 21 and 25 below. See below, Chapter V, ad 4:21.

[u]Or perhaps שְׁמָמָה/שַׁמָּה.

[v]Or perhaps תְּחִנָּתִי, or תְּפִלָּתִי.

4:21

אַל-תִּירְאוּ בָנִים[t] קִרְאוּ אֶל-אֱלֹהִים	θαρσεῖτε, τέκνα, βοήσατε πρὸς τὸν θεόν,

Fear not,[a] children! Cry out to God

וְיַצִּיל אֶתְכֶם מֵעֹשֶׁק מִיַּד אוֹיֵב	καὶ ἐξελεῖται ὑμᾶς ἐκ δυναστείας, ἐκ χειρὸς ἐχθρῶν.

So that he will deliver you from oppression, from the hand of the enemy.

4:22

וַאֲנִי אֶל-יהוה	ἐγὼ γὰρ ἤλπισα

As for me, I have entrusted

בָּטַחְתִּי לִישׁוּעַתְכֶם	ἐπὶ τῷ αἰωνίῳ τὴν σωτηρίαν ὑμῶν,

Your salvation to the Eternal;

וּבָאָה-לִי שִׂמְחָה מֵעִם-[w] קָדוֹשׁ	καὶ ἦλθέ μοι χαρὰ παρὰ τοῦ ἁγίου

And joy has come to me from the Holy One

עַל-[x] הַחֶסֶד יְבוֹאֲכֶם מְהֵרָה	ἐπὶ τῇ ἐλεημοσύνῃ, ἣ ἥξει ὑμῖν ἐν τάχει

Because of the mercy which quickly will come to you

מֵאֵת[w] יהוה מוֹשִׁיעֲכֶם	παρὰ τοῦ αἰωνίου σωτῆρος ὑμῶν.

From the Eternal, your Savior.

4:23

כִּי בְאֵבֶל וּבְכִי שִׁלַּחְתִּיכֶם	ἐξέπεμψα γὰρ ὑμᾶς μετὰ πένθους καὶ κλαυθμοῦ,

For I dismissed you with mourning and weeping,

---

[w]מֵעִם or מֵאֵת?

[x]Or perhaps חֶסֶד.

וְיָשִׁיב-לִי אֶתְכֶם (הָ)אֱלֹהִים   ἀποδώσει δέ μοι ὁ θεὸς ὑμᾶς

But God will return you to me

בְּשָׂשׂוֹן וְשִׂמְחַת עוֹלָם[y]   μετὰ χαρμοσύνης καὶ εὐφροσύνης εἰς τὸν αἰῶνα.

With joy and eternal gladness.

4:24

כִּי-כַאֲשֶׁר רָאוּ עַתָּה   ὥσπερ γὰρ νῦν ἑοράκασιν

For just as the neighbors of Zion

שְׁכֵנֵי צִיּוֹן שְׁבִיכֶם   αἱ πάροικοι Σιων τὴν ὑμετέραν αἰχμαλωσίαν,

Have now seen your captivity,

כֵּן יִרְאוּ מְהֵרָה   οὕτως ὄψονται ἐν τάχει

So shall they soon see

יְשׁוּעַת אֱלֹהֵיכֶם   τὴν παρὰ τοῦ θεοῦ ὑμῶν σωτηρίαν,

The salvation of your God,

תְּבוֹאֲכֶם בְּכָבוֹד גָּדוֹל   ἣ ἐπελεύσεται ὑμῖν μετὰ δόξης μεγάλης

Coming to you with great glory

וּבַהֲדַר יהוה   καὶ λαμπρότητος τοῦ αἰωνίου.

And with the splendor of the Eternal.

4:25

בָּנִים שְׂאוּ אַף-אֵל   τέκνα, μακροθυμήσατε τὴν παρὰ τοῦ θεοῦ

O children, bear patiently the wrath of God

הַבָּא עֲלֵיכֶם   ἐπελθοῦσαν ὑμῖν ὀργήν·

That has come upon you;

---

[y]Or perhaps וְשִׂמְחָה לְעוֹלָם.

רְדָפְךָ הָאוֹיֵב κατεδίωξέ σε ὁ ἐχθρός,

The enemy has harassed you,

וְתִרְאֶה בְאָבְדוֹ מַהֵר καὶ ὄψει αὐτοῦ τὴν ἀπώλειαν ἐν τάχει

But you will soon see their destruction

וְעַל צַוְּארֵיהֶם תִּדְרוֹךְ καὶ ἐπὶ τραχήλους αὐτῶν ἐπιβήσῃ.

And set foot upon their necks.

4:26

עֲנֻגַּי[z] הָלְכוּ דְרָכִים עֲקֻבִּים οἱ τρυφεροί μου ἐπορεύθησαν ὁδοὺς τραχείας,

My delicate ones have traveled rough roads;

נִשְּׂאוּ כְעֵדֶר גָּזוּל בְּיַד-אוֹיֵב ἤρθησαν ὡς ποίμνιον ἡρπασμένον ὑπὸ ἐχθρῶν.

They were taken away like a flock seized by the enemy.

4:27

אַל-תִּירְאוּ בָנִים θαρσήσατε, τέκνα,

Do not fear,[a] children,

וְזַעֲקוּ אֶל-אֱלֹהִים καὶ βούσατε πρὸς τὸν θεόν,

But cry out to God;

כִּי תִזָּכְרוּ בַּמֵּבִיא[aa] ἔσται γὰρ ὑμῶν

For you will be remembered by Him

הָרָעָה[bb] עֲלֵיכֶם ὑπὸ τοῦ ἐπάγοντος μνεία.

Who brought this evil[bb] upon you.

---

[z]Or perhaps בְּנֵי תַעֲנוּגָיִךְ, but see below, Chapter V, ad loc., and n. 310.

[aa]Or perhaps לַמֵּבִיא. For agentive *l*-, see below p. 237 and n. 408.

[bb]See Chapter V, ad loc., and cf. 4:18 and 4:29.

4:28

ὥσπερ γὰρ ἐγένετο ἡ διάνοια ὑμῶν	וְכַאֲשֶׁר הָיָה עִם-לְבַבְכֶם

Just as you had in mind

εἰς τὸ πλανηθῆναι ἀπὸ τοῦ θεοῦ,	לִתְעוֹת מֵאַחֲרֵי אֱלֹהִים

To stray away from God,

<οὕτω> δεκαπλασιάσατε	כֵּן[cc] עֶשֶׂר פְּעָמִים

So, return tenfold

ἐπιστραφέντες ζητῆσαι αὐτόν.	תָּשׁוּבוּ לְבַקְשׁוֹ

To seek him.

4:29

ὁ γὰρ ἐπαγαγὼν ὑμῖν τὰ κακὰ	כִּי הַמֵּבִיא הָרָעָה עֲלֵיכֶם

For the One who brought this evil upon you

ἐπάξει ὑμῖν τὴν αἰώνιον εὐφροσύνην μετὰ τῆς σωτηρίας ὑμῶν.	יָבִיא לָכֶם שִׂמְחַת-עוֹלָם בִּישׁוּעַתְכֶם

Will bring you eternal rejoicing with your salvation.'

4:30

θάρσει, Ἰερουσαλημ,	אַל תִּירְאִי יְרוּשָׁלַםִ

Fear not,[a] Jerusalem,

παρακαλέσει σε ὁ ὀνομάσας σε	יְנַחֲמֵךְ הַקּוֹרֵא-לָךְ שֵׁם

The One who named you will comfort you.

4:31-32

δείλαιοι οἱ σὲ κακώσαντες καὶ ἐπιχάραντες τῇ σῇ πτώσει,	שֹׁד לִמְעַנַּיִךְ וְלַשְּׂמֵחִים בְּנָפְלֵךְ[dd]

Wretched shall be those who maltreated you, and rejoiced at your fall;

[cc]Perhaps + עַתָּה (with G^{A}, νῦν). See Chapter V, ad loc.

[dd]Or בְּפִידֵךְ; see Chapter V, ad loc.

שֹׁד לֶעָרִים אֲשֶׁר־הֶעֱבִידוּ אֶת־בָּנָיִךְ	δείλαιαι αἱ πόλεις αἷς ἐδούλευσαν τὰ τέκνα σου,

ܕܘܝ̈ܢ ܡܕ̈ܝܢܬܐ ܗܠܝܢ ܕܫܥܒܕ ܠܒܢ̈ܝܟܝ

Wretched shall be the cities which enslaved your children,

שֹׁד לַלֹּקְחָה אֶת־בָּנָיִךְ	δειλαία ἡ δεξαμένη τοὺς υἱούς σου.

Wretched she who took away your sons.

4:33

[ee]כִּי־כַּאֲשֶׁר שָׂמְחָה בְּנָפְלֵךְ	ὥσπερ γὰρ ἔχάρη ἐπι τῇ σῇ πτώσει

For just as she rejoiced at your fall,

[ff]וְגָלָה[ee] בְּכָשְׁלֵךְ	καὶ εὐφράνθη ἐπὶ τῷ πτώματί σου,

And was glad for your disaster,

כֵּן תֵּעָצֵב עַל־חָרְבֹתֶיהָ	οὕτως λυπηθήσεται ἐπὶ τῇ ἑαυτῆς ἐρημίᾳ.

So will she be grieved at her own desolation.

4:34

וְאָסִיר מִמֶּנָּה מְשׂוֹשׂ הָמוֹן	καὶ περιελῶ αὐτῆς τὸ ἀγαλλίαμα τῆς πολυοχλίας,

I will remove her exuberant population,

וּתְהִי תְּהִלָּתָהּ לְאֵבֶל	καὶ τὸ ἀγαυρίαμα αὐτῆς ἔσται εἰς πένθος.

And her vaunted pride will turn to mourning.

[ee]The reverse verbal sequence (וְשָׂמְחָה . . . גָּלָה) is also a possibility; see Chapter V, ad loc.

[ff]This is pointed as a Niphal infinitive construct. A Qal infinitive construct (בְּכָשְׁלֵךְ) could perhaps be speculated, but such is unattested in BH. See below, Chapter V, and n. 374.

4:35 כִּי-אֵשׁ מֵאֵת-ʷ יהוה | πῦρ γὰρ ἐπελεύσεται αὐτῇ

For fire will come upon her

תָּבוֹא עָלֶיהָ | παρὰ τοῦ αἰωνίου

From the Eternal

לְיָמִים רַבִּים | εἰς ἡμέρας μακράς,

For many days;

וְתוּשַׁב לִשְׂעִירִים | καὶ κατοικηθήσεται ὑπὸ δαιμονίων

And she will be inhabited by demons

לְנֵצַח נְצָחִים | τὸν πλείονα χρόνον.

For a long, long time.

4:36

שְׂאִי-סָבִיב עֵינַיִךְ | περίβλεψαι

Look about you

מִזְרָחָה יְרוּשָׁלַםִ | πρὸς ἀνατολάς, Ἰερουσαλημ,

To the East, Jerusalem,

וּרְאִי הַשִּׂמְחָה הַבָּאָה-לָךְ | καὶ ἴδε τὴν εὐφροσύνην

And see the joy that is

מֵאֵתʷ אֱלֹהִים | τὴν παρὰ τοῦ θεοῦ σοι ἐρχομένην.

Coming to you from God.

4:37

הִנֵּה בָאוּ-לָךְ בָּנַיִךְ | ἰδοὺ ἔρχονται οἱ υἱοί σου,

ܗܐ ܐܬܝܢ ܠܟܝ ܒܢܝܟܝ

Behold, your sons are coming to you,

אֲשֶׁר שִׁלַּחַתְּ | οὓς ἐξαπέστειλας,

The ones you had sent away;

יָבֹאוּ נִקְבָּצִים ἔρχονται συνηγμένοι

They are coming, gathered

מִמִּזְרָח וּמִמַּעֲרָב ἀπὸ ἀνατολῶν ἕως δυσμῶν

From both East and West,

בִּדְבַר קָדוֹשׁ τῷ ῥήματι τοῦ ἁγίου

At the word of the Holy One,

שְׂמֵחִים בִּכְבוֹד-אֵל[gg] χαίροντες τῇ τοῦ θεοῦ δόξῃ.

Rejoicing in the glory of God.

5:1

פִּשְׁטִי יְרוּשָׁלַםִ ἔκδυσαι, Ἰερουσαλημ, τὴν
בִּגְדֵי-אֶבְלֵךְ וְעָנְיֵךְ στολὴν τοῦ πένθους καὶ τῆς
κακώσεώς σου

Strip off, Jerusalem, the clothing of your mourning and affliction,

וְלִבְשִׁי תִּפְאֶרֶת[hh] καὶ ἔνδυσαι τὴν εὐπρέπειαν
כְּבוֹד-אֵל לְעוֹלָם τῆς παρὰ τοῦ θεοῦ δόξης εἰς
τὸν αἰῶνα.

And put on forever the splendor of the glory of God!

5:2

עֲטִי מְעִיל περιβαλοῦ τὴν διπλοΐδα τῆς
צִדְקַת אֱלֹהִים παρὰ τοῦ θεοῦ δικαιοσύνης,

Wrap yourself in the cloak of God's righteousness;

שִׂימִי עַל-רֹאשֵׁךְ ἐπίθου τὴν μίτραν ἐπὶ τὴν
פְּאֵר-כְּבוֹד יהוה κεφαλήν σου τῆς δόξης τοῦ
αἰωνίου.

Put on your head the tiara of the glory of the Eternal.

[gg]Or אֱלֹהִים.

[hh]Or perhaps הֲדַר.

5:3

כִּי תַחַת כָּל-הַשָּׁמַיִם	ὁ γὰρ θεὸς δείξει

For everywhere under heaven

יַרְאֶה אֵל^{gg} הֲדָרֵךְ	τῇ ὑπ᾽ οὐρανὸν πάσῃ τὴν σὴν λαμπρότητα.

God will show your splendor;

5:4

וְקוֹרָא לָךְ שֵׁם	κληθήσεται γάρ σου τὸ ὄνομα

So your name will be

מֵאֵת[w] אֵל[gg] לְעוֹלָם	παρὰ τοῦ θεοῦ εἰς τὸν αἰῶνα

Forever called by God,

שְׁלוֹם צְדָקָה	Εἰρήνη δικαιοσύνης

'Peace of righteousness

וּכְבוֹד יִרְאַת-אֵל[gg]	καὶ δόξα θεοσεβείας.

And glory of godliness.'

5:5

קוּמִי יְרוּשָׁלַםִ וְעִמְדִי עַל-הַר-גָּבֹהַּ	Ἀνάστηθι, Ἰερουσαλημ, καὶ στῆθι ἐπὶ τοῦ ὑψηλοῦ

Arise, Jerusalem, and stand on the height,

וּשְׂאִי-סָבִיב עֵינַיִךְ מִזְרָחָה	καὶ περίβλεψαι πρὸς ἀνατολὰς

And look about you to the East,

וּרְאִי בָנַיִךְ נִקְבְּצוּ	καὶ ἴδε σου συνηγμένα τὰ τέκνα

And see your children gathered

[ii] מִמִּזְרַח שֶׁמֶשׁ עַד-מַעֲרָב   ἀπὸ ἡλίου δυσμῶν ἕως ἀνατολῶν

ܡܢ ܡܕܢܚܘܗܝ ܕܫܡܫܐ ܥܕܡܐ ܠܡܥܪܒܘܗܝ (Syh)

From East to West,

בִּדְבַר קָדוֹשׁ   τῷ ῥήματι τοῦ ἁγίου

At the word of the Holy One,

שְׂמֵחִים בְּזֵכֶר-אֵל[gg]   χαίροντας τῇ τοῦ θεοῦ μνείᾳ.

Rejoicing in the remembrance of God!

5:6

כִּי-רַגְלֵי מֵעִמָּךְ יָצְאוּ   ἐξῆλθον γὰρ παρὰ σοῦ πεζοὶ

For they went forth from you on foot,

נְהוּגִים בְּיַד אוֹיֵב   ἀγόμενοι ὑπὸ ἐχθρῶν,

Led captive by the enemy;

וִיבִיאֵם-לָךְ אֵל[gg]   εἰσάγει δὲ αὐτοὺς ὁ θεὸς πρὸς σὲ

But God will bring them back to you,

נְשׂוּאִים בְּכָבוֹד   αἰρομένους μετὰ δόξης

Carried in glory

כְּכִסֵּא מַלְכוּת   ὡς θρόνον βασιλείας.

As on a royal throne.

5:7

כִּי צִוָּה אֱלֹהִים   συνέταξε γὰρ ὁ θεὸς

For God has given the order

לְשַׁפֵּל כָּל-הַר גָּבֹהַּ   ταπεινοῦσθαι πᾶν ὄρος ὑψηλὸν

That every high mountain be lowered,

[ii] This sequence follows O, Sy, La^{L,S,V}, et al. Other possibilities for "West" are perhaps: וּמִמַּעֲרָבָה or עַד-מְבוֹא. The alternative (with G^B, et al.) is (מִזְרָחָה) מִמְּבוֹא הַשֶּׁמֶשׁ מִמִּזְרָחָה.

וְגִבְעוֹת עוֹלָם — καὶ θῖνας ἀενάους

Even the eternal hills,

וְגֵיאָיוֹת לְהִנָּשֵׂא — καὶ φάραγγας πληροῦσθαι

That the valleys be raised up

לְמִישׁוֹר הָאָרֶץ — εἰς ὁμαλισμὸν τῆς γῆς,

To level ground,

לְמַעַן יֵלֵךְ יִשְׂרָאֵל — ἵνα βαδίσῃ Ισραηλ

In order that Israel may walk

לָבֶטַח בִּכְבוֹד אֱלֹהִים — ἀσφαλῶς τῇ τοῦ θεοῦ δόξῃ

Securely in the glory of God.

5:8

סִכְּכוּ יְעָרוֹת — ἐσκίασαν δὲ καὶ οἱ δρυμοὶ
וְכָל-עֵץ רֵיחַ[jj] — καὶ πᾶν ξύλον εὐωδίας

The woods and every fragrant tree

עַל-יִשְׂרָאֵל בִּדְבַר אֱלֹהִים — τῷ Ισραηλ προστάγματι τοῦ θεοῦ·

Shade Israel at God's command.

5:9

כִּי-יֵלֵךְ אֱלֹהִים — ἡγήσεται γὰρ
לִפְנֵי יִשְׂרָאֵל — ὁ θεὸς Ισραηλ

For God will proceed before Israel

בְּשִׂמְחָה בְּאוֹר — μετ᾽ εὐφροσύνης τῷ
כְּבוֹדוֹ — φωτὶ τῆς δόξης αὐτοῦ

With joy, in the light of his glory,

בְּחֶסֶד וּבִצְדָקָה — σὺν ἐλεημοσύνῃ καὶ
מֵאִתּוֹ[kk] — δικαιοσύνῃ τῇ παρ᾽ αὐτοῦ.

With the mercy and righteousness that are from him.

[jj]Or perhaps בֹּשֶׂם.

[kk]Or perhaps מֵעִמּוֹ.

CHAPTER V

PHILOLOGICAL NOTES ON THE RECONSTRUCTED HEBREW TEXT OF THE CONSOLATION POEM OF BARUCH, 4:5-5:9

4:5

'al-tîrā' = *tharseite*

The verb *tharseō* is in limited use in the LXX. Among the twelve examples for which there are corresponding Hebrew texts all but two (both from Proverbs and both formed from the related root *tharreō*, Prov 1:21, 31:11) are used to represent the familiar Hebrew idiom--the negative plus the imperfect of *yārē'* ("fear not!").[1] This same combination of negative command + vocative appears in Isa 10:24, *'al-tîrā' 'ammî*.[2]

'ammî = *laos mou*

This represents an extremely regular equivalency throughout the LXX between *'am* and *laos*. A variant reading, *laos theou*, is found in texts of the Lucianic Recension group, noted in the margin of Syh within the *obeloi*, and reflected in La^{C,V}, and Sy.[3] This pattern of appearance plus the very character of the variant strongly suggest that it is the result of later (Lucianic?) correction to make clear at the outset of this poem that the vocative, "my people," refers to God's people rather than to Jerusalem's or the speaker's.

zēker = *mnēmosynon*

The "memorial of Israel" is to be understood as referring to that remnant which preserves, albeit scarcely, the very "remembrance" of the nation Israel. This is apparent from its common idiomatic use in the portrayal of national eradication as the "blotting out of a people's remembrance" in certain passages whose contexts reflect the horrendous consequences of military destruction; for example, Deut 32:26, Job 18:17, Ps 9:7, 34:17, 102:13, 109:15, and Deut 25:19.[4] In all these passages this same equivalency between *zēker* and *mnēmosynon* obtains.[5]

While the LXX does use *mnēmosynon* for two other Hebrew terms having the general sense of "memorial," *'azkārāh* and *zikkārôn*, neither is likely to have been found in the Hebrew original of this verse. This is because the first most pronouncedly is a cultic term used in the sacrificial sense (as in Lev 2:2 and passim) and the second has a similar, though less marked, connotation (cf. especially the clearly cultic use of the term in the Pentateuchal P-source). The Syriac equivalent in both texts, *dukrānā'*, is not only cognate but also corresponds semantically to *zēker*. It is in fact regularly in use for *zēker* in the Syriac Versions; cf., e.g., Ps 6:6, 9:7, 34:17, 112:6, 134:13, Exod 3:15, Deut 25:19.

The last citation interestingly yields the equivalence, *zēker = onoma = dukrānā'*, and underscores a further aspect of this "memorial" concept that often appears, namely, that *zēker* not only frequently appears in formal parallelism with *šēm* "name" but is even used synonymously on occasion (cf., e.g., Prov 10:7, Job 18:17, Exod 3:15, Ps 135:13, Isa 26:8, Sir 44:8-9, 46:11-12). The connotation for Bar 4:5, however, clearly has to be that of the "destruction" topos as the following verse demands--the remnant that God spared as a "memorial" preserves the "name" or "remembrance" of the nation.[6]

The next three verses, 6-8, have clearly been lifted directly from certain passages in Deut 32:15-30,[7] but in an abbreviated and eclectic patchwork-style that reassembles words and phrases from the Deuteronomy verses, often irrespective of context, to form the new sentences of Baruch. This is, of course, much in the manner of the Qumran hymnists.

<u>4:6</u>

(kî) = meṭul d- (Sy)

This is perhaps to be restored from Sy. Although there is no LXX textual support, nor thus in Syh, the presence of *meṭul d-* in Sy may reflect an original Hebrew *kî* which the LXX had stylistically (or accidentally?) omitted. Also if, as it appears, verse 6 is closely dependent on Esth 7:4,[8] the conjunctive *kî* would seem to be expected. But on the other hand, in the light of the LXX silence, it is probably equally as likely that this Syriac conjunctive is a stylistic addition.[9]

nimkartem laggôyīm = eprathēte tois ethnesin

Verse 6a seems clearly and decisively an allusion to Esth 7:4, *kî nimkarnû . . . lᵉhašmîd*, and reflects the same notion of selling people to their enemies in the sense of "giving them into their power." Here in Esth 7:4, *piprаskō* is the equivalent of the Niphal stem of *mākar* and even has the connotation "betrayed." Although *laggôyīm* or its equivalent is not specified it is clear that the expression is idiomatic and assumes some such understood referent. Other passages where *piprаskō* translates *mākar* are Ps 44:13, Judg 4:9, Isa 50:1, 52:3.[10] The same idea is expressed in Ezek 25:7 with the verb *nātan: ûnᵉtattîkā . . . laggôyīm*. Although the meaning is different, there is also a verbal parallel in CD 12:8, *'l ymkr . . . lgwym*. As noted above at 3:16, *ethnos* is the usual LXX equivalent for *gôy*.

lō' lᵉhašmîd = ouk eis apōleian

This is simply the negative counterpart of the last part of Esth 7:4 where *lᵉhašmîd = eis apōleian*. Cf. further the close parallel in 1 Macc 3:42, *poiēsai tō laō eis apōleian*.

wᵉya'an = dia de to

This reconstruction, "but because," is extremely tentative in that while causal clauses in BH are commonly introduced by *ya'an kî* (seven times), *ya'an 'ᵃšer* (thirty-two times), or *ya'an* (twenty-three times), the construction is even more often shortened simply to *'ᵃšer* or *kî*.[11] This may be illustrated by several examples. In Isa 37:29, *ya'an* introduces a causal clause in which the consequence of disobedience is going into captivity. The same context may be seen in Isa 30:12 (*ya'an*), 8:6, 3:16, 7:5, 29:13, 1 Kgs 21:29 (*ya'an kî*). Isa 30:12, 15:23, and Num 11:20 have in common the causal particle *ya'an* (= *hoti* in LXX), followed in each case by the verb *mā'as* which, in the context of creaturely disobedience provoking the wrath of the Creator, is semantically close to the verb *kā'as* of Bar 4:6.

Jer 48:7, dealing with a prophesied captivity for Moab, is the only MT example of the sequence *kî ya'an*. This is in fact the reconstruction of Kahana,[12] and if that *kî* were an actual adversative *kî*, such would be a plausible reconstruction.

However, its use in the Jer 48:7 passage is clearly asseverative. The Syriac there is of little help, rendering *kî ya'an* with the common idiom, *'al d-* "because," the same cliche used, for example, in the Syriac text of Isa 3:16 for Hebrew *ya'an kî*. Thus, from the welter of possibilities available in Hebrew (*ya'an*, *ya'an kî*, *ya'an 'ᵃšer*, *'ᵃšer*, *kî*, *taḥat*,[13] and *taḥat kî*)[14] and in Greek (*dioti*, *hoti*, *epeiper*, *anth' hōn*, and *dia to*) for the causal element "because," which yields equivalencies in the LXX according to no apparent patterns, it is simply not possible here to be more precise in reconstruction.

hak'îsᵉkem = parorgisai hymas

The Hiphil stem of *kā'as* "vex, provoke to anger" is normally the Hebrew equivalent rendered by *parorgizō* "provoke to anger" in the LXX,[15] and significantly this equivalence obtains in the key source-text, Deut 32:21.[16]

hosgartem laṣṣārîm = paredothēte tois hypenantiois

The parallel pairing, *mākar* (A) // *hisgîr* (B), appears in the Deuteronomy passage (32:30).[17] For the idiom *hisgîr + l-* (or the like), cf. Ps 78:48, *wayyasgēr labbārād*; 78:50, *laddeber hisgîr*; 78:62, *wayyasgēr laḥereb*; and Amos 1:9, *'al-hasgîrām . . . le'ᵉdôm*.[18] The common idiom *bᵉyad* is also often combined with *hisgîr* as, for example, in Ps 31:9, *wᵉlō' hisgartanî bᵉyad-'ôyēb*.[19] This combination is not likely here, however, since the Hebraism, "into the hand of," is usually represented literally in the LXX by the Greek, *eis tas cheiras*, or its equivalent.

That *hypenantios* represents Hebrew *ṣar* "adversary, enemy" is suggested by the overwhelmingly regular use of *echthros* in the LXX for the more common Hebrew term for "enemy," *'ôyēb*,[20] and by such parallels as that in the poetry of the Deut 32:27 source, where the pairing, *'ôyēb = echthros* (A) // *ṣar = hypenantios* (B), appears, and those in Isa 1:24 and Num 10:9 (prose) where the same equivalencies (but reversed in sequence) prevail.[21]

4:7

hiqnē'tem = *parōxynate*

The Greek verb *paroxynō* "provoke, vex" is most frequently used in the LXX for Hebrew *nā'aṣ*, and less so for *qānā'* and *kā'as*.[22] Intriguingly, the LXX displays undue economy in using this same Greek verb for each of these three different Hebrew verbs within the same limited context of Deut 32:16-21. The distinction between these verbs is briefly thus: *qānā'* is used in the Hiphil stem, always with instrumental *beth*, to mean "make jealous (*with* something)," and in Piel twice with a factitive sense and instrumental *beth*;[23] *nā'aṣ* is used in the Qal stem (cf. Deut 32:19) to mean "spurn, despise, contemn," and in the Piel to mean "treat without respect"; and *kā'as* is used in the Hiphil and Piel stems (cf. Bar 4:6) to mean "vex, aggravate, provoke, anger."

Nā'aṣ first of all seems improbable here since it has a somewhat different connotation from the other two, lacking the sense of "provoke to (some mood)." Further, as it is employed in Deut 32:19 it is in the Qal stem ("despise") with God as the subject, and thus not likely to have been the verb borrowed here. While *kā'as* would seem to satisfy the sense that the Baruch context demands--the people vex God to anger or aggravate him (as with the Hiphil and Piel forms in Deut 32:16, 21)--it remains true that this verb is yet more often translated in the LXX by *parorgizō* (as above in 4:6). Thus *qānā'* seems the most likely candidate by both such negative reasoning and the fact that it appears in the immediate context of *lō'-'ēl* in the source-text, Deut 32:21, with the very semantic sense that the Baruch context demands. Cf. Deut 32:21, *hēm qin'ûnî bᵉlō'-'ēl*, "they have provoked me to jealousy with what is no god"; and 32:16, *yaqnī'ūhû bᵉzārîm*, "they provoked him to jealousy with strange gods."

There is a syntactical problem in that *qānā'*, at least in the biblical examples where it has the causative sense in both Hiphil ("make jealous") and Piel ("provoke to jealous anger"),[24] is always idiomatically combined with instrumental *beth* to express the sense "*with* something." Good syntax would thus suggest that the Hebrew following the verb would have been *bizbāḥîm laššēdîm* or perhaps *bizbōaḥ laššēdîm* (i.e., instrumental *beth* with a substantive or temporal *beth* with an infinitive). However, since both Sy and Syh, featuring Peal perfect forms of the verb *dᵉbaḥ*, support the likely existence of a finite verb form in the original of verse 7b as opposed to a substantive or infinitive (or the LXX participle), it would perhaps be expected that the author of Baruch merely quoted Deut 32:17a verbatim, with only the slightest change of the person and tense of the initial finite verb. And, given the asyndetic character of the syntax of Deut 32:16-17, 21, one could reasonably expect the same syntactic style to have characterized the Baruch borrowing from it.

Further complicating the problem is the fact that both Syriac texts feature causal coordinators, that of Sy the more emphatic *'al d-* "because," and that of Syh simply *d-* (+ perfect verb) "for, on account of." While this could suggest the presence of a similar Hebrew coordinator in the original, it could also be no more than an example of the smooth transitions characteristic of good Syriac style. Also, the syntax of the LXX's participial construction could be construed as reflecting an asyndetic Hebrew syntax, but then it could also be an example of a non-literal rendering of a Hebrew coordination construction with instrumental or temporal *beth*.

There are thus several possibilities among which it is difficult to make a clear-cut decision: (1) the syntax was the more archaic asyndetic pairing of two parallel verbal clauses (as in Deut 32:16-21 and rather typically throughout Deuteronomy 32), yielding a Baruch text that would have conformed most closely to the source (though this does overlook the evidence for the regular use of *b-* with *qānā'*; (2) the syntax was that of a single verbal clause with *b-* coordinating the following substantive or infinitive, a solution which would have the advantage of taking into account the common use of *b-* with the causative forms of *qānā'* and yet the disadvantage of assuming considerably more drastic adjustment of the quoted source-text from an asyndetically coordinated finite verb to a syndetically coordinated substantive or infinitive; (3) the Syriac construction could possibly be construed as having derived from such (if not explainable satisfactorily as Syriac stylism) or perhaps as reflective of a more pronouncedly causal original construction with *kî* or the like.

The first alternative has been deemed best in that it accords most closely with its source's context in terms of syntactic style, features the least possible changes in its quoting of the source-text, and in its reconstruction of the finite verb for the LXX *thysantes* is supported in Semitic by both Syriac text traditions.

(ʾ^{e}lôᵃh)

Considerations of metre and balance suggest further the possibility that the *ʾ^{e}lôᵃh* of the phrase *ʾ^{e}lôᵃh ʿāśāhû* in Deut 32:15 may also have been borrowed by our author. The inclusion of this element does yield a well-balanced bicolon (9/9). It is at least possible, though not really probable, that the divine name may have been lost by influence of the following verse where *theon aiōnion* (Sy, *l[ʾ]allāhāʾ dalʿālam* and Hebrew, *ʾēl ʿôlām*) appears. Needless to say, this is very hypothetical and the occurrence in this verse of a vertical dittograph would more likely have eventuated than any sort of vertical haplography. Indeed, the appearance in verse 8 of the phrase *theon aiōnion* suggests itself as the source for the versional variants here in verse 7; Sy, *l(ʾ)allāhāʾ dalʿālam*, and La^{V,L}, *deum aeternum*. On the other hand, that the appearance of the divine name would not be at all unnatural here is witnessed by Deut 32:15, *ʾ^{e}lôᵃh ʿāśāhû*, and such parallels as Isa 44:2, *YHWH ʿōśekā*, and Isa 51:13, *wattiškaḥ YHWH ʿōśekā*.[25]

z^{e}baḥtem laššēdîm lōʾ ʾ^{e}lôᵃh = thysantes daimoniois kai ou theō

This, as already noted, is a direct quote from Deut 32:17. The matter of the finite form of the verb has already been discussed above; the equivalency is common in the LXX.[26]

Daimonion is a term rarely used in the LXX, having reference to the pagan idols that are represented by the comparably rare and obscure Hebrew terms: *šēd* (twice), *ṣiyyîm* (once), and *śāʿîr* (once).[27] In MT, *šēdîm* occurs only twice, in both instances translated by *daimonion* in the LXX.[28] One of these passages is the source-text, Deut 32:17; the other is a closely related parallel in Ps 106:37, *wayyizbᵉḥû 'et-bᵉnêhem wᵉ'et-bᵉnôtêhem laššēdîm*. The first, Deut 32:17, is simply a less explicit, though nonetheless obvious, reference to the same deplorable practice that the latter passage refers to--child sacrifice to pagan deities (i.e., "demons").

Happily, this one lone parallel does provide the needed interpretative clue for the end of the Baruch verse. Since the explicitness of Ps 106:37 makes clear that the point of reference of the Deut 32:17 source-text is not sacrifice in general but specifically child sacrifice, there can be absolutely no question about the intent of the phrase *lō' 'ᵉlōᵃh* there. It can only mean "non-deity" or "non-divinity" (i.e., literally "no-god"). It thus has reference to the nature and character of the heathen deities as "non-gods" and can in no way be legitimately construed as in the LXX translation: "sacrificing to demons and not to God." The LXX *theō* in both Deut 32:17 and Bar 4:7 is thus transparently interpretative on the part of the LXX translator(s). The other Versions have similarly erred interpretatively.[29]

<u>4:8</u>

wattiškᵉḥû ('ēl) mᵉḥôlelᵉkem = epelathesthe de ton tropheusanta hymas

The equivalence of the Qal stem of *šākaḥ* "forget" with the Greek verb *epilanthanō* "escape notice, forget" is regular in the LXX.[30] The Greek verb *tropheuō* is a rarity, however, occurring only here and in Exod 2:7 in the LXX. In Exod 2:7, it is employed to translate a Hiphil form of *yānaq* having the meaning "nurse" or "suckle." Obviously, the same sense here applied to *YHWH* would represent him in a most singular light. However, *tropheuō* happens to be a rare, late biform of *trephō* "nourish, rear, bring up," which has been ascribed this connotation, "suckle," by virtue of its singular association with Hebrew *yānaq* in Exod 2:7.[31] That the broader "parental" sense of *trephō* is the intent of Bar 4:8 can be deduced from the readings of both Sy (*mᵉdabrānākûn* "your guardian, governor," often the equivalent of Hebrew *nāgîd*) and Syh (*lᵉhaw dᵉrabbîkûn* "the one who brought you up"), and most significantly from the source-text, Deut 32:18, *kai epelathou theou tou trephontos se* = *wattiškaḥ 'ēl meḥōlelekā*. La^{V} also supports this interpretation with its reading: *qui nutrivit vos*. There is also one eleventh century LXX Minuscule of the G^{Q} group, #534, that offers a reading, *ton trephonta*, for Bar 4:8.[32]

There is only slight textual support for *'ēl* as the direct object of *wattiškeḥû*, preceding the participle ostensibly to specify (as if there really could be any doubt) who has been doing the "nourishing." Such a reading is reflected in La^{L,V} (*deum*), La^{S} (*dominum*), and Ar. But this element is noticeably wanting in all the more weighty Greek and Syriac exemplars. The only supportive argument of some consequence is the presence of *'ēl* as such an object in the closely quoted source-text, Deut 32:18. It would seem an unlikely omission, and yet with the author's addition of *'ēl 'ôlām* from elsewhere than Deuteronomy 32 it also seems superfluous.[33]

'ēl 'ôlām = theon aiōnion

This combination occurs in Gen 21:33 and Isa 40:28 as an epithet ascribed to *YHWH*, the latter being the more replete variant, *'elōhê 'ôlām*. In each case the LXX equivalent is the same as the above, though nominative. There is a similar expression in the Greek of Susanna 42, *ho theos ho aiōnios*, and in Hebrew alone the phrase *'l 'wlm* appears in 1QH 7:31. This element is lacking in La^{S,V} of Bar 4:8.[34]

'ap = de kai

Perhaps this should be reconstructed as *we'ap* with Kneucker,[35] but in none of the occurrences of *we'ap* in MT is it ever rendered in the LXX by *de kai*.

he'eṣabtem = elypēsate

Of the various Hebrew verbs that the LXX translates with some form of *lypeō* "pain, grieve," for example, *lā'āh* (Hiph) "make weary, exhaust," *qāṣap* (Hiph) "make wroth, enraged," *rā'a'* (Hiph) "injure, harm, do evil," and *'āṣab* (Hiph) "grieve, cause grief or pain," the one that is semantically closest to *lypeō* and most apt in the Bar 4:8 context is *ʿāṣab*. In the active voice, *lypeō* means "to give pain to, distress, grieve, vex, to cause pain or grief of body or mind."[36] Similarly, in the Hiphil stem (or Piel), *ʿāṣab* connotes the pain and distress of grief in its meaning of causing pain or anguish. Syh employs here the verb *ʿâq* which in the Aphel stem has the meaning "annoy, distress, grieve." It is cognate to Hebrew *ṣûq* (Hiph) "constrain, press, bring into straits." Sy has an Aphel form of *kᵉrāʾ* which, from a root meaning of "shorten," is commonly used metaphorically to mean "sadden, displease." The Vulgate verb, *contristo* "sadden, grieve," supports this same sense.

Of significance here also is Isa 54:6 where Jerusalem is personified in the role of a grieved wife with the Qal passive participle of *ʿāṣab*--*waʿᵃṣûbat rûᵃḥ*. Further support may be adduced in the fact that the related noun, *lypē* "pain," is the regular LXX equivalent for Hebrew *ʿeṣeb* "pain, grief, toil."[37] Thus the Hiphil stem of *ʿāṣab* (or perhaps Piel) is most probably to be reconstructed.

yôladtᵉkem yᵉrûšālayim = *tēn ekthrepsasan hymas Hierousalēm*

Although no known equivalence between *ektrephō* and *yālad* exists in the LXX, such is probable here by the parallel in the source-text, Deut 32:18, *mᵉḥōlᵉlekā // yᵉlādᵉkā*.[38] While such use of *yālad* to connote "rear" is not semantically impossible,[39] the more common equivalent of *ektrephō* is *gādal* (Piel or Qal) "raise, rear, bring up."[40] This latter is thus also a possibility here, since the second colon in Bar 4:8 is really a departure from Deut 32:18 (God and Jerusalem are the respective subjects of the cola of Bar 4:8, while in Deut 32:18 God is the subject in both).[41]

4:9

Here begins the portrayal of Jerusalem as the bereaved mother bewailing the unfortunate loss of her beloved children. Contextually, the frame of reference is the lamentable predicament of being a "byword" among the neighboring peoples--the "neighbors of Zion"--who have indeed witnessed the humiliation of the Hebrews and their God. But (cf. vs. 24) the author ultimately assures them in good prophetic fashion that the apparent powerlessness of *YHWH* is not at all what it might appear. Rather, he claims, this is all part of his disciplinary and purgative plan, and to be followed by its corollary, *YHWH*'s vindicating rescue from the ignominy of exile.

'ap-'ēl habbā' ʿᵃlêkem = tēn epelthousan hymin orgēn para tou theou

Here the problem is determining what lies behind *para* + genitive in the original Hebrew. Syh (*men 'allāhā'*) and Sy (*men qᵉdām māryā' 'allāhā'*), though the latter contains the typical expansionary "Lord," each suggest a prepositional phrase with *min*.[42] This is not altogether unlikely, but the Syriac style may be under Greek influence here. Retroversion into Hebrew on this tack yields an overly cumbersome phrase, and it is also true that within the general topos of the "wrath of God" (regardless of whether the precise term used is *'ap* or *ḥēmāh* or otherwise) the normal construction for joining "wrath" to "God" is genitival and not prepositional.[43] *Para* + genitive basically denotes motion "from the side of" and is commonly employed in combination with verbs of coming, going, and other such motions. In translating Hebrew constructions it is utilized to render a variety of expressions, frequently the common prepositional constructions with *b-* and *min* (or *mē'ēt*, *mēʿim*, etc.), but it is also often used simply as good Greek style with no actual equivalent in the Hebrew text. Oftentimes it renders a Hebrew genitive construction that inherently implies (as does the concept "wrath of God" here in Bar 4:9) "motion from" or "action from."[44]

There being no discernible specific source for this phrase, that *orgē* is the equivalent of *'ap* is likely but by no means certain. Since *orgē* is used in the LXX to render a plethora of Hebrew synonyms for "wrath, anger," other possibilities remain. In Hebrew, *'ap* and *ḥēmāh* are the most common, in Greek *orgē* and *thymos*. There is, however, no apparent consistency or pattern in the LXX's use of these two for translating the Hebrew counterparts. The Syriac, *rugzā'* similarly renders the Greek terms, *orgē* and *thymos*, and the Hebrew, *'ap* and *ḥēmāh*, interchangeably.[45]

Given the irregular translational pattern for the two Greek terms which do seem to be used interchangeably for the Hebrew terms without precise regard for semantic content, the fact that *orgē* (having its derivation in the verb *orgaō* "swell up, be rampant, be in heat") is semantically more akin to *ḥēmāh* "heat" and likewise *thymos* (derived from *thyō* "rush on as a wind," and meaning at the root or physical level "soul" or "breath,"[46] and thus ultimately "strong feeling, passion, anger") to *'ap* "breath, anger," would thus seem to carry little significance. The LXX translators seem rather to have operated on a more general level, using these terms as approximate synonyms with no particular concern to detect or preserve etymological niceties. Indeed, the Hebrew terms themselves appear often enough to have been employed by their users in a similar indiscriminate and general way as synonyms.

With regard to *ḥēmāh*, the concordances will show that the expression *ḥᵃmat YHWH* appears with some frequency (six times) in MT,[47] but also that there is in BH no such combination as *ḥᵃmat 'ēl*. On the other hand, concerning *'ap*, the expression *'ap-YHWH* is much more frequent (thirty-six times) in MT[48] and there are two examples there of the phrase *'ap 'ᵉlōhîm* (Num 22:22 and Ezra 10:14) as well as at least nine occurrences of the combination *'ap-'ēl* in the Qumran literature which is yet more contemporaneous with Baruch.[49] Thus it has been determined that *'ap* most probably stood in the original Hebrew.

šim'û 'ēlay = Akousate (mou?) = *šum'ūny* (Sy)

The reading with *mou*, "Listen *to me*," is not without significant textual support. All the texts of the Lucianic recension group offer *Akousate mou*,[50] and Sy, the chief Semitic witness, has the first person pronominal suffix. There being no particular source-text from which this passage is drawn but only the general imagery-reservoir of the lament and destruction topoi of classical prophetic poetry, and there being evidence of a great deal of similarity (in terms both of style and content) between this prophetic poem of Baruch and Deutero-Isaiah, it is surely of some significance that Deutero-Isaiah very typically employs this same stylistic feature of following the imperative of *šāma'* with *'ēlay* before the plural vocative. The following examples will illustrate this: Isa 46:3, *šim'û 'ēlay bêt ya'ᵃqōb*; 46:12, *šim'û 'ēlay 'ᵃbîrê lēb*; 51:1, *šim'û 'ēlay rōdᵉpê ṣedeq*; 51:7, *šim'û 'ēlay yōdᵉ'ê ṣedeq*.[51]

šᵉkēnê ṣiyyôn = hai paroikoi Siōn

This phrase is unique to Baruch, appearing three times in this poem only (vss. 9, 14, 24). *Paroikos* in its basic and original sense means simply "neighbor." By extension it came to mean also "foreigner, sojourner, alien." The latter is the more common meaning of the term in the LXX, as it is often used to translate Hebrew *gēr* "sojourner" and other similar terms. Both senses are to some extent involved in the common use of the Greek term by the classical authors to refer to neighboring cities or city-states. For example, cf. Aeschylus, *Persae*, 869, [*poleis* . . .] *paroikoi Thrēkiōn epaulōn*.[52] This is precisely the connotation *paroikos* has in Baruch--the neighboring (city-) states that surround Jerusalem.

Paroikos has exactly this political sense in Jer 49:18 (cf. 50:40) where it translates the Hebrew, *sᵉdōm wa'ᵃmōrāh ûšᵉkēnèhā*, "Sodom and Gomorrah and their neighbor cities."[53] The Hebrew equivalent is here seen to be *šākēn* "dweller, neighbor." Although the Greek is different, in Ezek 16:26 the Egyptians are similarly styled *šᵉkēnayik* with reference to Jerusalem. In Ps 79:4, 12, the context of Jerusalem's being a byword or reproach to her "neighbors" (*šᵉkēnîm*) implies that these are the surrounding nations.[54] The Syriac terms (Syh, *tawtābā'*, from *yᵉtab* "dwell," and Sy, *'āmûr*, from *'ᵉmar* "settle") have much the same range of meaning, "dweller, neighbor, sojourner, settler," or the like.[55]

'ēbel gādôl = penthos mega

Penthos is the regular LXX equivalent for Hebrew *'ēbel* with few exceptions.[56] The same may be said for the equivalence of *megas* and *gādôl*.[57] Properly and etymologically, *'ēbel* has the meaning "mourning," but by extension it can also connote more generally "grief" or "sorrow." Similarly, the Greek term is derived from the verb *pentheō*, meaning basically "mourn" or "lament." The Hebrew *'ēbel* thus closely matches this and also fits exactly the context of destruction and exile that is lamented by Jerusalem in this Baruch passage. The combination *'ēbel gādôl* is found elsewhere only in Esth 4:3. A similar expression, *'ēbel kābēd*, is found in Gen 50:11.

4:10

šᵉbî = aichmalōsian

This Greek noun is the normal LXX equivalent for *šᵉbî* "captivity, exile."[58] Both terms exhibit a comparable semantic range, being derived from or related to verbs meaning "take prisoner," and thus denoting firstly "captivity" or the state of captivity and secondly the collective sense of a "body of captives." Both Syriac texts offer the cognate, *šebyā'*. A less probable, yet possible, reconstruction is that of *gālût/gôlāh* "exile."[59]

YHWH = ho aiōnios

For *aiōnios*, cf. above, verse 8, where *theon aiōnion* appears. This occurrence in verse 10 is the first instance in Baruch of the absolute usage of *aiōnios* as a circumlocution for the deity, but it appears subsequently with great frequency throughout the remainder of this poem (vss. 14, 20, 22, 24, 35; 5:2). Such usage is almost without precedent in the LXX, being found elsewhere only in 2 Macc 1:25. Intriguingly, *Kyrios* is never used in either of these poems, though it does appear frequently in the prose section of Baruch. It is, then, a distinct possibility that *ho aiōnios* in this poem represents a circumlocution for the Tetragrammaton.[60] Kneucker,[61] noting that the epithet *'ēl 'ôlām* (LXX, *theos aiōnios*) is attributed precisely to *YHWH* (LXX, *Kyriou*) in Gen 21:33, concludes that "the Eternal One" is here a slight variation on that epithet, substituted for the divine name so common in the biblical sources and yet so eschewed in later post-biblical Judaism.

'Ēl 'ôlām itself could perhaps be considered a possibility here if the Greek, *ho aiōnios*, were construed as an abbreviated equivalent for it. But such a proposition has serious shortcomings. Not only is such an equivalence unprecedented, but

more significantly the combination of "eternal" and "God" is well-attested in the LXX, MT, and elsewhere (it appears in 4:8, above; cf. n. 34). In other words, it is much more likely that if the original Hebrew here had been *'ēl 'ôlām* the LXX translator would have used the much more common and precise equivalent, *theos aiōnios*.

It thus seems difficult to escape the conclusion that this does indeed stand for *YHWH* in this poem instead of the more usual and expected *Kyrios*, perhaps because of some peculiar predilection of the author. The use of circumlocutions for the Tetragrammaton is well-documented, especially in the later post-biblical period.[62] Also, the assumption of an original *YHWH* is supported by the content of the biblical sources from which some of the later Baruch passages containing *ho aiōnios* are borrowed or to which they manifest close affinity (cf. 4:20, 22, 24, 35; 5:2).

This conclusion, while not directly verifiable and thus hardly certain, appears all the more plausible when one considers that there is no living precedent in BH or at Qumran for the absolute use of *'ôlām*. It is always found in combination with other substantives (e.g., *'ēl*).[63] There is, however, precedent for such absolute use of the adjective *aiōnios* in Greek apocryphal and pseudepigraphical literature; cf. 2 Macc 1:24-25, *Kyrie Kyrie ho theos . . . ho monos dikaios, kai pantokratōr, kai aiōnios*, "O Lord, Lord God . . . the only just, almighty, and eternal One"; 3 Macc 6:12, *Sy de ho pasan alkēn kai dynasteian echōn hapasan, aiōnie, nun epide*, "Thou who art All-powerful and Almighty, O Eternal One, behold!"; and *Sib. Or.* (frg) 3:17, *aphthartos ktistēs aiōnios*, "(the) incorruptible Creator, (the) Eternal."[64] But since these writings were all probably composed in Greek it would be futile to speculate on such a basis whether or not there may have been a comparable absolute use of *'ôlām* current in the intertestamental period.

One other remote possibility is suggested by an obscure epithet in 1QS 11:4, *hww' 'wlm* (probably corrupt for *h^{a}yôt 'ôlām*), "Eternal Being," or the like.[65] Such a reconstruction as *h^{a}yôt 'ôlām* would perhaps be attractive but nonetheless impossible to substantiate with only a corrupt text and no other apparent examples. The reconstruction of the Tetragrammaton thus appears to represent the soundest alternative until further data are brought to light.

4:11

ki bᵉśāśôn giddaltîm = ethrepsa gar autous met' euphrosynēs

The Greek verb *trephō* "nourish, raise up" is not common in the LXX. Likewise, the use of the Piel stem of *gādal* in BH to mean "raise up children" is infrequent. In two instances, Num 6:5 and Dan 1:5, the verb *trephō* is used to translate the Piel stem of *gādal*, and with precisely the abovementioned meaning in the latter case. In two other examples (Isa 23:4 and Ezek 31:4) the "sea" and "waters" are the figurative subjects of "raising up young" and in both the LXX translates the Piel stem of *gādal* with *ektrephō*, meaning essentially the same as *trephō*. And, although the LXX uses another verbal root altogether, the Hebrew of Isa 1:2 is quite significant in that God himself is here described as "raising up young," *bānîm giddaltî*.

A common pairing in BH poetry is *śāśôn wᵉśimḥāh* "joy and gladness." Both terms (among others) are on occasion rendered in the LXX by *euphrosynē* "joy, gladness," the most frequent equivalency being that with *śimḥāh*.[66]

A good case can be made for *śimḥāh*. It occurs nineteen times in MT just in the particular phrase *bᵉśimḥāh*,[67] and in all all but three of these, the LXX equivalent is *en/met' euphrosynē(s)*.[68] It is further of some significance that the related verb, *euphrainō*, is regularly used to translate the Hebrew verb *śāmaḥ*.

Nevertheless, *śāśôn* is not lacking in support. In ten biblical occurrences it is translated also by *euphrosynē* in the LXX.[69] Significantly, in those instances where the fixed, conjunctive pairing *śāśôn wᵉśimḥāh* occurs in MT, the LXX, where its text does clearly correspond to that of the Hebrew, preserves this pairing with marked consistency in its *euphrosynē kai agalliama/chara*[70] (cf. Isa 22:13; 51:3, 11; Jer 15:16; 7:34; 33:11). The correspondence of *śāśôn* with *euphrosynē* is consistent in all of these. The LXX does, however, reverse its terms for this fixed Hebrew pairing in Ps 51:8, Zech 8:19, Jer 16:9, 25:10 (cf. Ps 105:43). Only in Esth 8:16,17 does BH ever reverse the members of this pairing and here the Greek still corresponds so that *euphrosynē* is the equivalent of *śāśôn*.[71]

Further, the term occurs twice in MT in the phrase *b^e^śāśôn* (Isa 12:3, Ps 105:43), and in Isa 12:3 is translated *met' euphrosynē* in Greek. In Isa 51:11, the Hebrew text has no preposition with *śāśôn* to correspond to the Greek rendering of *met' euphrosynē*. Finally, in several instances in MT *śāśôn* is pointedly contrasted with *'ēbel*; cf. Isa 61:3, *šemen śāśôn taḥat 'ēbel*; and Jer 31:13, *'eblām l^e^śāśôn*. All things considered, the more weight appears to be with *śāśôn* (cf. 3:34, but also 4:23, 29, 36 and 5:9).

bibkî = meta klauthmou

Klauthmos "weeping, wailing" is the term regularly employed in the LXX to translate Hebrew *b^e^kî* "weeping" with only a few exceptions.[72] The equivalency of *bibkî* and *meta klauthmou* is also found in LXX in Gen 45:2, Isa 15:3 and Ps 102:10 (cf. Jer 31:9, 48:5 with *en*).

šillaḥtîm = exapesteila

The Greek verb *exapostellō* "dismiss, dispatch, send away," though in somewhat limited use among classical authors, is found in quite frequent use in the LXX, and with extreme regularity there as the equivalent for the Piel stem of Hebrew *šālaḥ*.[73]

The object of the final verb, *autous* "them," lacking in the major Greek texts (G^B, G^A, G^V), is supported in Greek by G^Q, L', some minuscules of the C' group (87, 90, 91), and others (86, 233) of the Hexaplaric tradition.[74] Although Syh is like the major Greek Uncials in lacking an object, Sy does preserve it, *'enûn*. This element must surely have been original to the Hebrew text as the awkwardness of the Greek without *autous* alone will testify.

The syllabic balance of this bicolon is noticeably weighted in favor of the second colon. It is sheer speculation without any textual support (and must remain such), but it is obvious that a much improved balance, and parallelism, would obtain if the first colon had a pairing to match that of the second (e.g., *b^e^śāśôn w^e^śimḥāh*?). This verse also affords a clear example of rhyme.

4:12

'îš 'al = mēdeis

Examples of this equivalency may be compared in: 1 Sam 21:3, *'îš 'al-yēda'*; Exod 16:19, *'îš 'al-yôtēr*; 34:3, *wᵉgam-'îš 'al-yērā'*; 1 Kgs 18:40, *'îš 'al-yimmālēṭ*; Exod 16:29; and Hos 4:4 (cf. with *lō'*, Exod 34:3, Num 17:5 = LXX 16:40, Jer 40:15 = LXX 47:15).

yiśmaḥ lî = epichairetō moi

In the context of national or personal catastrophe in biblical literature, a prominent feature of the topos is the rejoicing of enemies over one's downfall or disaster (or vice versa). In BH this is usually expressed by the verb *śāmaḥ*; cf. Mic 7:8, *'al-tiśmᵉḥî 'ōyabtî lî*; Ps 35:19, 24, *'al-yiśmᵉḥû-lî*; 38:17, *pen-yiśmᵉḥû-lî*; Obad 12, *wᵉ'al-tiśmaḥ l-*; Prov 24:17; Job 31:29; Ezek 25:6. In all these examples of what BDB labels "rejoicing arrogantly"[75] over another's misfortune, the LXX translates with the verb *epichairō* which, in classical use, has precisely this connotation of "rejoicing over someone with malignant joy" and is only very rarely used in a favorable sense.[76]

hā'almānāh = tē chēra

This represents a regular equivalency in the LXX.[77] Both LXX and Syh preserve the definite article which doubtless reflects that of the Hebrew original. The definite article in such an appositional relationship in BH conveys a relative sense similar to that of *'ᵃšer*; that is, literally, "Let no one rejoice over me (in that I am) a widow."[78] *Chēra* in classical usage has essentially the same sense as in the LXX, "bereft, abandoned" (cf. Isa 49:21; Bar 4:16, 19). For Jerusalem as a widow, cf. also Lam 1:1 (Babylon is similarly styled in Isa 47:8). Sy does not have "widow" but the related abstract, "widowhood": *l(')armᵉlûtay*, "my widowhood."[79]

wa'ᵃzûbat hārabbîm = kai kataleiphtheisē hypo pollōn

The "and" element is lacking in several of the witnesses (viz., Sy, La^S, Ar, Arm). In the case of Sy, the most important of these, this is not overly significant since its reading is on the whole substantially different from that of the LXX.

The Greek verb *kataleipō* "abandon, leave behind" slightly more frequently translates forms of Hebrew *šā'ar* "remain, be left" than of *'āzab* "abandon, forsake," and its common prefixed variant, *egkataleipō* "leave behind" (as noted at 3:12), is in the LXX the normal equivalent of *'āzab*. The Hebrew verb *šā'ar* in the Niphal stem is applied in several instances in MT to a widow or desolate woman (cf. Ruth 1:3, 5; Isa 49:21; Dan 10:8), but always appearing as a finite verb form in these contexts. As a feminine participle, this verb connotes only the primary sense of the root--"remnant, remainder (of people, land, etc.)."

Thus *'ᵃzûbāh*, a common passive participle in BH, with precisely the requisite connotation, "forsaken, abandoned, bereft," appears as the obvious Hebrew original. This conclusion is confirmed by some significant Deutero-Isaianic parallels whose contexts clearly feature Jerusalem personified as a widowed mother: Isa 60:15, *hᵉyôtēk 'ᵃzûbāh* (LXX, *egkataleipō*; cf. above and 3:12); 54:6, *kᵉ'iššāh 'ᵃzûbāh* (LXX, *kataleipō*); and 62:4, *lō'-yē'āmēr lāk 'ôd 'ᵃzûbāh* (LXX, *kataleipō*). Further, both Sy and Syh employ the verb *šᵉbaq* (Ethpeel, "be deserted, left alone"), the usual Syriac equivalent for Hebrew *'āzab*.

The equivalency in the LXX between *polys* "many" and Hebrew *rab* "many, much" is very common and regular.[80] The phrase *'ᵃzûbat (hā)rabbîm*, as applied to a desolated Jerusalem, obviously means a city "forsaken of its populace." The manifestly interpretative reading of Sy, *waṣdît men 'ammā' saggî'ā'*, "and left desolate by many people," thus seeks to make this clear. On one level the Hebrew could easily be understood as "forsaken of many." This is how it was interpreted by the LXX (*pollōn*) and the Vulgate (*multis*) and this is satisfactory. But there is an additional factor in the semantic history of the term *rabbîm* that cannot be overlooked. That is that in late Hebrew it came into use as a technical term for "community" or "public" or the like, so that by the time that the Qumran community was producing its literature this usage was in full flower. In the *Damascus Document* (CD) 13:7 and 14:7, 12, *hārabbîm* "the Many" refers to the main body of the people, the *hoi pleiones* in contrast to the more select elders. The term appears profusely in the *Manual of Discipline* (1QS) and there clearly appears to be the *terminus technicus* for the community membership.[81] The roots of this usage are probably traceable back to biblical passages Dan 12:3, 11:33, 9:27, and Esth 4:3 where the *rabbîm* appear to be distinguished as the main body of the people as opposed to the Hellenizers.[82]

n^e šammôtî = ērēmōthēn

The Greek verb *erēmoō* "lay waste, make solitary, bereave of" is used for Hebrew *šāmam* "be desolate, solitary, depopulated" about twice as often as for *ḥārab* "be devastated, destroyed."[83] That the former equivalency obtains here is demonstrated by such passages as Isa 54:3, *w^e ʿārîm n^e šammôt* (in the very context of the central source, Isa 54:1-6, in which Jerusalem appears prominently as the bereft mother), Jer 33:10, *ûb^e ḥuṣôt ye rûšālayim hanšammôt* (again dealing with a desolate Jerusalem), Isa 33:8, Ezek 29:12, 32:15, Ps 69:25, Lev 26:22.[84]

The metre of this tricolon is difficult. As it stands, the first colon is only half as long as the other two. As mentioned, Kahana[85] has suggested a substantial, and unsupported, restoration to ease the difficulty. Another possibility is that the text of Sy may preserve a better reading. The major difference between it and the LXX text is its reading of the abstract noun *'almānûtî* "my widowhood" as the object of the verb in the first colon, coupled with the finite verb form for *ʿāzab* in the second colon. This would yield the following tricolon from Sy (3+3+2):

(12a) *'îš 'al-yiśmaḥ l^e 'almānûtî*
Let no one rejoice over my widowhood,

(12b) *ʿuzzabtî ûn^e šammôtî mērabbîm*
That I am forsaken and left desolate by many,

(12c) *'al-ḥaṭṭō't bānay*
Because of the sins of my children.

4:12d-13a

ya'an = dioti

Cf. 1 Kgs 21:20 with a similar context of rejecting God's way. The problem of determining equivalencies among these causal particles is an extremely complicated one and has been discussed above at 4:6.[86] This particular verse does seem to show dependence upon Job 34:27, however, particularly upon the Greek version which features a substantial change from the text of the MT. It could then perhaps be argued from this that the causal construction here would likely have been *'ᵃšer 'al-kēn* as in Job 34:27 (where the LXX has *hoti*), but such is not at all certain (nor metrically likely). Most probable would appear to be *ya'an*, or perhaps *kî*.

mittôrat-'ᵉlōhîm sārû = exeklinan ek nomou theou

Job 34:27 in the MT reads: *'ᵃšer 'al-kēn sārû mē'aḥᵃrāyw / wᵉkol-dᵉrākāyw lō' hiśkîlû*. The Syriac of Job 34:27 follows this quite closely: "Because they turned aside from (following) after him / and all his ways they did not consider." But the LXX diverges: *hoti exeklinan ek nomou theou, dikaiōmata de autou ouk epegnōsan*, "Because they turned aside from the law of God, and did not consider his ordinances." The LXX thus appears to be following a text tradition quite other than that preserved in MT Job.

Such a situation, however, is not surprising for the LXX Job whose production has long been viewed with unanimity by scholars as an exercise in translational liberty and free paraphrase, and whose text itself in its present state appears to be a composite of the earliest paraphrastic version (with about one-sixth of MT Job omitted) and the later one of Theodotian.[87] If there was a variant Hebrew text tradition for Job in addition to that reflected by MT, its origins are indeed obscure. The Qumran findings have shown, however, that such is at least not impossible.[88] It is nevertheless more likely that the tradition reflected in the LXX is secondary and interpretative (i.e., "his way" is the "law of God"). But be that as it may, the LXX of Job 34:27 is almost verbatim the equivalent of this Baruch passage.[89]

The verb *sûr* "swerve, turn aside, rebel," at least, seems to be certain from its use in MT and especially from a parallel in CD 16:9, *lswr m[n htw]rh*, "to swerve fr[om the l]aw." Cf. also 1QS 1:15 and the concept of swerving from the "way" or "path" in CD 1:13, 5; 8:4, 16; Exod 32:8; Deut 9:12; and Judg 2:17.[90] For the equivalence of *sûr* and *ekklinō* in the LXX, cf. also Mal 3:7, *sartem meḥuqqay wᵉlōʼ šᵉmartem = exeklinate nomima mou* . . . ; 1 Sam 12:20; Deut 17:11; Josh 23:6; et al.[91]

With regard to the source-text, Job 34:27, the LXX rendition is consistent throughout the bicolon with its legal imagery --swerving from the "law" and disregarding the "ordinances"-- whereas the Hebrew of that same passage expresses disobedience through the pedestrian imagery of straying from "following after" God and disregarding his "ways." The Sy text for Job 34:27 (i.e., the Peshiṭta) closely follows MT, but for the derived Baruch passage, Sy here presents a curious mixture of both sorts of imagery: *meṭul dasṭaw men ʼûrᵉḥeh dᵉmāryāʼ ʼallāhāʼ / wᵉpuqdānaw(h)y wᵉdînaw(h)y lāʼ ʼîdʻaw*, "because they swerved from his paths[, those of the Lord God],[92] / and did not consider his statutes and judgments." The pairing "statutes and judgments" doubtless represents a conflation of variants.

The Syriac of our Baruch passage thus suggests the possibility that the parallelism in the Hebrew of Job 34:27 may well have originally been between *ʼrḥw* (or *ʼrḥtyw*) and *drkyw*, "path(s) and ways" (cf. MT, *ʼḥryw*), subsequently being obscured by metathesis in the first member perhaps under the influence of the common cliché, *mēʼaḥᵃrê*.[93] The Sy text of Bar 4:12d-13a, at any rate, has the earmarks of an eclectic, committee-like resolving of the textual dilemma by a translator(s?) who had before him two quite different versions of this same verse, one in Hebrew with the imagery of paths and ways, and the other the Greek with its divergent imagery of law and ordinances.

It is noteworthy, however, that in Baruch the following bicolon, verse 13b-c, features the same path and way imagery, suggesting that for Bar 4:12d-13a the LXX arrangement of parallel legal terms more probably represents the original Hebrew structure. The borrowing thus seems clearly to have been from the LXX tradition of Job 34:27 (or perhaps from a comparably phrased Targumic version?),[94] even though that does not accurately represent, and is doubtless secondary to, the MT reading in the Job source. Since the textual authority for Bar 4:12d-13a favors the reading of the LXX, it is best to follow on this more certain ground.

ûmišpāṭāyw lō'-yādā'û = kai dikaiōmata autou ouk egnōsan

The equivalence of *yāda'* and *gi(g)nōskō* is extremely regular in the LXX. Six examples have already been encountered in the Wisdom poem of Baruch (3:9, 14, 20, 23, 31, 32).[95] In both the Greek and Hebrew, the verb here then has the connotation "regard, take note of, observe."[96] That "to have regard for" the statutes here has the sense of "to observe" the statutes is confirmed in Greek by the interpretative G^A variant (followed by Ar), *ephylaxan*, from the verb *phylassō* "keep, observe (a law)." *Phylassō* (= Hebrew, *šāmar*) is the more usual verb in this idiom; cf., e.g., Deut 6:2, *lišmōr 'et-kol-ḥuqqōtāyw*.

Dikaiōma most commonly translates *ḥōq/ḥuqqāh* and *mišpāṭ* in the LXX, the former more frequently by a ratio of almost 2:1.[97] The use of such a verb of "knowing" or "perceiving" or "observing" is unusual with *ḥuqqôt* or *mišpāṭîm*. Rather, both "statutes" and "judgments" (as well as their other common synonyms, "laws," "commandments," and "testimonies") are usually: (1) "pronounced" (*dābar*), (2) "made/done" (*'āśāh*), (3) "heard" (*šāma'*), (4) "kept" (*šāmar*), (5) "commanded" (*ṣiwwāh*), (6) "walked in" (*hālak*), or (7) "given" (*nātan*). The Hebrew of Job 34:27 uses the verb *śākal* for "perceiving his ways," but there is no precedent in the entire LXX for the translation of that verb by *gi(g)nōskō*. The original Hebrew verb must surely have been *yāda'*, for not only is it the normal equivalent for *gi(g)nōskō* but also it is supported by Sy. Whereas the Peshiṭta reading in Job 34:27 is *s^ekal*, here in Bar 4:13a Sy has *y^eda'*.

Nevertheless, there are few parallels for such use of *yāda'* with these legal terms. The closest parallels are those of CD 9:15, *ky l' yd' mwṣ'yh 't mšpṭh*, "For the one who found it does not know the rules regarding it"; CD 15:10, *w'l ywdy'hw 'yš 't hmšpṭym*, "let no man let him know the rulings";[98] and Ezek 20:11, *wa'ettēn lāhem 'et-ḥuqqôtay w^e'et-mišpāṭay hôda'tî 'ōtām = kai edōka autois ta prostagmata mou, kai ta dikaiōmata mou egnōrisa autois.*[99]

With the verb *śākal*, one might compare the sense of Neh 8:13, *ûl^{e}haśkîl 'el-dibrê hattôrāh*, Dan 9:13 and Job 34:27. The sense of this Baruch passage as a whole is well paralleled by Amos 2:4b, *'al-mo'^{o}sām 'et-tôrat YHWH w^{e}ḥuqqāyw lō' šāmārû* (cf. also the sense of Ps 89:31).

An approach from the point of view of parallelism is not especially helpful. *Tôrāh* in BH poetry appears as an A-word to the B-word, *ḥōq/ḥuqqāh*, in three instances: Amos 2:4, Isa 24:5, and Mal 3:22; but the reverse order prevails in one instance: Ps 105:45. Similarly, *tôrah* is the A-word to the B-word, *mišpāṭ*, four times: Isa 51:4, Hab 1:4, Ps 89:1, and Mal 3:22; but the reverse sequence is found twice: Deut 33:10 and Isa 42:4. Thus there is no consistent pattern perceivable here to help to confirm one or the other of the B-word alternatives for this passage, *ḥuqqāh* or *mišpāṭ*. Sy is reflective of this same dilemma with its conflate reading of *puqdānā'* and *dînā'*. The former agrees with *ḥuqqāh* and the latter with *mišpāṭ* (Syh has *puqdānā'*).[100]

Thus, in the light of the BH and Qumran parallels cited, and against the attested ratio of translation frequency for *ḥōq/ḥuqqāh* in the LXX, *mišpāṭ* has been reconstructed here. Needless to say, the alternative may have equal claim to originality.

<u>4:13</u>

b^{e}darkê miṣwôt '^{e}lōhîm lō' hāl^{e}kû = oude eporeuthēsan hodois entolōn theou

The LXX translational equivalencies for this colon are all of exceptional regularity: *poreuomai = hālak* (= Sy, *h^{e}lak*);[101] *entolē = miṣwāh* (= Sy, *puqdānā'*);[102] and *hodos = derek* (= Sy, *'ûr^{e}ḥā'*).[103] The closest BH parallels are: Ps 119:32, *derek-miṣwôtèkā 'ārûṣ*; 2 Chr 17:6, *hālak b^{e}darkê YHWH*; 2 Sam 22:22; Ps 138:5; 2 Kgs 21:22; Ps 119:14, 35; cf. also Bar 3:13, *hālaktā b^{e}derek '^{e}lōhîm*.

ûnᵉtîbôt mûsar ṣidqātô lō' dārākû = oude tribous paideias en dikaiosynē autou epebēsan

This is now the fourth occurrence of the equivalency between *tribos* and *nᵉtîbāh* in the Baruch poetry. *Nᵉtîbôt/tribous* has previously appeared as the B-word to *derek/hodos* in Bar 3:21, 23, 31, and now appears in the same configuration here. *Nᵉtîbāh* was still in common use at Qumran (though in MH it gave way to *šᵉbîl*), and indeed the expression *ntybwt ṣdq(h)* appears in both CD 1:16 and 1QH 7:14.[104]

Paideia is in the LXX the regular equivalent of *mûsār*, an important term in Wisdom literature meaning "discipline, instruction, correction," or the like. There is no BH parallel for "paths of instruction" or "instruction of righteousness" or, for that matter, "paths of the instruction of his righteousness."[105] For the idea of "instruction *in* righteousness," cf. 2 Tim 3:16, *pros paideian tēn en dikaiosynē*. The regular LXX correspondent for *ṣᵉdāqāh/ṣedeq* is *dikaiosynē*.[106]

There is slight textual evidence for combining *autou* with *paideias* (LXX Minuscule 26 of the G^Q group, and $La^{S,V}$). Kneucker[107] thus contends that this would better correspond to proper Hebrew usage if the phrase were *ûnᵉtîbôt mûsārô biṣdāqāh lō' dārākû*, "and the paths of *his* instruction they did not tread in righteousness," rather than "and they did not tread the paths of instruction in his righteousness." Sy omits *autou*, reading (with an apparent conflation of *dikaiosynē* and *alētheia* lying behind it): "They did not even tread the paths of the instruction of truth [i.e., "true instruction"][108] in righteousness." G^V omits the phrase *en dikaiosynē* altogether.

Nevertheless, from the point of view of Hebrew parallelism a solution is apparent. The problem is really the *en* which, though present in all the LXX witnesses and both Sy and Syh (*b*-), appears actually to be only a product of the LXX translator's style. By means of this preposition he apparently sought to smooth out what was for him an awkwardness in the Hebrew. The precise structuring of the individual cola so that each unit of the first corresponds exactly to a counterpart in the second, which arrangement is quite transparent when the Hebrew is reconstructed, makes it clear that the original construction was most probably a construct chain of three members[109] that precisely paralleled that of the first colon. Cf. the following literal translation of the two Hebrew cola:

In the ways	And the paths
of the commandments	of the instruction
of God	of his righteousness
they did not walk,	they did not tread.

There is hardly sufficient textual support for placing the suffix "his" after *mûsār* instead of *ṣ*^{e}*dāqāh* to be able to contend that *mûsārô* was the original reading and that the LXX translator in effect shifted the suffixal element. Rather, it is much easier to contend that the suffix was indeed originally after *ṣ*^{e}*dāqāh*, with the vast majority of the witnesses, but that the LXX translator, through some influence or inadvertency, missed the precision of this parallelism and inserted *en*.[110]

The Greek verb *epibainō* "tread on, mount on" which most commonly translates Hebrew *rākab* "mount" in the LXX, is also frequently used there to render *dārak* in the sense of "tread" or even "enter (e.g., a path)."[111] *Dārak* appears elsewhere as the B-word for *hālak* in Isa 42:16.

4:14

bō'û = elthatōsan

The equivalency between *erchomai* and *bô'*, both meaning "come, go," is extremely regular in the LXX.[112]

š^{e}*kēnê ṣiyyôn = hai paroikoi Siōn*

This has been discussed above at verse 9.

zikrû = mnēsthēte

Mimnēskō "call to mind, remember" in the LXX is with very few exceptions the regular equivalent for Hebrew *zākar* "remember."[113]

The rest of this verse is the same as in verse 10 above. The major problem here is the apparent imbalance of the three cola, the first being markedly shorter. Sensing this deficiency, Kahana[114] has offered a totally unsupported restoration, [*yōš*ᵉ*bôt s*ᵉ*bîbôtèhā*], apparently suggested by the parallelism of Ps 79:4 (= 44:14), *liškēnênû* (A) // *lisbîbôtênû* (B). Such would yield a 3+2 metre and a balanced parallelism for the first part of the verse and leave the remainder as a 4+4 bicolon. However, such a measure has no textual support; there is no trace of such a major haplography.

The Sy reading, *'a(n)tūn* "ye (neighbors of Zion)," is probably best explained as the result of an intra-Syriac corruption from *t*ᵉ*wūn* "come ye!"[115] But there is at the very beginning of this verse in Sy a phrase, *'ā(w)'eṯṯ*ᵉ*pîsw* "Oh be persuaded!" This is, however, marked as a gloss by Lagarde.[116] The verb is a denominative from *pîs* "persuasion" which here in the Ethpeel stem means "be persuaded, consent, make up one's mind," or something similar. Thus the imperative could be rendered: "make (ye) up your minds (and come)!" This is approximately the equivalent of the reflexive Hithpolel stem of *bîn* "discern" in Hebrew; for example, as in Jer 9:16, *hitbôn*ᵉ*nû w*ᵉ*qir'û*, "consider in your own mind and call!"[117]

Speculatively, then, reconstruction of the first colon along these lines would yield: *hitbôn*ᵉ*nû (w*ᵉ*)bô'û š*ᵉ*kēnê ṣiyyôn*. This, when joined to the remaining cola, would result in a well-balanced 4+4+4 tricolon. Satisfying as this may appear, it rests unfortunately on very insecure textual grounds. It may nevertheless represent the best of a poor set of alternatives for reconstructing this verse.

One other possibility, also not satisfying in that it runs counter to the indicated divisions of both the Greek and Syriac texts, is a reconstruction which ignores such divisions and includes "remember" with the first colon:

> *bô'û š*ᵉ*kēnê ṣiyyôn w*ᵉ*zikrû*
> *š*ᵉ*bî bānay ûb*ᵉ*nôtay*
> *'ᵃšer hēbî' 'ᵃlêhem YHWH*,

metrically 4+3+4.

Thus this verse ultimately remains deficient and problematic. As it stands from the Greek, it is textually satisfactory but weak metrically:

bô'û š^e^kēnê ṣiyyôn
zikrû š^e^bî bānay ûb^e^nôtay
'^a^šer hēbî' '^a^lōhem YHWH,

a 3+4+4 tricolon (syllabically, 7/9/10). The tentative restoration from Sy, on the contrary, is metrically sound but textually uncertain. Thus the reading of *hitbôn^e^nû* in the reconstructed text is manifestly offered as a very tentative possibility.

4:15

This verse is borrowed, almost verbatim, from Deut 28:49-50.

kî nāšā' '^a^lêhem gôy mērāḥôq = epēgage gar ep' autous ethnos makrothen

This may be compared to the beginning of Deut 28:49, *yiššā' YHWH 'ālèkā gôy mērāḥôq*. The Greek verb *epagō* "bring upon, let loose," which elsewhere in Baruch (4:9, 10, 18, 27, 29) appears in its normal equivalency with *bô'* (Hiph),[118] is here shown most certainly to have been the equivalent of *nāšā'*. Likewise, *ethnos*, which appeared for *'am* in Bar 3:16, 4:3, and for *gôy* in 4:6, is here seen to have been representing *gôy*.[119]

gôy 'az-pānîm = ethnos anaides

Again, cf. Deut 28:50, where *gôy 'az-pānîm* is translated even more literally by the Greek, *ethnos anaides prosōpō*, "a nation, bold of countenance" (i.e., "an insolent nation"). Further parallels may be compared in Dan 8:23, *melek 'az-pānîm = basileus anaides prosōpō*, Eccl 8:1, Prov 7:13, and Isa 25:3.

'imqê šāpāh = alloglōsson

This term does not appear in the LXX of the source-text, Deut 28:49-50, but it does appear to be the functional equivalent of the Hebrew there, *'^a^šer lō' tišma' l^e^šōnô*, "whose speech is unintelligible." *Alloglōssos* "of foreign tongue" is extremely rare in the LXX, appearing only here and in Ezek 3:6 where it glosses *allophōnos* (itself a hapax legomenon in the LXX!) as the equivalent of the Hebrew idiom, *'imqê šāpāh* "thick-lipped" (i.e., "unintelligible of speech"). This same Hebrew idiom also appears in a passage the context of which is very similar to that of Bar 4:15 and Deut 28:49-50, namely, Isa 33:19, *'am 'imqê śāpāh miššᵉmôaʿ nilʿag lāšôn 'ên bînāh*, "a people too thick-lipped [unintelligible] to understand, too stammering of tongue [barbarous of speech] to comprehend." Here the idiom *'imqê śāpāh* is rendered in the LXX by *bathyphōnos*, literally, "deep of speech" (i.e., "beyond comprehension"). The parallel expression, *nilʿag lāšôn*, was misunderstood by the LXX translator, but that *bathyphōnos* is the equivalent of *'imqê śāpāh* is certain from the correspondence between the two initial elements signifying "deep," *bathy-* and *'ēmeq*.

What has apparently happened is that our author, in search of a more poetic or idiomatic alternative to what he had in the Deuteronomy 28 passage, selected the expression "thick-lipped," familiar as it no doubt was from the foreign-menace topos. Kahana[120] has restored the other roughly synonymous phrase from Isa 33:19 (which occurs only there in MT), *nilʿag lāšôn*, apparently only *ad sensum*. But this expression has no textual association with the LXX, *alloglōssos*, as does the other. Thus in effect the author of Baruch has in this one part of Deut 28:49 paraphrased the Hebrew before him with the shorter, more workable, *'imqê śāpāh*.[121]

pᵉnê zāqēn lō' nāśā'û = hoi ouk ēschynthēsan presbytēn

This Hebrew idiom, *nāśā' pānîm* "lift the face," has the sense in BH of "show respect to" or "be considerate of."[122] From this is derived the related social status designation *nᵉśū' pānîm* "the distinguished."[123] These idioms no doubt arose from some sort of symbolic action of lifting the faces of those prostrate in humility along with the granting of a boon or royal favor, and thence became idiomatic. The *pānîm lᵉzāqēn* of Deut 28:50 is really only periphrastic for *pᵉnê zāqēn*.[124] The latter has been reconstructed here but the former cannot be ruled out altogether. Job 32:21 and 34:19 are the only other passages where the LXX uses *aischynō* "feel shame before" (i.e., "respect") to render this idiom.[125] That it does so here also seems certain from the Deut 28:50 source.

w^{e}na'ar lō' ḥānānû = oude paidion ēleēsan

This too has been adopted directly from Deut 28:50, with only minor adjustment of the verb. Cf. Lam 4:16, *p^{e}nê kōh^{a}nîm lō' nāśā'û / z^{e}qēnîm lō' ḥānānû*, for the same verbs in parallel.

Kneucker[126] has observed that in Deut 28:49-50 the subject corresponding to Baruch's *ho aiōnios* is *YHWH*. This fact would appear to be a significant confirmation of this assumed equivalence in the poem at hand. The *hoi* of the LXX at the beginning of verse 15c need be no more than the effect of Greek style, as assumed in the above restoration, but the variant *hoti*, of $G^{B,Q,V}$, et al.,[127] strongly suggests the possibility of the presence of *'^{a}šer* in the original Hebrew, as in the Deut 28:50 source.

<u>4:16</u>

w^{e}hôlîkû = kai apēgagon

The Greek verb *apagō* has the meaning "carry off" or "lead away." A number of Hebrew synonyms come to mind as potential correspondents. One is *gālāh* "remove, carry off (into exile)," but it is translated only once in the LXX by *apagō* (as a Hophal participle in Jer 40[47]:1).[128] Further, *gālāh* is regularly translated in the LXX by another Greek verb, *apoikizō* "emigrate, transplant, colonize."[129] In several instances, *apagō* translates Hebrew *nāhag* (Qal and Piel) "drive (off), lead (away)" with the particular connotation "lead captive." For example, cf. Gen 31:26, *kai apēgages tas thygateras mou hōs aichmalōtidas machaira;* = *watt^{e}nahēg 'et-b^{e}nōtay kišbûyôt ḥāreb*, "and [why] have you led away my daughters as captives (taken) with the sword?" Cf. similarly, Deut 28:37. A phrase in Lam 3:2, *'ôtî nāhag wayyōlak*, reveals, however, a different pattern of equivalency; *nāhag* is there rendered by *paralambanō*[130] and *hālak* (Hiph) by *apagō*. It is indeed this latter equivalency with the Hiphil stem of *hālak* that proves to be the most common for *apagō*.[131] In addition to Lam 3:2, other examples may be adduced: Deut 28:36, *yôlēk YHWH 'ōt^{e}kā*; 1 Kgs 1:38, *wayyōlîkû 'ōtô 'al-giḥôn*; 2 Kgs 6:19, *w^{e}'ôlîkāh 'etkem* and *wayyōlek 'ôtām*; 2 Kgs 17:27, *hôlîkû šāmmāh*; 24:15, *hôlîk gôlāh* (// *wayyegel*); and 2 Chr 36:6, *l^{e}hôlîkô bābelāh* (// *hēbî'*).[132]

'et-y^e^dîdê hā'almānāh = tous agapētous tēs chēras

This phrase, "the beloved sons [// *thygaterōn*] of the widow," appears to be unique to Baruch. Kahana[133] has reconstructed *'^a^hûbê* (Qal passive participle, plural) for the Greek verbal adjective *agapētous*. This is despite the fact that only once in the LXX is *agapētos* "beloved" ever employed to translate a form of the verb *'āhab* "love," in Zech 13:6, where it represents the Piel active participle, *m^e^'ahēb*.[134] This equivalency in Zech 13:6 appears to be an abnormality resulting from the LXX's mistranslation of the Hebrew.[135] There are fifteen occurrences of *agapētos* in the LXX and fifteen occurrences of the Piel active participle of *'āhab* in MT, and this is the only example of such convergence. Further, the connotations of the Piel active participle "friends, lovers" often carry overtones of carnality and are thus to a large extent incongruous with the sense of the passive Greek term "beloved."

Of the five occurrences of the Qal passive participle of *'āhab* in MT, four are feminine forms.[136] The only one that is masculine and therefore apropos is that in Neh 13:26, designating Solomon as "beloved of God," *'āhûb lē'lōhāyw*. This sense would be generally adequate for Bar 4:16, but there is no real support from parallels or from LXX equivalencies.

The term *yādîd* "beloved" is likewise not a common lexical item in BH, but within its limited frequency it is the equivalent of the Greek verbal adjective, *agapētos*, five times (Ps 45:1, 60:7, 84:2, 108:7, 127:2) and of the like-meaning passive participle of *agapaō*, *ēgapēmenos*, four times in Deut 33:12, Isa 5:1, Jer 11:15, and once in Baruch (3:36).[137] Further, both Sy and Syh offer *ḥabîb* "beloved," the usual Syriac equivalent for *yādîd*.[138]

The term for "widow," *chēra*, always represents Hebrew *'almānāh*,[139] except in one instance, Isa 49:21, where it renders the rare BH word *galmûdāh* "barren" (in MH, "lonely"). Both Sy and Syh have the cognate, *'armaltā'*.

w^e^'et-hayy^e^ḥîdāh = tēn monēn

In the LXX, *monos* "alone, only" quite frequently serves to render the common Hebrew adverbial *l^e^bad* (or *bādād*), where it has the comparable sense of "alone, only." Here it is clearly substantival as the direct object of the verb, literally "the alone one, the solitary one." In combination with a genitive (or as here with a prepositional phrase), *monos* can have the connotation "bereft" or "deprived."[140] The Hebrew equivalent must thus be something else.

The Sy equivalent, *îḥîdūtā'* "the lonely (woman), the solitary (woman),"[141] suggests the cognate BH substantive, *yāḥîd/ yᵉḥîdāh* "lone, solitary," as a distinct possibility. This term appears only twelve times in MT. In at least nine of these occurrences the connotation is specifically that of "only child."[142] This familial nuance is so strong that in half the examples the LXX translates the term with *agapētos* "beloved" (Jer 6:26; Amos 8:10; Zech 12:10; Gen 22:2, 12, 16) and in one other (Prov 4:3) with *agapōmenos* "beloved." In the remaining five instances the translation is made four times with *monogenēs* "only child, only-begotten" (Ps 25:16, 22:21, 35:17, Judg 11:34) and once with *monotropos* "solitary" (Ps 68:7).[143] In both Ps 22:21 and 35:17 where the feminine form *yᵉḥîdāh* appears in BH, the Syriac equivalent is *îḥîdūtā'*, as in the Sy text of Bar 4:16. Further, the Hebrew adverb from this same root, *yaḥad*, is translated twice in the LXX by the phrase *kata monas* (Ps 33:15, 141:10).

Another possibility, proposed by Kahana,[144] is that of *galmûdāh*, a very rare word in BH that seems basically to mean "barren." It appears three times in Job, figuratively applied to the night of his birth (3:7), hypocrites (15:34), and friends (30:3), with the sense of "barren" or "unproductive." The only other occurrence is in Isa 49:21, where it more aptly figures Zion as a bereaved and barren woman, *wa'ᵃnî šᵉkûlāh wᵉgalmûdāh* = *egō de ateknos kai chēra*. This is, as noted above, the only instance of *chēra* being used in the LXX for anything other than *'almānāh*.

In MH this term came to mean, quite exclusively, "lonely, solitary."[145] The term is not as yet attested in the Qumran literature. Intriguing as this proposal may be, it nevertheless has no textual associations with the Greek term *monos* or its combined forms, as does the alternative, *yᵉḥîdāh*.

heḥ^e^rîbû mibbānôt = apo tōn thygaterōn . . . ērēmōsan

In the active voice, the Greek verb *eremoō* has the meaning "leave bereft, desolate, desert." It has already been encountered at Bar 4:12 above, where it was seen to represent Hebrew *šāmēm*. This Hebrew verb, in the Hiphil stem, exhibits a similar range of meaning, "desolate, devastate, wipe out." As noted above, this is the most common equivalency for *eremoō*, but it is also used with some frequency for Hebrew *ḥārēb* "lay waste, desolate, depopulate."[146]

Šāmēm, as previously noted, frequently appears in the imagery of devastated cities and lands. Thus in Bar 4:12 the Greek aorist passive form was found to be representing Hebrew *n^e^šammôtî* "I am destitute" in the personified Jerusalem's self-description. Similarly, in Isa 54:1, again with reference to Jerusalem, there is found the phrase *b^e^nê šômēmāh = ta tekna tēs erēmou.*[147]

There is, however, considerable support in this case for *ḥārēb*. This verb is also applied to devastated cities and lands. Cf., for example, Jer 26:9, *w^e^hā'îr hazzō't teḥ^e^rab mē'ēn yôšēb = kai hē polis hautē erēmōthēsetai apo katoikountōn* (of Jerusalem); and (where the LXX equivalent is not *eremoō* but the slightly stronger *exeremoō* "utterly devastate") Zeph 3:6, *heḥ^e^rabtî ḥûṣôtām = exerēmōsō tas hodous autōn*; and Ezek 19:7, *w^e^'ārêhem heḥ^e^rîb wattēšam 'ereṣ = kai tas poleis autōn exērēmōse, kai ēphanise gen.*[148] It is also noteworthy that the Hebrew noun *ḥorbāh* "desolate place" is applied to Jerusalem in her devastated condition in Isa 52:9 (LXX, *erēma*) and Dan 9:2 (LXX, *erēmōseōs*),[149] as is the adjective *ḥārēb* (LXX, *erēmos*) in Jer 33:10.

Sy here has the cognate *ḥ^e^reb* in the Aphel stem, as it does also in Zeph 3:6, Ezek 19:7, and Judg 16:24.[150] Thus, while the evidence is not decisive between the two possibilities, a reconstruction of the Hiphil stem of *ḥārēb* seems in the light of the above the more likely.

The Greek preposition *apo* "from" commonly translates Hebrew *min* (as, for example, in Gen 4:3, 4) and that equivalency underlies the above reconstruction (cf. also Syh, *men b^e^nātā'*). But in the light of such passages as Jer 26:9, 33:10, and Zeph

3:6, *mē'ēn* or *mibbᵉlî* could perhaps be considered. "Daughters" is suffixed in Sy; in all the other witnesses it is indeterminate.[151]

4:17

The "mother," Jerusalem, now addresses comfort to her "children," and the rhetorical question with which she begins is one that implies a negative answer (a familiar literary device in BH): "But I, how shall I be able to help you?" That this is the case is confirmed by the reading of Sy which presents not a question but a declaration: "As for me, I am not able to help you."[152] The form of the rhetorical question is without doubt the original form, and the reading of Sy a secondary development from it, as is witnessed by the other Versions; cf. LXX, *ego de ti dynatē boēthēsai hymin*; Syh, *'enā' den mānā' maṣyā' (')nā' lam'addārū lᵉkūn*; and La^{V}, *ego autem quid possum adjuvare vos.*

wa'ᵃnî = egō de

This equivalency is exemplified, for example, in Ps 2:6.

māh = ti

For this equivalency, cf. Eccl 8:4, *ti poieis = mah-ta'ᵃśeh*; Job 31:2, *kai ti = ûmāh*; 2 Kgs 4:2, *ti . . . ti = māh . . . māh*; Deut 10:12, *ti = māh*; and Judg 8:3, *kai ti edynēthēn poiēsai = ûmah-yyākōltî 'ᵃśôt*. The last citation is particularly enlightening for the equivalency between the verbs, *dynamai* and *yākōl*.

'ûkal = dynatē (G^{A}, *dynamai*)[153]

The LXX manuscript authorities are here in disagreement between the adjectival construction with *dynatos* and the verbal one with *dynamai*, both of which appear commonly in the LXX with a following infinitive to convey the sense of "being able to (do something)." Both constructions are, however, employed to translate the same Hebrew construction--*yākōl* + infinitive.

For the Greek construction with the adjective, *dynatos*, + infinitive, cf. Num 22:38, *dynatos esomai lalēsai ti*; = *hᵃyākōl 'ûkal dabbēr mᵉ'ûmāh*, and Dan 3:17, *dynatos exelesthai hēmas = yākil lᵉšêzābûtānā'* (Aram).[154] For the verbal construction with *dynamai* + infinitive, cf. Num 13:31, *hoti ou mē dynōmetha anabēnai = lō' nûkal laʻᵃlôt*; Sir 34(31):10, *tis edynato parabēnai = my ywkl lswr*; Eccl 8:17, *ou dynēsetai tou eurein = lō' yûkal limṣā'*; and Judg 8:3 (cited above).[155]

lᵉʻozrᵉkem = boēthēsai hymin

The Greek verb *boētheō* "aid, help, come to the rescue" is most frequently used in the LXX to represent Hebrew *ʻāzar* "help, succor" (at least forty-one times).[156] It also translates a number of other Hebrew verbs, the most frequent of which (six times) is *yāšaʻ* (Hiph). This latter verb, very common in BH, is regularly translated in the LXX by *sōzō* "save."[157] Both Sy and Syh employ forms of the verb *ʻᵉdar* "help," cognate to Hebrew *ʻāzar*. Examples of this equivalency, *laʻᵃzōr = boēthēsai*, may be compared in 2 Chr 28:16, Jer 37:7, Dan 10:13, and 2 Sam 8:5.[158]

It seems possible from the brevity of verse 17 and its amenability to a ready parallel[159] that this verse as presently preserved could constitute the first half of a bicolon, the parallel half to which would have to be assumed lost. But with no versional traces of such an assumed lost colon, any attempt at restoration could only be a guess.[160] It is perhaps more plausible that verse 17 actually constitutes the first colon of a tricolon that is completed by verse 18. The latter verse, after all, provides the answer to the rhetorical question posed in verse 17.

Curiously, the above reconstruction of verse 17 approximates very closely, almost verbatim, the reading of Syh for this verse[161] since the Syriac verb *mᵉṣā'* "find, be able," while cognate to Hebrew *māṣā'* "find," nevertheless functions also as the semantic equivalent of Hebrew *yākōl* "be able, capable."

4:18

kî = gar

This equivalency is certainly not uncommon and it is found regularly throughout Baruch. Attention is called to it here only because Kahana[162] has chosen not to reconstruct *kî*. The reading of *gar*, however, has complete textual support in the Versions (cf., e.g., *ger* in both Sy and Syh, and *enim*, the precise Latin equivalent for Greek *gar*, in La^{V}).

hammēbî' = *ho epagagōn*

This is the common and usual equivalence of *epagō* and *bô'* (Hiph) as found elsewhere in Bar 4:9, 10, 27, 29.

'ᵃlêkem = *'alaykûn* (Sy) = [*hymin*] (LXX)

The presence of this element in the LXX text is a matter of judgment. It is included in the Rahlfs Edition,[163] but not in the more recent Göttingen Edition.[164] *Hymin* is not found in G^{B}, 106', O, Syh, La^{C,L}, Bo, Arm. It is found in G^{A} and L' after *ta kaka*; the remainder of the witnesses, most significantly Sy (*'alaykūn bîšātā'*) and La^{V} (*super vos mala*), offer the equivalent of *hymin ta kaka* as in Bar 4:29. The notation, + *'alaykūn (hymin)*, is also recorded between *obeloi* in the margin of Syh.

Thus the versional witness for the authenticity of "upon you" is both of ample quantity and distribution and of significance in quality, even though it is not attested in the Codex Vaticanus. It is also apparent from the following parallels that this element is regular in such constructions; cf. Jer 32:42, *hēbî'tî 'el-hā'ām hazzeh 'ēt kol-hārā'āh haggᵉdôlāh hazzō't kēn 'ᵃnōkî mēbî' 'ᵃlêhem* = *epēgagon epi ton laon touton panta ta kaka ta megala tauta, houtōs egō epaxō ep' autous*; 1 Kgs 9:9, *'al-kēn hēbî' YHWH 'ᵃlêhem 'ēt kol-hārā'āh hazzō't* = *dia touto epēgage Kyrios ep' autous tēn kakian tautēn*; and Job 42:11, *kol-hārā'āh 'ᵃšer-hēbî' YHWH 'ālāyw* = *pasin hois epēgagen ep' autō ho Kyrios*.[165] It may be observed as well that the presence of this element in the Hebrew text is metrically desirable.

From the abundant biblical sources of this "evil-bringing" theme it is clear that *'al-* is indeed an integral part of the construction. Its absence in the Hebrew text would thus be unlikely.[166]

hārā'āh = ta kaka

Another pattern, of great significance for accurate reconstruction, emerges from the above collecting of the sources; namely, that, at least within the confines of this "bringing evil upon (someone)" convention, the translating of the singular, *hārā'āh*, by the plural, *ta kaka*, prevails in the LXX with only one exception (1 Kgs 9:9). It is thus likely as well that the original Hebrew text offered *hārā'āh* rather than the apparent plural, *hārā'ôt*, as reconstructed by Kneucker, contra Kahana.[167] This equivalency is very common and regular in the LXX.[168]

[*hû'*?]

The emphatic pronoun is perhaps to be reconstructed here. It is not found in any of the LXX witnesses, nor in most other Versions, but it is included in the readings of Sy (*hū pāreq lᵉkūn*), La^{V} (*ipse vos eripiet*), and Bo (*ṅthof on* "yet he"),[169] in each case being pre-verbal.

yaṣṣîl = exeleitai

This is an extremely regular equivalency in the LXX. Only once is *exaireō* used for *hôšîᵃ'* (Jer 49:11).[170]

miyyad 'ôyᵉbêkem = ek cheiros echthrōn hymōn

Echthros is the normal and very frequent translational equivalent for Hebrew *'ôyēb*, as already in Bar 3:10 (cf. also 4:21, 25, 26; and 5:6, below).[171] Surely, no clearer Hebraism could obtain than the expression "from the hand of" to indicate "power of" or "control of." And thus the idiom "to deliver from the hand of (someone)" is very common in BH (*haṣṣîl miyyad-*). Examples of the stereotypical combination of the Hiphil stem of *nāṣal* + *miyyad* + *'ôyēb* are the following: Judg 8:34, *miyyad kol-'ōyᵉbêhem = ek cheiros pantōn tōn thlibontōn autous*; Ps 31:16, *miyyad 'ôyᵉbay = ek cheiros echthrōn mou*; 1 Sam 12:10 (cf. 11), *miyyad 'ōyᵉbênû = ek cheiros echthrōn hēmōn*; and 2 Kgs 17:39, *miyyad kol-'ōyᵉbêkem = ek pantōn tōn echthrōn hymōn*.[172]

The metrical balance of this tricolon may be seen to be a neat 9/10/10 arrangement according to syllable count, thus lending additional support to the reading of *ʿᵃlêkem* and the interpretation of the whole as a tricolon.

4:19

lᵉkû bānîm = badizete, tekna

The Greek verb *badizō* appears here and in 5:7 in Baruch; it literally means "walk on foot" and thus generally "go." Of the approximately fifty LXX occurrences with Hebrew equivalents, in only three is anything other than *hālak* being translated.[173] Cf. Ps 34:12, *lᵉkû bānîm = deute tekna*, and Isa 26:20, *lēk ʿammî = badize laos mou*. Syh offers the cognate *hallēk* and Sy the synonymous *ʾezal*.

The equivalence of *teknon* and *bēn* is very common and regular in the LXX[174] and in Baruch (cf. above 4:12, and below vss. 21, 25, 27, 32; 5:5).

kî ʾᵃnî ḥorbāh = egō gar . . . erēmos

Erēmos appears only here in Baruch. Elsewhere in the LXX it is most commonly the equivalent for MT *midbār* "desert."[175] With specific reference to ruined places or devastated lands it is also used with frequency to render the Hebrew substantives *ḥorbāh* (or *ḥᵃrēbāh*) "waste, ruin, desolation," and *šᵉmāmāh* (or *šammāh*) "devastation, waste, ruin."[176]

For *ḥorbāh* applied specifically to Jerusalem, cf. Isa 52:9, *ḥorbôt yᵉrûšālayim = erēma Hierousalēm*; Ezek 5:14, *lᵉḥorbāh = eis erēmon*; Jer 44(51):2, *ḥorbāh = erēmoi*; Isa 51:3 (of Zion), *kol-ḥorbôtèhā = panta ta erēma autēs*; for *ḥᵃrēbāh*, cf. Neh 2:17, *bāh ʾᵃšer yᵉrûšālayim ḥᵃrēbāh = pōs Hierousalēm erēmos*; Jer 33(40):10, *bammāqôm hazzeh . . . ḥārēb* [masc.] *hûʾ = en tō topō toutō . . . erēmos estin.*[177]

The terms *šᵉmāmāh* and *šammāh* are not often applied specifically to Jerusalem in MT, but nevertheless offer some good parallels. Cf. Isa 24:12 (taking particular note of the verb with reference to what follows below), *nišʾar bāʿîr šammāh = kataleiphthēsontai poleis erēmoi*; Isa 62:4 (of Jerusalem), *lō'-yē'āmēr 'ôd šᵉmāmāh = kai ouketi klēthēsē kataleleimmenē;* and Jer 34(41):22 (of the cities of Judah).

Thus, although *ḥorbāh* is better supported (note as well that the cognate, *ḥarbᵉtā'*, is found in both Sy and Syh), *šᵉmāmāh/šammāh* cannot be entirely ruled out as a possibility.

niš'artî = kateleiphthēn

The Greek verb *kataleipō* "leave behind, abandon" most frequently renders Hebrew *šā'ar* "be left over (Niph), leave over (Hiph)" and *'āzab* "abandon," but at a ratio of about 2:1 in favor of the former.[178] The most striking parallel is Isa 49:21, the context of which is the same sort of lament over her lost children by the personified widow, Jerusalem: *hēn 'ᵃnî niš'artî lᵉbadî = egō de kateleiphthēn monē.*[179]

For the possibility of the Niphal stem of *'āzab*, cf. Isa 62:12, *wᵉlāk yiqqārē' dᵉrûšāh 'îr lō' ne'ᵉzābāh = ouk egkataleleimmenē;* Ezek 36:4; and Isa 27:10.[180]

4:20

pāšaṭtî // lābaštî = exedysamēn // enedysamēn

This is both a common parallel and equivalence between the LXX and MT. Cf. the same in Lev 16:23; 6:4; Cant 5:3; Ezek 26:16; 44:19; Bar 5:1; Num 20:26, 28 (Hiph); and in Greek only, 1 Macc 10:62; Jdt 10:3; Add Esth 4:1-3.[181]

bigdê šālôm = tēn stolēn tēs eirēnēs

In the LXX, *stolē* is used most frequently to render Hebrew *beged* "garment, robe, clothing," or actually most often its plural, *bᵉgādîm.*[182] The other noun, *eirēnē* "peace," is almost always the equivalent of Hebrew *šālôm* in the LXX.[183] While this precise phrase has no exact parallels, other data may be adduced in support. Particularly interesting is the semantic parallel in *Pss. Sol.* 2:21 where Jerusalem is said, in the context of destructive conquest, to have "girded on sackcloth instead of comely raiment" (*periezōsato sakkon anti endymatos euprepeias*).[184]

There is also in the Bible a close association of *stolē/beged* with priestly vestments (forty+ times); cf., for example,

Exod 28:2, 4, *stolēn hagian* = *bigdê-qōdeš*, and Exod 31:10, *tas stolas tas leitourgikas* = *bigdê haśśᵉrād*. In later times, this vesture began to assume eschatological overtones and is thus described in Sir 45:7 and 50:11, for example, as the *stolē doxēs* = *bgdy kbwd*.[185] Especially in the Jewish Apocalyptic literature the *stolē doxēs* is figurative for all the goodness that God has readied for the elect upon their entry into the new age; cf. *1 Enoch* 62:15-16, where the "robe of glory" is also labeled a "garment of life"; *T. Levi* 8:5, *stolēn hagian kai endoxon*; and *Pss. Sol.* 11:8 (of Jerusalem): *endysai, Hierousalēm, ta himatia tēs doxēs sou, hetoimason tēn stolēn tou hagiasmatos sou*, "put on, O Jerusalem, your glorious garments, make ready your holy robe!"[186]

Although the phrase appears to be unique to Baruch, there is hardly any question according to the equivalencies that the Hebrew would have been *bigdê šālôm*.

wᵉśaq taḥᵃnûnay = *de sakkon tēs deēseōs mou*

There is no difficulty with the equivalency between *sakkos* and *śaq*, which, as might be expected, is invariable in the LXX.[187] What precisely is to be judged the Hebrew equivalent of *deēsis* "supplication" is, on the contrary, quite problematic.

The original sense of *deēsis* is "lack" as it is for its cognate verb, *deomai* "lack, want."[188] This, however, diminished with the passage of time and by logical extension the verb came to mean "ask, seek, entreat," and the substantive similarly, "prayer, petition, supplication." There appear to be only traces of the original sense remaining in the LXX (perhaps, e.g., Job 17:1) for *deēsis* is predominantly nuanced there as a "request to God," and thus "supplication." By the time of the NT, it appears in the latter sense exclusively.[189]

Thus in the LXX, *deomai* is used in the majority of cases for forms of the Hebrew verb *ḥānan* (Hithp) "seek or implore favor,"[190] and *deēsis* renders either of the cognate substantives, *taḥᵃnûnîm* or *tᵉḥinnāh*, both meaning "supplication for favor," in roughly half of its LXX occurrences.[191] Similarly, it is used nine times for *rinnāh* "cry of entreaty" and seven for *tᵉpillāh* "prayer, intercession," six times for *šûᵃʿ* "cry for help," and three times for *ṣ*^e^*ʿāqāh* "cry of distress." In the four remaining instances it renders *ʾ*^a^*rešet* "request," *r*^e^*wāḥāh* "respite," *śî*^a^*ḥ* "complaint," and *ʿ*^e^*nût* "affliction." Only in this last example (Ps 22:25) does the Hebrew equivalent have a markedly different sense from the general semantic range of *deēsis*.

The consistency of the supplicative connotation in all of these is apparent. It becomes even more so when one is aware that the *ʿ*^e^*nût* of Ps 22:25 is a hapax legomenon in MT and may instead be the infinitive construct of *ʿānāh* I "respond" or of *ʿānāh* IV "chant" (as well as of *ʿānāh* III "be afflicted"). In any event, the LXX choice of *deēsis* here is odd and may have been determined by the sense of one of the other *ʿānāh* roots than the one with the meaning, "afflict."[192]

Nevertheless, this last is the equivalency seized upon by many scholars who have dealt with the problem of the LXX Baruch and its Hebrew *Urtext*, basing themselves on the assumption that the concept "sackcloth of affliction" offers a more precise antonymical parallel to "robe of peace" than does "sackcloth of supplication."[193]

Kneucker and the others of his position, noting late evidence of such a "garment of prayer," the Talmudic *ṭallît* "cloak, covering"[194] (overlooking any figurative sense here), find no proper antithesis between "sackcloth of petition" and "robe of peace" and on this basis dismiss the predominant meaning of the term *deēsis* in favor of this supposed nuance, "affliction," derived (not at all securely) from the obscure *ʿ*^e^*nût* in Ps 22:25. Add Esth 4:2,[195] [*Esthēr*] *enedysato himatia stenochorias kai penthous*, "[Esther] put on garments of anguish and mourning," is commonly cited in support of this interpretation but is surely no convincing parallel.

Such a criterion as antithesis alone, in the light of the overwhelmingly contrary textual and lexical evidence certainly cannot be said to suffice. The above interpretation of *deēsis* as connoting "petition" and probably presupposing *taḥ*^a^*nûnay* or *t*^e^*ḥinnātî* in the original Hebrew is further reinforced by the Syriac evidence. In both Sy and Syh the substantive, *bāʿūtāʾ* "petition, intercession," from the root *b*^e^*ʿāʾ* "seek, pray," stands for *deēsis*. La^{V} likewise offers *sacco obsecrationis*, "sackcloth of prayer."

bᵉyāmay 'eqrā' 'el-YHWH = kekraxomai pros ton aiōnion en tais hēmerais mou

The bulk of this phrase appears to derive from Ps 116(114):2, where *ûbᵉyāmay 'eqrā' = kai en tais hēmerais mou epikalesomai*. It is worth noting at least that in the immediate context (116:1) the equivalence *taḥᵃnûnay = deēseōs mou* may be found (cf. verse 20b, above). For "in my days," cf. Isa 39:8 (= 2 Kgs 20:19), *bᵉyāmāy = en tais hēmerais mou*.[196] *Qārā'* is the Hebrew verb regularly translated in the LXX by the Greek verb *krazō*.[197]

The major problem here as in verses 10 and 14 above is that of determining what in the original Hebrew was represented by the Greek, *ho aiōnios*. For support for the reading of *YHWH*, see the discussion at verses 10 and 14 above. For the expression "I will call upon *YHWH*," cf. 2 Sam 22:4, 7 (= Ps 18:4, 7), *'eqrā' YHWH*; 1 Sam 12:17 and Ps 3:5, *'eqrā' 'el-YHWH*; Joel 1:19 (Ps 28:1, 30:9), *'ēlèkā YHWH 'eqrā'*.[198]

<u>4:21</u>

'al-tîrᵉ'û bānîm = tharseite, tekna

For the discussion of this same imperative (or negative command) + vocative, see Bar 4:5 above (cf. also 4:27, 30). For the exact phrase, cf. Tob 7:18. Sy reads *bᵉnay* "my sons," but is echoed in this only by Sa. For the absolute use of *bānîm* in the vocative (with imperative), cf. Jer 3:14, 22; Ps 34:12; Prov 4:1; 5:7, 24; 8:32; and Tobit passim.

qir'û 'el-'ᵉlōhîm = boēsate pros ton theon

The three most frequent equivalencies for *boaō* "shout, cry out" in the LXX are: (1) *qārā'* (Qal), thirty-five times; (2) *zā'aq* (Qal), twenty-five times; (3) *ṣā'aq* (Qal), eighteen times.[199] Of these, *ṣā'aq* is never used in BH specifically for crying out to *'ᵉlōhîm*. It is, however, in common use with reference to *YHWH* as, for example, in Num 12:13, *yiṣ'aq 'el-YHWH*.[200]

Significant parallels in support of *zā'aq* are: 1 Chr 5:20, *lē'lōhîm zā'ᵃqû = pros ton theon eboēsan*; Jonah 1:5, *wayyiz'ᵃqû 'îš 'el-'ᵉlōhāyw = aneboēsan . . . pros ton theon autou*; and

Judg 10:14, *lᵉkû wᵉzaʿᵃqû ʾel-hāʾᵉlōhîm = boēsate pros tous theous.*[201] For *qārāʾ*, however, an almost exact parallel is found in 2 Sam 22:7, *wᵉʾel-ʾᵉlōhay ʾeqrāʾ = kai pros ton theon mou boēsomai.*[202]

Sy and Syh both offer *gᵉʿāʾ* "cry out," but this verb appears to have been used in Syriac rather fluidly for any or all of the above Hebrew verbs (e.g., for *ṣāʿaq* in Num 11:2, for *qārāʾ* in 2 Kgs 20:11, and for *zāʿaq* in Ps 22:6) and is thus not of appreciable help in determining the Hebrew original. In the light of the close parallel cited for *qārāʾ*, this verb has been employed in the reconstruction, but it should also be clear from the other citations that *zāʿaq* in particular appears to have good claim to originality as well.

The second part of verse 21, with the exception of the phrase *ek dynasteias*, and the lacking possessive pronoun *hymōn*, is exactly the same as the second part of verse 18 above.[203] The major problem here, as will subsequently become apparent, is the phrase *ek dynasteias*, which means literally "from power."

wᵉyaṣṣîl ʾetkem mēʿōšeq miyyad ʾōyēb = kai exeleitai hymas ek dynasteias, ek cheiros echthrōn

The witness of the LXX Codices and the various Versions for this line is in manifest disarray. The above Greek reading is that of G^B and the majority of the LXX Uncials and Minuscules. It is followed by Syh (with an expansion of meaning in its equivalent for *dynasteia*, *ʿᵉšūmᵉyāʾ* "oppression"): "He will deliver you from 'oppression,' from the hand of enemies." G^A (+ the Lucianic minuscule #311), however, lacks precisely *ek dynasteias*. This suggests the possibility of haplography in either the Greek (*ek . . . ek*) or the Hebrew (*min . . . min*), or, less plausibly, the possibility that G^B and the majority of the LXX witnesses preserve a conflate text in which *ek dynasteias* may have been a Greek editorial variant elaborating or explaining the Hebraism (or, conversely, *ek cheiros* the marginal addition of a later editor who perhaps sought to restore the literal sense as opposed to the initial translator's rather free rendition of Hebrew "hand" as "power"?).

It seems very improbable that the Hebrew text itself would have been conflate.[204] It is perhaps within the realm of possibility that *ek cheiros/miyyad* itself represents a gloss added under the influence of verse 18, but if so it would have been such already in the Hebrew for this phrase is consistently represented in all the LXX and other versional witnesses.

Sy clearly presents a conflate reading: "from the hand of the mighty, from the hand of rulers, from the hand of the enemy." This involves a conflation of two variants for *ek dynasteias*: "from (the hand of) the mighty / from (the hand of) rulers," both of which meanings are allowed by the sense of *dynasteia*, plus the expected equivalent for *ek cheiros echthrōn*, "from the hand of the enemy." It appears that "hand of" has been expanded laterally from the last phrase to both the preceding ones. But the ultimate import of this is that it tends to support the authenticity of *ek dynasteias* by virtue of the fact that it already has these two variants which do not in any way compete with the final phrase, "from the hand of the enemy" (as they would were *dynasteias* a variant for *cheiros*), but rather support the originality of both phrases of the LXX.

La[V] offers yet another variation: *et eripiet vos de manu principum inimicorum*, "and will deliver you from the hand of enemy rulers." This Latin arrangement is doubtless best explainable as the result of the influence of good Latin style over wooden literality; that is, combining into a unified concept what in the Greek amounts to a duality of the general and specific designations of a particular thing. The process of corruption probably explains the Coptic (Sa) reading: "And he will save you from the iniquity/violence [*či ngons̄*][205] that is in the hand of the enemy."

This ultimately boils down to three basic possibilities: (1) that *ek dynasteias* is authentic to the text and is in parallel with the following phrase; (2) that it is a gloss for *ek cheiros* so that the Hebrew would presumably have been *w^e^yaṣṣîl 'etkem miyyad 'ôyēb*; or (3) that *miyyad* was already a gloss in the Hebrew so that the original reading would have been something like *mē'ôšeq 'ôyēb*, "from the oppression of the enemy," or perhaps, *mimmemšelet 'ôyēb*, "from the dominion of the enemy" (cf. 1QM 18:10), depending on the determination of the proper meaning. It can be seen that the first has the most support, the second appears at best "dubious" from the evidence, and the third must remain speculative.

Determination of the Hebrew equivalent of *dynasteia* is yet more problematic. This Greek substantive expresses the abstract sense, "power, sovereignty, dominion, exercise of political power," or the like, that derives from the verbal root, *dynasteuō* "hold power, exercise lordship." In the LXX, *dynasteia* is with few exceptions the regular equivalent of Hebrew *g^e bûrāh* "power, might, valor."[206] Both these terms, the Greek and the Hebrew, are decidedly neutral and non-pejorative in character, as are most of the other Hebrew words that *dynasteia* translates.[207] The same may be said for the Latin equivalent, *princeps* "chief, ruler,"[208] and for those given in the text of Sy: *'aššînē'* "the mighty" and *šallîṭānē'* "the rulers." All this stands in marked contrast with the clearly pejorative character of the translational equivalents in Syh, *'^e šūm^e yā'* "oppression," and Sa, *či ngonš* "iniquity, violence."[209] Indeed, the context of a hoped-for deliverance from foreign domination would also seem to require a pejorative sense.

Thus Kneucker[210] has contended for *'ōṣer* "coercion, pressure" as the original Hebrew term. But the only possible parallels for this rather rare word are in Isa 53:8, where *'ōṣer* = *tapeinōsei* "humiliation, affliction" (the usual LXX equivalent for Hebrew *'^o nî* "affliction"), and Ps 107:39, where *'ōṣer* = *thlipsis* "pressure, affliction" (the usual LXX equivalent for Hebrew *ṣar/ṣārāh* "pressure, distress").[211] In both cases it is the only time the Greek term is used for *'ōṣer*, and further, *dynasteia* itself is never used to translate *'ōṣer* in the LXX.

If then we should consider the neutral, non-pejorative character of *dynasteia* to be determinative for the recovery of the original Hebrew, we are left with the related Hebrew terms *mimšāl* "realm" and *memšālāh* "dominion, imperium,"[212] or perhaps even the usual, though not apparently political, equivalent for *dynasteia*, *g^e bûrāh*.[213]

Prima facie *g^e bûrāh* would appear an unlikely candidate, usually denoting little more than personal "might" or "valor," and yet the term is employed in clearly political contexts by the Deuteronomistic redactor of Kings in his reign-evaluation formulary; cf., for example, 1 Kgs 16:5, *w^e yeter dibrê Ba'^a šā' wa'^a šer 'āśāh ûg^e bûrātô h^a lō'-hēm k^e tûbîm*, etc.[214] Such usage cannot be merely propagandistic on the part of the Deuteronomistic redactor for it is applied there in eight of ten instances to kings who did not merit his favorable judgment.[215] It is thus difficult to resist finding *g^e bûrāh* nuanced here with a technical-political connotation of greater precision than is offered by such translational terms as "success" or "prowess." One might perhaps conjecture the sense of "dominion" or "sovereignty."[216]

Yet on the other hand, one does not find this sense in evidence in the Qumran literature even though the term itself is in very common use there. Its use at Qumran appears to be generally comparable to its normal use in BH. It means simply "might, power," except that at Qumran it often has an even more pronouncedly militaristic nuance as "battle-prowess," especially with regard to God or the hand of God.[217] The supposed political nuance does not appear to be in evidence in the later Rabbinic literature either.

If *g^e bûrāh*, then, were to be considered a possibility for reconstruction, it would demonstrably have to carry this sort of extended political connotation of "dominion" or "political control" (obviously, from the context, of foreign origin).

There is, however, a term in BH which means precisely "dominion" or "imperium," and that is *memšālāh* (a more rare biform is *mimšāl*). In two instances in the LXX, *memšālāh* is translated by *dynasteia* and has precisely this meaning: Dan 11:5, *ûmāšāl mimšāl rab <mi>memšaltô = kai dynasteusei dynasteia megalē hē dynasteia autou* (Dn, G), "and he will rule a great(er) dominion <than>[218] his dominion"; and Ps 103:22, *b^e kol-m^e qōmôt memšaltô = en panti topō tēs dynasteias autou*, "in every place of his dominion."[219]

This term, *mmšlh*, is quite common at Qumran and a further enlightening parallel may be found in 1QM 18:10, where God is called upon to "show us the hand of your mercies . . . so as to remove the dom[in]ion of the enemy, to be no more, and the hand of your might . . ." (. . . *lhsyr mm[š]lt 'wyb l'yn 'wd wyd gbwrtkh* . . .). The association here of *memšālāh* with *'ôyēb* would appear also to be significant for our problem,[220] but the really telling argument against considering *memšālāh* for reconstruction here is that there is no real precedent in Hebrew for such use of the term in the absolute state as would be required.

In short, then, if *dynasteia* does in fact demand some sort of non-opprobrious political term as its Hebrew *Vorlage*, that word would have to be the politically neutral *memšālāh*. Yet there is the very serious objection that such use of the term in the absolute state would be unprecedented.[221] This solution is clearly unsatisfying.

The only remaining alternative is to assume, as did Kneucker unsuccessfully, that *dynasteia* is used here in an expanded and untypically opprobrious sense so that we might expect the Hebrew original to have been a term sufficiently political in tone and evil in connotation as to satisfy the context of our passage. The only Hebrew term that will suffice is *ʿōšeq* "oppression, violence."[222]

There is only one example in the LXX of the Greek verb *dynasteuō* translating the Hebrew verb *ʿāsaq* "oppress, tyrannize, extort" (1 Chr 16:21), but this is the only instance of *dynasteuō* being used in a deprecative sense in the LXX.[223]

Very significantly, however, the cognate, *katadynasteuō* "oppress" (literally, "overpower"), is used in the LXX seven times for *ʿāšaq*.[224] Also, the derived noun, *katadynasteia* "oppression," appears twice for *ʿōšeq*[225] and once for *ʿᵃšûqîm*.[226] Both the verb *katadynasteuō* and the noun *katadynasteia* appear first in the LXX in Exodus where they are used in relation to the political oppression practiced by the Egyptian government on the Hebrew minority, though in neither case do they represent *ʿāšaq* or *ʿōšeq*.[227]

For the use of *ʿāšaq* or *ʿōšeq* in a particularly political sense, cf. Jer 6:6; Ezek 22:7, 12, 29(?); Eccl 5:7; Jer 22:17; Isa 30:12; 54:14.[228] A further suggestive parallel from Qumran is found in 1Q27 1:I:10-11.

(10) *my gwy ḥpṣ ʾšr yʿwšqnw ḥzq mmnw*
my (11) *yḥpṣ ky ygzl bršʿ hwnw*
my gwy ʾšr lwʾ ʿšq rʿhw,

(10) What nation is glad to be oppressed by
one stronger than itself?
What one (11) is glad that its wealth is
wickedly plundered?
Yet what nation does not oppress its
neighbor?[229]

It would thus appear that the LXX translator, either inadvertently or by virtue of a deficient *Sprachgefühl*, employed the neutral *dynasteia* when he had really intended the opprobrious sense of the more fitting *katadynasteia*, and most subsequent Versions followed suit, oddly with the notable exception of Syh (usually rather slavishly close to the Greek of G^B)[230] and Sa. It is also possible that the prefixal element *kata-* may have dropped out inadvertently early in the process of transmission.

4:22

wa'ᵃnî 'el-YHWH bāṭaḥtî = egō gar ēlpisa epi tō aiōniō

The LXX uses *elpizō* "hope, trust" by far most frequently for Hebrew *bāṭaḥ* "trust" (forty-seven times),[231] even though *pepoitha* (perfect middle of *peithō*) "trust, rely on" is actually more common yet for *bāṭaḥ* and its derivatives.[232] *Elpizō* also represents Hebrew *ḥāsāh* "take refuge" (twenty times)[233] and *yāḥal* "await, expect, hope for" (ten times in the Piel stem and five in the Hiphil). It occurs twice for Hebrew *qāwāh* "wait for, hope for," and the equivalence of the related nouns *tiqwāh* and *elpis* is quite common, especially in Job and Proverbs (but the much more common LXX equivalent for *qāwāh* is *hypo-/perimeinō* "wait patiently for"). The use of *elpizō* for other Hebrew verbs such as *gālal* (Ps 21:9) is rare and exceptional.

In the MT in general, these terms, particularly *bāṭaḥ*, *qāwāh*, *ḥāsāh*, and their derivatives, are used somewhat synonymously. There is a certain fluidity about this concept that allows one to be used in one instance while in another place one or the other will appear in the same sense. For example, Ps 91:2, *'ebṭaḥ bô = elpiō ep' auton*, may be compared with Ps 18:3, *'eḥseh bô = elpiō ep' auton.*[234]

It is very significant that when one lines up all the passages with *elpizō*, generally whether the Hebrew verb is *bāṭaḥ*, *ḥāsāh*, *qāwāh*, or *yāḥal*, the Greek construction is consistently *elpizō epi* + dat. or acc. This is, despite its commonness in the LXX, rather odd Greek.[235] In classical Greek, *elpizō* is not used with *epi*, or even *eis* or *en* as sometimes in the LXX, but rather in good style is used only with the dative ("to hope in")[236] or the accusative ("to hope for, expect").[237] This aberrant Greek syntax is without doubt due to the impact of the Hebrew phrasing which rarely states what is the object of hope but rather affirms the source of it (i.e., God). The Hebrew idiom is not "to hope for something," but "to hope/trust in God" (using *b-*, *'el-*, *'al-*, etc.). This can thus be counted among those Greek stylisms in the Baruch poetry which unavoidably reflect the Hebraisms behind them.

Kneucker[238] proposes that the Hebrew idiom involved is the rather rare (and textually questionable) one of Ps 22:9 that uses the verb *gālal* "roll," *gōl 'el-YHWH* = *ēlpisen epi Kyrion*. The same reading appears elsewhere only in Prov 16:3, but there it has no LXX counterpart. The verb *gālal* itself means "roll," and in these passages the Hebrew expression is usually understood by some sort of semantic expansion to mean "roll to *YHWH*" or thus, "commit to *YHWH*," "entrust to *YHWH*," one's way or self. That this sense must be involved is clear from the one remaining (slightly varied) occurrence of the expression in Ps 37:5, *gôl 'al-YHWH darkekā ûb^{e}ṭaḥ 'ālāyw*, where *gôl* is in parallel with *b^{e}ṭaḥ*. Yet the LXX text of this same passage yields a different perspective: *apokalypson pros Kyrion tēn hodon sou kai elpison ep' auton*. Here the LXX translator obviously understood himself, whether or not correctly, to be dealing with the Hebrew verb *gālāh* "reveal, disclose," indeed making better sense than *gālal*. The resultant equivalencies are: *b^{e}ṭaḥ* = *elpison* and *gôl* = *apokalypson*. Thus not only is this idiom in very restricted use in MT, but also the verb is textually in question, and the parallelism of Ps 37:5 argues instead for *bāṭaḥ* as the more likely equivalent of *elpizō*. In short, Kneucker's solution seems highly improbable.

Of the two instances where the equivalent of *elpizō* is *qāwāh*, only Isa 25:9 has significance for this problem: *hinnēh '^{e}lōhênû zeh qiwwînû lô w^{e}yôšî'ēnû / zeh YHWH qiwwînû lô nāgîlāh* *w^e^nismᵉḥāh bîšû'ātô = idou ho theos hēmōn eph' hō ēlpizomen, kai sōsei hēmas houtos Kyrios, hypemeinamen autō kai ēgalliōmetha kai euphranthēsometha epi tē sōtēria hēmōn*, "Behold, this is our God; we have waited for him [LXX, "in whom we have trusted"] and he will save us; / this is *YHWH*, we have waited for him; we will be glad and rejoice in his salvation."

The two Hebrew occurrences of *qāwāh* are identical in this text, but the LXX employs *elpizō* for one and *hypomeinō* for the other. The close semantic equivalence ("wait for") in the second instance, and also the fact of that being the far more common equivalence, suggests that *hypomeinō* is what the LXX translators considered to be the normal equivalent for Hebrew *qāwāh* and that here the use of *elpizō* in the first instance is stylistic variation. There is, nonetheless, a significant correspondence of content between Isa 25:9 and Bar 4:22 that cannot be discounted (e.g., lexically with *elpizō epi* and *sōtēria*, and semantically with other terms). This is in fact the verb used in the Kahana rendering,[239] but as will be seen, there are closer parallels to be found than that of Isa 25:9.[240]

The closest and most numerous parallels obtain, however, for *bāṭaḥ* as might be expected from the frequency of its translation by *elpizō*. Four examples in particular may be compared, each featuring the same structure with the pleonastic pronoun: Ps 31:7 (an almost exact parallel, especially if the *ho aiōnios* of Baruch is in fact a circumlocution for the Tetragrammaton), *wa'ᵃnî 'el-YHWH bāṭāḥtî = egō de epi tō Kyriō ēlpisa*; Ps 13:6, *wa'ᵃnî bᵉḥasdᵉkā bāṭaḥtî yāgēl libbî bîšû'ātekā = egō de epi tō eleei sou ēlpisa agalliasetai hē kardia mou en tō sōtēriō sou* (also revealing a high degree of correspondence in content with the whole of Bar 4:22); Ps 31:15, *wa'ᵃnî 'ālèkā bāṭaḥtî YHWH = egō de epi soi ēlpisa, Kyrie*; and Ps 55:24, *wa'ᵃnî 'ebṭaḥbāk = egō de elpiō epi se, Kyrie*.[241]

The Syriac verb *sᵉbar* (Pael) "hope, trust" is used much as *elpizō* for the various Hebrew terms, but mostly for *bāṭaḥ*.[242] In the light of all the above evidence, *bāṭaḥ* appears to be the most probable Hebrew original. Also, from the numerous parallels that support *bāṭaḥ*, it appears very likely that in this instance (if not the others as well), *ho aiōnios* does in fact stand for the Hebrew Tetragrammaton.

lîšûʿatkem = tēn sōtērian hymōn

As mentioned, while it is customary for the Greek to use *elpizō* + acc. (as here, *tēn sōtērian hymōn*) to express the idea "hope *for*" (i.e., the actual thing hoped for), a similar arrangement is not common in Hebrew. The verbs of "hoping" and "trusting" in Hebrew are usually content to express the source of the hope (God) and indicate this with *b-*, *ʾel-*, or *ʿal-* (as may be seen from the above citations). When and if an object of the hope is mentioned, it is not expressed directly as in the Greek but rather indirectly by means of *l-*, as both the Syriac texts witness to be the Semitic style. Cf. Sy, *(ʾ)nāʾ ger sabbᵉret ʿal ḥay ʿālᵉmēʾ lᵉpurqānākūn.*[243]

Statistically, *sōtēria* appears in the LXX mostly (eighty-one times) for the Hebrew root *yāšaʿ* (Hiph) "save, deliver." For example, it represents *yᵉšûʿāh* thirty-nine times and *tᵉšûʿāh* twenty-five times, *yēšaʿ/yešaʿ* fourteen times, but *pᵉlêṭāh* only six times and others still less.[244] In the LXX, the Hebrew verb *yāšaʿ* and its derived nouns are with only minimal exceptions rendered by the Greek verb *sōzō* or one of its derivatives. Cf. the following ratios: the verb *yāšaʿ* (Hiph), by *sōzō* 121 times :: 22 times for verbs other than *sōzō*; the substantives *yēšaʿ/yešaʿ*, by *sōzō* derivatives 33 times :: 3 times for non-*sōzō* derivatives; *yᵉšûʿāh* 78 :: 0; and *tᵉšûʿāh* 31 :: 3.[245] Thus *yᵉšûʿāh* appears most likely, but *tᵉšûʿāh* is also quite possible for the Hebrew original. It is also very typical for the term *sōtēria* in the Apocrypha to refer to God's deliverance; cf. Bar 4:24, 29; 1 Macc 3:6; Jdt 8:17; Wis 18:7; Sir 46:1; et al.

ûbāʾāh-lî śimḥāh = kai ēlthe moi chara

The Hebrew term *śimḥāh* "gladness" has been discussed at some length above at 4:11, especially with respect to its patterns of equivalency in the fixed pairing with *śāśôn*, and that may now be referred to for support.

In the LXX, *chara* "joy" represents *śimḥāh* seven times (1 Chr 29:22, Esth 9:22, Ps 21:6, Prov 14:13, Jonah 4:6, Jer 15:16, and Esth 8:16). Jer 15:16 features the parallel pairing *śāśôn/euphrosynē* (A) // *śimḥāh/chara* (B), while Esth 8:16 displays the same equivalencies but in reverse sequence. In four instances *chara* translates *śāśôn*: Joel 1:12, Zech 8:19, Jer 16:9, 25:10, the last three of which exhibit the parallel relationship *śāśôn/chara* (A) // *śimḥāh/euphrosynē* (B). Just as *śāśôn* has already been reconstructed for *euphrosynē*, so here *śimḥāh* is assumed for *chara*, but as can readily be ascertained, there are enough passages divergent from the usual pattern so as plausibly to contend for *śāśôn* as the equivalent here.[246]

The Greek verb *erchomai* is very consistently and very frequently a LXX equivalent for the Hebrew verb *bô'*.[247]

mē'im qādôš = para tou hagiou

The erstwhile relatively little used Greek adjective *hagios* "holy" was used almost invariably by the LXX translators to render the Hebrew *qādôš* "holy." Classical Greek was able to distinguish between the taboo aspects of holiness with *hagios* and its positive value with *hieros*, but the Semitic root *qdš* does not so discriminate.[248] Yet it was *hagios* that was selected by the LXX translators, almost exclusively, and pressed into the service of Hebrew *qādôš* in so thoroughgoing a fashion that the Semitic background of the *hagios* concept in the LXX is everywhere apparent.[249]

The designation of God as "holy," or particularly the "holy One of Israel," or simply the "holy One," appears to have been the creation of, and favorite epithet of, Isaiah (cf., e.g., 6:3f.). *YHWH* appears as *qᵉdôš yiśrā'ēl* twelve times in First Isaiah, thirteen times in Second Isaiah, and about six more times in what are probably derivative passages elsewhere.[250] He is also styled as *qᵉdôš ya'ᵃqōb* in Isa 29:23. In Isa 43:15, *YHWH* is said to be *qᵉdôšᵉkem* (LXX, *ho hagios hymōn*), "your holy One," and in Isa 10:17 and 49:7, *qᵉdôšô* (in both these last instances misread by the LXX translator). The closest parallels are, however, in Isa 40:25, *qādôš = ho hagios*; Hab 3:3, *qādôš = ho hagios* (// *'ᵉlôᵃh = ho theos*); and Job 6:10, *'imrê qādôš*, "the words of the holy One."[251]

For *mē'im*, see below, verse 22.

ʿal-haḥesed yᵉbôʾᵃkem = epi tē eleēmosynē hē hēxei hymin

Basically, *eleēmosynē* means "mercy" or "pity." It appears twenty times in the books corresponding to the Hebrew canon, almost evenly split in its equivalencies with *ḥesed* (eight times) and *ṣᵉdāqāh* (nine times).[252] It occurs, however, with even greater frequency (thirty-eight times) in just three Apocryphal works: Sirach (thirteen times), Tobit (twenty-three times), and Baruch (twice). In Proverbs it appears invariably for *ḥesed* (seven times: 3:3, 14:22, 15:27, 19:22, 20:28, 21:21, 31:26); elsewhere its use is limited but consistent for *ṣᵉdāqāh* (three times in Psalms, three in Isaiah, two in Deuteronomy and one in Daniel).

Prov 21:21 reveals the pairing *ṣᵉdāqāh/dikaiosynēs + ḥesed/eleēmosynēs*. As has been observed (4:13 above), *dikaiosynē* is quite regularly the equivalent of *ṣᵉdāqāh*, especially insofar as the latter conveys its usual meaning, "righteousness." *Eleēmosynē*, commonly "mercy, pity," has another more technical connotation, displayed prominently in Tobit and Sirach, and exclusively in the NT,[253] that of "almsgiving, benevolence, charity." This later connotation that pervades Tobit and Sirach is consistent with other contemporary teaching in late post-biblical Judaism.[254]

It can be seen from Sirach where there is an extant Hebrew text that such use of *eleēmosynē* is an exact counterpart to the technical use of Hebrew *ṣᵉdāqāh* in this late period as "benevolence" or "charity."[255] Indeed, it appears that the Greek term developed this connotation (which by NT times had become its exclusive meaning) through the LXX translation of these few books of the Apocrypha that thoroughly utilized this technical usage of *ṣᵉdāqāh*.[256] This connotation appears to be thoroughgoing in Sirach; the correspondence between *eleēmosynē* and *ṣᵉdāqāh* is invariable so far as the extent of the Hebrew text allows ascertainment.[257] Sir 40:17 even offers an interesting pairing with *ḥesed--ḥsd/charis* ("grace") // *ṣdqh/eleēmosynē* ("benevolence")--in which the sense is that these are the eternal verities of human society. It goes almost without saying then that this connotation for *ṣᵉdāqāh* was operative at least as early as Sirach (cf. also Dan 4:24).

Both meanings of *ṣ*^{e}*dāqāh* appear to be operative at Qumran; cf. 1QS 8:2, *l'śwt 'mt wṣdqh wmšpṭ w'hbt ḥsd whṣn' lkt 'yš 'm r'hw*, "to practice truth, benevolence/righteousness, justice, love of mercy, and walking humbly each with his neighbor,"[258] and 10:25, *lṣdqt 'l*, "from God's righteousness." Cf. also 1QH 1:26 and 4:31 for *m'śy ṣdqh*,"deeds of righteousness" (or "acts of benevolence"?).[259]

Ḥesed is also prominent in the Qumran literature.[260] Mic 6:8 was popular and often quoted. For its relationship to *y*^{e}*šû'āh*, cf. 1QS 11:12, *ḥsdy 'l yšw'ty l'd*, "the mercies of God are my salvation forever."[261]

That *eleēmosynē* represents an original *ḥesed* (and not *ṣ*^{e}*dāqāh*) in Bar 4:22 is thus supported by several lines of evidence: (1) the general pattern of this equivalency elsewhere (as, e.g., in Proverbs) and the close semantic correspondence between the two terms, *ḥesed* being the sort of "mercy" that characterizes the grace of a superior; (2) also the fact that the frequent equivalency between *ṣ*^{e}*dāqāh* and *dikaiosynē* in the LXX represents the primary and normal one for each of those terms; and (3) the fact that this passage deals with God as the source of the "mercy" here hoped for, and not with the concept of "pious benevolence" (*eleēmosynē* does not represent *ṣ*^{e}*dāqāh* where it connotes "righteousness").

The Greek verb *hēkō* "come" is the equivalent of Hebrew *bô'* in the LXX with extreme regularity.[262]

m^{e}*hērāh = en tachei*

This phrase occurs fifteen times in the LXX[263] but in only five of these instances is there a Hebrew counteraprt: *bim'aṭ* in Ps 2:12, *m*^{e}*hērāh* in Deut 11:17 and Josh 8:19, and *mahēr* in Deut 9:3 and 28:20 (cf. also 1QM 15:11). There are no particularly close parallels upon which to draw within this limited range of equivalencies, but support for *m*^{e}*hērāh* may be found in two MT passages where it is the equivalent, not of *en tachei*, but of closely related cognate forms. Cf. Josh 10:6, *'alēh 'ēlênû m*^{e}*hērāh* [LXX, *totachos*] *w*^{e}*hôšî'āh lānû*, "Come up to us quickly, and save us," and Isa 5:26 (also featuring the combination with *bô'*), *w*^{e}*hinnēh mehērāh* [LXX, *tachy*] *qal yābô'*, "and behold, he comes very quickly."

mē'ēt YHWH môšî'ᵃkem = para tou aiōniou sōtēros hymōn

The Greek construction, *para* + genitive, is common in the LXX for Hebrew *mē'ēt* (cf., e.g., *para Kyriou = mē'ēt YHWH* in 1 Sam 16:14, Ps 24:5, Ezek 33:30 and Ps 118:23)[264] or *mē'im* (cf., e.g., *para Kyriou = mē'im YHWH* in Isa 29:6, and in Ps 121:2 following the verb *hēkō/bô'*).[265] This construction appears with great frequency from this point on in the poem (4:25, 35, 36; 5:4, 6). *Mē'ēt* is much more commonly found in combination with *YHWH* in MT and has thus been used in the reconstruction here. *Mē'im* has been used with *qādôš* immediately above in verse 22c, but without precedent since *qādôš* used in the absolute state as a divine epithet appears only rarely in the MT and is never combined there with either *mē'ēt* or *mē'im*. Ultimately, either prepositional combination is possible in each case.

The LXX uses the agentive noun *sōtēr* "savior" only for terms from the Hebrew verb *yāša'* "save" (i.e., twelve times for *yēša'*, seven times for *môšîᵃ'*, and a few times for *yᵉšû'āh*).[266] Clearly its only true equivalent should be the Hiphil active participle *môšîᵃ'* "savior," for the other two equivalents that it does appear for are really abstract nouns meaning "salvation."

In the passages where *sōtēr* appears for *yēša'*, it is almost always in the stock phrase *'ᵉlōhê yiš'î* (with varying suffix), "God of my salvation." The Greek rendering of this is typically *ho theos ho sōtēr mou*, "God, my Savior" (cf. Ps 24:5, 25:5, 27:9, 79:9, Sir 51:1, et al.). With the exception of Ps 27:1, *YHWH 'ôrî wᵉyiš'î* (LXX, *sōtēr mou*), *'ᵉlōhê = ho theos* is a constant in this idiom ("God my salvation") which in its Greek version is always a rather free and imprecise rendering of the Hebrew otherwise ("salvation" translated as "Savior"), for whatever the reasons of the LXX translators. Now, if *tou aiōniou* in our passage does indeed represent a circumlocution for *YHWH* (cf. vss. 10, et al.), then *môšîᵃ'* is again put forward as the probable Hebrew original in view of the numerous Deutero-Isaianic passages which designate *YHWH* as the *môšîᵃ'* of Israel.[267]

It seems likely that the original Hebrew text would have featured the Tetragrammaton, for if the stock phrase *'ᵉlōhê yiš'î*, were involved the translator would surely have used *tou theou* according to the usual pattern and not *tou aiōniou*. The Deutero-Isaianic parallels indicate that if *YHWH* is to be read, his proper designation is *môšîᵃ'*, and not *yēša'*.[268]

<u>4:23</u>

kî šillaḥtîkem = exepempsa gar hymas

The LXX uses the verb *ekpempō* "send out" only for the Hebrew verb *šālaḥ* "send," and always the Piel stem when active.[269]

bᵉ'ēbel ûbᵉkî = meta penthous kai klauthmou

This pairing has already appeared in Bar 4:11 where the equivalencies were seen to be between *penthos* and *'ēbel*, *klauthmos* and *bᵉkî*. However, there the sequence was the reverse of what it is here. Unfortunately the two Hebrew terms are not paired in MT so that there is no apparent sequence preference.[270] The closest parallel is that of Deut 34:8, *yᵉmê bᵉkî 'ēbel mōšeh = hai hēmerai penthous klauthmou Mōysē*, even though the usual equivalency pattern is reversed here. The Lucianic text group offers slight evidence for the transposition of the two synonyms, but this itself probably represents a harmonization in accord with 4:11.

For "mourning" in its total context being contrasted with "joy," cf. Jer 31(38):13, *wᵉhāpaktî 'eblām lᵉśāśôn = kai strepsō to penthos autōn eis charmonēn*; Isa 61:3, *šemen śāśôn taḥat 'ēbel = aleimma euphrosynēs tois penthousi*; and 1QH 18:15, *w'blym lśmḥt 'wlm*, "and mourning into eternal rejoicing."

Both Syriac texts present the same pairing here, with each member of the pairing cognate to the Hebrew term expected from the known LXX equivalencies, and also in each case in the same sequence as that of the LXX (Sy, *be[']blā' wᵉbabkātā'*, and Syh, *'am 'eblā' wabkātā'*).

wᵉyāšîb-lî 'etkem (hā)'ᵉlōhîm = apodōsei de moi ho theos hymas

The Greek verb *apodidōmi* "give back, return" is common in the LXX, appearing approximately fifty times as the equivalent of Hebrew *šûb* (Hiph). It also appears often, but with less frequency, for *mākar* (Qal) and *šālēm* (Piel).[271] For its use in the context of returning captives, cf. 1 Macc 9:70, *apodounai autois tēn aichmalōsian*, "to return the captives to them" (cf. also 9:72 and 10:9). For the same sense in the Hebrew idiom, cf. Jer 30(37):3, *wᵉšabtî 'et-šᵉbût 'ammî* (but the LXX equivalent is *apostrephō* "turn back"), and similarly Jer 30:18; 33:7, 11; Ps 14:7; 53:7; et al. Sy preserves the indirect object (*lay*), as does La^{V} (*mihi*) and the vast majority of the LXX witnesses (*moi*), but the Hexaplaric tradition lacks this element.[272]

bᵉśāśôn wᵉśimḥat 'ôlām = meta charmosynēs kai euphrosynēs eis ton aiōna

Charmosynē "rejoicing" is a very rare word, appearing only seven times in the LXX:[273] for Hebrew *śimḥāh* in 1 Sam 18:6, Jer 48(31):33, 33(40):11, and for *tôdāh* in Lev 22:29 (in Judg 8:6, Bar 2:23, 4:23, the Hebrew is not extant). Though limited in use, its association with *śimḥāh* is quite apparent. As has already been observed, *euphrosynē* occurs often (and somewhat interchangeably) for both *śāśôn* and *śimḥāh* in the LXX, thus far in the Baruch poetry with most likelihood for *śāśôn* (cf. above, Bar 3:34, 4:11; but also cf. below, 4:29, 36 and 5:9). It has also been noted elsewhere that *śāśôn wᵉśimḥāh* is a fixed A-B pair in BH that is extremely consistent in this sequence, being reversed only in Esth 8:16. It is probable, then, that the sequence here would be the usual even though that means that *euphrosynēs* represents *śimḥāh* and *charmosynēs* stands for *śāśôn*.

In the first instance this constitutes a departure from the thus far regular equivalence in our poetry of *euphrosynē* and *śāśôn*, and in the second there is simply no precedent in the LXX for such an equivalence (in three of its four verifiable occurrences *charmosynē* is the equivalent of *śimḥāh*). Such imprecision could be attributable to either the conscious or unconscious decision of the LXX translator.

But perhaps a more significant factor is the existence of the Hebrew idiom *śimḥat 'ôlām* "eternal gladness," which very probably represents the original Hebrew here. This phrase appears in Isa 61:7, 51:11 and 35:10, in each case rendered in the LXX by *euphrosynē aiōnios*. It also appears at Qumran in

1QH 18:15, *w'blym lśmḥt 'wlm*. This expression, if indeed original to Bar 4:23, would serve to verify the equivalence there of *euphrosynē* and *śimḥāh*. The LXX reading would then be a somewhat free translation through another familiar enough idiom, *eis ton aiōna* "forever," which elsewhere in the LXX often renders Hebrew *lᵉ'ôlām* "forever," or the like. This phrase, *eis ton aiōna*, has already appeared in the Baruch poetry (3:13, 32; 4:1) and it suggests that another possible reconstruction would be: *bᵉśāśôn wᵉśimḥāh lᵉ'ôlām*, "in joy and gladness forever." Cf. also La, Sy, and Syh.

<u>4:24</u>

ka'ᵃšer . . . kēn = hōsper . . . houtōs

This same Greek comparative coordination appears again in 4:33 and 4:28 (G^A only). The construction corresponds to the Hebrew comparative clause pattern in which *ka'ᵃšer* "just as" in the protasis corresponds to *kēn* "thus," so" in the apodosis.[274]

'attāh = nyn

This is an extremely regular correspondence in the LXX.[275] It also appears below in verse 28 (G^A only).

rā'û = heorakasin

The equivalency between *horaō* and *rā'āh* is also very common and very regular in the LXX,[276] and in these poems as well (cf. Bar 3:22, 37; 4:25).

šᵉbîkem = tēn hymeteran aichmalōsian

For this equivalency, cf. verse 10 above. The precise Hebrew form is paralleled in Num 31:19, *ûšᵉbîkem*, and the LXX counterpart there utilizes the much more common possessive pronoun *hymōn* (*hē aichmalōsia hymōn*). *Hymeteros* "your (plural)" appears very rarely in the LXX though it is not at all uncommon in the classical literature. Altogether it is found only five times in the LXX, here and in Gen 9:5, Job 8:21, Prov 1:26, and Amos 6:2. The difference between its use here and the much more common use of *hymōn* elsewhere appears to be simply a matter of style.

kēn = houtōs

This equivalency is very common in the LXX.[277]

y^{e}šû'at '^{e}lōhêkem = tēn para tou theou hymōn sōtērian

For the equivalency between *sōtēria* and *y^{e}šû'āh*, cf. verse 22 above. The Greek syntax in this phrase is just ambiguous enough to have given rise to subsequent translational divergencies. *Hymōn* would appear properly to modify *tou theou*, but it could also be construed with *sōtērian*. The various Versional witnesses are in disagreement. The Greek witnesses are practically unanimous in support of the above syntax, but Sy, Syh, L' (-#62), La^{V}, Ar, and Arm support instead a transposed reading of *sōtērian hymōn*. Cf., for example, La^{V}, *salutem vestram a Deo*, "your salvation from God," and Syh, *l^{e}purqānā' dîl^{e}kūn d^{e}men 'allāhā'*, "your salvation which is from God."

But close biblical parallels make clear from the corresponding Greek and Hebrew there what sort of relationship is involved here, namely, the Greek construction *para* + genitive, representing the Hebrew construct or genitive relationship (cf. above, vs. 9). This may be illustrated with a particularly close parallel to our passage, Isa 52:10, *w^{e}rā'û kol-'apsê-'āreṣ 'et y^{e}šû'at '^{e}lōhênû = kai opsontai panta akra tēs gēs tēn sōtērian tēn para tou theou hēmōn*, "and all the ends of the earth shall see the salvation of our God."[278] Cf. also a similar passage, Exod 14:13, *'al-tîrā'û hityaṣṣ^{e}bû ûr^{e}'û 'et-y^{e}šû'at YHWH = tharseite, stēte, kai horate tēn sōtērian tēn para tou Kyriou*, "Fear not, stand still, and see the salvation of *YHWH*."

t^{e}bô'^{a}kem b^{e}kābôd gādôl = hē epeleusetai hymin meta doxēs megalēs

The Greek verb *eperchomai* "go or come toward" most frequently in the LXX translates Hebrew *bô'* "come or go in"[279] and is common in this poem (4:9, 24, 25, 35, 36). *Doxa* in the classical literature often had the meaning "opinion," "honor," or "reputation." But in the LXX (and subsequently in the NT), these connotations virtually disappeared because through the very process of the LXX translation itself the Greek term had been so thoroughly colored by its regular Hebrew equivalent, *kābôd*, particularly in the latter's distinctive sense of denoting the honor, glory or "divine radiance" of the deity.[280] The Greek adjective *megas* "great" has already been observed to be the regular LXX equivalent for Hebrew *gādôl* (cf. above, 3:24, 25 and 4:9).

ûbahᵃdar YHWH = kai lamprotētos tou aiōniou

The Greek term *lamprotēs* "splendor, brilliancy" is also used metaphorically to mean "distinction" or "munificence."[281] It is an extremely rare term in the LXX, occurring in addition to the two appearances in Baruch (here and in 5:3) only four times, and in each instance representing a different Hebrew term or expression: in Ps 90:17, *nō'am* "pleasantness," in Ps 110:3, *hādār* "splendor, ornament, array,"[282] in Isa 60:3, *nōgah zeraḥ* (// *'ôr*) "brilliant shining, burst of light," and in Dan(Th) 12:3, *zōhar* "shining."[283]

The Hebrew equivalent here is not very likely to have been *zōhar*. That term appears in Dan 12:3, applied not to God but to the "shining" of the firmament, and elsewhere only a few times in Ezekiel (1:27, 8:2), there applied to the numinous apparition appearing to the prophet. *Nō'am* is ascribed to *YHWH* twice, in Ps 27:9 and 90:17,[284] but it never manifests the semantic content that our passage requires.

Hādār is used in MT primarily to express the "majesty" or "splendor" of God. It is often paired with *hôd*, also meaning "majesty, splendor."[285] Of particular significance for our Baruch passage is the fact that *hādār* is often associated with *kābôd* (clearly the original Hebrew behind *doxa* in this verse), as in Ps 145:5, *hᵃdar kᵉbôd hôdekā*; 145:12, *ûkᵉbôd hᵃdar malkûtô = tēn doxan tēs megaloprepeias tēs basileias sou*, "the glorious majesty of his/your kingdom"; and the double parallel of Isa 35:2 (a passage significantly utilizing *kābôd* and *hādār* as the manifestations of *YHWH*'s powerful presence in leading a triumphant return of his people), *kᵉbôd hallᵉbānôn nittan-lāh hᵃdar hakkarmel wᵉhaššārôn / hēmmāh yir'û kᵉbôd-YHWH hᵃdar 'ᵉlōhênû*.[286] *Hādār* is also closely associated with *kābôd* at Qumran; cf. 1QS 4:8, *wklyl kbwd 'm mdt hdr*, "and a crown of glory together with raiment of majesty";[287] 1QH 12:15, *hdr kbwdkh*; and Barthélemy and Milik (DJD I, 19, 13:2), *nś' bhdr kbwd wtp'rt*.

In Ps 90:16, *hādār* is ascribed to *YHWH: wahᵃdārᵉkā ʿal-bᵉnêhem*, "and your majesty upon their sons." Here the LXX misread *hdrk* as the Hiphil stem of *drk*, translating *kai hodēgēson tous huious autōn*, "and guide their sons." In Ps 29:4, *hādār* is paralleled by *kōᵃḥ* "strength."[288] In Mic 2:9, the term is used in the enigmatic statement about taking away *YHWH*'s splendor forever: *hᵃdārî lᵉʿôlām*.[289] In Ezek 16:14, it is applied to Jerusalem: *bahᵃdārî ʾᵃšer śamtî ʿālayik*, "with the splendor which I [*YHWH*] put on you." Similarly, in Lam 1:6 it is said of the devastated Jerusalem, *wayyēṣēʾ min-bat-ṣiyyôn kol-hᵃdārāh*, "All her splendor has departed from the daughter of Zion." And finally in Ps 110:3 it is applied to the king who proceeds *bᵉhadrê qōdeš*, "in the splendor of holiness/in holy array" (or perhaps, "in the splendor of the holy One").[290] It is only in this last example that the equivalence between *hādār* and *lamprotēs* occurs in the LXX. Nevertheless, it appears quite likely from the above evidence regarding *hādār* that it would have stood parallel to *kābôd* in the original Hebrew of Bar 4:24.

However, Isa 60:2-3 reveals the significant equivalency, *lamprotēti* = *nōgah zarḥek*, and suggests that this too may have a reasonable claim to originality here. This passage also deals with the restoration of Jerusalem and employs the markedly theophanic terms *zāraḥ* "shine forth" and *nōgah* "flash of light, brilliance" in doing so. These are, in fact, the same terms used in the great biblical theophanies of Deut 33:2 (*zāraḥ*), Ezek 10:4 (*nōgah kᵉbôd YHWH*), and Ps 18:13 (*minnōgah negdô*),[291] and it seems clear that in our passage the "great glory" and the "splendor of the Eternal" also represent the theophanic presence of the One who is restoring and leading his people by his glorious presence.[292] The sense of the passage is that the neighboring principalities will now witness the glorious and splendid restoration ("salvation") about to be shaped by God.

Unfortunately, *zeraḥ* "shining forth, sunburst" is a hapax legomenon in MT, yet its parallelism with "light" and "glory" is striking in its only occurrence in Isa 60:2-3, *wᵉʿālayik yizraḥ YHWH ûkᵉbôdô ʿālayik yērāʾeh / wᵉhālᵉkû gôyim lᵉʾôrēk ûmᵉlākîm lᵉnōgah zarḥēk* = *epi de se phanēsetai Kyrios, kai hē doxē autou epi se ophthēsetai. Kai poreusontai basileis tō phōti sou, kai ethnē tē lamprotēti sou*, "And *YHWH* will shine forth upon you and his glory will be visible upon you; / and nations will walk to your [Jerusalem's] light, and kings to the brilliance of your shining."

Thus this term also could claim with some degree of merit to have been the original in our passage, yet it has the disadvantage of being so rare and thus difficult to establish for lack of parallels. *Hādār* then would seem to have here both the more impressive accumulation of support and the more persuasive.

The problem of *tou aiōniou* is the same as that already encountered at verses 10, 14, 20 and 22.[293]

<u>4:25</u>

bānîm = tekna

For this vocative use of *bānîm* with the imperative, cf. 4:19 and 21, above. Sy again, as in verse 21, has the suffixed form "my children."[294]

śeʾû ʾap-ʾēl habbāʾ ʿalêkem = makrothymēsate tēn para tou theou epelthousan hymin orgēn

This Greek verb appears ten times in the LXX but in only three of these instances are Hebrew equivalents detectable: Eccl 8:12, *maʾarîk* "prolong"; Prov 10:11, *heʾerîk ʾap* "be patient"; and Sir 35:22(32:18), *ytʾpq* "restrain oneself."[295] The usual Greek construction is *makrothymeō epi* + dat., "be patient toward/with (someone or thing),"[296] or simply the intransitive use of the verb without an object, "be patient, endure."[297] Here in Baruch, unlike the usage elsewhere, this verb is used transitively with the object following directly in the accusative.[298] The sense is thus to "bear (something) patiently."

The usual Hebrew idiom, *heʾerîk ʾap* "be patient" (literally, "prolong or postpone anger" or "make oneself slow to anger"), clearly does not suffice for our passage. As a self-contained construction it does not take an object.[299]

Sensing this inadequacy, Kahana[300] has proposed the Hebrew verb *bālag* (Hiph) "smile, be cheerful" as the equivalent. This is a very rare verb, occurring only four times in MT (Job 9:27, 10:20, Amos 5:9, Ps 39:4). Amos 5:9 is very problematic and obscure, but of the other passages also only in Ps 39:4 is the meaning really clear, and only in that one did the LXX translators come close to grasping the sense of *hablîg*.[301] But the major difficulty with this is that "cheerfulness" is simply not involved in the semantic content of *makrothymeō*, nor in that of the other Versional equivalents. Rather, the basic sense is everywhere "patience, (dogged) endurance."

The older suggestion of Kneucker[302] appears then in the above light to be the best: that the Hebrew verb was probably *nāśā'* "raise, bear, carry," used here in the same manner as it is in Mic 7:9, *zā'ăp YHWH 'eśśā'*, "I will bear the anger of *YHWH*."[303] This would then necessitate the assumption of a heretofore unencountered equivalency for *makrothymeō*, but such an eventuality is neither impossible nor unlikely.

For the remainder of this bicolon, cf. 4:9, above.

r^{e}dāp^{e}kā hā'ôyēb = katediōxe se ho echthros

The Greek verb *katadiōkō* "pursue closely" is used in all but seven of its seventy-eight LXX occurrences with Hebrew equivalents to translate the Hebrew *rādap* "pursue, harass."[304] The cognate, *r^{e}dap*, is featured in Sy, *r^{e}dapāk b^e'eld^{e}bābāk*, "your enemy has pursued you." For the combination *rādap 'ôyēb*, cf. Ps 143:3 and 7:6; for the reverse concept, "pursue the enemy," cf. Jos 10:19.[305]

w^{e}tir'eh b^e'obdô mahēr = kai opsei autou tēn apōleian en tachei

The form of *opsei* is second person singular, future indicative, whereas the prior imperative in verse 25a is plural. This represents a rather incongruous, but biblically not unprecedented, intra-verse shift in person--the *tekna* of verse 25a, still the referent in 25b, is now construed collectively as singular. Nonetheless, all the LXX and other Versional witnesses, with the sole exception of La^S (*videbitis*), concur.

Apōleia "destruction" occurs elsewhere in Baruch only in 4:6 where, quoted from Esth 7:4, it is found in the idiom "sold for destruction" (*eis apōleian = l^{e}hašmîd*). But in this case a different equivalency appears likely, namely, one with the Hebrew infinitive construct *'^{a}bōd* "perishing, destruction." The author here appears to have borrowed from Deut 28:20, 22, *'ad-'^{a}bodkā* *mahēr = apolesē se en tachei*, and *ûr^{e}dāpûkā 'ad 'obdekā = katadiōxontai se heōs an apolesōsi se.*[306]

Dependence on Esth 8:6 is also apparent: *w^{e}rā'îtî b^e'obdan môladtî*. This passage exemplifies the MT use of *rā'āh + b-*, which appears to have been the construction utilized also in the Hebrew original of Bar 4:25.[307] It also suggests that *'obdān / 'abdān* "destruction" is a distinct possibility for reconstruction. Both Sy and Syh offer the cognate noun *'abdānā'*.

w^e'al ṣaww^e'rêhem tidrôk = kai epi trachēlous autōn epibēsē

Here our author has drawn primarily from Deut 33:29. There the MT, with reference to *'ōy^{e}bêkā*, has *w^e'attāh 'al-bāmôtêmô tidrôk*, "and you shall tread upon their backs." The LXX, however, has *kai sy epi ton trachēlon auton epibēsē*, "and you shall tread upon their *necks*." The image is, of course, that age-old submissive posture of subjection, bowing the neck to the conqueror's foot. This important symbol of triumph is well illustrated in Josh 10:24, where as the climax of the post-victory ceremonial carefully orchestrated by Joshua it is said of the leaders of the Israelite forces, *wayyāśîmû 'et-raglêhem 'al-ṣaww^e'rêhem = . . . epi tous trachēlous autōn* , "and they put their feet upon their necks."[308] *Trachēlos* appears very regularly in the LXX for Hebrew *ṣawwā'r* "neck."[309] The verb *epibainō* "tread" has already been encountered at 4:13 where it was also found to be the equivalent for Hebrew *dārak*; cf. ad loc.

4:26

'^{a}nuggay = hoi trypheroi mou

The Greek adjective *trypheros* has the meaning "delicate, dainty." In six of its nine occurrences in the LXX, Hebrew equivalents are verifiable, and five of those six are substantives derived from the verbal root *'ānag* "be delicate, dainty."[310]

In Deut 28:54, the "tender and delicate people," *hā'îš hārak b^{e}kā w^{e}he'ānōg m^e'ōd = . . . kai ho trypheros sphodra*, are singled out as those whose more elite lifestyle has left them totally unprepared for the harsh realities of disaster.[311] In Mic 1:16, the prophet instructs Jerusalem, in the course of his prophetic lament over her impending doom, that the populace should shave their heads "for the sake of your delicate children ['*al-b e nê ta' a nûgāyik = epi ta tekna ta tryphera sou*][312] . . . for they will go from you into captivity." In Isa 47:1, Babylon is depicted as a dethroned queen left squatting in the dust and is told that she will never again be called *rakkāh wa' a nuggāh* (= . . . *kai tryphera*). And finally, in Jer 6:2, Jerusalem herself is referred to as "the dainty one," *hamm e 'unnāgāh*.[313]

hāl e kû d e rākîm ' a qubbîm = eporeuthēsan hodous tracheias

Trachys "rough, rugged, harsh" is another rare word in the LXX, occurring there eight times. In only two of these can its Hebrew equivalencies be determined with any certainty, and both are of significance. Wisdom in Sir 6:20 is said to be "harsh [*tracheia* = *'qwbh*] to the foolish." In Isa 40:4 is found the equivalency *tracheia* = *har e kāsîm* ("impasses"?), parallel to *skolia* = *he'āqōb* ("rugged places"). The precise phrase *hodou tracheias* is found in the LXX of Jer 2:25, but the Hebrew there is quite different. *Hodous tracheias* also appears in the Greek only in *Pss. Sol.* 8:19 in the context of Jerusalem's downfall. Though there is indeed little to go on the Qal passive participle of *'āqab* appears most probably to have been the original.[314]

Hodos is extremely regular in the LXX as the equivalent of Hebrew *derek*.[315] Likewise, *poreuomai* is almost always the equivalent of Hebrew *hālak*, as already in 3:13, 33 and 4:13 (cf. ad loc.).

niśś e 'û k e 'ēder gāzûl b e yad-'ôyēb = ērthēsan hōs poimnion hērpasmenon hypo echthrōn

The Greek verb *airō* "lift up, carry (off), take away" is an extremely regular equivalent for Hebrew *nāśā'*, possessing also a very similar range of meaning.[316] An illustrative paraparallel is found in Mic 2:2 where *nāśā'* is also paired with *gāzal* "seize, snatch away," *w e ḥām e dû śādôt w e gāzālû ûbāttîm w e nāśā'û*, "And they covet fields and seize them; and houses and take them away."[317] Judg 21:23 also reveals this sense for *nāśa'* as well as its pairing with *gāzal*: *wayyiś'û nāšîm l e mispārām min-hamm e ḥōl e lôt ' a šer gāzālû = kai elabon gynaikas eis arithmon autōn apo tōn choreuousōn hōn hērpasan*, "[The depopulated Benjaminites lay in wait] and carried off wives according to their number, snatching them away as they danced."[318] For the passive sense in Niphal, cf. 2 Kgs 20:17 (= Isa 39:6), *w^e niśśā' kol-'ᵃšer b^e bêtekā*, "everything in your house will be taken away." Cf. also Bar 5:6, below.[319]

As would be expected from the abbve citations, *harpazō* "snatch up, carry away" is most frequently the equivalent of Hebrew *gāzal*.[320] The key source here is Job 24:2, *'ēder gāz^e lû = poimnion . . . harpasantes*, "they carried off the flock." So, while *poimnion* in the LXX almost equally represents *'ēder* and *ṣō'n*,[321] this combination secures *'ēder* as our Hebrew original. For the use of the Qal passive participle of *gāzal*, cf. Jer 21:12 (and 22:3), *w^e haṣṣîlû gāzûl miyyad 'ôšēq = kai exelesthe diērpasmenon ek cheiros adikountos*, "and rescue the stolen from the oppressor's hand." Cf. also Deut 28:29.

Hypo echthrōn most probably represents *b^e yad 'ôyēb*, with the instrumental *b-*. Such a combination as *b^e 'ôyēb* does not occur in MT, and *b^e yad 'ôyēb* (or plural) there always has the sense "*into* the enemy's hand" (cf. Lev 26:25, Ps 31:9 and Lam 2:7). But this construction is probably comparable to that of Exod 16:3 where *b^e yad YHWH = hypo Kyriou*, "by the hand of *YHWH*" (cf. also Deut 33:29, Isa 45:17 and 1 Sam 28:6).

The text of Sy is rather heavily expanded in this verse. In the first colon, for example, Sy reads: "My delicate ones have gone into captivity and have traveled on hard, rough roads." The first expansion is clearly explanatory but the second may be due to the influence of the MT source in Isa 40:4, representing both of the rare Hebrew terms there, *'āqōb* and *rekes*. The second colon is likewise expanded: "They have been scattered on difficult paths; they have been scattered like the flock which is snatched up by enemies."

<u>4:27</u>

'al tîr^e 'û bānîm w^e za'ᵃqû 'el-'^e lōhîm = tharsēsate, tekna, kai boēsate pros ton theon

This colon is virtually the same as the first of verse 21 above, with the exception that here the Hebrew verb *zā'aq* has been used in the reconstruction for *boaō* instead of *qārā'* as in verse 21.[322] This has been done particularly in the light of the Sy reading, *w(')az'eqw*. In verse 21, Sy read *g*ᵉ*'aw*, as does Syh in both verses 21 and 27. It may also be noted that Sy again offers the suffixed form, "my sons."

kî tizzākᵉrû bammēbî' hārā'āh 'ᵃlêkem = estai gar hymōn hypo tou epagontos mneia

Mneia "remembrance" occurs here, in 5:5, and thirteen other times in the LXX.[323] In those instances where the Hebrew equivalent can be determined, it is always either a verbal form of *zākar* "remember," or the derived noun *zēker*. The Syriac equivalent here is, in both Sy and Syh, the cognate *dukrānā'* "remembrance."

Although there is no exact parallel, the literal equivalent for *estai gar hymōn mneia* would appear quite plausibly to be *kî yihyeh lākem zēker* "for there is remembrance of/for you."[324] Indirect support may perhaps be adduced from such cult-oriented passages as Num 10:10, *wᵉhāyû lākem lᵉzikkārôn lipnê 'ᵉlōhêkem = kai estai hymin anamnēsis enanti tou theou hymōn*, "and they/there shall be a memorial for you before your God," or Exod 30:16, *wᵉhāyāh libnê yiśrā'ēl lᵉzikkārôn lipnê YHWH = kai estai tois huiois Israēl mnēmosynon enanti Kyriou*, "and it will be to the Israelites a memorial before *YHWH*."

While the overall effect of these passages may appear similar to that of this Baruch passage, comparison of the Greek texts reveals that in detail they do not jibe. Significantly, *mneia* is not used in these, and in fact is never used for the more cultic *zikkārôn* in the LXX (cf. 4:5, above). Also, *lipnê = enanti* is not at all what Bar 4:27 expresses by *hypo* + genitive (i.e., the agentive force of "by" or "through"). It thus seems quite unlikely that such a construction, lifted almost verbatim from these sources, could have been the original Hebrew of this Baruch passage.[325]

There is better support for a passive construction utilizing the Niphal stem of *zākar*. Several examples will show that this verbal form alone may be rendered in Greek by *mneia* + a form of *eimi* "to be" or *gi(g)nomai* "to be or become" + a pronoun in the genitive case: Zech 13:2, *lō' yizzāk^{e}rû 'ôd = ouketi autōn estai mneia*, "they will no longer be remembered," or "there will no longer be a remembrance of them"; Ezek 21:37, *lō' tizzākērî = ou mē genētai sou mneia*; Num 10:9, *w^{e}nizkartem lipnê YHWH '^{e}lōhêkem = kai anamnēsthēsesthe enanti Kyriou*; 1QM 10:7, *wnzkrtmh lpny 'lwhykm*; Isa 23:16; and Ezek 25:10. Thus a reconstruction of *kî tizzāk^{e}rû* appears to have the best support for the first part of this colon.

The agentive force of *hypo* here strongly suggests the comparable use of Hebrew *b-* (or *l-*). The verb *epagō* is quite common in this poem, having already appeared (as it does frequently in the LXX) for the Hiphil stem of *bô'* (cf. 4:9; 10, 15, 18 and 29). It is also quite likely that the reading of the major LXX Uncials, *epagontos* (present active participle), is wrong and should rather be, as suggested in the margin of Syh (and supported as well in Greek by G^{Q,V}, L', and Minuscules 26, 46, 86, 130, 239, 410, 544, 538), the second Aorist participle, *epagagontos*, as it is in the very similar verses 18 and 29. The difference could be easily explained by the assumption of a simple haplography of the syllable *-ag-*. The reconstruction of *bammēbî'*, "by the One who brought," is thus very certain.

That notwithstanding, the end of the verse is very uncertain. The Greek, followed by Syh, supplies no object and thus ends quite abruptly and awkwardly. There is, however, a Semitic Version (Sy) that is complete with both the direct and indirect objects: *men haw d(')aytî '^{e}laykūn hālēn*, "from the One who brought these things upon you." The ellipsis of one or the other of these, or perhaps even both, would not be impossible (or necessarily unlikely) for Hebrew poetry, but the imbalance of the latter half of the bicolon without these elements suggests strongly that such were original but inadvertently lost (La^{V} does have the indirect object, *vos*).

This would then assume for the verse end an original Hebrew reading: *bammēbî' '^{a}lêkem 'ēlleh*. Supportive parallels for such absolute usage of *'ēlleh* with the precise connotation of "these things (that have disastrously come from YHWH)" abound. Cf., for example, Ezek 23:30 (where the context, verses 23ff., is the threatened invasion of Babylon), *'āśōh 'ēlleh l^{e}kā*; Ps 15:5, *'ōśēh-'ēlleh*; Jer 5:19, *taḥat meh 'āśāh YHWH '^{e}lōhēnû lānû 'et-kol-'ēlleh*; and Jer 30:15, *'āśîtî 'ēlleh lāk*.[326] This solution has a very serious drawback, however, in that *'ēlleh* in this idiom appears almost exclusively with the verb *'āśāh* (+ *l-*, "to do these things to"), and never with *hēbî'* or *mēbî'*.

An alternate solution is suggested by comparison of this with the initial cola of verses 18 and 29:

(29) *ho gar epagagōn hymin ta kaka* =
kî hammēbî' hārā'āh '^{a}lêkem;

(18) *ho gar epagagōn <hymin> ta kaka* =
kî hammēbî' hārā'āh '^{a}lêkem

(27) *hypo tou epag<ag>ontos* =
bammēbî'.

The Greek of the last is different only by being in the genitive case, and the missing object, even if deliberate ellipsis be granted, is here clearly seen to be those disastrous events summed up in *ta kaka*. Indeed, a survey of the MT reveals that the literary image of *YHWH* as the *mēbî'* of the people's woes is quite common and that what he "brings" upon his people is frequently described as *rā'āh* "evil," for which *ta kaka* in the LXX is the extremely regular equivalent. Cf., for example, 2 Kgs 21:12, *hinnî mēbî' rā'āh 'al-y^{e}rûšālayim = idou egō pherō kaka epi Hierousalēm*; and Jer 19:3, *hinnî mēbî' rā'āh 'al-hammāqôm hazzeh = idou egō epagō epi ton topon touton kaka*.[327]

It thus seems best in the light of the above evidence to assume that what was lost was *hymin ta kaka/hārā'āh '^{a}lêkem*,[328] and that the reading of Sy very likely represents a more or less neutral attempt to smooth over the felt loss.

The following then are the basic alternatives for reconstruction:

(1) assuming the haplography and the nominal *zēker*,

kî yihyeh lākem zēker
bammēbî' hārā'āh '^{a}lêkem;

(2) assuming the haplography and the passive verbal construction,

kî tizzāk^{e}rû bammēbî'
hārā'āh '^{a}lêkem;

(3) assuming ellipsis and no haplography,

(a) *kî yihyeh lākem*
bammēbî' zēker, or

(b) *kî tizzāk^{e}rû bammēbî'*.

On the basis of the abovementioned evidence, the second alternative appears to be the more meritorious.

4:28

ka'^{a}šer . . . kēn = hōsper . . . <*houtō*> (G^{A})

For this construction, cf. above, verse 24, and below, verse 33. Only G^{A} (cf. also Ar) offers *houtō nyn* "so now."[329] *Ka'^{a}šer* uncoordinated by *kēn* (following the syntax of G^{B}, et al.) would have the equally plausible sense of "because, since, in so much as." Cf., for example, Mic 3:4, and Sy. *Kēn* has thus been used in the reconstruction because its presence in the original Hebrew appears probable from both syntactical and metrical criteria and is supported in the Greek by the Codex Alexandrinus.

hāyāh 'im-l^{e}babkem lit'ôt = egeneto hē dianoia hymōn eis to planēthēnai

Lexically, this phrase consists entirely of very regular correspondences: *gi(g)nomai* is used in the LXX with frequency and regularity for *hāyāh* (especially in the Qal stem);[330] *dianoia* "mind" is likewise regular for Hebrew *lēb/lēbāb* "heart, mind," as is *planaō* "wander, stray" for Hebrew *tā'āh* "stray."[331]

For the idiom "to have in mind to do something," cf. 1 Kgs 8:17, *wayhî 'im-l^{e}bab dāwid . . . libnôt = kai egeneto epi tēs kardias*; 1 Chr 22:7, *hāyāh 'im-l^{e}bābî libnôt = emoi egeneto epi psychē tou oikodomēsai*; and 2 Chr 24:4, *hāyāh 'im-lēb Yô'āš l^{e}ḥaddēš = kai egeneto epi kardian Iōas episkeuasai*.[332]

For the combination of *lēbāb* and *tā'āh* with reference to Israel's erring ways, cf. Ps 95:10, *wā'ōmar 'am tō'ê lēbāb hēm = kai eipa, aei planōntai tē kardia*; and Isa 21:4, *tā'āh l^{e}bābî = hē kardia mou planatai*. Cf. also *tō'ê rû^{a}ḥ* in Isa 29:24.

mē'aḥ^a^rê 'e^lōhîm = apo tou theou

For the combination of this phrase with *tā'āh*, cf. Ezek 14:11, *l^e^ma'an lō'-yit'û 'ôd bêt-yiśrā'ēl mē'aḥ^a^ray = hopōs mē planatai eti ho oikos to Israēl ap' emou.*[333]

tāšûbû l^e^baqq^e^šô = epistraphentes zētēsai auton

Epistrephō "turn about, return" is used very regularly in the LXX for the Qal stem of Hebrew *šûb* "return, turn" (cf. above, 4:2), as is *zēteō* "seek" for that of *bāqaš* "seek."[334] These equivalencies are certain.

For the negative command construction with the imperfect + infinitive "let you return to . . .," cf. Deut 24:19, *lō' tāšûb l^e^qaḥtô*; 1 Kgs 13:17, *lō'-tāšûb lāleket*; and Job 7:7, *lō'-tāšûb 'ênê lir'ôt.*[335]

'eśer p^e^'āmîm = dekaplasiasate

This imperative of *dekaplasiazō* "multiply by ten" is the only LXX example of this late and rare Greek verb.[336] Since *epistrephō* in the II Aorist passive has the meaning "turn oneself around" or "be turned" (i.e., "repent"), the sense of this imperative + vocative plural II Aorist passive participle + infinitive is literally "turn yourselves around ten times over to seek him."

Kneucker,[337] in reconstructing the original Hebrew for this phrase, contends for the Piel imperative of *'iśśēr* as the equivalent of *dekaplasiasate*. He claims that *'iśśēr* is used here "in der neuhebräischen Bedeutung 'verzehnfachen.'"[338] But *'iśśēr* is only attested in BH, as are other numeral-derived verbs such as *šillēš* and *ḥimmēš*,[339] with a divisional sense. Indeed, in both BH and MH, *'iśśēr* means "take the tenth part, tithe, divide into tenths."[340] While there does appear to be evidence for numeral-derived verbs in Ugaritic with the meaning "do for the nth time,"[341] such is not evident in BH or MH with the exception of *šānāh* "repeat, do again."[342]

Kahana[343] has rendered *dekaplasiasate* with the phrase *pî-'^a^śārāh*, as in the modern Hebrew idiom *pî-N* "N times." This idiom does not occur in BH or MH but there is a similar expression, *pî-šᵉnayim*, traditionally translated "a double share, double amount." This itself occurs only three times in the MT: Deut 21:17, 2 Kgs 2:9, and Zech 13:8, but it is still very much debated by scholars whether the phrase really means "two times" or rather "two-thirds."[344] Both philology and simple logic are on the side of the latter. Indeed, the modern Hebrew dictionary, Eben-Shoshan, *Millon Ḥadaš*, states that the modern Hebrew idiom *pî-N* is based on misinterpretation of the phrase *pî-šᵉnayim* in BH as "two times" when it is really always the term for "two-thirds."[345] It is thus very unlikely that such would have constituted the original Hebrew here.

Whitehouse[346] has suggested the possibility of the adverbial multiplicative **ʿeśrātayim* for "ten times" on the model of BH *ʾarbaʿtayim* "four times, fourfold" (2 Sam 12:6) or *šibʿātayim* "seven times, sevenfold" (Isa 30:26, Prov 6:31). However, such a term never appears in BH and given the highly derivative character of the Baruch poetry this proposal also seems unlikely.

There is yet to be considered the most common method of expressing "N times" in BH, and that appears to offer the most plausible reconstruction. That is the well-attested and well-understood idiom that combines the required cardinal number with *pᵉʿāmîm* ("times"). In 2 Kgs 5:10, Naaman is told to wash *šebaʿ-pᵉʿāmîm* (LXX, *heptakis*); in 2 Kgs 13:18-19 three examples of the idiom occur: *šᵉlōš pᵉʿāmîm*, *ḥāmēš ʾô šēš pᵉʿāmîm* (LXX, *tris*, *pentakis*, *hexakis*); and in Neh 6:4 a message is sent *ʾarbaʿ pᵉʿāmîm*.

But most significantly, the precise combination *ʿeśer pᵉʿāmîm* "ten times" occurs three times in BH: Num 14:22, *way-nassû ʾōtî zeh ʿeśer pᵉʿāmîm*, "and have tempted me these ten times"; Neh 4:6, *wayyōʾmᵉrû lānû ʿeśer pᵉʿāmîm*; and Job 19:3, *zeh ʿeśer pᵉʿāmîm taklîmûnî*, "these ten times you reproach me." The LXX in each of these instances is unfortunately either lacking an equivalent or simply not literal in its translation.[347]

In each case, "ten" is the purposely round number of repeated action, so that this idiom is metaphoric for doing something over and over again, continually and persistently. This is, in fact, the very point of our author: "so, continually return to seeking him."

4:29

kî hammēbî' hārā'āh 'ᵃlêkem = ho gar epagagōn hymin ta kaka

Cf. the same phrase in verse 18 above, and Jer 32:42 cited there.

śimḥat-'ôlām = tēn aiōnion euphrosynē

Cf. above, verse 23, and especially Isa 35:10, 51:11, 61:7 and 1QH 18:15. *Euphrosynē* also appears above in 3:34, 4:11 and below in 4:36 and 5:9.

bîšû'atkem = meta tēs sōtērias hymōn

Cf. above, verses 22 and 24, and the evidence cited there for *yᵉšû'āh*. The Greek preposition *meta* is frequently the equivalent of Hebrew *b-*, as, for example, in Exod 1:14, *bᵉpārek = meta bias*. Cf. also Ps 149:4, *bîšû'āh = en sōtēria*; 1 Sam 2:1 (also Ps 21:6 and 106:4), *bîšû'ātekā = en sōtēria sou*; and Tob 5:16, *meta sōtērias*.

4:30

'al tîrᵉ'î yᵉrûšālayim = tharsei, Hierousalēm

This is a clear borrowing from Zeph 3:16, *bayyôm hahû' yē'āmēr lîrûšālayim 'al-tîrā'î*. Cf. the same pattern in verses 5, 21, and 27 above.

yᵉnaḥᵃmēk = parakalesei se

The Greek verb *parakaleō*, with the sense of "summon, invoke" in classical Greek, has a unique connotation in the translational Greek of the LXX--"comfort, console." This is doubtless due to its close association with the Hebrew verb *nāḥam* "comfort."[348] As might be expected, this concept of "comfort" is intimately associated in the Bible with the personified and desolated Jerusalem, and the influence here of Deutero-Isaiah is quite prominent. Several examples will serve to illustrate not only this equivalency, but also the association with Jerusalem and thus the likelihood of the above reconstruction: Isa 51:3, *kî niḥam YHWH ṣiyyôn = kai se nyn parakalesō Siōn*; 51:12, *'ānōkî 'ānōkî hû' m^e naḥemkem* = *egō eimi, egō eimi ho parakalōn se*; and Sir 48:24 (itself dependent on Isa 40:1 and 61:2-3), *wynḥm 'bly ṣywn* = *parakalesai tous penthountas en Sion.*[349]

haqqôrē'-lāk šēm = *ho onomasas se*

Interestingly, although *onoma* "name" occurs over a thousand times in the LXX (almost exclusively for Hebrew *šēm*), the derived verb *onomazō* is comparatively rare, occurring less than thirty times.[350] The usual pattern for "naming" or "giving a name" in Hebrew is *qārā'* + *šēm* (or the name itself in the accusative) + *l*- for the person or thing named, as in Gen 2:20, *wayyiqrā' hā'ādām šēmôt l^e kol-habb^e hēmāh*, or Gen 1:8, *wayyiqrā' 'ᵉlōhîm lārāqîᵃ' šāmāyim.*[351] An extremely rare BH alternative is the idiom found only in Dan 1:7 and 2 Kgs 17:34, *sîm šēm l*-, "to set the name for (someone), to name (someone)," but this is never rendered in the LXX by *onomazō*. This is, in fact, the idiom used by Sy in Bar 4:30, *haw man d^e sām leky š^e mā'*, "the One who set your name."

Of the twenty-seven occurrences of *onomazō* in the LXX, fifteen have Hebrew equivalents. In three instances it represents Hebrew *qārā'*, twice in the Qal stem (Gen 26:18, Deut 2:20) and once in the Niphal (Jer 25:29). Our Baruch passage appears to allude to the last, Jer 25:29, where Jerusalem appears as a target of *YHWH*'s wrath and is described there as *'îr 'ᵃšer niqrā'-š^e mî 'ālèhā* = *polei en hē onomasthē to onoma mou ep' autēn*, "the city on which my name has been pronounced."[352]

Other passages with *qārā'* illustrate this idiom even though the LXX uses the common *kaleō* "call" as the equivalent. It would be difficult, for example, to exclude such a passage as Isa 62:2 (cf. also Isa 62:4, 12) from our author's sources even though *kaleō* rather than *onomazō* is used by the LXX: *w^e qōrā' lāk šēm ḥādāš 'ᵃšer pî YHWH yiqq^o bennû* = *kai kalesei se to onoma to kainon, ho ho Kyrios onomasei auto*, "And you will be called by a new name which the mouth of *YHWH* shall designate."[353]

The common name-giving idiom with *qārā'* appears in the above light to represent the most plausible reconstruction.[354] Also, the structure of this phrase in the Greek gives every appearance of being a literal rendering of the Hebrew in both syntax and form so that the Greek participle may doubtless be assumed to reproduce a Hebrew participle.

4:31

šōd l- = deilaioi

The Greek adjective *deilaios* "fearful, wretched" is quite rare in the LXX, appearing only five times.[355] Our author appears to have drawn this concept from Hos 7:13, where *deilaios* translates Hebrew *šōd* "ruin, devastation" in the parallel construction *'ôy lāhem // šōd lāhem = ouai autois // deilaioi eisin* (the latter being a free rendition on the part of the LXX translator). In Nah 3:7 *deilaia* represents a passive verbal form of the cognate verb *šādad* "despoil (violently), bring to ruin": *šodd^e dāh Nîn^e wēh = deilaia Nineuē*.[356]

Since both *šōd* and *deilaios* are each rarely employed in BH and the LXX respectively, parallels are in short supply. The close association of *deilaios* with the Hebrew root *šādad* substantiates the claim of Hos 7:13 to have been our author's source, and of *šōd l-* to have been the precise expression borrowed. The Greek translation, if this be so, is clearly free, and it is at least possible that this adjectival use of *deilaioi* may represent the Hebrew nominal equivalent plus the copula--*šōd yihyeh l-*. Literally (with or without the copula), this idiom would mean: "there will be ruination/wretchedness for (someone)," or better, "(someone) will be ruined/wretched." The use of the copula is unsubstantiated for this idiom in the severely limited parallel material and is, in fact, grammatically superfluous and improbable.[357]

lim'annayik = hoi se kakōsantes

The Greek verb *kakoō* "maltreat, harm" with almost equal frequency represents both Hebrew *'ānāh* III (Piel) "afflict, maltreat" and *rā'a'* (Hiph) "do evil, harm."[358] The original Hebrew would clearly have featured a suffixed plural participle "those who maltreated you." The Hiphil plural participle of *rā'a'*, *m^e rē'îm*, occurs sixteen times in BH,[359] but in only one instance (Ps 27:2) is it rendered by *kakoō*. *M^e rē'îm* also is never suffixed in BH and never denotes anything more than the very general "evildoers" or "wicked" so common in the Psalms.

On the other hand, the Piel plural participle of *'ānāh* III occurs twice in BH, both times suffixed (*mᵉ'annayik*) and both times the suffix referent is personified Jerusalem herself, just as in our Baruch passage. In both of these passages, Isa 60:14 and Zeph 3:19, the context is one of prophetic consolation to the beleaguered Jerusalem. The latter is, in fact, part of a message labeled *bayyôm hahû' yē'āmēr lîrûšālayim*, and beginning, as does our Baruch section, with *'al-tîrā'î* (Zeph 3:16). It reads: *hinnî 'ōśeh 'et-kol-mᵉ'annayik bā'ēt hahî'*, "See, at that time I will deal with all who maltreated you."[360] The other example (Isa 60:14) concerns Jerusalem's future fortune when the *bᵉnê mᵉ'annayik* (LXX, *huioi tapeinōsantōn se*) will come doing homage to Jerusalem and will designate her the "city of *YHWH*" (*wᵉqārᵉ'û lāk 'îr YHWH*).

Even though neither of these parallels reveal LXX equivalencies with *kakoō*, it seems inescapable that they are the sources for our author's allusions. Such an equivalency in this passage would not be at all improbable in the light of the frequent association elsewhere of *kakoō* with *'ānāh* III (Piel).[361]

wᵉlaśśᵉmēḥîm bᵉnoplēk = kai epicharantes tē sē ptōsei

For the equivalence of *epichairō* and *śāmaḥ* in the figure of rejoicing over another's misfortune, cf. above, 4:12 (cf. also Ps 35:15, 26).

Determining the original Hebrew for *ptōsis* "downfall" is a problem. The parallels suggest four possible equivalents. (1) In Prov 24:17 the Qal infinitive construct *nᵉpōl* "falling, downfall" is represented in the Greek by the II Aorist subjunctive of *piptō* "fall" (*ean pesē*, "if he should fall"): *binpōl 'ôyᵉbèkā(K) 'al-tiśmāḥ = ean pesē ho echthros sou, mē epicharēs autō*, "Do not rejoice over the fall of your enemy." Heavily favoring this possibility is the fact that *ptōsis* itself is most commonly the equivalent of some form of the Hebrew root *nāpal*,[362] and the cognate verb *piptō* is almost exclusively the LXX equivalent for the Hebrew verb *nāpal*.[363] Also, the noun *pesos* "fall," synonymous with *ptōsis* (4:31) and *ptōma* (4:33) is derived from the II Aorist of the same verbal root, *piptō*.

(2) In Job 31:29, *pîd* "ruin"[364] appears as the Hebrew equivalent of *ptōma*, cognate and synonymous with *ptōsis*, and also in combination with *śāmaḥ*: *'im-'eśmaḥ b^e pîd m^e śan'î* = *epicharēs egenomēn ptōmati echthrōn mou*, "If I rejoice over the ruin of those who hate me." (3) A similar figure appears in Prov 17:5, *śāmē^a ḥ l^e'êd* = *epichairōn apollymenō*, "he who is glad at disaster." But *'êd* "disaster" has only its association here with *sāmaḥ* to recommend it for there is no equivalency here with *piptō* or its derivatives.[365]

(4) A slight possibility is *mappelet* "downfall" which is translated by *ptōsis* six times in the LXX of Ezekiel, and always applied there to the overthrow of cities or kings.[366] But despite the frequency of its association with *ptōsis*, *mappelet* is never found in combination with *śāmaḥ* in this figure of "rejoicing over a fall."

Of the four possibilities, the first, *noplēk*, seems best substantiated. The second, *pîd*, also has some merit.

<u>4:32</u>

šōd l- = *deilaiai/deilaia*

For this equivalency, cf. above, verse 31.

le'ārîm '^a šer he'^e bîdû 'et-bānayik = *hai poleis hais edouleusan ta tekna sou* (LXX) = *m^e dînātā' 'aylēn d^e ša'bed labnayky* (Sy)

The reconstruction follows the internal arrangement of Sy in which the "cities" are the subject and not the object of the verb "serve." The above reading of Sy, "the cities which enslaved your children," stands in marked contrast with that of LXX (followed by Syh), "the cities which your children served." That of Sy represents not only the more logical and expected arrangement,[367] but it also offers a better parallel with the second half of the verse in which "the city" (the understood feminine subject) is the subject and the "children" are again the object of the verb. The verbal parallel is much more exact and artful between "the cities which enslaved your children" and "she who took away your children." Reconstruction from the Greek yields *'^a šer '^a bādûm bānayik*.[368]

The equivalency between *douleuō* and *'ābad* is certain. There are only three exceptions to this among the one hundred plus occurrences of *douleuō* in the LXX.[369] Both Sy and Syh offer here the cognate *'ᵉbad*.

lallōqᵉḥāh 'et-bānayik = hē dechamenē tous huious sou

The Greek verb *dechomai* "take, accept, receive" is by far most commonly used for the Hebrew *lāqaḥ* "take, receive" in the LXX.[370] The sense of "receive," while passive and less than forceful, is yet possible for Bar 4:32 (cf. Sy, *qᵉbel*, meaning "receive, accept" in the Pael stem), but it is more likely from the parallel context that in the original Hebrew the other sense of *lāqaḥ* "take (away)" was expressed. For examples of this meaning of *lāqaḥ* in similar contexts, cf., for example, Gen 14:12, *wayyiqḥû 'et-lôṭ wᵉ'et-rᵉkūšô*, "and they carried off Lot and his belongings"; Jer 48:46, *kî-luqqᵉḥû bānêkā baššebî*, "for your sons are taken into captivity"; and Gen 43:18, *wᵉlāqaḥat 'ōtānû la'ᵃbādîm*, "and to take us for slaves."

For the Greek pairing *tekna . . . huious*, it is very likely that the original Hebrew utilized the same word, *bānîm*, in each case. *Huios*, innumerably and almost exclusively, represents Hebrew *bēn* in the LXX.[371] *Teknos*, while hardly so numerous, is nonetheless also used with great regularity for *bēn*.[372] In addition, it appears a few times for Hebrew *ṭap* "children" and *'ôlēl* "youngster," but these are not likely here in that when paired in MT, *ṭap* is paired idiomatically with *nāšîm* "women" and *'ôlēl* similarly with *yônēq* "suckling."[373] *Teknos* does represent *yeled* "child" eight times in the LXX, but in the lone example of *yeled // bēn* in Isa 9:5, the LXX has *paidion // huios*. Further, significant support for the sequence *bānayik . . . bānayik* in Bar 4:32 is found in the cognate Syriac texts, both of which have this same sequence, repeating the same term (*bᵉnay*).

4:33

ka'ᵃšer . . . kēn = hōsper . . . houtōs

For this construction, cf. above, verses 24, 28.

śāmᵉḥāh bᵉnoplēk wᵉgālāh bikkāšᵉlēk[374] = *echarē epi tē sē ptōsei kai euphranthē epi tō ptōmati sou*

The Greek verb *chairō* "rejoice" usually represents Hebrew *śāmaḥ*. This equivalency appears sixteen times in the LXX; next in frequency are its equivalencies with *gîl* "rejoice" (eight times) and *śîś* "rejoice" (four times).[375]

Euphrainō, the parallel verb, is used for Hebrew *śāmaḥ*, however, with far greater frequency and regularity.[376] That *euphrainō* is the equivalent of *śāmaḥ* in our passage appears quite certain from the following evidence. In the nine passages in which *chairō* and *euphrainō* are translationally paired in the LXX (either in parallel or conjunctively, and regardless of the A-B sequence), in only one instance (Hos 9:1) does *euphrainō* ever represent anything other than *śāmaḥ*. In seven of these nine examples, this pairing is the equivalent of the Hebrew *śāmaḥ-gîl* pairing; the sequence *euphrainō* (A) // *chairō* (B) = *śāmaḥ* (A) // *gîl* (B) obtains in Zech 10:7, Prov 2:14 and 23:25, and the same sequence pattern prevails in the conjunctive pairing of Hab 1:15. In the parallel pairing of Hos 9:1, the reverse sequence in Greek corresponds to the above Hebrew sequence, and in the two examples of conjunctive pairing in Joel 2:21, 23, the sequence *chairō* (A) // *euphrainō* (B) = *gîl* (A) // *śāmaḥ* (B) is found. In the two remaining cases (Lam 4:21, Isa 66:10), the Hebrew equivalent of *chairō* is *śîś*, but there again *euphrainō* consistently represents *śāmaḥ*.

In addition, it is significant that in the twelve other passages in MT where the pairing *śāmaḥ-gîl* occurs, either in parallel or conjunctively,[377] the LXX, though always using *agalliazō* "rejoice" for Hebrew *gîl*, also consistently represents *śāmaḥ* with *euphrainō* in every case.[378]

From the above information, then, not only does *śāmaḥ* appear confirmed as the equivalent for *euphrainō* in our passage, but also *gîl*, its common parallel or pair member, emerges as a very probable candidate for the equivalent of *chairō*. Of significance here are the Joel parallels with their close contextual similarities to the context of Bar 4:33 (e.g., *tharsei* as in 4:30, and *ta tekna Sion*, similar to 4:32); cf. Joel 2:21, *tharsei, gē, chaire kai euphrainou* = *'al tîrᵉ'î 'ᵃdāmāh gîlî ûśᵉmāḥî*, and

Joel 2:23, *kai ta tekna Sion, chairete kai euphrainesthe* = *ûbᵉnê ṣiyyôn gîlû wᵉśimḥû.*

Gîl, then, by its frequency as A- or B-word to *śāmaḥ*, is most plausibly a part of the original Hebrew here. This conclusion is reinforced by a comparison of Prov 24:17 which, although none of its Greek terms correspond exactly to those of Bar 4:33, does feature the Hebrew pairing *śāmaḥ* (A) // *gîl* (B), within the same contextual setting as that of our Baruch passage--rejoicing over the enemy's "fall" // "downfall." Cf. Prov 24:17, *binpōl 'ôyᵉbèkā(K) 'al-tiśmāḥ / ûbikkāšᵉlô 'al-yāgēl libbekā*, "Do not rejoice in the fall of your enemy, / and let not your heart be glad over his downfall."

As noted, *śîś* is translated twice by *chairō* when paired with *śāmaḥ* (Lam 4:21, Isa 66:10) and it remains an outside possibility.

For the equivalency between *ptōsis* and *nᵉpōl*, cf. above, verse 32. The term in parallel with *ptōsis* "fall" is the synonymous and cognate noun *ptōma* "fall, disaster." This latter term appears twelve times in the LXX with Hebrew equivalents, none of the equivalencies occurring more frequently than twice.

The reconstruction of *pîd* "ruin, disaster" as the original Hebrew is suggested by Job 31:29, *'im-'eśmaḥ bᵉpîd mᵉśan'î* = *ei de kai epicharēs egenomēn ptōmati echthrōn mou*, "If I was glad at the ruin of my enemy." But *pîd* is never used in parallel with *nāpal* in MT, and in the only instance of its appearing in parallel with anything it is paired with *'êd* (Prov 24:22), and the Greek equivalents are wholly different from those of Bar 4:33.[379]

More fruitful it seems is the twice-appearing equivalency between *ptōma* and derived nouns of the Hebrew verb *kāšal* "stumble, fall."[380] For *kāšal* does appear with frequency in MT in parallel with *nāpal* (cf., e.g., Isa 3:8, 8:15, 31:3, Jer 8:12, 46:12, 50:32, Ps 27:2, and Prov 24:17), more commonly as the A-word in relation to *nāpal*. It is thus likely that the arrangement of the pairings in Bar 4:33 is the same as that in Prov 24:17, which appears to be the primary source of the "fall" // "disaster" parallelism. Cf. *binpōl . . . tiśmāḥ // bikkāšᵉlô . . . yāgēl* in Prov 24:17 and *śāmᵉḥāh bᵉnoplēk // wᵉgālāh bikkāšᵉlēk* in Bar 4:33.

The equivalence of *ptōsis* with the Hebrew root *nāpal* and of *ptōma* with the root *kāšal* appears all the more certain since *ptōsis* never occurs in the LXX for the Hebrew *kāšal* or derivatives as does *ptōma*. But the sequence of the other parallel pairing is problematic. As demonstrated above, it is to a high degree likely that *śāmaḥ* is the equivalent of *euphrainō* and *gîl* of *chairō*. But this would mean that these two Hebrew verbs would appear in Bar 4:33 in the reverse sequence of that of the Prov 24:17 source. Analysis of the MT pairing of *śāmaḥ* and *gîl* in parallel, however, reveals that *śāmaḥ* (as in Prov 24:17) is by far more commonly the A-word in relation to *gîl*. The overall MT ratio is 15:5 in favor of this sequence, and 7:1 in the Psalms.[381]

The above reconstruction has thus assumed that the LXX translator either deliberately or inadvertently reversed the usual sequence of terms. If this should not be so the reconstruction would then follow the sequence *gîl* (A) // *śāmaḥ* (B), which sequence could perhaps be justified on the basis of influence from the Joel parallels mentioned above.

tēʿāṣēb = *lypēthēsetai*

For the equivalency between the Greek *lypeō* and Hebrew *ʿāṣab* "pain, grieve," cf. above, 4:8. Clearly, the Greek future passive form would have rendered the Hebrew Niphal imperfect as in Gen 45:5, *ʾal-tēʿāṣ*^{e}*bû*, and 2 Sam 19:3, *neʿ*^{e}*ṣab hammelek*.[382]

ʿal-ḥorbōtèhā = *epi tē heautēs erēmia*

The Greek verb *erēmoō* "make desolate" is related to two common nouns, *erēmia* "desolation" and *erēmos* "desert." Both nouns have essentially the same meaning and are somewhat interchangeable, but the former (that of Bar 4:33) appears only six times in the LXX while the latter is quite common there, regularly representing Hebrew *midbār* "desert."

Of the four instances where the Hebrew equivalents of *erēmia* are known,[383] Ezek 35:4 offers the best parallel: *ʿārèkā ḥorbāh ʾāśîm w*^{e}*ʾattāh š*^{e}*māmāh tihyeh* = *kai tais polesi sou erēmian poiēsō, kai sy erēmos esē*, "I will make your cities a desolation and you will be devastated." The Sy text at Bar 4:33

also offers the cognate *ḥurbāh* "her desolation." The use of *erēmia* for *š^e^māmāh* in Ezek 35:9 suggests that this is also a possibility (cf. the discussion above at 4:19 where *erēmos* was deemed to be representing an original *ḥorbāh*). The plural has been used in the reconstruction here since the singular, *ḥorbāh*, never appears suffixed in MT. For the suffixed plural form, cf. Isa 51:3 and 44:26, in both of which the LXX offers the plural of *erēmos*.

The readings of both Sy and Syh reveal no more than the noun plus suffix; the reflexive *heautēs* of the LXX would thus appear to be an embellishment peculiar to the LXX. It may be noted finally that Sy lacks half of the parallel in the protasis, but adds an expansion in the apodosis.

4:34

w^e^'āsîr mimmennāh = kai perielō autēs

The Greek verb *periaireō* "strip off, take away from" appears over fifty times in the LXX, but only here in Baruch.[384] Kneucker[385] has contended for an equivalency here with the Hiphil stem of *'ābar* "bring over," which on occasion is used with the sense "take away, remove."[386] The MT examples reveal that this verb in the causative stem is used for the removing of sin, the withdrawal of rulership, but most often for more mundane operations such as the removal of rings, articles of clothing, and the like. It is clearly not the verb used in the prophetic rhetoric of BH to express the divinely ordained destruction of a city under the figure of removal of its teeming and noisy population.

There appears to be a better case for the causative stem of *šābat* "cause to cease, bring to an end," for it is found in BH in this very figure and often with *hāmôn* "population, (city-)noise" or *māśôś* "merriment." Cf. Ezek 30:10, *w^e^hišbattî 'et-h^a^môn miṣrayim = apolō plēthos Aigyptiōn*, "and I will make Egypt's population(-noise) cease"; Ezek 26:13 (of Tyre), *w^e^hišbattî h^a^môn šîrāyik*, "and I will silence the noise of your songs"; Isa 24:8, *šābat m^e^śôś tuppîm*, "the merriment of the timbrels has ceased"; and Lam 5:15 (the lament of the surviving population after the Jerusalem debacle), *šābat m^e^śôś libbēnû* /

nehpak l^{e}'ēbel m^{e}ḥōlēnû = katelyse chara kardias hēmōn, estraphē eis penthos ho choros hēmōn, "The merriment of our hearts has come to an end; / our dancing has turned to mourning."[387]

Significantly, these stereotypical expressions with *šābat* (Hiph or Qal) quite consistently include either *hāmôn* or *māśôś*, both of which terms were probably in the original Hebrew of Bar 4:34. The likelihood of an equivalency with *periaireō* thus appears strong.

Yet there remains a major obstacle to such a reconstruction --the LXX always translates *šābat* in these instances with *apollyō* or *katalyō* "destroy," and nowhere in the LXX is *periaireō* ever used for *šābat*.

The Hiphil stem of the verb *sûr* "remove, take away" suggests itself above all from a survey of the equivalency statistics for *periaireō*.[388] Of the fifty-six occurrences in the LXX for which there are Hebrew equivalents, thirty are with the Hiphil stem of *sûr*.[389] This alone is impressive and *hāsîr* is frequently used in BH to speak of divine removal, but still parallels involving this figure of depopulation in which *hāsîr* = *periaireō* are not plentiful. Cf. Zeph 3:11 (of Jerusalem), *'āsîr . . . 'allîzê ga'^{a}wātēk = perielō . . . ta phaulismata tēs hybreōs sou*, "I will remove . . . your arrogantly proud (people)"; and Amos 5:23, *hāsēr mē'ālay h^{a}mōn šîrèkā*, "Remove from me the noise of your songs." There are also other references to depopulation using *hāsîr*, particularly with regard to Jerusalem (cf. 2 Kgs 23:27, Ezek 16:50, Jer 32:31, and Isa 3:1), but in none of them is *periaireō* the LXX equivalent.[390]

In the light of the LXX's silence on the possibility of *periaireō* standing for *šābat* and the attested preponderance of its use for the Hiphil stem of *sûr*, the latter has been used in the reconstruction.

m^{e}śôś hāmôn = to agalliama tēs polyochlias

The Greek noun *polyochlia* "crowd of people"[391] occurs only three times in the LXX--this passage, Job 31:34 (*kî 'e'^{e}rôṣ hāmôn rabbāh*, "because I was awed by the large population"), and Job 39:7 (*yiśḥaq lah^{a}môn qiryāh*, "It scorns the populous city"). In each of these two instances it renders Hebrew *hāmôn*.

This Hebrew term basically means "noise" or "din," and from its consistent use in BH with regard to that produced particularly by teeming cities it has also come to mean "crowd" or "populace" or the like. The Greek and Hebrew terms are thus semantically close and this equivalency can be counted as certain.[392]

Agalliama "delight, joy" is used in the LXX for all the common BH synonyms for "joy."[393] The likelihood of *māśôś* "exultation, joy" is suggested by the common appearance of that term in the city-depopulation figure. It is also worthy of note that this is the only appearance of *agalliama* in Baruch, and that the other common synonyms for "joy" that occur in Baruch (viz., *euphrosynē, charmosynē, chara*) generally appear to have fairly regular equivalencies with Hebrew terms for "joy" other than *māśôś* (viz., *śimḥāh, śāśôn, gîl*). It is significant that *māśôś* does appear in the Lam 5:15 parallel with respect to Jerusalem, and similarly is frequently applied to Jerusalem elsewhere in MT (cf., e.g., Isa 60:15, Ps 48:3, Lam 2:15, Jer 49:25, and Isa 24:8).[394]

ûtᵉhî tᵉhillātāh lᵉʾēbel = kai to agauriama autēs estai eis penthos

Here the Kahana translation[395] follows the Lam 5:15 parallel quite closely, retroverting *ʾehᵉpōk lᵉʾēbel*, "I will turn to mourning." This is,,in fact, a familiar BH idiom that is paralleled several times with *ʾēbel*; cf. Amos 8:10, *hāpaktî ḥaggêkem lᵉʾēbel = kai metastrepsō tas heortas hymōn eis penthos*, and the reverse in Jer 31:13, *wᵉhāpaktî ʾeblām lᵉśāśôn = kai strepsō to penthos autōn eis charmonēn*. *Hāpak l-* is a common idiom in BH for the "turning" of one thing into another; cf. Ps 66:6, 78:44, 114:8, Amos 5:7, and 6:12. Nevertheless, the LXX without exception has (*meta-/ek-*)*strephō* "change" as the equivalent of *hāpak* in the examples of this idiom. Thus if a form of *hāpak* were assumed to have been in the original Hebrew of Bar 4:34, it would be exceedingly odd for the LXX not to have represented it in the translation.

There is, however, an alternative means of expressing this same concept of changing one thing into another that involves the use of *hāyāh l-* "become." This is indeed suggested by the

Greek reading *estai* which, although not in G^B and Syh, is represented in all the other textual witnesses. Two examples with *'ēbel* confirm this: 2 Sam 19:3, *watt^ehî hatt^ešû'āh . . . l^e'ēbel* = *kai egeneto*[396] *hē sōtēria . . . eis penthos*, "and the victory became [was turned into] . . . mourning"; and Job 30:31, *wayhî l^e'ēbel kinnōrî* = *Apebē de eis penthos mou hē kithara*, "my harp has turned into mourning."[397]

The Greek noun *agauriama* "insolence" appears rarely in the LXX. In addition to this passage it is used in Job 13:12 for Hebrew *zikkārôn* "memorial," and in Isa 62:7 (and Jer 48[31]:2?) for *t^ehillāh* "renown, fame" (as here in Baruch also with the LXX variant *gauriama* "exultation, pride"). This term is part of a set of related Greek words deriving ultimately from *gauros* "haughty."[398] The Hebrew *t^ehillāh* derives from the verb *hālal* II "be boastful, give praise," and is frequently used with the connotation "fame, renown," glory."[399] Thus semantic content alone suggests a likely correspondence.

But in addition it may be noted that in those instances where *t^ehillāh* denotes "renown" it is most commonly applied to cities as is the case in our passage. Cf. Isa 62:7, *w^e'ad-yāśîm 'et-y^erûšālayim t^ehillāh bā'āreṣ* = *kai poiēsē Hierousalēm agauriama epi tēs gēs*, "until he makes Jerusalem famous throughout the earth"; and Jer 48(31):2, *'ēn 'ôd t^ehillat Mô'āb*, "Moab is no longer renowned" (*gauriama* appears in some LXX mss. as an apparent conflation).[400] *T^ehillāh* would thus, in this light, appear to have been the original Hebrew rendered in the LXX by *agauriama*, having the sense of "(boasted-)renown" or "vaunted pride."

4:35

kî-'ēš mē'ēt-YHWH tābô' 'ālèhā = *pyr gar epeleusetai autē para tou aiōniou*

The LXX employs *pyr* "fire" with extreme regularity for Hebrew *'ēš*.[401] Likewise, *eperchomai* is commonly the equivalent of Hebrew *bô'* (as elsewhere in this chapter, vss. 9, 24, 25, 36). When used in the sense of "come upon," *bô'* usually affixes its object pronoun directly or attaches it to the combined preposition *'al-* "upon."[402] Either alternative is possible, although the lack of *epi* (or its equivalent) in the LXX text would seem to favor the suffixed verb form. But on the other hand, the more replete form with *'al-* seems to be demanded from the standpoint of the metrical balance of the tricolon.

For the identification of *ho aiōnios* with *YHWH*, see the discussion above at 4:10 (and cf. 4:14, 22, 24, 25; 5:2). Here the construction *mē'ēt-* (or perhaps *mē'im-*) *YHWH* as the equivalent of *para tou aiōniou* appears to be required by the close parallel in Gen 19:24, *wᵉYHWH himṭîr 'al-sᵉdōm wᵉ'al-'ᵃmōrāh goprît wā'ēš mē'ēt YHWH min-haššāmāyim* (LXX, . . . *kai pyr para Kyriou ex ouranou*).

For the threat of fire against the city of Babylon, cf. Isa 34:10, Jer 50:32, 51:30, and 51:58,(*ûšᵉ'ārèhā haggᵉbōhîm bā'ēš yiṣṣattû*).[403]

lᵉyāmîm rabbîm = eis hēmeras makras

Of the eighteen occurrences of the Greek adjective *makros* "long, far, much" in the LXX, only ten have Hebrew equivalents, and among those there appears to be no particular pattern of predominance.[404] In one instance, Deut 19:6, *makroterōs* (the comparative degree of *makros*) represents the Hebrew verbal root *rābāh* "be many, be great," but never does *makros* occur in the LXX for the adjective *rab* "much, many." But despite this lack of precedent, it is quite likely that in our passage the original Hebrew did have the adjective *rab*, and that the precise idiom was *yāmîm rabbîm* "many days," an expression used frequently in BH (approximately thirty times).[405] The usual LXX equivalent for *lᵉyāmîm rabbîm* is *eis hēmeras pollas*. It is significant that Bar 4:35 features this same adjectival construction with only a change in synonyms (*makros* in lieu of *polys* "much, many").

The only other likely possibility would involve the verbal root *'ārēk* (Hiph) "be long, grow long," for which there is at least closer semantic correspondence with *makros*. The Hebrew adjective *'ārōk* "long" is on one occasion in the LXX represented by *makros* (Job 11:9) where it has the comparative sense "longer." This adjective, however, never occurs in combination with *yôm*. The LXX also reveals that in one instance *makros* represents the

Hebrew adjective *'ārēk* "long" and once also a form of the verb *'ārēk*, but in neither case is there any association with *yôm*. There is, however, one instance in the LXX where *makros* is the equivalent of the related noun *'ōrek* "length." That passage is Job 12:12 (G^A only) and there it is found in the familiar idiom *'ōrek yāmîm* "length of days" (i.e., "long life").[406]

While such is an intriguing correspondence, this nominal construction, which the LXX usually translates *makrotēta hēmerōn* (or *pollō biō*) is not at all the same as the adjectival one. Its meaning is always either "long life" or "forever." This idiom, then, could hardly have been a part of the original Hebrew of Bar 4:35 as it is a nominal construction consistently connoting a long, indefinite period of time such as a lifetime or eternity. The original Hebrew, then, could only have been *yāmîm rabbîm*, since this is exactly the adjectival construction that is required by the Greek and it also connotes precisely the similarly required "long but terminable" period of time.

wᵉtûšab liś'îrîm = kai katoikēthēsetai hypo daimoniōn

Katoikeō "inhabit" is the regular and frequent LXX equivalent for Hebrew *yāšab* "dwell, inhabit"[407] (as already in Bar 3:13, 20, above). This use of the Greek future passive + *hypo* suggests that the original Hebrew was a Hophal imperfect verb form as in Isa 44:26 (of Jerusalem), *tûšab = katoikēthēsē*, or Ezek 35:9, *tûšabnāh(!) = katoikēthōsin* (also of cities). A Niphal form is also a possibility; cf. Jer 22:6 (of cities), *nôšābû(!) = katoikēthēsomenas*; Ezek 36:10 (of cities), *nōšᵉbû = katoikēthēsontai*; and Ezek 12:20.

The preposition *l-* is used in combination with passive verbs in BH (though admittedly not ever with the passive forms of *yāšab*) to denote the agent or subject of the action; for example, cf. Gen 31:15, *hᵃlô' nokriyyôt neḥšabnû lô*, "Are we not counted by him as foreigners?"[408]

The noun *daimonion* "demon" appears infrequently in the LXX, nine times in Tobit and ten times elsewhere (including twice in Baruch). In Bar 4:7 its Hebrew equivalent was found to have been *šēd* "demon," but such an equivalency is unlikely here. The context of this passage is particularized to that limited BH topos of ruined city-sites that are haunted by various wild beasts and, supposedly, by cavorting preternatural "demons" as well. This then narrows the field to the *ṣiyyîm* "desert beasts" and the *śᵉʿîrîm* "satyrs," each of which appear once as equivalents of *daimonia* within this very topos in Isa 13:21 and 34:14.[409]

In Isa 34:14, *ûpāgᵉšû ṣiyyîm ʾet-ʾiyyîm wᵉśāʿîr ʿal-rēʿēhû yiqrāʾ*, the LXX equates *ṣiyyîm* with *daimonia* and *śāʿîr* is completely misread. In Isa 13:21, *ṣiyyîm* is rendered in the LXX by *thēria* "beasts," while *śᵉʿîrîm* is there equated with *daimonia*. That the latter contains the proper equivalencies is confirmed by the Sy equivalent in our passage, *šîʾdēʾ* "demons," the same Syriac term that serves as the equivalent of *śāʿîr/śᵉʿîrîm* in the Peshiṭta of these two Isaianic passages.[410]

lᵉnēṣaḥ nᵉṣāḥîm = ton pleiona chronon

This final phrase also appears to have derived from the ruined city-site topos. The specific terms, *polys* and *chronos*, have already been encountered (cf. above, 3:13, 32; 4:12). In Isa 34:10 it is said that not even a traveler will pass over the long-smouldering ruins of Edom "forever and ever" (*lᵉnēṣaḥ nᵉṣāḥîm = eis chronon polyn*). Cf. also Isa 13:20 where it is said of Babylon that, like Sodom, she would never again be inhabited "forever" (*lānesaḥ = eis ton aiōna chronon*).

<u>4:36</u>

śᵉʾî-sābîb ʿênayik mizrāḥāh yᵉrûšālayim ûrᵉʾî = periblepsai pros anatolas, Hierousalēm, kai ide

While there is no precedent in the LXX for such an equivalency with the rare verb *periblepō* "look around,"[411] several very close BH parallels support it. Cf. Deut 3:27, *wᵉśāʾ ʿênèkā yammāh wᵉṣāpōnāh wᵉtêmānāh ûmizrāḥāh ûrᵉʾēh = kai anablepsas tois ophthalmois sou kata thalassan kai Borrhan kai Liba kai anatolas kai ide*; and Gen 13:14, *śāʾ nāʾ ʿênèkā ûrᵉʾēh . . . ṣāpōnāh wānegbāh wāqēdᵉmāh wāyāmmāh = anablepson tois ophthalmois sou, kai ide . . . pros Borrhan kai Liba kai anatolas kai thalassan.*

Even more pertinent are two passages which, like Bar 4:36, also have the maternal Jerusalem as their subject and whose contexts similarly depict Jerusalem's joyful anticipation of her children's return: Isa 49:18, *śᵉʾî-sābîb ʿênayik ûrᵉʾî kullām niqbᵉṣû bāʾû lāk* = *Aron kyklo tous ophthalmous sou, kai ide pantas, idou synēchthēsan kai ēlthosan pros se*, and Isa 60:4 (the same in the Hebrew and only slightly different in the Greek text).

These are clearly source-texts for Bar 4:36. It appears as well that this peculiar Isaianic use of *sābîb* "round about" within the common idiom *śāʾ ʿênèkā* (LXX, *anablepson*) stimulated our translator to press into service the rare *periblepō*, thereby achieving the "round about" nuance that he needed.[412]

haśśimḥāh habbāʾāh-lāk mēʾēt ʾᵉlōhîm = *tēn euphrosynēn tēn para tou theou soi erchomenēn*

A significant parallel here is Jer 13:20, *śᵉʾî ʿênêkem ûrᵉʾî habbāʾîm miṣṣāpôn* = *analabe ophthalmous sou Hierousalēm, kai ide tous erchomenous apo Borrha*. This is the fifth of six occurrences of *euphrosynē* in the Baruch poetic corpus (cf. also 3:34; 4:11, 23, 29; 5:9). As already noted, it is difficult to determine without direct parallels whether it represents in a given instance Hebrew *śimḥāh* or *śāśôn*. In this case it could well be either, but the former has been used in the reconstruction since it is the more common Hebrew equivalent for *euphrosynē*.

Erchomai is regularly the LXX equivalent for Hebrew *bôʾ* (cf. 4:14, 22, 37). For the correspondence between *para tou theou* and *mēʾēt* (or *mēʿim*) *ʾᵉlōhîm*, cf. 4:22, 35 and 5:2, 4. In contrast to verses 24, 25, and 9 above, where such stock genitival expressions as the "salvation of God" and the "wrath of God" are rendered in the Greek with *para tou theou*, there is no such BH combination as the "joy of God." Thus, as in verses 22, 35, and elsewhere, the Hebrew original here without doubt also involves the prepositional phrase *mēʾēt* or *mēʿim* (cf. Sy, *dᵉmen ʾallāhāʾ*).

A significant parallel to this verse (and the following one) may be found in the Greek only in *Pss. Sol.* 11:3-4, *stēthi Hierousalēm eph' hypsēlou, kai ide ta tekna sou apo anatolōn kai dysmōn synēgmena eisapax hypo kyriou. apo Borrha erchontai te euphrosynē tou theou autōn, ek nēsōn makrothen synēgagen autous to theos,* "Stand up on high, O Jerusalem: and behold thy children gathered from the East and the West together by the Lord. From the North they come in the gladness of their God: from the islands afar off hath God gathered them."[413]

4:37

hinnēh yābō'û-lāk bānayik 'ᵃšer šillaḥat = idou erchontai hoi huioi sou, hous exapesteilas

The equivalencies in this bicolon are already familiar and require no further comment (cf. above, 4:11, 23). For the dative, *lāk*, cf. Sy.

yābō'û niqbāṣîm = erchontai synēgmenoi

As is much of the content of verse 36, this also is drawn from Isa 49:18 and 60:4, where it is said of Jerusalem's dispersed children: *kullām niqbᵉṣû bā'û-lāk = synēchthesan kai ēlthosan pros se.* For the plural participle, cf. Jer 40:15, where *hanniqbāṣîm = hoi synēgmenoi.*[414]

mimmizrāḥ ûmimma'ᵃrāb = apo anatolōn heōs dysmōn

Here Isa 43:5 is clearly the primary source: *mimmizrāḥ 'ābî' zar'ekā ûmimma'ᵃrāb 'ᵃqabbᵉṣekā = apo anatolōn axō to sperma sou, kai apo dysmōn synaxō se.* Cf. also Ps 107:3, *ûmē'ᵃrāṣôt qibbᵉṣām mimmizrāḥ ûmimma'ᵃrāb miṣṣāpôn ûmiyyām = kai ek tōn chōrōn synēgagen autois apo anatolōn, kai dysmōn, kai Borrha kai thalassēs;* Isa 45:6 and Zech 8:7.

bidbar qādôš = to rhēmati tou hagiou

The Greek noun *rhēma* "word" is an extremely frequent and regular equivalent in the LXX for Hebrew *dābār* "word."[415] A much more limited equivalency with *'ēmer* "word" offers about twenty examples in BH, including in Job 6:10 the combination *'imrê qādôš = rhēmata hagia theou mou* (the LXX either misreads here or follows a different text tradition, "holy words of my

God"). However, *rhēmati* in Bar 4:37 is in case and number dative singular, and the Hebrew *'ēmer*, with only once exception in BH (the probably corrupt Job 20:29), always occurs in the plural.[416]

In Isa 5:24 the phrase *'imrat qᵉdôš yiśrā'ēl* suggests the possibility of the Hebrew noun *'imrāh* "word" as the Hebrew equivalent. But this term is very rarely represented by *rhēma*. In only three of the 400+ occurrences of *rhēma* in the LXX does it represent *'imrāh*. Indeed, in Isa 5:24 the LXX equivalent is *logion* "declaration," itself the normal LXX equivalent for *'imrāh*.[417] Thus, although a precise parallel is wanting, *dābār* is the obvious choice.

śᵉmēḥîm bikbôd-'ēl = chairontes tē tou theou doxē

For the equivalency between *chairō* and *śāmaḥ*, cf. above, 4:33, as well as the parallel passage in 5:5. The participial construction is consistent in the Versions (cf. LXX, Sy, Syh, La^V) and may be compared with the parallel in 1 Kgs 8:66, *wayyēlᵉkû . . . śᵉmēḥîm = apēlthon . . . chairontes*, "they went . . . rejoicing." For the equivalency between *doxa* and *kābôd*, cf. above, 4:3, 24, and below, 5:1, 2, 4, 6, 7, 9. The concept of the divine "glory" that accompanies and leads the returnees may be found in similar contexts in Deutero-Isaiah (cf. 40:5, 43:7, 48:11, 58:8, 59:19, 60:1, 66:18, et al.). For the precise parallel *kᵉbôd-'ēl = doxa theou*, cf. Ps 19:2. Also the equivalency *kᵉbôd 'ᵉlōhîm = doxa theou* is found in Prov 25:2, indicating that such is equally a possibility here.[418]

5:1

For the same verbal sequence, *ekdyō . . . endyō = pāšaṭ . . . lābaš*, in combination with *stolē/beged*, cf. 4:20, where the disconsolate Jerusalem removed the "clothing of peace" and put on sackcloth. Now the mourning garments are removed in favor of the splendor of God's glory (cf. Isa 52:1, Ezek 16:14).

bigde- eblēk wᵉ onyēk = stolēn tou penthous[419] *kai tēs kakōseōs kakōseōs sou*

The equivalency between *penthos* and *'ēbel* is now well-attested (cf. 4:9, 11, 23, 34). *Kakōsis* "ill-treatment, affliction" has discernible Hebrew equivalents in thirteen of the eighteen instances of its use in the LXX. Six of these are with Hebrew *rāʿāh* "evil," and three are with *ʿŏnî* "affliction." The available parallels tend to support the latter term as it carries with it especially the overtones of the Egyptian captivity, that notorious and paradigmatic affliction that provides a more apt and precise connotation for the Baruch context than could the more general *rāʿāh*.[420]

Several examples will illustrate this. In Exod 3:7, *YHWH* says, "I have seen the affliction of my people who are in Egypt" (*rāʾōh rāʾîtî ʾet-ʿŏnî ʿammî ʾăšer bᵉmiṣrāyim = Idōn eidon tēn kakōsin tou laou mou tou en Aigyptō*). In Exod 3:17, God declares, "I will bring you up out of the affliction of Egypt" (. . . *mēʿŏnî miṣrayim* = . . . *ek tēs kakōseōs tōn Aigyptiōn*). The same allusion is involved in the *leḥem ʿōnî* (LXX, *arton kakōseōs*) of Deut 16:3.

For the Semitic pattern of suffixing the possessive pronoun to each coordinated substantive, cf. the conflate Sy, *ʾesṭᵉlāʾ d(ʾ)ebleky wadbîšᵉteky wadḥaššeky*, and Syh, *ʾesṭᵉlāʾ d(ʾ)eblāʾ dîleky wadmūkākāʾ dîleky*.[421]

tipʾeret = tēn euprepeian

This would appear to have derived from Isa 52:1 where the context is again that of the exuberant mother-Jerusalem welcoming back her children: *ʿûrî ʿûrî libšî ʿuzzēk ṣiyyôn / libšî bigdê tipʾartēk yᵉrûšālayim ʿîr haqqōdeš = exegeirou exegeirou Siōn, endysai tēn ischyn sou Siōn, kai sy endysai tēn doxan sou Hierousalēm polis hē hagia*, "Awake, awake, put on your strength, O Zion; put on your glorious garments, O Jerusalem, the holy city" (LXX, ". . . put on your glory . . ."). But *tipʾeret* is here represented in the LXX by *doxa*, and the equivalency assumed above with *euprepeia* "beauty, comeliness, majesty," though semantically likely (*tipʾeret* also has the sense of "beauty, glory") and seemingly apt, is nevertheless unprecedented in the LXX.

There is, however, considerable support for *hādār* "splendor" as the equivalent here, and it may well be the better choice. Of the ten occurrences of *euprepeia* with Hebrew equivalents in the LXX four are with *hādār* (and another is probable in Sir 47:10). The remaining six occurrences are spread over five different words.[422]

In two instances of this equivalency, *euprepeia* is combined with the verb *endyō* in the LXX: Ps 104:1 (of *YHWH*), *exomologēsin kai euprepeian enedysō = hôd wᵉhādār lābāštā*, "You have clothed yourself with praise and splendor"; and Prov 31:25 (of the ideal woman), *Ischyn kai euprepeian enedysato = ʿōz-wᵉhādār lᵉbûšāh*, "She is clothed with strength and splendor." The two other passages, while not featuring the verb *endyō*, do however deal with Jerusalem: Lam 1:6, *wayyēṣēʾ min-bat-ṣiyyôn kol-hᵃdārāh*, "all her splendor has dissipated from the daughter of Zion"; and Ezek 16:14, *bahᵃdārî ʾᵃšer-śamtî ʿālayik*, "the splendor with which I bedecked you."

Despite the above support for *hādār*, *tipʾeret* has been used in the reconstruction largely because of the parallel in Isa 52:1 and the already established equivalency between *hādār* and *lamprotēs* in 4:24 (and in 5:3 below). Clearly, though, *hādār* is here equally as possible as the original Hebrew.[423]

5:2

ʿᵃṭî mᵉʿîl ṣidqat ʾᵉlōhîm = peribalou tēn diploïda tēs para tou theou dikaiosynēs

With only slight embellishment, this phrase is borrowed directly from Isa 61:10, *kî hilbîšanî bigdê-yešaʿ / mᵉʿîl ṣᵉdāqāh yᵉʿāṭānî*. The LXX translation of this verse is free and contains no equivalent for the second verb. Also, *mᵉʿîl* "cloak" is rendered in this Isa 61:10 passage by the Greek *chitōn* "tunic," the only instance of such an equivalence in the LXX. With but four exceptions in thirty occurrences, *chitōn* otherwise consistently represents Hebrew *kᵉtōnet/kuttōnet* "tunic" in the LXX, and *diploïs* "cloak" in each one of its LXX occurrences with a discernible Hebrew equivalent stands for Hebrew *mᵉʿîl* "cloak, robe."[424]

The Greek verb *periballō* "put on, wrap around," while actually more common in the LXX for Hebrew *kāsāh* "cover," appears five times for Hebrew *ʿāṭāh* "wrap around, envelop," including the very significant parallel in Ps 109:29, *wᵉyaʿᵃṭû kamʿîl boštām = kai peribalesthōsan hōs diploïda aischynen autōn*, "and let them wrap on their shame like a cloak."[425]

The LXX employs *dikaiosynē* "righteousness, justice" with great regularity for the common Hebrew *ṣedeq/ṣᵉdāqāh* "righteousness, justice." While the precise combination *ṣedeq/ṣidqat 'ēl/'ᵉlōhîm* does not appear in BH, nevertheless the deity is often the referent for the suffixed forms of these Hebrew nouns.[426] The phrase is in use in the Qumran literature, however; cf. 1QS 10:25 and 11:12, *ṣdqt 'l*, and 1QM 4:6, *ṣdq 'l*. Also in the Qumran material suffixed forms frequently refer to God. The longer *'ᵉlōhîm* has been used in the reconstruction here instead of *'ēl*, *metri causa*.

śîmî 'al-rō'šēk pᵉ'ēr-kᵉbôd YHWH = epithou tēn mitran epi tēn kephalēn sou tēs doxēs tou aiōniou

The Greek verb *epitithēmi* "put upon, set upon" occurs only here in Baruch. In the LXX it is most commonly the equivalent for the Hebrew verbs *śîm* and *nātan*.[427] *Nātan* "give" has a wide range of meaning in BH and is at times nuanced to express precisely the sense of *śîm*, "put, set." This is especially true when combined with *'al-* "upon"; cf., for example, 1 Sam 17:38, *wᵉnātan qôba' nᵉḥōšet 'al-rô'šô* (the LXX lacks the verb here), "and he put a bronze helmet upon his head."[428]

Yet *śîm* is the more natural and logical equivalent here as several parallels reveal: Zech 3:5, *yāśîmû ṣānîp ṭāhôr 'al-rô'šô = kai epithete kidarin katharan epi tēn kephalēn autou*, "Let them put a clean turban upon his head"; and Exod 29:6, *wᵉśamtā hammiṣnepet 'al-rô'šô = kai epithēseis tēn mitran epi tēn kephalēn autou*, "and put the turban upon his head."[429] This very expression appears in the Greek only in Jdt 10:3, *kai epetheto mitran ep' autēs* (cf. also 16:8).

The primary source-text, Isa 61:10, has no doubt also considerably influenced this part of Bar 5:2. After the above-cited portion it continues: *keḥātān yᵉkahēn (yākîn!)*[430] *pᵉ'ēr = hōs nymphiō peritheke moi mitran*, "as a bridegroom knots on a turban." Here *peritithēmi* functions as the equivalent of *epitithēmi* except that it more explicitly nuances the "wrapping around" or "putting around" aspect of donning a turban or similar headgear. Thus the bridegroom's *pᵉʾēr* (LXX, *mitra*), a striking symbol of exuberant joy (the very opposite of mourning garb; cf. Isa 61:3, *pᵉʾēr taḥat ʿēper*) in this exulting speech of Jerusalem herself, appears to be precisely the equivalent required by the context of Bar 5:2.

Statistically, *mitra* represents Hebrew *miṣnepet* "turban" in eight of its nine LXX occurrences that reveal a Hebrew equivalent, and the equivalency with *pᵉʾēr* in Isa 61:10 occurs only there.[431] Nevertheless, *miṣnepet* is quite restricted in its usage, almost exclusively appearing in descriptions of the priestly paraphernalia,[432] while *pᵉʾēr* in its general usage[433] more closely approximates the connotation of *mitra* here in Baruch, especially its use in the source-text, Isa 61:10.[434] The Greek noun *kephalē* "head" is very regularly used for Hebrew *rôʾš* in the LXX.[435]

The combination *kᵉbôd YHWH* occurs significantly in Isa 60:1 and altogether thirty-five times in MT,[436] and is very probably the original Hebrew here.[437]

5:3

The equivalencies in this verse are all clear. For *lamprotēs* = *hādār*, cf. above, 4:24. The Greek verb *deiknymi* "show, point out" is very regularly used in the LXX for the causative stem of the Hebrew verb *rāʾāh* "see" (cf. Sir 45:3).[438]

taḥat kol-haššāmayim = *tē hyp' ouranon pasē*

This Hebrew idiom appears in Gen 7:19, Deut 2:25, 4:19, Job 28:24, 37:3, 41:3, and Dan 9:12. The meaning of the phrase "under the whole heaven" is exactly what would be meant in current English by "everything under heaven." This can be seen in Deut 2:25, for example, where Israel is told that its terror and fear will be held up before *hāʿammîm taḥat kol-haššāmāyim*, "all the peoples under heaven"; Job 41:3, *taḥat kol-haššāmayim lî-hûʾ* = *pasa hē hyp' ouranon emē estin*, "everything under the heavens is mine"; and Job 28:24, *taḥat kol-haššāmayim yirʾeh* = *tēn hyp' ouranon pasan ephora*, "He sees everything under heaven."[439]

The text of Sy for Bar 5:3 (followed only by Sa in changing the essence of the idiom from "under heaven" to "upon earth") reads: *l^{e}kulnaš d^{e}ʿal kullāh ʾarʿāʾ*, "to every person on the whole earth." Syh offers *l^{e}kullāh hāy datḥet š^{e}mayyāʾ*, "to everything which is under heaven." These might appear to suggest an alternative Hebrew expression such as *l^{e}kōl taḥat haš-šamayim*, but more probably they rather reflect the predilection of their language for handling such an idiom (cf. also La^V, *omni quae sub caelo est*).

5:4

w^{e}qôrāʾ lāk šēm mēʾēt ʾēl l^{e}ʿôlām = klēthēsetai gar sou to onoma para tou theou eis ton aiōna

The primary source for this verse is Isa 62:2, *w^{e}rāʾû gôyim ṣidqēk w^{e}kol-m^{e}lākîm k^{e}bôdēk / w^{e}qōrāʾ lāk šēm ḥādāš ʾ^{a}šer pî YHWH yiqq^{o}bennû = kai opsontai ethnē tēn dikaiosynēn sou, kai basileis tēn doxan sou, kai kalesei se to onoma to kainon, ho ho Kyrios onomasei auto*, "And nations will behold your righteousness and all kings your glory; / and you shall be called by a new name, which the very mouth of the Lord will pronounce." Isa 43:1 offers a variation of the same idiom: *qārāʾtî b^{e}šimkā = ekalesa se to onoma sou* (cf. also 1QpH 8:9, *nqrʾ ʿl šm hʾmt*, "called by the name of truth").

The equivalency between *kaleō* and *qārāʾ* in the LXX is very common[440] and has already appeared in Bar 3:33, 34. That the required passive verb form in the original Hebrew was the Qal passive is indicated by Isa 62:2. This is confirmed also by several other Deutero-Isaianic name-giving passages: Isa 58:12, *w^{e}qôrāʾ l^{e}kā gôdēr pereṣ*, "and you will be called 'repairer of the breached wall'"; 61:3, *w^{e}qôrāʾ lāhem ʾêlê haṣṣedeq*, "and they will be called 'trees of righteousness'"; Isa 48:8 and 65:1.

The Greek construction *klēthēsetai gar sou* undoubtedly represents the *w^{e}qôrāʾ lāk* construction as in Isa 62:2, literally, "it will be called to/of you" (i.e., "you will be called"). This is also the arrangement in Sy--*netq^{e}rēʾ leky ger*--suggesting that for the Greek the dative, *soi*, would perhaps more accurately represent the Semitic construction.[441]

The LXX employs *onoma* "name" both extensively and regularly for Hebrew *šēm* "name." Curiously, this very common biblical word occurs only here in the Baruch poetry.[442] For the use of *para tou theou* for *mē'ēt 'ēl/'ᵉlōhîm*, cf. above, 4:22, 35, 36. For *lᵉ'ôlām*, cf. above, 4:1, 5:1 and Isa 32:17. It may be noted that in this instance Sy presents the very same word order for this bicolon as does the LXX: *netqᵉrē' leky ger šᵉmā' men lᵉwāt 'allāhā' lᵉ'ālam*, "For the name will be pronounced for you from the presence of God forever."[443]

šᵉlôm ṣᵉdāqāh ûkᵉbôd yir'at-'ēl = Eirēnē dikaiosynēs kai doxa theosebeias

The equivalencies in this bicolon are all highly regular in the LXX.[444] The term *theosebeia* "godliness, fear of God" (= Latin, *pietas*) appears eight times in the LXX, but in only two of these is there a Hebrew equivalent.[445] In both cases the Hebrew is a genitival construction with *yir'āh* "fear." The first, Gen 20:11, exemplifies the literal equivalent of the Greek, *yir'at 'ᵉlōhîm* (cf. also 1 Sam 23:3 and Neh 5:5). The other, Job 28:28, is a secondary variation, *yir'at 'ᵃdōnāy*. The former is mirrored at Qumran in 1QSb 5:25, *wyr't 'l*.[446] The latter probably reflects the combination *yir'at YHWH* which is far more numerous in MT.[447]

5:5

This verse repeats much of the substance of Bar 4:36-37 and thus is also heavily dependent upon Isa 49:18 (= 60:4).[448] However, two additional Deutero-Isaianic sources are apparent here: Isa 51:17, *qûmî yᵉrûšālayim = anastēthi Hierousalēm*; and Isa 40:9, *'al har-gābōᵃh 'ᵃlê-lāk = ep' oros hypsēlon anabēthi*.

qûmî yᵉrûšālayim = Anastēthi Hierousalēm

The equivalency in the LXX between *anistēmi* "rise up" and *qûm* "arise" is quite regular.[449] The source is Isa 51:17, cited above (cf. also Isa 60:1, *qûmî 'ôrî*, with reference to Jerusalem).

wᵉ'imdî 'al-har-gābōᵃh = kai stēthi epi tou hypsēlou

Although *histēmi* "stand" is employed by the LXX to represent some thirty-seven different Hebrew equivalents, the normal, or most common, equivalent is *'āmad* "stand."[450] An example of this equivalency is Jer 48:19, *'el-derek 'imdî = eph' hodou stēthi*, "stand by the road!" In Job 29:8 the same verbal sequence appears: *qāmû 'āmādû*.

The source-text for *epi tou hypsēlou* and its Hebrew counterpart appears to be another Deutero-Isaianic passage, Isa 40:9 (quoted above). This same phrase appears also in Isa 57:7 and (with the slight addition of *kol*) in Isa 30:25 and Jer 3:6. In each of these the LXX equivalent is quite literal--*ep' oros hypsēlon*. It might be assumed with Kneucker[451] that the original Hebrew for Bar 5:5 would have lacked *har* since the corresponding LXX element, *oros*, is lacking. However, this Greek adjective is used as a substantive in the absolute sense as "height" or "high place"[452] much more frequently than is the Hebrew *gābō^{a}h*.[453] So it would have been far easier and more natural for the LXX translator to have omitted an equivalent for *har* and used *hypsēlos* absolutely than it would have been for the original author to have omitted *har* and used *gābō^{a}h* absolutely. The Hebrew synonym *mārôm* "height" might also be considered a possibility but its connotations are usually more metaphorical or theological.[454]

ûś^{e}'î-sābîb 'ênayik mizrāḥāh ûr^{e}'î = kai periblepsai pros anatolas kai ide

With the exception of the missing vocative, *y^{e}rûšālayim*, this is exactly the same as its counterpart in 4:36, both derivative of Isa 49:18 (= 60:4). Sy expands, *walma'rābā'*, "and to the west."

bānayik niqb^{e}ṣû = sou synēgmena ta tekna

For this phrase, cf. above, 4:37 and Isa 60:4. Sy adds *w(')ātēn leky*, "and coming to you."

mimmizrah šemeš 'ad-ma'^{a}rāb = men madn^{e}ḥaw(h)y d^{e}šemšā' 'edammā' l^{e}ma'rābaw(h)y (Syh)

In this portion of the verse, G^{B} and the major LXX Uncials (and most Minuscules) offer the reading *apo hēliou dysmōn heōs anatolōn*, "from the west unto the east." This would appear to presume a Hebrew original such as that in Kneucker's reconstruction, *mimma'ᵃrab (haš)šemeš ûmimmizrāḥāh.*[455] However, there being no such combination in MT as *mimma'ᵃrab šemeš*, a more probable alternative would appear to be the common BH idiom for "west," *mābô' haššemeš.*[456]

In marked contrast to this reading, however, stands that of the Hexaplaric text-tradition, O (= primarily LXX Ms. 88 + Syh): *apo anatolōn hēliou mechri dysmōn.* Indeed, it is this reading that is reflected in most non-Greek Versions; cf. Sy, *men madnᵉḥaw(h)y dᵉšemšā' wa'dammā' lᵉma'rābaw(h)y*, two Vetus Latina codices and the Vulgate ($La^{L,S,V}$), *ab oriente sole (et) usque ad occidentem*, Bo, Arm, and Irenaeus.[457] This is also in substantial agreement with Bar 4:37, and it would presume as the original Hebrew: *mimmizraḥ šemeš 'ad-ma'ᵃrāb.*[458]

The evidence of Hebrew parallelism is supportive of this latter reading also over that of G^B et al. Wherever in BH the terms "east" and "west" are paired, either conjunctively or in parallel, with only one exception out of thirteen examples (Isa 59:19) *mizrāḥ* "east" is always the A-word, not only in relation to *ma'ᵃrāb*, but also to *mābô' (haššemes)* and *yāmmāh* as "west."[459]

In both Ps 50:1 and 113:3 this very same Greek phrase, *apo anatolōn hēliou mechri dysmōn*, renders the Hebrew, *mimmizraḥ-šemeš 'ad-mᵉbō'ô.* Two very close Deutero-Isaianic parallels with contexts similar to that of Bar 5:5 also present this same sequence of east to west: Isa 45:6, *mimmizraḥ-šemeš ûmimma'ᵃrābāh = ap' anatolōn hēliou kai . . . apo dysmōn*; and Isa 43:5, *mimmizrāḥ . . . mimma'ᵃrāb = apo anatolōn . . . apo dysmōn.* In the whole of BH only in Isa 59:19 is the sequence otherwise, *mimma'ᵃrāb . . . ûmimmizraḥ-šemeš = apo dysmōn . . . kai . . . apo anatolōn hēliou*, and except for sequence even this does not correspond precisely to the usual LXX reading in Bar 5:5.

It has thus been deemed best to follow at this point the text-tradition of the Hexaplaric, Syriac, and Latin Versions vis-à-vis G^B and the other Greek witnesses. It is perhaps possible that the terms, east and west, were reversed at some point in the LXX tradition but preserved in their normal sequence elsewhere.

bidbar qādôš śᵉmēḥîm bᵉzeker-'ēl = tō rhēmati tou hagiou chairontas tē tou theou mneia

This is repeated verbatim from 4:37 with the sole exception of the final word, *mneia = zēker* "remembrance." For that equivalency, cf. above, 4:27.

5:6

kî raglî mē'immāk yāṣᵉ'û = exēlthon gar para sou pezoi

The Greek verb *exerchomai* "go out," which appears only here in the Baruch poetry, is used in the LXX with extreme regularity for Hebrew *yāṣā'* "go out."[460] *Pezos* "afoot" in every LXX occurrence with a Hebrew equivalent represents Hebrew *raglî* "on foot."[461] Indeed, this is the term used in Exod 12:37, *wayyis'û bᵉnê-yiśrā'ēl . . . raglî*, with reference to the exodus from Egypt. Another possibility is perhaps *bᵉregel* "on foot," as in Ps 66:6 and Judg 4:15, 17.

nᵉhûgîm bᵉyad 'ôyēb = agomenoi hypo echthrōn

The LXX uses *agō* "lead, bring, carry off" most frequently for the Hiphil stem of Hebrew *bô'*.[462] But there is another less frequent equivalency with the Piel (and Qal) stem of *nāhag* "drive off, lead captive" that appears even more apropos here. The basic sense of this Hebrew verb is that of "driving" as applied, for example, to herds (Exod 3:1, Ps 78:52) or chariots (Exod 14:25, 2 Kgs 9:20). In other passages this "driving away" becomes metaphorical for "leading into captivity." Cf. Isa 60:11, *ûmalkêhem nᵉhûgîm = kai basileis autōn agomenous*, "and their kings led captive"; and Isa 20:4, where it is said of the king of Assyria that he will "lead captive" (*yinhag = axei*) the captives of Egypt (cf. also Nah 2:8, 1 Sam 30:2).

wîbî'ēm-lāk 'ēl = eisagei de autous ho theos pros se

The contrast between the humiliating departure and the glorious return is made quite sharp. This theme of returning "carried" is especially Deutero-Isaianic; cf. Isa 49:22, *wᵉhēbî'û bānayik bᵉḥōṣen ûbᵉnōtayik 'al-kātēp tinnāśe'nāh* (the LXX verbal equivalents are *agō* and *airō*); Isa 60:9, *lᵉhābî' bānayik mērāḥôq = agagein ta tekna sou makrothen* (cf. Isa 60:4); and Isa 66:20, *wᵉhēbîʾû . . . ûbaṣṣabbîm*, "and they will bring back . . . and in palanquins." The Greek verb *eisagō* "lead in" is very regularly used in the LXX for the Hiphil stem of *bôʾ*,[463] as is *agō*. The above examples also reveal that the Hebrew verb for "bringing back" the carried returnees is certainly *hēbîʾ*.

nᵉśûʾîm bᵉkābôd = airomenous meta doxēs

The use of *airō* "lift, raise, bear" for Hebrew *nāśāʾ* is extremely regular in the LXX.[464] This equivalency is found in the Isa 49:22 source (cited above) in which the returnees are depicted as being "carried upon the shoulder." It is also found in a similar restoration context in Isa 66:12, *wînaqtem ʿal-ṣad tinnāśēʾû = ta paidia autōn epʾ ōmōn arthēsontai*, "their infants will be carried on the hip" (cf. Isa 60:4). This equivalency appears also in Isa 46:7 where the verbs have the same sense with respect to carrying idols in exalted procession: *yiśśāʾūhû ʿal-kātēp = airousin auto epi tou ōmou*. For the Qal passive participle form, cf. Isa 46:3; for the association of *nāśāʾ* with *kissēʾ*, cf. Isa 6:1.

Another possibility for reconstruction might perhaps be a Hophal participle from the verb *yābal*,[465] as in Isa 55:12, but such really has more the connotation of "be conducted" than "be borne." Also, *airō* is never used in the LXX for *yābal*.

kᵉkissēʾ malkût = hōs thronon basileias

The author's conception of a triumphant return by Jerusalem's children is expressed here through the figure of heroes borne by bearers in a royal sedan chair or palanquin.[466] The Greek phrase, *hōs thronon*, admits only the meaning "as a throne." Thus the earliest commentators were disposed to interpret this figure to mean that the returnees would be carried as royal thrones are carried (by implication, with dignity). An example is Fritzsche's rendering into German, "getragen . . . wie ein Thron des Königreiches."[467]

Kneucker[468] recognized this as a Hebraism, comparable to those "elliptical" prepositional phrases in BH that are introduced by what has been traditionally termed the "pregnant" use of the preposition *k-*. From an available wealth of biblical examples he cited Isa 9:3, 1:25, and 1 Sam 15:22, in each of which the single preposition carries, as it were, a double force. This so-called "pregnant *k*-" phenomenon is perhaps better understood as a comparative particle that conveys itself the fuller sense, "as in, as on, as with."[469]

That this Hebrew construction often proved puzzling to the Greek translators is evident from various examples. For instance, in Isa 9:3 *k*^{e}*yôm midyān* is rendered in the LXX *hōs tē hēmera tē epi Madiam*, and in 1 Sam 15:22 *kišmō*^{a}*ʿ b*^{e}*qôl YHWH* becomes in the LXX *hōs to akousai phōnēs Kyriou*. In both this peculiar (yet common for BH) "pregnant" sense of the comparative particle was missed, yielding recognizable Hebraisms in the LXX text.[470]

It would appear then that *hōs thronon basileias* also represents one of these Hebraisms and that the Hebrew behind it was *k*^{e}*kissēʾ*[471] *malkût*, "as on a royal throne." This is after all the sense demanded by the context (as well as the Deutero-Isaianic parallels noted above), and it would be a very strange use of this figure indeed if the author's analogy were here assumed to be with the bearing or lifting of portable thrones rather than with the dignified and stately manner in which royalty are carried on such.[472]

Further confirmation of this may be found in the clearly secondary Alexandrinian variant *(hōs) huious basileias(-ias)*, "(as) royal sons" (G^{A}, G^{Q}, $La^{C,S,V}$, et al.).[473] This reading betrays the reasoning of attempted clarification; those who are carried on thrones "of the kingdom" are royal personages, to be sure, royal sons in this context. The reading of Sy, *ʿal kurs*^{e}*yāʾ d*^{e}*malkūtāʾ*, "upon the royal throne," is thus also a translational facilitation that attempts to render the easily obscured Hebrew sense more obvious.

There are several possible equivalents for *basileia* "kingdom":[474] *mamlākāh* is combined with *kissēʾ* five times in BH (2 Chr 23:30, Deut 17:18, 2 Sam 7:13, 1 Kgs 9:5, Hag 2:22), *malkût* is found in the same combination five times (1 Chr 28:5, 22:10, 2 Chr 7:18, Esth 1:2, 5:1), and *m*^{e}*lûkāh* occurs thus once (1 Kgs 1:46). The choice among these is by no means clear-cut, but the second is favored by the lateness of the writings it appears in, by the fact that it is five times more prominent than either of the others in the extra-biblical Qumran literature,[475] and by the fact that both Sy and Syh offer the precise cognate, *malkūtā'*.

5:7

This verse gives evidence of clear derivation from Isa 40:4, but there is enough expansion beyond that to suggest further influence, perhaps from a Jewish midrash. The Sy text confirms this biblical source by its additional inclusion of "and the rough places will become smooth and level." Other sources are yet involved in this patchwork verse, as will be noted, but none so basically or extensively as Isa 40:4.

kî ṣiwwāh 'ᵉlōhîm lišpal kol-har gābōᵃh wᵉgib'ôt 'ôlām = synetaxe gar ho theos tapeinousthai pan oros hypsēlon kai thinas aenaous

Syntassō "arrange, put in order" is used with extreme regularity in the LXX for Hebrew *ṣiwwāh* "command, order."[476] This element is not derived from Isa 40:4 itself but rather gives every indication of being a midrashic elaboration consonant with such. Biblical examples of this sort of subordination of the Hebrew infinitive construct to *ṣiwwāh* may be compared in Exod 35:29, *'ᵃšer ṣiwwāh YHWH la'ᵃśôt = hosa synētaxe Kyrios poiēsai*, "which *YHWH* had ordered to be done"; Exod 35:1, 36:5, and Lev 7:36. Comparable subordination to *'āmar* may be found in Esth 9:14, *wayyō'mer hammelek lᵉhē'āśôt kēn*, "So the king gave orders for this to be done"; Esth 1:17, 1 Chr 13:4, et al.[477]

The equivalency between *tapeinoō* "make low, humble" and Hebrew *šāpēl* "become low, be humbled" is clear from its appearance in the Isa 40:4 source.[478] The same is true with respect to *oros* and *har*, both common for "mountain."[479]

The substantive *hypsēlos* has over a dozen possible Hebrew equivalents,[480] but after *bāmāh* (a BH term largely used in a highly specialized manner for the "high places" of the historical narratives, and thus unlikely here) the most frequent is *gābōᵃh* "high, lofty." The cinching evidence, however, is that in BH it is only this term that appears in combination with *har* to express the conception of "high or lofty mountain(s)."[481]

The phrase *thinas aenaous* "everlasting hills" does not appear as such in Isa 40:4, but the synonymous *bounos* "hill" (MT, *gib'āh* "hill") does. It would thus appear that this is an elaboration of the Isa 40:4 source under the influence of the familiar cliche, "everlasting hills," drawn from such passages as Gen 49:26, *gib'ōt 'ôlām = thinōn aenaōn* , and Deut 33:15, *gib'ôt 'ôlām = bounōn aenaōn*. Both *this* "hill" and *aenaos* "everlasting" are extremely rare words in the LXX, but within their limited use these equivalencies are very consistent. *This* occurs only three times in addition to its occurrence here,[482] but in each instance for Hebrew *gib'āh*. And, of the four occurrences of *aenaos* with discernible Hebrew equivalents, three represent *'ôlām*.[483]

w^e gê'āyôt l^e hinnāśē' = kai pharaggas plērousthai

Both equivalencies are again clear from Isa 40:4--*pharagx* "valley" = *gay'* "valley"[484] and *plēroō* "fill up" = *nāśā'* "raise up." *Plēroō* is normally the equivalent in the LXX of *mālē'* (Piel) "fill up"[485] but in one lone instance in the LXX it does stand for *nāśā'*--in the Isa 40:4 source! This information not only serves to confirm the source-text, but could also suggest the degree of carefulness with which the LXX translator checked his biblical source.

l^e mîšôr hā'āreṣ = eis homalismon tēs gēs

The Greek denominative verb *homalizō* "make even, level" occurs three times in the LXX, only twice with Hebrew equivalents. In Isa 28:25 it renders *šāwāh*(Piel) "smooth out, level" and in Isa 45:2 it represents *yāšar*(Piel) "make smooth, straight."[486] The related substantive *homalismos* "a leveling" occurs only here and in Mic 7:12. In the latter instance it is very probably a mistranslation and unfortunately lacks a Hebrew equivalent. Given the dependent character of Bar 5:7, it is highly probable that *eis homalismon* here represents the *l^e mîšôr* "(to) a leveling, level place" of the Isa 40:4 source-text.[487]

yēlēk = badisē

Out of fifty LXX occurrences with Hebrew equivalents, in only three does *badizō* "go, walk" ever represent anything but Hebrew *hālak* (cf. also Bar 4:19).[488]

lābeṭaḥ = asphalos

The adverb *asphalōs* "securely" appears only six times in the LXX, once (Gen 34:25) with a Hebrew equivalent, *beṭaḥ*.[489] The alternative BH forms, *beṭaḥ* and *lābeṭaḥ*, are equally possible here. Each appears in BH in combination with *hālak*; cf. Prov 3:23, *tēlēk lābeṭaḥ*, and Prov 10:9, *yēlēk beṭaḥ*.

bikbôd ʾᵉlōhîm = tē tou theou doxē

This phrase is the same as that in 4:37 and doubtless alludes to the glorious presence of God, the "Light" that guided Israel through the wilderness; cf. Bar 5:9, 4:37, 4:2, Job 29:3, Isa 60:1-3, 40:5, 42:16-17, and *Pss. Sol.* 11:7. This is a prominent figure in Deutero-Isaiah.[490]

5:8

sakkû yᵉʿārôt = eskiasan de kai hoi drymoi

The Greek verb *skiazō* "shade" appears eight times in the LXX with Hebrew equivalents. In three of these instances the Hebrew verb is *sākak* "overshadow, screen off"; cf. Exod 37:9, 1 Chr 28:18, and Job 40:22.[491] Never in the LXX does it represent the Hebrew verb *ṣālal* "shade."[492] For the use of *sākak* in combination with *ʿal-*, cf. Exod 40:3, 21; 33:22; 1 Kgs 8:7; Ps 5:12 (and cf. Sy); for its use with *l-*, cf. Ps 91:4, 140:8 (and cf. Syh).

Kahana,[493] apparently *ad sensum*, has rendered the Greek Aorist active indicative *eskiasan* "they have overshadowed" with a Hebrew imperfect verb form *yāsōkkû* "they will overshadow," even though the LXX and the other Versions consistently witness past tense for this verb. The original Hebrew was thus undoubtedly a perfect verb form, probably the so-called *perfectum propheticum*.[494]

For the Greek *de kai*, cf. above, 4:8. In the light of Sy which has here neither conjunction nor conjunctive particle, *de kai* probably represents a facilitation of the more asyndetic Hebrew on the part of the LXX translator.

The Greek noun *drymos* "coppice, grove, wood" is used with great regularity in the LXX for Hebrew *ya'ar* "forest, thicket,"[495] and the equivalency is virtually certain here.

w^{e}*kol-'ēṣ rê*^{a}*ḥ = kai pan xylon euōdias*

Of paramount importance here are the parallels for *y*^{e}*'ārôt w*^{e}*kol-'ēṣ* in Isa 44:23, *ya'ar w*^{e}*kol-'ēṣ bô*, and Ps 96:12, *kol-'*^{a}*ṣê yā'ar = panta ta xyla tou drymou*. The Greek noun *xylon* "tree, timber" is the frequent and normal equivalent for Hebrew *'ēṣ* "tree" in the LXX[496] and its reconstruction here may be considered certain. The remainder of this phrase, *euōdia* "fragrant," is, however, problematic.

In the LXX, *euōdia* always represents Hebrew *nîḥō*^{a}*ḥ* "soothing, appeasement,"[497] mostly in the cultic *terminus technicus*, *rê*^{a}*ḥ nîḥō*^{a}*ḥ* "odor of soothing," used to indicate a pleasing sacrifice. *Rê*^{a}*ḥ nîḥō*^{a}*ḥ* is usually rendered in the LXX by *osmēn euōdias* "smell of sweetness." Clearly this association of *euōdia* with *nîḥō*^{a}*ḥ* is a semantic mismatch and thus an interpretative equivalency. But not only is this LXX equivalency thus an interpretative one, it is also very unlikely to have occurred here in Bar 5:8. For *nîḥō*^{a}*ḥ* would hardly have been applied to trees in order to designate them as odoriferous. The term *rê*^{a}*ḥ* "odor, scent" (usually translated in the LXX by *osmē* "odor, smell")[498] is, however, commonly used with reference to the fragrance of trees, plants, and the open country in such biblical passages as Cant 1:12; 2:3, 13; 4:11; 7:14; Hos 14:7; and Gen 27:27. In two of these the *rê*^{a}*ḥ l*^{e}*bānôn* "fragrance of Lebanon" (i.e., that of its renowned trees) is the point of reference. The fragrant tree (*to dendron euōdias*) appears also as a sign of divine blessing in the Gizeh Greek fragment of *1 Enoch* 25:4.[499]

The use in both Sy and Syh of nouns related to the verb *b*^{e}*sem* "be fragrant, sweet" suggests that Hebrew *bōśem* "balsam, perfume, sweet odor" is also a possibility here (cf., e.g., Cant 8:14 and 6:2). Sy has *w*^{e}*kul qîs d*^{e}*besmā'*, "and every fragrant tree," and Syh has *wᵉkul qaysā' bassîmūt rîḥā'*, "and every tree, fragrant of odor."[500]

'al-yiśrā'ēl bidbar 'ᵉlōhîm = tō Israēl prostagmati tou theou

Although *prostagma* "commandment" is normally the equivalent of *ḥōq/ḥuqqāh* in the LXX, and less often of *miṣwāh* (cf. Bar 4:1), it nevertheless appears with some frequency, especially in the late Daniel, for *dābar* "word, order."[501]

This passage has a close parallel (undoubtedly dependent on it)[502] in *Pss. Sol.* 11:6-7, *hoi bounoi ephygon apo eisodou auton, hoi drymoi eskiasan autois en tē parodō autōn / pan xylon euōdias aneteilen autois ho theos, hina parelthē Israēl en episkopē doxēs theou autōn*, "The hills fled before their entering in, the woods gave them shelter as they passed by. / Every tree of sweet savor did God make to spring up before them: that Israel might pass by in *the day when* the glory of their God shall visit them."[503]

<u>5:9</u>

kî yēlēk 'ᵉlōhîm lipnê yiśrā'ēl bᵉśimḥāh = hēgēsetai gar ho theos Israēl met' euphrosynēs

The Greek verb *hēgeomai* "lead, go before, precede" appears in the LXX for thirty-five different Hebrew equivalents.[504] Very frequent as a participle, it most often represents various Hebrew substantives such as *rô'š*, *nāgîd*, *śar*, et al., terms that express the attitude or position of leadership. Here the picture is that one familiar from the Exodus journey (and from its reappropriation in Deutero-Isaiah) of *YHWH* himself "going before" (*hōlēk lipnê*) his homebound people as their protective vanguard.[505]

Exod 13:21 reveals this equivalency clearly: *wᵉYHWH hōlēk lipnêhem yômām = Ho de theos hēgeito autōn hēmeras*, "And *YHWH* went before them by day." This and its counterparts in Deutero-Isaiah are no doubt the sources for this passage; cf. Isa 52:12, *kî-hōlēk lipnêkem YHWH ûmᵉ'assipkem 'ᵉlōhê yiśrā'ēl*, "*YHWH* will proceed before you, the God of Israel will be your rearguard"; and Isa 58:8, *wᵉhālak lᵉpānêkā ṣidqekā kᵉbôd YHWH ya'aspekā*, "Your righteousness will be your vanguard, and the glory of *YHWH* your rearguard." It may be noted finally that Sy has for Bar 5:9 a different combination, "For the God of Israel will go before you," which appears to correspond even a little more closely to these sources.

For the equivalency between *euphrosynē* and *śimḥāh*, cf. above, 4:23, 29, 36, 11 and 3:34.

bᵉ'ôr kᵉbôdô = tō phōti tēs doxēs autou

Phōs "light" appears with great regularity in the LXX for Hebrew *'ôr*.[506] This equivalency has already been encountered in 3:14, 20, 33 and 4:2, above. For the association of "light" with "glory," cf. Isa 60:1, *ûkᵉbôd YHWH 'ālayik zārāḥ*; 58:8; 55:12; Bar 4:24, 37; and Ps 56:14.

bᵉḥesed ûbiṣdāqāh mē'ittô = syn eleēmosynē kai dikaiosynē tē par' autou

With approximately equal frequency, *eleēmosynē* "mercy" represents both *ḥesed* "mercy" and *ṣᵉdāqāh* "righteousness, alms" in the LXX.[507] Since *dikaiosynē* "righteousness," the frequent and normal LXX equivalent for *ṣᵉdāqāh*, does stand in this passage conjunctively paired with *eleēmosynē*,[508] it is thus reasonably certain that *ḥesed* lies behind *eleēmosynē* in this instance.[509]

NOTES TO CHAPTER V

[1]Cf. Gen 35:17; Exod 14:13; 20:20; 1 Kgs 17:13; Jdt 7:30; 11:1, 3; Sir 19:10; Tob 5:9; 7:18; 8:21; 11:11; Joel 2:21-22; Zeph 3:6; Hag 2:5; Zech 8:13, 15.

[2]The same pattern of negative command/imperative + vocative may be compared in Tob 5:9; 7:18; 8:21; Jdt 11:1, 3; Isa 44:2; Dan 10:12; Gen 15:1; Jer 30:10, 46; 27:28; Ruth 3:11; and Isa 41:14 (cf. also 1QM 10:3). Sy uses *bᵉyā'* which in the Ethpaal stem has the sense "be comforted." This verb form is in fact regularly the equivalent in Syriac for the passive Hebrew Niphal stem of *nāḥam* "comfort," as in Deut 32:36, et al. It is clearly not the same as the vigorously positive LXX imperative *tharseite* "be confident," but the Syh, *lᵉbab*, can mean similarly "take heart, be encouraged, be consoled." The Sy reading would appear to represent an editorial interpretation, very possibly under the influence of the LXX, rather than a real variant.

[3]See Ziegler, 462.

[4]Cf. also the semantic parallel in Isa 14:22 where the same thought is expressed in terms of the wiping out of a nation's name, remnant, and seed.

[5]This equivalency can also be observed in Hos 12:6, Ps 6:6, 112:6, Esth 9:28, and frequently in Sirach (41:1, 44:9, 45:1, 46:11, 49:1). In addition, the Greek synonym *mnēmē* is sometimes employed in the LXX to represent *zēker*, as in Ps 30:5, 97:12, 145:7, Eccl 9:5, Bar 4:27, 5:5.

[6]Kahana (360) has apparently assumed that a misread imperative lay behind the LXX reading *mnēmosynon* and has thus rendered the verse: *'al-tîrā' 'ammî*
zᵉkōr yiśrā'ēl.

There is, to be sure, no biblical precedent for the expression *zēker yiśrā'ēl*, but neither is there any for the assumed parallel between *'al-tîrā'* and *zᵉkōr*, or even the combination *zᵉkōr yiśrā'ēl*. There is, however, the significant prophetic (especially Isaianic) concept of the *šᵉ'ār/šᵉ'ērît yiśrā'ēl* "remnant of Israel" (cf. Isa 10:20, 1QM 14:9, et al.), which is (semantically) what the poet had in mind here as the "memorial of Israel."

[7]Kneucker (318) in comparing the lexical items (Hebrew and Greek) extracted from this section of Deuteronomy, concluded: "Zugleich beweisen diese Parallelen, besonders klar die letzte, dass unsere griechischen Verse nicht aus LXX zu Deut. 32, sondern unmittelbar aus hebräischen Originale hier geflossen sind." Indeed, the Hebraic character of the composition is especially prominent here.

[8]See the section immediately below for the discussion of Esth 7:4.

[9]For the equivalence *meṭul d-* = *kî* = *hoti*, cf., e.g., Num 15:25, Ps 1:6, 2 Kgs 19:3, Joel 3:1, Isa 7:16.

[10]Cf. other passages where the same semantic idea is conveyed, but in which *mākar* is represented by *apodidonai* "give back, deliver over (into slavery)": Ezek 30:12 (G^{A} only); Deut 32:30 (where the same parallel pairing, *mākar* [A] // *hisgîr* [B], occurs); Judg 2:14, 3:8, 4:2; 1 Sam 12:9. Cf. also Jdt 7:25.

[11]See *GKC*, §158, p. 492.

[12]Kahana, 360.

[13]Cf., e.g., Isa 60:15.

[14]Cf., e.g., Deut 4:37.

[15]See HR II, 1072.

[16]Cf. also Judg 2:12, 17; 1 and 2 Kgs passim; and the Aramaic of Ezra 5:12.

[17]Note the same parallel in 1 Sam 23:7 where, although MT has *nikkar*, the LXX reading assumes the verb *mākar*. A further semantic parallel is found in Job 16:11.

[18]Similarly, + *'el-*, cf. Job 16:11, *yasgîrēnî 'ēl 'el 'awîl*; and Deut 23:16, *lō'-tasgîr 'ebed 'el-'adōnāyw*.

[19]Cf. also Lam 2:7; 1 Sam 23:7, 11, 20; 30:15.

[20]See HR I, 589. *Echthros* has already been observed to be the normal equivalent of Hebrew *'ōyēb* in Bar 3:10, above; cf. further Bar 4:18, 21, 25, below.

[21]The equivalence of *ṣārîm* and *hypenantion* is found also in Josh 5:13. The Syriac evidence in our verse is ambiguous in that the *be'eldebābā'* "enemy" of the Sy text sometimes represents *ṣar* (as in Job 16:9, Ps 81:15, 8:2, 10:5) but equally *'ōyēb* (as in Lev 26:7, 36; Mic 4:10; Ps 3:7; Bar 3:10).

[22]See HR II, 1072.

[23]The Hiphil forms are found in Deut 32:16, 21b; Ps 78:58; and the Piel in Deut 32:21a, 1 Kgs 14:22. Elsewhere in BH the Piel stem is non-factitive, "be jealous."

[24]The five BH passages cited above in note 23 constitute the total of the causative or factitive examples for the verb *qānā'*, and in each case the verb is combined with instrumental *beth* to express the meaning "provoke to jealous anger (*with* something)."

[25]Cf. further Gen 41:25, 28; 1 Sam 12:16; 2 Kgs 7:2, 19; Isa 44:24; 45:7; Jer 9:23; 33:2; Amos 9:12; Zech 10:1; Ps 77:15. Kneucker (319-20, 357), in dealing with this difficulty, decided that the phrase *ton poiēsanta hymas thysantes daimoniois*

kai ou theō. (8) *epelathesthe de*, was an interpolative gloss by a later copyist who was familiar with the original source in Deuteronomy 32 and perhaps then first introduced this addition into the margin from whence with time it gravitated into the text proper. This was argued mainly on the basis of the supposedly unorthodox syntactical use in BH of the participle without a preceding subject to which it would stand in apposition (as in Deut 32:15, 18), and on the likelihood that the verb *šākaḥ* would have been a weak, and thus improbable, parallel to the more vigorous and more naturally paired verbs, *qānā'* and *'āṣab*. Kneucker thus understood vss. 7-8:

kî qinnē'tem ['ôšêkem lizbōaḥ laššēdîm lō'-'elôaḥ

(8) *wattiškeḥû*] *('ēl) meḥōlelekem 'elōhê 'ōlām*

we'ap 'iṣṣabtem yōladtekem yerûšālayim.

But this contention is quite unlikely in that such direct and non-appositional use of the participle in BH is not uncommon (cf., e.g., Job 31:15, 40:19, Isa 45:18, Hos 8:14, *wayyiškaḥ yiśrā'ēl 'et-'ōśēhû*). In addition, even if Kneucker were correct, he would not thereby prove the existence of such an interpolation, but more probably the abovementioned possibility that the divine name was originally here as in Deut 32:15. His contention is especially dubious on the basis of the second argument because *wattiškaḥ* is precisely the verb form used in Deut 32:18 with *'ēl meḥōlelekā*, and not at all an unlikely parallel for *'āṣab* (cf. the above-cited Isa 51:13 and Hos 8:14).

[26] See HR I, 659.

[27] Ibid., 283.

[28] See L. Koehler and W. Baumgartner, *Lexicon in Veteris Testamenti Libros*, 2nd ed. (Leiden: E. J. Brill, 1958) 949 (hereafter cited as KB), and cf. the Akkadian cognate *šēdu*, a favorable "demon" or "genie."

[29] For further amplification of the clarity of this striking Hebrew idiom used to express the idea "non-entity" or "non-existence," by means of a simple negation of a substantive, cf. *GKC*, §152a, n. 1, p. 478, and the following examples: Deut 32:21, *belō'-'ēl . . . belō'-'ām*, "with a non-god . . . with a non-people"; Jer 5:7, *belō' 'elōhîm*, "with non-divinities"; 2 Chr 13:9, *lelō' 'elōhîm*; Jer 2:11 (16:20), *lō' 'elōhîm*; and with other substantives: Amos 6:13, *lelō' dābār*, "for nothing"; Ps 44:13, *belō' hōn*; Isa 55:2, *belō'-leḥem*; Isa 10:15, *lō'-'ēṣ*; and 31:8, *lō'-'îš*.

[30] See HR I, 524.

[31] See LSJ, 1827, and Frisk, *Wörterbuch* II, 926.

[32] This would seem to correspond with the marginal notation found at this verse in Syh--*detarsîkûn* "who nourished you" (either the Pali or Taphel stem of *resî* "nourish, rear"). This Syriac verb is commonly used to render the Pilpel stem of Hebrew *kûl* "supply nourishment, rear, support," as well as the Greek *trephō*. Cf., e.g., Gen 50:1, Ps 55:22, Isa 7:21.

[33]Kneucker (320) suggests that either the LXX translator, the glossator he assumes, or even the original author (in using his Deuteronomy 32 sources), saw *'ēl* but actually read *'et-*.

[34]In Greek, cf. the following biblical and extra-biblical examples: Isa 26:4, *ho theos ho megas, ho aiōnios*; Rom 16:26, *tou aiōniou theou*; Sir 36:22, *ho theos ton aiōniōn*; *1 Enoch* 1:4, *ho theos tou aiōnos*; Philo, *De Plantatione*, trans. F. H. Colson and G. H. Whitaker (LCL, III; London: W. Heinemann, 1930) 73-74, pp. 250-51, *theou aiōniou* and *theon aiōnion*. See also Hermann Sasse, "*aiōn, aiōnios*" (*TWNT* I, 201) for the idea that the Greek genitive construction was modeled on the Hebrew *status constructus*.

[35]Kneucker, 320.

[36]See LSJ, 907.

[37]It is also for its other Hebrew equivalents, *'aṣṣebet* "hurt, pain" and *'iṣṣābôn* "pain, toil." Cf. Sir 14:1, 36:25, and see HR II, 889-90. Cf. also Ps 78:40 where the Hiphil stem of *'āṣab* is used of *YHWH*, and Bar 4:33, below.

[38]This is the verb that has consistently been used in reconstruction by those who have previously attempted such. Cf. Kneucker, 357; Kahana, 360; and Harwell, 58.

[39]Note that both *yālad* and *ḥûl*, verbs characterizing the act of giving birth more precisely than rearing, are in Deut 32:18 rather startlingly applied to God!

[40]See HR I, 443-44.

[41]God is represented in Deut 32:18 as both the "father" who "begot" his people and the "mother" who "travailed" with them. For the combination of these two figures elsewhere, cf. Jer 2:27 and Job 38:29. S. R. Driver (*Deuteronomy* [ICC, V, 1895; reprinted, Edinburgh: T. & T. Clark, 1965] 363) suggests that, although such a combination with reference to one and the same subject, particularly God, is rather bold, the figure of the mother was necessitated by the parallelism and the need to stress *YHWH*'s tender affection for his people. Cf. also Ps 90:2. The rendering of Kahana, *y^erûšālayim zô yôladt^ekem*, seems quite dubious. This use of the Mishnaic pronoun, *zô*, which is found only twice in MT (and in only one of these two instances, Ps 132:12, used relatively), in a relative construction supposedly beginning with the direct object, *y^erûšālayim*, appears to be clearly counter to the syntax consistently presupposed here by the Versions. Cf., e.g.,

LXX, *tēn ekthrepsasan hymas Hierousalēm*
"the one who reared you, Jerusalem";

Sy, *lamrabyānît^ekûn 'ûrišlem*
(accus.) "your nursemaid, Jerusalem";

Syh, *walhāy d^erabbîkûn 'ûrišlem*
(accus.) "and her who raised you, Jerusalem";

La^V, *nutricem vestram Hierusalem*
"your nourisher, Jerusalem."

It is immediately clear from these examples that the direct object, Jerusalem, always occupies final position in the word order, and is always preceded by the modifying phrase or term expressive of her "rearing" of the people. This is decidedly Hebraic (abc // a'b'c') and accords with the usual ordering of post-verbal modifiers in BH. Cf. the evidence for this presented by Francis I. Andersen in "Studies in Hebrew Syntax" (I, 255-406). The Kahana rendering implies that the author of Baruch here slipped pronouncedly from the usual syntax patterns of BH, from which he manifestly draws virtually all his material, into the mode of his own time with its increased usage of relatives, and here employed a Mishnaism. This style, whether or not legitimate, seems out of place and disintegral to its context which is so largely a "biblical pastiche." This is one of the examples that reveals the character of the Kahana work more as a translation into currently comprehensible Hebrew than an actual reconstruction. Other passages depicting Jerusalem in the role of a mother include Isa 54:1-6, 13; 49:14f.; 50:1; 51:17f.; 52:1; 60:1f.; 61:10f.; Job 13:9; Lam 1:5, 16. For a similar picturing of *YHWH* as a "parent," cf. Isa 1:2.

[42]Cf., e.g., Isa 54:10, 51:4, 49:25, Sir 41:4, Lam 2:9, Ezek 33:30, Exod 29:28, Job 20:29.

[43]See the lexica and concordances for such combinations as *'ap-'ēl*, *'ap-YHWH*, *ḥ^a^mat-YHWH*, etc.

[44]Cf., e.g., in Deutero-Isaiah: Isa 63:14, *rû^a^ḥ YHWH* = *pneuma para Kyriou*; Isa 46:13, *ûtᵉšû'ātî lō' tᵉ'aḥēr* = *kai tēn sōtērian tēn par'emou ou bradynō*; and Isa 52:10, *wᵉrā'û 'et yᵉšû'at 'ᵉlōhênû* = *kai opsontai tēn sōtērian tēn para tou theou hēmōn*. The alternative, the prepositional construction, would most likely follow the reconstruction of Kneucker (p. 357): *kî rā'^a^tāh hā'ap habbā' '^a^lêkem mē'ēt 'ᵉlōhîm*, yielding perhaps a balance of 4+3 (8/8).

[45]E.g., in Job 14:13 and Ps 2:5, *orgē* = *'ap* (= *rugzā'* in Syriac); in Ps 6:1, *thymos* = *'ap* and *orgē* = *ḥēmāh*; in Isa 51:17, *thymos* = *ḥēmāh*; in Ezek 43:8, *thymos* = *'ap* (but this instance is quite a rarity in Ezekiel where the equivalence, *thymos* = *ḥēmāh*, is both regular and frequent). Also of some help is Ezra 10:14, *ḥ^a^rôn 'ap-'ᵉlōhênû* = *orgēn thymou theou hēmōn*.

[46]I.e., as the Latin, *anima*.

[47]See Mandelkern I, 402. Cf. also 2 Kgs 22:13, Isa 51:20, Jer 6:11, 2 Chr 28:4, 34:21, 36:16.

[48]Ibid., 135, and cf., e.g., Exod 4:4, Num 11:10.

[49]Cf. 1QS 2:15, 1QM 4:1, 6:3, CD 1:21, 3:8, 8:13, 10:9, 19:20, 20:16.

[50]LXX Minuscule 96 reads *moi*.

[51]Cf. also Judg 9:7, *šim'û 'ēlay ba'^a^lê šᵉkem*; and the expression *šᵉma'-lî* in Job 15:17; 33:31, 33; 32:10.

[52]Literally, "[cities (l. 865). . . .] neighbors to Thracian places." See Aeschylus, *Persae*, ed. H. D. Broadhead (Cambridge: Cambridge University, 1960) l. 869, p. 28. Cf. also Herodotus, *Historiae* (trans. A. D. Godley (LCL, III; London: W. Heinemann, 1928] vii, 235, pp. 550-51) for the concept of war with "neighbors" (*paroikou de polemou*), and other citations in LSJ (1342).

[53]In the LXX, 29:18 (and 27:40).

[54]Cf. similarly, Ps 31:12, 44:14, 80:7, and 89:42.

[55]Kahana (360) has here retroverted the feminine plural, *š*^{e}*kēnôt*, as in Ruth 4:17, even though the use of the masculine plural is consistent in the MT application of *šākēn* to denote neighboring cities or states. While the Greek *hai paroikoi* is indeed feminine it does not follow that the Hebrew counterpart must have thus been feminine as well (cf. further La^{V}, *confines Sion*). The evidence of MT is quite to the contrary. Where BH uses the plural of *šākēn* to indicate neighboring cities it is always masculine. As a *nomen regens* in a bound relationship to a proper noun in such a phrase as *š*^{e}*kēnê ṣiyyôn*, it is of course definite without the need of any preposed article. The LXX *hai* is thus only an intra-Greek phenomenon, serving in fact to express this precise connotation, "neighbor(-cities)," *hai (poleis) paroikoi*. This expression, with its implication of *poleis*, must thus be feminine. That the Hebrew equivalent is nevertheless masculine is proved by Jer 49(29):18 where *k*^{e}*mahpēkat s*^{e}*dōm wa'*^{a}*mōrāh uš*^{e}*kēnèhā = Hosper katestraphē Sodoma kai Gomorrha kai hai paroikoi autēs*. Further, the Sy reading, *'āmûrē' d*^{e}*ṣehyûn*, is also masculine plural.

[56]See HR II, 1118.

[57]Ibid., 902-07.

[58]Ibid., I, 38-39. *Aichmalōsia* appears thirty-seven times in the LXX for Hebrew *š*^{e}*bî* and about twenty-two times altogether for the cognate synonyms, *š*^{e}*bît*, *š*^{e}*bût*, and *šibyāh*.

[59]Kneucker (322) very dubiously contends for *gālût* on the ground that as the Greek term supposedly denotes the act of being led into captivity rather than the state of being in captivity, so *gālût* is favored as the equivalent by a supposed similar sense. *Gālût* is surely a possible reconstruction but such a delineation between *š*^{e}*bî* and *gālût* is hardly so clear. *Aichmalōsia* is the equivalent for *gôlāh* twelve times in the LXX, mostly in Ezekiel in such expressions as *hālak baggôlāh*, *bô' 'el-haggôlāh*, or *k*^{e}*lî gôlāh*, and for *gālût* ten times, in Ezekiel always in date formulae and in Daniel always in the cliché *b*^{e}*nê-gālûtā'*. See HR I, 38-39.

[60]See Kneucker, 320. Gifford ("Baruch," 253) comments: "Also in the latter part of iv.22 (*para tou aiōniou sōtēros hymōn*) it [*aiōnios*] probably has the same sense, 'the Eternal your Savior,' corresponding to 'the Lord (Jehovah) your Savior' in Isa. xlix.26; lx.16."

[61]Kneucker, 320.

[62]Cf., e.g., the post-biblical use of *haššēm* and *'ᵃdōnāy*, the biblical use of *hammāqôm* in Esth 4:14, the use of "Heaven" in 1 Macc 4:24, the practice of CD in its biblical citations regularly to omit *YHWH* or substitute *'ēl* for it, the frequent rendering of *YHWH* by *theos* in the LXX, and the interpretative circumlocutions of Philo (e.g., *ho ōn*, as noted by William Brownlee, *The Dead Sea Manual of Discipline* [*ASOR* Supp., nos. 10-12; New Haven: ASOR, 1951] 43). For background, see Werner Foerster, "*Kyrios*," *TWNT* III, 1081-98, esp. 1082-83.

[63]For background, see Frank M. Cross, *Canaanite Myth and Hebrew Epic: Essays in the History of the Religion of Israel* (Cambridge: Harvard University, 1973) 48 et passim. Cross has persuasively shown that *'ôlām* was used absolutely in the early Hebrew literature, as in that of Canaan, as a divine name, "the Eternal" (cf., e.g., Deut 33:27, *zr'wt 'wlm*). That this use of *'ôlām* had become obscured by the time of the book of Baruch is implicit in the fact that both the Hebrew tradition and the LXX translators have understood *'ôlām* in such examples attributively as "eternal" or adverbially as "forever."

[64]Johannes Geffcken, *Die Oracula Sibyllina* (Leipzig: J. C. Hinrichs, 1902) frg. 3:17, p. 231.

[65]See Brownlee, *The Dead Sea Manual of Discipline*, 43.

[66]See HR I, 582-83.

[67]Cf. Gen 31:27, Deut 28:47, 1 Sam 18:6, 2 Sam 6:12, Isa 55:12, Zeph 3:17, Ps 21:7, 68:4, 100:2, Eccl 2:1, 9:7, Ezra 3:12, 6:22, 1 Chr 15:25, 29:17 and 22, 2 Chr 20:27, 23:18, 30:21. In both Gen 31:27 (*wā'ᵃšallēḥᵃkā bᵉśimḥāh*) and Isa 55:12 (*bᵉśimḥāh tēṣē'û*), the concept of "sending/going away with gladness" is found. Here in the destruction-lament context of Bar 4:11 the exact opposite is presented--"sending away in grief."

[68]Cf. 1 Sam 18:6, Ps 21:7, 1 Chr 29:22. In these instances the equivalent is *chara* "joy" or a related noun.

[69]Cf. Isa 12:3, 22:13, 51:3, 61:3, Esth 8:16, Jer 15:16, 38:13, 40:9 and 11, Sir 34:31, 37:4. *Śāśôn* is also translated in its few remaining occurrences by other Greek synonyms of *euphrosynē*, such as *agalliama* and *chara*.

[70]All other nouns appearing as the second member in this Greek pairing are, like *chara*, derivates from *chairō*.

[71]This Hebrew pairing appears once in the Qumran material where it is also reversed; cf. 1QH 9:24, *lśmḥh wśśwn*.

[72]See HR II, 767.

[73]Ibid., I, 488-89; and see LSJ, 586. Here the context is that of the reluctant dismissal of those taken prisoner. Cf.

Polybius, *The Histories* (trans. W. R. Paton [LCL, II; London: W. Heinemann, 1960] iv, 84, 3, pp. 500-01) for the use of this verb in dismissing a prisoner, though without the tone of reluctance. This Greek verb is the equivalent of *šālaḥ* even in those passages where the latter has the connotations "expel" (Gen 3:23) and "divorce" (Deut 24:4).

[74]See Ziegler, 463.

[75]BDB, 970.

[76]See LSJ, 672. Cf. further Bar 4:31 and 33; Sir 8:7; 23:3; and with the verb *euphrainō*, Hos 9:1; Isa 14:29; Jer 50:11; Ps 35:15; 2 Sam 1:20+. In the light of this particular topos, especially as it is reflected in the parallelism of such BH passages as Obad 12, Ezek 35:13, and even Zeph 2:8, 10, and the obvious imbalance of the three cola of the tricolon (i.e., vs. 12a,b,c, 12d being in reality the first colon of a bicolon formed with vs. 13a), Kahana (360) has proposed the restoration of a supposedly lost parallel that, while unsubstantiated by any textual evidence in the Versions, is nevertheless attractive by comparison with Obad 12. The effect of such a restoration would be to yield for verse 12a a short bicolon of a 3 + 2 metre, each colon numbering five syllables:

(12a) *'îš 'al-yiśmaḥ-lî* "Let no one rejoice over me,
[*we'al-yagdēl pîw*] [Nor make taunting boasts!"].

Cf. Obad 12, *we'al-tiśmaḥ libnê-yehûdāh beyôm 'obdām / we'al-tagdēl pîkā beyôm ṣārāh;* and Ps 137:7, 38:17, Ezek 35:13.

[77]See HR II, 1468.

[78]See *GKC*, §§131, 138g,i,k.

[79]See below, p. 170.

[80]See HR II, 1181-85.

[81]Cf. also 1QH 4:27 and 1QSb 4:27. See also Joachim Jeremias, "*polloi*," *TWNT* VI, 536-45.

[82]See further Chaim Rabin, *The Zadokite Documents*, 2nd rev. ed. (Oxford: Clarendon, 1958) 65 n. 7.6, 69 n. 9.1; Brownlee, *The Dead Sea Manual of Discipline*, 23 n. 2; S. Holm-Nielsen, *Hodayot: Psalms from Qumran (Acta Theologica Danica*, II; Aarhus: Universitetsforlaget, 1960) 85 n. 64; Kuhn, *Konkordanz zu den Qumrantexten*, 198-99; G. H. Dalman, *Aramäisch-Neuhebräisches Handwörterbuch zu Targum, Talmud und Midrash* (1901; reprinted, Hildesheim: Georg Olms, 1967) 395; and Jastrow, *A Dictionary of the Targumim* II, 1438.

[83]See HR I, 546-47.

[84]For the possibility of *ḥārabtî* or *neḥerabtî*, cf. Jer 26:9 and Isa 44:27.

[85]Kahana, 360; see above, n. 76.

[86]Other possibilities for *dioti* are by no means ruled out. In such passages as 1 Kgs 11:34; Ezek 13:9; 23:34; 25:5, 6, 7, 11; et al., *dioti* is simply the equivalent of *kî*. In Lev 26:43; Ezek 13:8, 10; 23:35; 25:6, 8, 12; et al., *yaʻan* is rendered by *anth' hōn*. In Ezek 35:10, *yaʻan* is represented in the LXX by *dia to*, as in Bar 4:6 above. In 1 Sam 30:22, *dioti* is the equivalent of *yaʻan 'ᵃšer*, but in 1 Kgs 11:33, *yaʻan 'ᵃšer* is represented by *anth' hōn*. See further, Bar 4:6 above.

[87]See Thackeray, *The Septuagint and Jewish Worship*, 13; and Marvin Pope, *Job*, 3rd ed. (AB 15; Garden City: Doubleday, 1979) xliii-iv.

[88]The Job Targum from cave 11 at Qumran suggests that the Hebrew parallelism in Job 34:27 was originally between "path(s)" and "way(s)," even though other Targumic evidence indicates agreement with the LXX's "law-ordinances" parallelism. See J.P.M. van der Ploeg and A. S. van der Woude, *Le Targum de Job de la Grotte XI de Qumrân* (Leiden: E. J. Brill, 1971) 60-61. With regard to the Job fragment (Job 33:28-30) from cave 2 (DJD III, 15, Pl. XIII, p. 71), its editors have declared: ". . . l'identification est sûre et suppose un texte de type massorétique"; see M. Baillet, J. T. Milik, and R. de Vaux, *Les 'Petites Grottes' de Qumran* [DJD III; Oxford: Clarendon, 1962] p. 71); see also Frank M. Cross, Jr., *The Ancient Library of Qumran* (London: Gerald Duckworth, 1950) 26 n. 48.

[89]Cf. Job 34:27 (LXX), *hoti exeklinan ek nomou theou, dikaiōmata de autou ouk epegnōsan*, and Bar 4:12d-13a (LXX), *dioti exeklinan ek nomou theou, kai dikaiōmata autou ouk egnōsan*.

[90]For the expression, *sûr mē'aḥᵃrê . . .*, as in the MT of Job 34:27, cf. 1 Sam 12:20, *'al-tāsûrû mē'aḥᵃrê YHWH = mē ekklinēte apo opisthen Kyriou*; and CD 16:5, *yswr . . . m'ḥryw*.

[91]See HR I, 433-34. There is some support as well for the verb *nāṭāh* "bend, turn aside," also translated on occasion in the LXX by *ekklinō*. Cf. this equivalence in 1 Sam 8:3; 1 Kgs 11:9; Ps 44:19, *wattēṭ 'ᵃšūrênû minnî 'orḥekā = kai exeklinas tas tribous hēmōn apo tēs hodou sou*; and especially Ps 119:51, *mittôrātᵉkā lō' nāṭîtî = apo de tou nomou sou ouk exeklina*. Cf. also CD 17:1, 4.

[92]The phrase, "those of the Lord God," is patently a gloss.

[93]Cf. the reading of the Job Targum from Qumran cave 11 (11QtgJob) for Job 34:27, *'r]ḥh wbkl sbylwhy l' hstk[lw*, "*parce qu'ils se sont détournés de*] sa [vo]ie et n'ont obser[vé] aucun de ses sentiers," in van der Ploeg and van der Woude, *Le Targum de Job* (60-61). The editors, noting that the "law of God" is plausibly interpretative for "his way," conclude: "La coïncidence de Tg 1 [11QtgJob] et G rend probable qu'ils ont lu en hébreu *m'rḥyw* au lieu de *m'ḥryw*; il se pourrait, cependant, qu'ils se soient permis des libertés pareilles en traduisant" (p. 60 n. 3).

[94]Cf. the targumic reading for Job 34:27 in *Hagiographa Chaldaicae* (ed. P. de Lagarde [Leipzig: B. G. Teubner, 1873] 111): *dmṭwl hykn' zrw mbtrwhy wkl 'wrḥtyh l' 'skylw.* See also L. H. Brockington, "LXX and Targum," *ZAW* 66 (1954) 80-86.

[95]See further, HR I, 267-70.

[96]Cf. Ps 1:6, 37:18, Amos 3:2, et al.

[97]See HR I, 334-35.

[98]The translations are those of Chaim Rabin (*The Zadokite Documents*, 46, 72).

[99]There are numerous parallels for "knowing (*yāda'*) the way (*derek*)": of "wisdom" (Bar 3:20, 23, 31, 27, 36; Job 28:23, 12-13; of "peace" (Isa 59:8); and of *YHWH* (Jer 5:4-5; Ps 95: 10). Cf. also Ps 119:152, *yāda'tî mē'ēdōtèkā*, "I have perceived from your testimonies"; and Jer 38:24.

[100]Harwell (23) judges the first to have been the work of the original translator and the second a later marginal correction, it being in his judgment the more literal rendering of the Greek. But this is debatable and the evidence is ambiguous at best.

[101]See HR II, 1189-94. Cf. also Bar 3:13, 33 and 4:26.

[102]Ibid., I, 479-80.

[103]Ibid., II, 962-66. Cf. also Bar 3:13, 20, 23, 27, 31, 36 and 4:26.

[104]Cf. also *1 Enoch* 92:3, Jub 1:20, and 1QH 6:24.

[105]A very remote parallel might be adduced from 1QH 6:4, *lmwsr mwkyḥy ṣdq*, "for the instruction/correction of the determiners/reprovers of righteousness."

[106]Cf. below, 5:2, 4, 9, and see HR I, 332-34.

[107]Kneucker, 324, 358.

[108]Sy *qušṭā'* "truth" (Syh^{mg}, *š^erārā'*) is the equivalent of the Greek *alētheia* "truth." According to a marginal notation in Syh, this conflate reading is attributable to Theodotian.

[109]Cf., e.g., the construct chains in Gen 3:2, 47:9, Job 2:24, and Isa 10:12.

[110]For the nuances of *mûsār/paideia*, cf. Prov 22:15, 23:13 ("correction"); Jer 2:30 ("discipline"); Prov 1:2, 7; et al. ("instruction"). There is some support for the variant *alētheias* (= BH, *'^emet*) in place of *paideia*, namely in C', LXX Minuscules 239 and 613, and $La^{L,S,V}$. The conflate reading of Sy, + *qušṭā'* (= *alētheia*), is supported also by G^{Q}, LXX Minuscules

106', and La^{C}. The passage in 1 Kgs 3:6, *hālak . . . be'^{e}met ûbiṣdāqāh*, has been suggested as supportive of the concept of "walking in truth and righteousness" (Whitehouse, "1 Baruch," 592), but such is not the syntax of the Greek or the Syriac in our verse.

[111]For this sense of the Hebrew verb, cf. Deut 1:36, 11:25, 33:29, Josh 1:3, 14:9, 1 Sam 5:5, Ps 91:13, Amos 4:13, Mic 1:3, 5:4 and 5. See also HR I, 515-16.

[112]See HR I, 548-53. Cf. also below, Bar 4:22, 36, 37.

[113]See HR II, 927-29. Cf. also above, Bar 3:23.

[114]Kahana, 360.

[115]See Whitehouse, "1 Baruch," 592.

[116]*LVTAS*, 99.

[117]Cf. further Isa 43:18, *tizk^{e}rû* (A) // *titbōnānû* (B); and Job 37:14.

[118]See HR I, 503-04, and M. L. Margolis, "The Greek Preverb and its Hebrew-Aramaic Equivalent," *AJSL* 26 (1909-10) 49.

[119]See HR I, 368-73.

[120]Kahana, 360.

[121]Cf. further Jer 5:15, Isa 28:11.

[122]Cf. 2 Kgs 3:14, Gen 19:21, Prov 6:35, Lam 4:16, 5:12, and also Isa 13:18, 47:6.

[123]Cf. Isa 3:3, 2 Kgs 5:1, Isa 9:14, Job 22:8.

[124]See S. R. Driver, *Deuteronomy*, 315.

[125]See HR I, 36-37.

[126]Kneucker, 325.

[127]*Hoti* has considerable support here; viz., G^{B,Q,V}, Minuscules 86', 106, 534, 538, 613, O, C', and Bo. See Ziegler, 463.

[128]See HR I, 115.

[129]Ibid., 131.

[130]This equivalency itself is not very common in the LXX; see HR II, 1061. *Paralambanō* usually renders Hebrew *lāqaḥ* in the LXX.

[131]See HR I, 115. *Apagō* appears in the LXX seven times for forms of *nāhag* and twelve times for those of *hālak*. See also Margolis, "The Greek Preverb," 44.

[132]Cf. also Job 12:17 where *môlîk* is rendered in the LXX by *diagōn* (Aq, *apagōn*). An imperfect consecutive form is perhaps also a possibility--*wayyôlîkû*.

[133]Kahana, 360.

[134]See HR I, 7.

[135]Cf. MT, *bêt mᵉʾahᵃbāy*, "the house of my lovers" (i.e., "idols"?), with LXX, *tō oikō tō agapetō mou*, "my beloved house." But, cf. G^{A}.

[136]Three of these designate the "favorite wife" status, *ʾᵃhûbāh* (Deut 21:15-16), and the other an adultress as "beloved of a friend," *ʾᵃhûbat rēᵃʿ* (Hos 3:1).

[137]Note that one LXX Minuscule, #239 of the Vaticanus group, offers *ēgapēmenous* here in Bar 4:16.

[138]Cf., e.g., Deut 33:12, Isa 5:1, Jer 11:15, Ps 60:7, 84:2, 108:7, 127:2, and Bar 3:36. See also PS, 1170.

[139]See HR II, 1468. Cf. also Bar 4:12, above.

[140]See LSJ, 1145.

[141]Cf. in Syh the use of the Shaphel participle of the same verbal root, *yᵉḥad*, to achieve the same sense. This Shaphel participle is also preserved by Sy in its conflate text.

[142]Cf. "only child" (Prov 4:3), "only son" (e.g., Jer 6:26, Amos 8:10), "only daughter" (e.g., Judg 11:34).

[143]It is notable that such a reading, *monogenēn*, is supported for Bar 4:16 by $G^{A,V}$, Minuscules 106, 130, 544, and Ar.

[144]Kahana, 360.

[145]It is commonly used in MH to describe menstruating women as being isolated or solitary. Cf. the references to the various tractates of the Talmudim and Midrashim given in Jacob Levy, *Neuhebräisches und Chaldäisches Wörterbuch* (4 vols.; Leipzig: F. A. Brockhaus, 1876) I, 336, and Jastrow, *A Dictionary of the Targumim*, 250. Especially to be noted among them are: *Talmud Babli*, *Soṭah*, 42a, "in the coastal towns they call a menstruating woman *galmûdāh*" (*qwryn lnydh glmwdh*); and *Talmud Yerushalmi*, *Ta'anith*, I, 64d, "make your wife lonely" (*ʿśh ʾštk glmwdh*). Also in *Midrash Bereshith Rabbah*, 79, the meaning of *galmûdāh* in Isa 49:21 is explained by equating it with *niddāh*, again in reference to menstruation.

[146]See HR I, 546-47. *Eremoō* is never used in the LXX for two other Hebrew verbs that would seem semantically appropriate: *ʿāzab* "abandon, desert" and *šākal* (Piel) "bereave of children."

[147]Cf. also Isa 54:3 and the other passages cited in support of this equivalency at 4:12, above. Additional pertinent examples of this equivalency are Job 16:7, *hešimmôtā kol-ʿadātî* and Jer 10:25 (= Ps 79:7), *weʾet-nāwēhû hēšammû* (of Jacob).

[148]Cf. also Ezek 19:17, 6:6, and 12:20.

[149]It is similarly applied twice to Edom in Ezek 35:4 (LXX, *erēmos*) and 36:10 (LXX, *ērēmōmenē*).

[150]Syh uses the verb *gaz* (cognate to Hebrew *gāzaz*) "cut off, deprive," and by extension, "bereave."

[151]Cf. Kahana, 360: *mibbenôtèhā*.

[152]The Syriac idiom, *lāʾ meškeḥāʾ* "it is impossible," combined with the personal pronoun yields, for example: *lāʾ meškeḥāʾ (ʾ)nāʾ* "I cannot."

[153]*Dynamai* is supported altogether by the uncial G^A, and the Minuscules 106 of the G^A tradition, 51, 62, 449, and 538 of the Lucianic group, and 534 of the G^Q tradition. See Ziegler, 463.

[154]A similar equivalency is that of *kai dynatos esē = wattûkāl* in Gen 32:29.

[155]Cf. also Jer 15:20, *ou mē dynōntai = lōʾ yûkelû*, and several passages in Job in which correspondence between the LXX and MT is either vague or non-existent: Job 4:20, *para to mē dynasthai autous heautois boēthēsai apolonto*, "they have perished from being unable to help themselves"; 20:14, *kai ou mē dynēthē boēthēsai heautō*, "and he will be unable to help himself"; 7:20, *ti dynēsomai praxai = māh ʾepʿal*; Job 35:6, *ti dynasai poiēsai = māh tipʿal*; and Wis 13:16, *adynatei heautō boēthēsai*. It is noteworthy that the Greek infinitive *boēthēsai* "to help," appearing in several of these parallels, is the same as that in Bar 4:17.

[156]See HR I, 223.

[157]Ibid., II, 1328-30.

[158]Cf. also in Greek only, Jdt 8:15. The correspondence between *ʿāzar* and *boētheō* in general is further illustrated by such passages as 1 Kgs 1:7, 20(21):16, 2 Sam 21:17, 2 Chr 19:2, Ps 20:2, 44:25, 46:5, 86:17, Isa 41:10, Josh 10:33, Hos 13:9. The particular combination of the infinitive *ʿazōr* (*boēthēsai*) with the verb *yākōl* (*dynamai*) has been examined above; cf. especially n. 155 above, and Job 20:14 (LXX). Parallels with the semantically similar Hebrew verbs *nāṣal* (Hiph) "deliver, rescue" and *yāšaʿ* (Hiph) "save," are available also. Jer 14:9 is particularly striking: *hōs anēr ou dynamenos sōzein = kegibbôr lōʾ-yûkal lehôšîaʿ*. Cf. also 2 Kgs 18:29, *hoti ou mē dynatai hymas exelesthai = kî-lōʾ yûkal lehaṣṣîl ʾetkem* (Isa 36:14 is practically the same). In 2 Chr 32:13-15 the combination *yākelû . . . lehaṣṣîl* occurs four times.

[159]Note the parallelism of such passages as: Ps 109:26, *ʿozrēnî/boēthēson* (A) // *hôšîʿēnî/sōson* (B); Ps 71:2, *taṣṣîlēnî/rhysai* (A) // *hôšîʿēnî/sōson* (B); Ps 119:117, *s^{e}ʿādēnî/boēthēson* (A) // *ʾiwwāšēʿāh/sōthēsomai* (B); Jer 15:20, *l^{e}hôšîʿ^{a}kā/sōzein se* (A) // *l^{e}haṣṣîlekā/exaireisthai se* (B); and etc. Cf. also n. 160, below.

[160]Nevertheless, sensing the possibility of such a deficiency, Kahana (360) has proposed the restoration of a parallel colon (to a differently reconstructed verse 17) as follows:

(17a) *waʾ^{a}nî mah-kōḥî kî ʾôšîʿ^{a}kem*

[17b] [*w^{e}kî ʾaṣṣîl^{e}kem miyyad b^{e}nê-nēkār*].

The sources for this reconstruction are apparently in the main: Job 6:11, *mah-kōḥî kî-ʾ^{a}yaḥēl ûmah-qqiṣṣî kî-ʾaʾ^{a}rîk napšî = tis gar mou hē ischys, hoti hypomenō; tis mou ho chronos, hoti anechetai mou hē psychē*; Judg 16:6, *bammeh kōḥ^{a}kā gādôl ûbammeh tēʾāsēr l^{e}ʿannōtekā = en tini hē ischys sou hē megalē, kai en tini dethēsē tou tapeinōthēnai se*; Judg 6:14, *lēk b^{e}kōḥ^{a}kā zeh w^{e}hôšaʿtā ʾet-yiśrāʾēl mikkap midyān = poreuou en tē ischyi sou tautē, kai sōseis to Israēl ek cheiros Madiam*; and Ps 144:11, *w^{e}haṣṣîlēnî miyyad b^{e}nê-nēkār = kai exelou me ek cheiros huiōn allotriōn*. This entire reconstruction, not merely the restored lost parallel colon, is quite remote from the Greek and Syriac of our Baruch passage, lacks the sort of close textual parallels that obtain for the above reconstruction, and thus appears to be quite unlikely.

[161]See above, p. 184, for citation.

[162]Kahana, 360.

[163]Rahlfs, *Septuaginta* II, 754:

[164]Ziegler, 463-64: *ho gar epagagōn ta kaka*.

[165]Cf. further: Jer 36:31, *hēbēʾtî ʿ^{a}lêhem . . . kol-hārāʿāh = kai epaxō epʾ auton . . . panta ta kaka*; Jer 44:2, *kol-hārāʿāh ʾ^{a}šer hēbēʾtî ʿal-y^{e}rûšālayim = panta ta kaka ha epēgagon epi Hierousalēm*; Jer 49:37, *w^{e}hēbēʾtî ʿ^{a}lêhem rāʿāh = kai epaxō epʾ autous kaka*; Ezek 14:22, *ʿal-hārāʿāh ʾ^{a}šer hēbēʾtî ʿal-y^{e}rûšālayim = epi ta kaka ha epēgagon epi Hierousalēm*; and with objects other than *hārāʿāh*, cf. Gen 20:9; 26:10; 27:12; Exod 11:1; 32:21; Lev 26:25; Deut 29:26; Jer 25:9, 13; 49:8, 36; Ezek 5:17; 11:8; 14:17; 33:12.

[166]Kneucker (327) has observed that *ʿ^{a}lêkem* could easily have fallen out of the Hebrew text *per lapsum oculi* as the same suffix appears (again) closely thereafter.

[167]Kneucker (358) reconstructs *hārāʿāh*; Kahana (360) has *hārāʿôt*.

[168]See HR II, 709-11.

[169]See Brugsch, "Das Buch Baruch, Koptisch," *ZÄS* XI (1873) 20.

[170]See HR I, 484-85.

[171]Ibid., 589-91.

[172]For this same expression with the ellipsis of *yad* in Hebrew, cf. Ps 59:2, 143:9, 2 Sam 22:18 (= Ps 18:18). For the same idiom with *kap* instead of *yad*, cf. Ps 18:1 (= 2 Sam 22:1), *mikkap kol-'ōyebāyw* = *ek cheiros pantōn tōn echthrōn autou;* 2 Sam 19:10, *mikkap 'ōyebênû* = *apo pantōn tōn echthrōn hēmōn;* and Ezra 8:31, *mikkap 'ôyēb* = *apo cheiros echthrou.* For the same idiomatic use of *haṣṣîl + miyyad-* with reference to other terms, cf., e.g., Gen 32:12; Exod 2:19; 18:9, 10; 34:27; Deut 25:11; 1 Sam 7:14; 17:37; 2 Sam 12:7; Jer 15:21; Ps 82:4; 144:11.

[173]See HR I, 188.

[174]Ibid., II, 1340-42. See also n. 294 below.

[175]*Erēmos* in classical usage has the meaning "desolate, lonely, solitary," and is commonly applied to persons or places. In the case of the latter, it also commonly designates "desert parts." See LSJ, 687.

[176]See HR I, 545-46.

[177]For its application to cities in general, cf. Lev 26:31, 33; Ezra 9:9; Isa 44:26; 61:4; Ezek 36:33+.

[178]See HR II, 736-37.

[179]More remotely, cf. Ruth 1:3, 5; 2 Kgs 25:11, 22; Ezra 1:4; Neh 1:2, 3; Jer 21:7; 34(41):7; Dan 10:8.

[180]Note that both Sy and Syh have the verb *šebaq* (Ethpe) "be left, deserted," which may tend to support *'āzab* for the Hebrew. See PS, 4037-38. From the evidence of all the Versions, the pleonastic personal pronoun *'ant* seems a secure part of the original Hebrew text, but it is at least noteworthy that without it this bicolon would be in perfect balance according to syllable count (6/6).

[181]Cf. also Neh 4:17, 1 Sam 19:24, and Isa 32:11; and see HR I, 423, 471.

[182]See HR II, 1291-92.

[183]Ibid., I, 401-02. Cf. also Bar 3:13, 14 and 5:4. It may also be noted that since *eirēnē* is used in the LXX almost exclusively for *šālôm* it is only a matter of course that the meaning of that Greek term has there been affected and expanded by the Hebrew sense which would naturally have penetrated into it to some extent. Thus the basic Greek sense of "peace" as a "state of rest" (vis-à-vis *polemos* "war") has throughout the LXX been further colored by the Hebrew social and religious overtones of "well-being" and "salvation." See further Foerster, "*eirēnē*," 405-07.

[184] Ryle and James, *Psalmoi Solomontos*, 18-19.

[185] Cf. also Sir 6:29, 31 and Wis 18:24.

[186] Cf. also *2 Enoch* 22:8f., 56:2, 62:14, 71:16f., Apocalypse of Abraham 13; and Jdt 16:8, *stolēn chēreuseōs*, "robe of widowhood."

[187] See HR II, 1257, and Bickerman, "The Septuagint as a Translation," 22.

[188] See LSJ, 372, 383.

[189] Saint Paul, e.g., uses *deēsis* at times simply to express general piety, but at other times to convey the particular sense of "intercession" (cf. Rom 10:1). See also Heinrich Greeven, "*deomai, deēsis*," *TWNT* II, 39-40.

[190] See HR I, 288.

[191] Ibid., 285-86.

[192] The LXX has other terms for "affliction," particularly *tapeinōsis* which is used regularly for Hebrew *ʿonî/ʿānî* "affliction"/"afflicted." The cognate verb *tapeinoō* is regular in the LXX for *ʿānāh* III. See HR II, 1334-36.

[193] See Kneucker (328 and 358, *weśaq ʿenûtî*, "den Sack meines Elends"), who cites the previous authorities, Fritzsche, Reusch, and Ewald, for the same position. See also Gifford, "Baruch," 282, n., "sackcloth of my affliction," and Kahana, 360, *weśaq ʿenûtî*. To the contrary, see Whitehouse, "1 Baruch," 593, "sackcloth of my petition"; Bissell, *The Apocrypha*, 431, "sackcloth of my prayer"; NEB, Bar 4:20, "sackcloth of a suppliant"; and RSV, Bar 4:20, "sackcloth of my supplication."

[194] See Kneucker, 329.

[195] In the Rahlfs edition of the LXX, 4:17K; in that of Ziegler, C13.

[196] Cf. other similar, though not so precise, parallels in 2 Kgs 25:30, Jer 52:34, and Ps 104:33.

[197] See HR II, 781-82.

[198] Similarly with *'elōhîm*, cf. 2 Sam 22:7, *we'el-'elōhay 'eqrā'*; Ps 55:17, *'el-'elohîm 'eqrā'*; 57:3, *lē'lōhîm 'eqrā'*; 22:3, *'elōhay 'eqrā'*. Kahana (360), noting what again appears to be a deficiency in the parallelism for the third colon of this verse, has suggested, without textual warrant, an additional colon to balance it: [*we'el-'elōhîm 'ārîm qôlî*].

[199] It is employed also with less frequency for other stems of these verbs as well as a few other verbs.

[200]Cf. also Exod 8:8, 15:25, 17:4, Num 12:13, 1 Chr 13:14, and Lam 2:18 (*'el-'ᵃdōnāy*).

[201]For *zā'aq* with reference to *YHWH*, cf. Judg 6:7; 10:10; 1 Sam 7:8; 12:8, 10; 15:11; Neh 9:4; and in general Hab 1:2 and 2 Chr 20:9.

[202]Other parallels for *qārā'* with reference to *YHWH* are: Deut 15:9, Judg 15:18, 16:28, 2 Sam 22:7, 2 Kgs 20:11, 21:26, 2 Chr 14:10, and Jonah 2:3. Parallels in Greek only from LXX passages lacking extant Hebrew *Vorlagen* may also be adduced: Tob 6:7, *boēsate pros ton eleēmona theon*; Jdt 4:9 (+ 4:12, 10:1, LXX Esth 1:1), *eboēsan . . . pros ton theon*; LXX Esth 10:3, *ho boēsantes pros ton theon*.

[203]Thus, see the discussion and citations given there, but especially note the parallels for this whole concept in: 2 Kgs 17:39, *wᵉhû' yaṣṣîl 'etkem miyyad kol-'ōyᵉbêkem*; 1 Sam 7:3, *wayyaṣṣēl 'etkem miyyad pᵉlištîm*; Judg 9:17, *wayyaṣṣēl 'etkem miyyad midyān*; 1 Sam 12:11, *wayyaṣṣēl 'etkem miyyad 'ōyᵉbêkem*. For the absolute use of *'ôyēb* in essentially the same idiomatic expression, cf. Ps 106:10, *wayyig'ālēm miyyad 'ôyēb = kai elytrōsato autous ek cheiros echthrou*; and Ezra 8:31, *wayyaṣṣīlēnû mikkap 'ôyēb = kai errhysato hēmas apo cheiros echthrou*. Cf. also the use of *ôyēb* in the absolute state in the antithetical concept with *bᵉyad-* in Lam 2:7, Lev 26:25, Ps 31:9.

[204]The Hebrew idiom, *miyyad-* (or *bᵉyad-*), is extremely common and pervasive in BH.

[205]See Kasser (*Papyrus Bodmer XXII*, 316-17), who renders *či ngonš*, "iniquité." This Coptic compound, however, possesses an even more basic sense of "violence" (literally, "doing of violence, evil"), a feature which will assume some significance for determining the Hebrew equivalent of *dynasteia* below. See Walter E. Crum, *A Coptic Dictionary* (Oxford: Clarendon, 1939) 822.

[206]See HR I, 354-55.

[207]This Greek term occurs forty-seven times in the LXX where the Hebrew equivalent can be determined. In thirty-three of these, it stands for Hebrew *gᵉbûrāh*. No other equivalency occurs more than three times. The other equivalencies and their frequencies are: *gibbôr* "mighty-hero" (two), *gᵉdûllāh* "greatness" (one), *mimšāl* "dominion" (one), *memšālāh* "rule, dominion," (two), *mā'ôz* "stronghold" (one), *'ôz* "strength" (three), *'ᵉzûz* "might" (one), *siblāh* "burden (of forced labor)" (one), *'āṣûm* "mighty, numerous" (one), *ṣābā'* "host, armed forces" (one).

[208]Contrast, e.g., *rex* "king" and the semantic overtones that it carries.

[209]See n. 205 above. It is also worthy of note that Crum (*A Coptic Dictionary*, 822) indicates that the Coptic verb *či ngonš* "do violence, evil" is used as the translational equivalent for the Greek *dynasteuō* in 1 Chr 16:21 (cf. MT, *'āšaq* "oppress"), and for the related *katadynasteuō* in Wis 2:10.

[210]Kneucker, 329.

[211]See HR II, 1335-36, and I, 652-53.

[212]Cf. Dan 11:4-5, Ps 103:22, Prov 19:10, and Sir 48:12.

[213]See n. 207 above for the frequency of this equivalency.

[214]*Gebûrāh* thus gives every indication in this Kings formula of being nuanced in a technical-political sense. The lexica at least suggest that in this formulaic usage in Kings the term does seem to have a specialized sense. Koehler and Baumgartner (KB, 3rd ed., 165) suggest the meaning *Erfolg* ("success"). It may also be noted that the term in this formulaic usage consistently appears in the singular, commonly: *ûgᵉbûrātô* for kings Baasha, Omri, Jehoahaz, Joash, and Jeroboam II (cf. 1 Kgs 16:5, 27; 2 Kgs 13:8, 12; 14:15, 28); the rather odd *wᵉkol-gᵉbûrātô* for kings Asa, Jehu, and Hezekiah (cf. 1 Kgs 5:23, 2 Kgs 10:34, 20:20); and the more expanded *ûgᵉbûrātô 'ᵃšer-'āśāh* for King Jehoshaphat (cf. 1 Kgs 22:46).

[215]Indeed, his evaluation of the various kings' performances was markedly unfavorable in several of the most notorious examples!

[216]1 Chr 29:30 is suggestive: *'im kol-malkûtô ûgᵉbûrātô = peri pasēs tēs basileias autou kai tēs dynasteias autou*, "concerning all his reign and 'dominion'(?)." This is, however, usually interpreted as a case of hendiadys, "his all-powerful reign." Cf. also Ps 145:12, *lᵉhôdîᵃ' libnê hā'ādām gᵉbûrōtāyw ûkᵉbôd hᵃdar malkûtô = tou gnorisai tois huiois tōn anthrōpōn tēn dynasteian sou, kai tēn doxan tēs megaloprepeias tēs basileias sou*, "To make known to the sons of men his/your 'sovereignty'(?), and the glorious majesty of his/your kingdom."

[217]Cf. 1QM 11:11; 13:13, 14; 16:1; 18:10; et al.

[218]The supposition of a highly probable haplography here greatly improves the sense of the passage. Note also that the Hebrew *mimšāl* in this same passage is translated as well by *dynasteia* with no appreciable differentiation in meaning.

[219]Cf. further two other LXX passages where forms of the Hebrew verb *māšal* "rule, exercise dominion" are translated by the Greek verb *dynasteuō*: Prov 19:10, *mᵉšōl = dynasteuein*; and Sir 48:12, *mšl = dynasteusen* (G^S). This meaning of *memšālāh* may also be clearly seen in some of its other occurrences; cf., e.g., Jer 51(28):28, *wᵉ et kol- eres memšaltô* = (G^A) *pasēs tēs gēs exousias autou*, "and all the land(s) of his dominion"; and 2 Kgs 20:13, *ûbᵉkol-memšaltô = kai en pasē tē exousia autou*, "and in all his dominion." Also cf. Isa 22:21 and 1 Kgs 9:19, where the LXX does not follow the Hebrew. The Greek term *exousia* "power, authority" is more frequently associated with the Hebrew *šālaṭ/šallîṭ* "rule/ruler." See HR I, 500-01.

[220]In addition, the typically non-political use of *gᵉbûrāh* in the immediate following context also offers its own sort of negative confirmation regarding that term.

[221]This term is always modified in some way in BH, e.g., "remove the domionion of the enemy," "of his dominion," etc., but never "of dominion," "from dominion," or the like.

[222]Kahana (360 [*mē'ōšeq*]) has also arrived at this conclusion.

[223]Indeed, a lone example such as this is open to interpretation as a mere translator's quirk, for if *'ōšeq* were assumed to have been in the Hebrew *Vorlage*, one might rather have expected something more like *tyrannos* "tyranny," a term very common in the Maccabean literature, or *katadynasteia* "oppression" to appear in the Greek. Cf. nn. 205 and 209 above, with reference to the use of the Coptic compound verb *či ngonš* in translating *dynasteuō* in 1 Chr 16:21.

[224]Cf. 1 Sam 12:3, Hos 5:11, 12:8, Amos 4:1, Zech 7:10, Jer 7:6, 50(27):33.

[225]Cf. Jer 6:6, Ezek 22:12.

[226]Cf. Mic 3:9.

[227]Cf. Exod 1:13, *'ābad* (Hiph), and 6:7, *siblāh*. Cf. also LSJ, 890.

[228]For the similar terms *'ōšēq* and *'āšōq* "oppressor," cf. Jer 22:3, 12; Amos 3:9; Eccl 4:1; and perhaps Job 35:9.

[229]See Barthélemy & Milik, DJD I, 27, 1:I:10-11, p. 103. The translation is that of Millar Burrows, *More Light on the Dead Sea Scrolls* (New York: Viking, 1958) 398.

[230]See Kneucker, 176, and Harwell, 5.

[231]See HR I, 453-54. Note that the corresponding noun, *elpis*, represents *bāṭaḥ* seven times, *mibṭāḥ* nine times, and *beṭaḥ* fourteen times in the LXX.

[232]Ibid., II, 1114-15.

[233]It also occurs seven times for *maḥseh* "refuge." *Pepoitha* is used for *ḥāsāh* nine times in the LXX.

[234]Cf. also Ps 55:24, *wa'ănî 'ebṭaḥ bô* = *egō de elpiō epi se*, with Ps 71:14, *wa'ănî . . . 'ayaḥēl* = *egō de . . . elpiō*. Note also that in Ps 25:2-3 *bāṭaḥ* and *qāwāh* are synonymous in parallel cola, and in Ps 71:5-7 the three substantives *tiqwāh*, *mibṭāḥ*, and *maḥseh*, appear in this way.

[235]Rudolf Bultmann,("*elpis*, *elpizō*," *TWNT* II, 519) characterizes it as "im Griech ungebräuchlichen."

[236]Cf. Thucydides, *History of the Peloponnesian War*, Vol. III, trans. Charles F. Smith (LCL, II; London: W. Heinemann, 1920) 97:2, pp. 172-73: *tē tychē elpisas*, "hoping in good fortune."

[237]See LSJ, 537.

[238]Kneucker, 329.

[239]Kahana, 360.

[240]*Ḥāsāh* is also a possibility and a number of suggestive parallels can be adduced in its support. Cf. Ps 7:2, *YHWH 'elōhay bekā ḥāsîtî hôšî'ēnî = Kyrie ho theos mou, epi soi ēlpisa, sōson me*; Ps 31:2 (= 71:1), *bekā YHWH ḥāsîtî = epi soi Kyrie ēlpisa*; Ps 141:8, *bekāh ḥāsîtî = epi soi ēlpisa*; Ps 18:3, *'eḥseh-bô = elpiō ep' auton*; Ps 16:1 and 25:20, *kî ḥāsîtî bekā = hoti epi soi ēlpisa/hoti ēlpisa epi se*; Ps 37:40, *kî ḥāsû bô = hoti ēlpisan ep' auton*; and Ps 17:7, *môšîa' ḥôsîm = ho sōzōn tous elpizontas epi se*. But, cf. also Ps 118:8-9, *ṭôb laḥasôt beYHWH mibbeṭōaḥ bā'ādām / ṭôb laḥasôt beYHWH mibbeṭōaḥ bindîbîm = Agathon pepoithenai epi Kyrion, ē pepoithenai ep' anthrōpon. Agathon elpizein epi Kyrion, ē elpizein ep' archousi.* Whereas the Hebrew in this last passage offers parallel terms within each colon, the Greek glides over the slight semantic differences between the Hebrew infinitives in each colon and instead presents the same sort of verbal counterposition, but between the cola. For *yāḥal*, there is one parallel that has the same rather idiomatic beginning with the pleonastic pronoun as in Bar 4:22, viz., Ps 71:14 (Piel), *wa'anî tāmîd 'ayaḥēl = egō de diapantos elpiō*. Also two examples in the Hiphel stem are worthy of comparison: Ps 38:16, *kî-lekā YHWH hôḥāltî = hoti epi soi Kyrie ēlpisa*; and Ps 130:5, *hôḥāltî napšî la'dōnāy = ēlpisen hē psychē mou epi ton Kyrion.*

[241]Cf. further examples of this equivalency in Ps 56:4, 91:2, 26:1, 52:10, 56:12, 143:8, 78:22, 22:5, and 86:2.

[242]Cf. Ps 4:5, 9:10, 21:7, 33:21, 37:3, 40:3, Isa 32:9-11, et al. See also PS, 2510-11.

[243]Cf. also Syh, *(')nā' ger sabberet 'al haw dal'ālam lepurqānā' dîlekūn*. Also, although the Greek uses *hypomeinō* and the Hebrew *yāḥal*, the ending and the general sense of Lam 3:26 offers a helpful parallel: *ṭôb weyāḥîl wedûmām litšû'at YHWH = agathon kai hypomenei, kai hēsychasei eis to sōtērion Kyriou*. Cf. also Job 2:9 (LXX).

[244]See HR II, 1331-32.

[245]See Georg Fohrer, "*sōzō, sōtēria*," *TWNT* VII, 970-71.

[246]*Chara* also occurs rarely in a few other equivalencies, e.g., with *rinnāh* in Isa 55:12 (where it also appears to represent *šālôm*), or *gîl* in Joel 1:16.

[247]Cf. Bar 4:14, above, and see HR I, 548-53.

[248]Bickerman ("The Septuagint as a Translation," 22 n. 46) has observed in this regard that such a statement as that in Exod 31:13, *egō ho Kyrios ho hagiazōn hymas*, "heard by a Greek

contemporary with the 'Seventy' would have meant to him that the owner of the Jews had marked them off as untouchables but not that their Deity had made them holy."

[249] It may be noted that this pattern is so thoroughgoing that the normal Greek term for temple, *hieron*, never even appears in the LXX, but instead the temple sanctuary is always designated *to hagion* (or *ta hagia*), clearly a Hebraism. Bickerman ("The Septuagint as a Translation," 22 n. 46) contends that this translational predilection for *hagios* on the part of the "Seventy" may be traced back to the practice already established by the dragomans, but he admits only to puzzlement as to why *hagios* and not *hieros* was chosen to express the Hebrew conception. Some scholars have theorized that the choice of *hagios* as the equivalent of the Hebrew *qādôš* was probably the result of a careful search for a word that would have been unfreighted with any of the connotations of the pagan cults and yet an apt equivalent. Yet, see Martin Flashar, "Exegetische Studien zum Septuagintapsalter" (*ZAW* 32 [1912] 245 n. 2), who notes nevertheless that already in a temple edict of Ptolemy III Euergetes *to hagion* is used with reference to a pagan temple. See further Otto Procksch, "*hagios*," *TWNT* I, 87-97; Bickerman, "The Septuagint as a Translation," 22; and H. S. Gehman, "*Hagios* in the Septuagint, and its Relation to the Hebrew Original," *VT* 4 (1954) 337-48.

[250] See BDB, 872.

[251] Cf. also Bar 4:37, 5:5, and other Greek apocryphal references to God as *hagios*: 2 Macc 14:36, 3 Macc 2:2, Sir 23:9, Tob 12:12, 15, et al.

[252] It also appears once each for *ṣedeq*, *ṣidqāh*, and *'emet*. See HR I, 450.

[253] See Rudolf Bultmann, "*eleos*, *eleeō*, *eleēmōn*, *eleēmosynē*," *TWNT* II, 482-83. It may also be observed that *eleēmosynē* appears to have the ordinary sense of "mercy" where it appears in the Ptolemaic Zenon Papyri, *Pros se oun kataphygganomen hina eleēmosynēs tychomen*, "Thus we have fled for refuge to you that we may obtain mercy." See Campbell Cowan Edgar, ed., *Zenon Papyri* (*Catalogue général des antiquités égyptiennes du Musée du Caire*, no. 85), Vol. III (Le Caire: Imprimerie de l'Institut français d'archéologie orientale, 1928) no. 59495, p. 210; and Bickerman, "The Septuagint as a Translation," 20 n. 41.

[254] Cf. especially Sir 3:14, 30; 29:8-9, 12, for the doing of benevolence works as a covering for sin, and *Talmud Babli*, *Baba Bathra*, 9a, where Rabbi Assi is quoted to the effect that "charity is equivalent to all the other religious precepts combined."

[255] See also *Talmud Babli*, *Sukkah*, 49b, and Matt 6:12, for this conception of the giving of alms as righteousness par excellence.

[256] See Franz Rosenthal, "*Sedaka*, Charity," *HUCA* 23/1 (1952) 428-29.

[257]Cf. Sir 3:14, 30; 7:10; 12:3; 16:14; 40:17, 24.

[258]Cf. the source, Mic 6:8, where the MT has "with God."

[259]Cf. further 1QH 4:37, 16:9, 17:20, CD 20:20, and many other Qumran passages too numerous to cite.

[260]See Kuhn, *Konkordanz*, 74-75.

[261]Cf. also 1QH 2:23, *wbḥsdykh twšy' npšy*, "and by your mercies you save my life." The combination *ḥsdkh 'wḥyl*, "I await your mercy," appears in 1QH 7:18, 9:10, 11:31.

[262]See HR I, 605-06. It appears only here in Baruch.

[263]See HR II, 1338.

[264]Cf. also 2 Sam 3:13, Exod 29:28, Esth 7:7, Josh 11:20, and other examples cited in BDB, 86-87, sec. 4c.

[265]Cf. also Gen 41:32 with *'ᵉlōhîm*, and Exod 9:33, 1 Sam 16:14, where the LXX has *apo* instead of *para*, and other examples cited in BDB (768-69, sec. d).

[266]See HR II, 1331.

[267]Isa 45:21, *hᵃlô' 'ᵃnî YHWH . . . 'ēl-ṣaddîq ûmôšîᵃ'* = *egō ho theos* [sic] . . . *dikaios kai sōtēr*; Isa 45:15 (also of *YHWH*), *'ᵉlōhê yiśrā'ēl môšîᵃ'* = *ho theos tou Israēl sōtēr* (cf. 45:17); Isa 43:11, *'ānōkî 'ānōkî YHWH wᵉ'ên mibbal'āday môšîᵃ'* (LXX, *sōzōn*); Isa 49:26 (and 60:16), *kî 'ᵃnî YHWH môšî'ēk* (LXX, *ho sōzōn se*). Cf. similarly, Isa 43:3; 63:8; Hos 13:4; Jer 14:8; 30:10; Neh 9:27; Judg 3:9, 15; 1 Sam 10:19; 2 Sam 22:3; Ps 106:21; and etc.

[268]But note that three times in 3 Maccabees *ho theos* is referred to as *sōtēr* (6:29, 32 and 7:16), in the first instance as *ton hagion sōtēra*, "holy Savior," and in the last as *aiōniō sōtēri*, "eternal Savior."

[269]See HR I, 439.

[270]Jackson (41) has shown that *bᵉkî* is always the A-word in parallel with terms other than *'ēbel*.

[271]See HR I, 126-27.

[272]Another possible reconstruction for this colon is perhaps *wîšîbᵉkem lî 'ᵉlōhîm*. Cf. the rendering of Kahana (360).

[273]See HR II, 1455-56.

[274]See *GKC*, §161b, p. 499; and BDB, 455, 486. For examples, cf. Jer 31(38):28, *wᵉhāyāh ka'ᵃšer šāqadtî 'ᵃlêhem lintôš . . . kēn 'ešqōd 'ᵃlêhem libnôt* = *kai estai hōsper egrēgoroun ep' autous kathairein . . . houtōs grēgorēsō ep' autous tou*

oikodomein, "And it will come to pass that just as I watched over them to pull down . . . so will I watch over them to rebuild"; Isa 55:10-11, *kî ka'ᵃšer yērēd haggešem . . . kēn yihyeh dᵉbārî = hōs gar an katabē ho hyetos . . . houtōs estai to rhēma mou*, "For just as the rain descends . . . so will my word be"; Jer 13:11; Judg 1:7; Exod 7:6; Num 14:28; Isa 31:4.

[275] See HR II, 951-52.

[276] Ibid., 1005-07.

[277] Ibid., 1035-39.

[278] This source-passage may be as well the source for the common pronominal variant in our Baruch passage (*hēmōn* "our" instead of *hymōn* "your"), as especially in G^A, 106', Sy, La^C, LXX Minuscules 567, 49, 90, 764, and 239 of the Catenae group, and the Hexaplaric 233. See Ziegler, 464.

[279] See HR I, 509-10.

[280] See Gerhard Kittel, "*dokeō, doxa*," *TWNT* II, 245-48. It is significant that *doxa* represents *kābôd* in approximately 180 of its 280+ occurrences within the LXX books that correspond to the Hebrew canon. The remaining occurrences represent 24 other Hebrew words, some quite rare, having either the same or nearly the same sense as *kābôd*. See also HR I, 341-43) and observe that *kābôd* is extremely common in this second Baruch poem, occurring 9 times in all (4:3 in the first poem and 4:24, 37 and 5:1, 2, 4, 6, 7, 9 in the second).

[281] See LSJ, 1028.

[282] For a discussion and evaluation of the varying interpretations of this term, and support for the sense of (divine-) splendor, see P. R. Ackroyd, "Some Notes on the Psalms," *JTS* 17 (1966) 393-96. For the interpretation (following Ugaritic *hdrt*) "appearance, vision, theophany," see Cyrus H. Gordon, *Ugaritic Textbook* (Analecta Orientalia 38; Rome: Pontificum Institutum Biblicum, 1965) 389 n. 752; F. M. Cross, "Notes on a Canaanite Psalm in the Old Testament," *BASOR* 117 (1950) 21; and Mitchell Dahood, *Psalms* I (AB 16; Garden City: Doubleday, 1966) 176, and *Psalms* III (AB 17A; Garden City: Doubleday, 1970) 116. See also H. J. Kraus, *Psalmen* 2 (BKAT 15/2; Neukirchen: Neukirchener, 1961) 752-53) for the commonly adopted emendatory solution (following Sym, Hi, and numerous Hebrew mss.), *bᵉharrê qôdeš*.

[283] The related adjective, *lampros* "brilliant, radiant," appears seven times in the LXX, always in Apocryphal works for which there is no extant Hebrew *Vorlage* with the exception of two of these instances, Sir 30:25(33:13) and 31:23(34:23). In each of these two instances, *lampros* represents Hebrew *ṭwb* in an extended use of the term to mean "generous" or "expansive" (in the first case, *lampra kardia = lb ṭwb*, "an expansive heart," and in the second, *lampron ep' autois = ṭwb 'l lḥm*, "generous about food"). Clearly, such a far-extended meaning

of "brilliant(-light)" is not helpful here. Sym employs the cognate verb *lamprynō* in Ps 119:9 and Prov 20:9, in both instances to represent Hebrew *zākāh* "be pure," also quite an extension of the basic sense of the verb. The related noun *lampsin* is a LXX hapax legomenon appearing only in Bar 4:2 where it probably represents Hebrew *nōgah* (cf. ad loc.). These various related terms are thus ultimately of little avail in determining the Hebrew equivalent here in Bar 4:24.

[284]Syh translates *nō'am/lamprotēs* in Ps 90:17 with *naṣṣîḥûtā'* "splendor," the very same term that it uses for *lamprotēs* in Bar 4:24 and 5:3. See PS, 2439.

[285]Cf. *hôd wehādār* ascribed to *YHWH* in Ps 96:6, 104:1, 111:3, and 1 Chr 16:27, and to *'Ēl* in Job 40:10. The derivations of these two terms suggest that they are properly differentiated semantically by the fact of *hôd* being essentially an auditory phenomenon and *hādār* a visual one.

[286]The LXX translates *kābôd* in this passage consistently with *doxa*; *hādār*, however, is not rendered with *lamprotēs* but with other general synonyms (*timē* "honor" and *hypsos* "height"). In the abovementioned passages in which *hādār* appears paired with *hôd*, the LXX usually renders the former by *megaloprepia* "splendor."

[287]This translation is by Brownlee, *Dead Sea Manual of Discipline*, 16.

[288]Similarly, *'ōz* "might" is a parallel term several times: Ps 96:6, 1 Chr 16:27.

[289]Here the LXX translator apparently misread *resh* for *daleth* in the Hebrew text and translated *oresin aiōniois*, "everlasting mountains."

[290]The precise interpretation of this phrase is a matter of some dispute. See n. 282 above for the commonly proposed solutions and the basic literature appertaining thereto, especially Ackroyd ("Some Notes on the Psalms," 393-96).

[291]But it should be observed that *nōgah* is quite regularly rendered in the LXX by the Greek *pheggos* "light, lustre." See HR II, 1426.

[292]Cf. 4:37 and 5:9 below, where the "glory of God" and the "light of his glory" similarly are indicative of God's guiding personal presence.

[293]The omission of *tou*, resulting in the sense "eternal splendor," is found in the Greek in a few LXX Minuscules (nos. 46, 233) but is especially reflected in the Latin ($La^{L,S,V}$), *splendore aeterno*.

[294]See Bickerman ("The Septuagint as a Translation," 23 n. 48) for documentation of the Hellenistic usage of the independent vocative in expressing the familiar terms of parentage:

e.g., "father" (without any pleonastic pronoun) for "my father," or etc.

[295]See HR II, 893. The cognate adjective *makrothymos*, in thirteen of its sixteen LXX occurrences, translates the Hebrew *'erek 'appayim*, "patience, patient" (Sir 5:4, Exod 34:6, Num 14:18, Neh 9:17, Ps 86:15, 103:8, 145:8, Prov 14:29, 15:18, 16:32, Joel 2:13, Jonah 4:2, Nah 1:3), and in addition, the similar *'erek rûaḥ* (Eccl 7:8), *qar rûaḥ* (Prov 17:27), and *'arkā'* (Dan 4:24). The cognate noun *makrothymia* has Hebrew equivalents in three instances, similarly: *'ōrek 'appayim* (Prov 25:15), *'erek 'appayim* (Jer 15:15), and *'erek rûaḥ* (Sir 5:11). See also Johannes Horst, "*makrothymia, makrothymeō, makrothymos, makrothymōs*," *TWNT* IV, 377-90.

[296]See LSJ, 1074, and cf. Sir 18:11, 29:8, 2 Macc 6:14.

[297]For examples, cf. Job 7:16, Prov 19:11, Sir 2:4, 2 Macc 8:26.

[298]See LSJ, 1074, which cites Bar 4:25 as its lone example of *makrothymeō* + acc.

[299]Cf. Isa 48:9, Prov 19:11, and the similar, more common idiom *ya'arîk yāmîm* "endure, live long" (literally, "prolong the days"), as, e.g., in Deut 17:20, et al.

[300]Kahana, 360.

[301]The LXX translates it in Job 9:27 with *stenachō* "groan"! Kahana also has to assume an unsubstantiated *'al-* to convey the sense "be cheerful concerning . . .," whereas this verb does not use *'al-* (except perhaps in the very problematic Amos 5:9).

[302]Kneucker, 332.

[303]For the similar use of *nāśā'*, cf. Job 21:3, Isa 1:14, 53:4, Ezek 16:52, et al. The synonymous *sābal* "carry, bear a burden" could also be considered. It is often used metaphorically of "bearing sorrows or iniquities." Cf. Isa 53:4, 11; 46:4; and especially Lam 5:7.

[304]See HR II, 730-31. Cf. also Deut 28:20 (especially in relation to its following context), Jdt 16:3, et al. There is, it should be noted, considerable support for *gar* (= Hebrew, *kî*) after *katediōxe*, particularly in G^A, La^V, and numerous LXX Minuscules (see Ziegler, 464), but the Syriac Versions (which of all would be the most likely to have or even add such) are unanimous in lacking any such conjunctive particle.

[305]Codex Vaticanus stands virtually alone here in maintaining the absolute state of *echthros* (= *'ôyēb*). All other witnesses attest modification with the second person singular possessive pronoun or pronominal suffix (*echthros sou*). But it remains true that in MT, *'ôyēb* is more commonly found in the absolute state than suffixed (e.g., cf. Lam 1:9, 16; 2:7; Ezek 36:2; Bar 3:10, 21; etc.). See also Mandelkern (I, 41), where

one may count fifty+ examples of *'ôyēb* :: less than ten of *'ôyibkā*. It may also be noted that the addition of just such a suffix or possessive pronoun is one of the most natural and expected types of editorial insertions that creep into texts.

[306] Cf. also Obad 12, *bᵉyôm 'obdām = en hēmera apōleias autōn*. For this infinitive construct + suffix, cf. Deut 7:20, Prov 11:10, Josh 23:13, and Prov 28:28. For the use of the Hebrew verb *'ābad* with reference to the destruction of other nations, cf. Deut 7:20, Jer 10:15, 51:18, Ps 2:12, 10:16, 83:18, Amos 1:8, Isa 41:11, 60:12, Jonah 3:9. See also HR I, 151-52.

[307] Cf. also Obad 13, Ps 22:18, Jer 29:32, and Mic 7:9.

[308] Cf. also Amos 4:13, Mic 1:3, and the thought of Isa 51:23, 26:6, Jer 27:12, and Mic 2:3. In addition, cf. 1QM 12:10, *qwmh gbwr sbh sbykh . . . tn ydkh b'wrp 'wybykh wrglkh 'l bmwty ḥll*, "Arise, mighty one, take your captives, . . . put your hand upon the neck of your enemies and your foot upon the bodies of the slain"; and Gen 49:8.

[309] It does so about 70% of the time. See HR II, 1370.

[310] These are: *'ānōg* "daintiness" in Deut 28:54, 56; Isa 47:1; *'ōneg* "dainty, delicate" in Isa 58:13; and *ta'ᵃnûg* "daintiness" in Mic 1:16. In the remaining instance, the equivalent is *'ādîn* "voluptuous" (applied to personified Babylon in Isa 47:8). See HR II, 1377.

[311] Cf. Deut 28:56 for the same applied to the women.

[312] This is obviously a distinct possibility for Bar 4:26, but one might expect *tekna* there also.

[313] Another possibility, but a very dubious one, is that proposed by Kahana (360)--*bᵉnê ṭippûḥay*, "my dandled[?] children." His sources are Lam 2:20, *'ōlᵃlê ṭippūḥîm*, "children of dandling[?]," and Lam 2:22, *'ᵃšer ṭippaḥtî wᵉribbîtî 'ōyᵉbî killām*, "whoever I dandled[?] and raised up my enemy destroyed." Only in these two places in BH is this expression found, and in both cases the LXX either misunderstands or offers a different reading. But this idiom is unsatisfactory for Bar 4:26 because it does not provide at all the proper contrast with the "rough roads" depiction that follows. Also, the sense of "dandle" for *ṭpḥ* is uncertain. From its parallel with "raise up," it connotes youthfulness but not delicateness.

[314] Another possibility perhaps is that suggested by Kahana (360), *'ᵒrāḥôt 'ᵃqalqallôt*, "crooked paths." This expression occurs in MT only in Judg 5:6 where the LXX translates *hodous diestrammenas*, "crooked paths." Cf. also Sir 4:17 which depicts Wisdom as "walking crookedly" (or "disguisedly") with a person in order to test his mettle: *hoti diestrammenōs poreuetai met' auton = ky bhtnkr 'lk 'mw*. But the root sense of the verb *'āqal* is "twist, distort" and this "crookedness" simply does not offer the proper parallel, in this case with "delicate." Further, *tracheia* is never used in the LXX for Hebrew *'ᵃqalqāl* "crooked."

[315]Cf. Bar 3:13, 20, 21, 23, 27, 31, 36; and 4:13, above. Note that out of 600+ occurrences, the next highest in frequency is *'ōraḥ* "path" with 33. See HR II, 962-66.

[316]See HR I, 34-36.

[317]The LXX does not follow this closely, "They desire land, carry off [*diarpazō*] orphans, and oppress [*katadynasteuō*] homes."

[318]Cf. as well 1 Kgs 15:22, 18:12, Lam 5:13, Jer 40:29, Isa 40:24, 41:16.

[319]Kahana (360) has *hûbᵉlû*, the Hophal perfect of *yābal* "lead (away)," as the Hebrew here. This passive form is used in Jer 11:19 and Isa 53:7 for the image of being led like a sheep to the slaughter. But it also has a positive connotation as in Isa 55:12 where it expresses the idea of being led away (triumphantly) out of exile. But, *airō* is never used in the LXX for this Hebrew verb.

[320]See HR I, 160. It is also used almost as frequently for Hebrew *ṭārap* "tear or seize prey," but this verb belongs to a distinctly different topos involving animals of prey. Insight into the criminal overtones of this term can be gained from the fact of its extremely common biblical pairing with *'ōšeq* "oppression, extortion." It thus often means "steal."

[321]See HR II, 1169-70.

[322]See the data given there regarding these verbs as common equivalents for *boaō*. Cf. also Jer 11:12.

[323]See HR II, 931.

[324]Note the support for *hymin* ("for you" as opposed to "of you") in the LXX Minuscules 86', 534, Sy, Bo, Ar, and Arm.

[325]Nonetheless, this is apparently the assumption of Kahana (360) who translates *wᵉhāyāh lākem zikkārôn lipnê hammēbî'*. It would, however, be plausible that such passages may have served as models for something like *kî yihyeh lākem zēker*.

[326]Cf. further, Lam 5:17; Ezek 4:6; 17:12, 15; Isa 40:26; 44:21; 45:7; 48:14; Jer 4:18; 5:25; 13:22.

[327]Cf. also especially 1 Kgs 14:10; 2 Kgs 22:16, 20; Jer 4:6; 6:19; 11:11; 42:17; 45:5; 49:5; 51:64.

[328]The *ta* of the LXX reading suggests that the Hebrew noun was in this case determined (*hārā'āh*), although in most of the above cited examples it is not (usually, *mēbî' rā'āh*). Also, the normal internal sequence for this idiom appears to be: *mēbî' rā'āh 'al-*.

[329]See Ziegler, 465.

[330]Cf. above, 3:21, 26, and see HR I, 256-57.

[331]See HR I, 306-07, and 1139-40.

[332]Cf. also 1 Kgs 8:18, 1 Chr 28:2, 2 Chr 1:11, 29:10, 1 Sam 14:7, 2 Sam 7:3, 2 Kgs 10:30, Isa 10:7. Note also that in Jer 31(38):33, *kardia* appears in parallel with *dianoia*.

[333]Other possibilities are: *mē'al* as in Ezek 44:15, *bit'ōt bᵉnê yiśrā'ēl mē'ālay* (cf. 44:10), or *min-* as in Prov 21:16, *tō'eh midderek = planōmenos ex hodou*, or Ps 119:110, *lō' tā'îtî mippᵉqûdèkā = ek tōn entolōn sou ouk eplanēthēn.*

[334]See HR I, 531-33, and 597-98.

[335]Similarly, cf. Hos 11:9, *lō' 'āšûb lᵉšaḥēt 'eprāyim;* Dan 10:20, *wᵉ'attāh 'āšûb lᵉhillāḥēm 'im-śar pārās.* Cf. also 1 Sam 27:4, *wᵉlō' yāsap lᵉbaqšô.*

[336]It appears elsewhere in Philo,(*De Migratione Abrahami*, trans. F. H. Colson and G. H. Whitaker (LCL, IV; London: W. Heinemann, 1932) 169, pp. 230-31. See also LSJ, 376, which lists only these examples.

[337]Kneucker, 336.

[338]Ibid.

[339]Cf. Deut 19:3, 1 Kgs 18:34, Gen 41:34, et al.

[340]See Jastrow, *Dictionary of the Targumim*, 1127; BDB, 797.

[341]See Gordon, *UT*, §7.73, p. 52.

[342]Dahood (*Psalms* I, 142), with regard to Ps 22:26, proposes vocalization of consonantal *m'tk* as *mī'ētīkā*, "a piel denominative verb from *mē'āh*, 'hundred,' followed by a datival suffix." The translation he proposes is: "One hundred times will I repeat to you."

[343]Kahana, 360.

[344]In the first of these passages the inheritance share of the firstborn is stipulated to be *pî-šᵉnayim* of the father's estate. In the second case, Elisha requests *pî-šᵉnayim* of the spirit of Elijah. But in the Zechariah poem, *pî-šᵉnayim* stands indubitably in parallel with *haššᵉlîšît* "the third (part)," and is thus usually understood there to mean "two-thirds." In the light of this last example from BH, and of the Akkadian *šinipatu* "two-thirds," many would take *pî-šᵉnayim* in all three of its BH occurrences to be the Hebrew term for "two-thirds." See Ch. Clermont-Ganneau, "Deux inscriptions israélites archaïques de Gezer," *Recueil d'Archéologie Orientale*, Vol. VIII (Paris: E. Leroux, 1924) 105-12; Anton Jirku, "Zur magischen Bedeutung der Kleidung in Israel," *ZAW* 37 (1917-18) 110; and KB, 753-54.

[345]See A. Eben-Shoshan, *Millôn Ḥādāš* (Jerusalem: Kiryat Sepher, 1964) 1260.

[346]Whitehouse, "1 Baruch," 573.

[347]BH expresses the same thing on occasion with the plural of *mōneh* "unit, time" (cf. *ʿaśeret mōnîm* "ten times," only in Gen 31:7, 41) or the plural of *yad* "hand, unit" (cf. *ʿeśer yādôt* "ten times," in Dan 1:20, and *ḥāmēš yādôt* "five times," in Gen 43:34).

[348]See O. Schmitz and G. Stählin, "*parakaleō*," *TWNT* V, 771-90.

[349]Numerous other examples include: Isa 40:1; 49:13; 51:19; 52:9; 61:2; Lam 2:13; 1:2, 9, 16, 17, 21; Ezek 14:23.

[350]*Kaleō* "call" is much more common perhaps because Hebrew *šēm* has no derived verb. See Hans Bietenhard, "*onoma, onomazō*," *TWNT* V, 263, 252, and 251 n. 84.

[351]Cf. also Gen 5:2, 31:47, et al. The use of the double accusative is also sometimes found (e.g., Isa 60:8).

[352]The other examples are also enlightening: Gen 26:18, *wayyiqrā' lāhen šēmôt kaššēmôt 'ašer-qārā' lāhen 'ābîw* = *kai epōnomasen autois onomata kata ta onomata ha ōnomasen ho patēr autou*; Deut 2:20, *yiqrā' lāhem zamzummîm* = *(ep)onomazousin autous Zochommin*.

[353]Cf. further Jer 11:16, 33:16, et al. Isa 62:2 suggests yet another possibility, *nāqab*, which is translated five times in the LXX by *onomazō*. This Hebrew verb normally means "pierce, bore" but in an extended sense it is used in Isa 62:2 and 1 Chr 12:31 (= 2 Chr 31:19) with the meaning, "designate, name," and in Lev 24:16, "name (abusively)." But such usage is really quite rare vis-à-vis the normal pattern with *qārā'* + *šēm*. The other seven equivalencies of *onomazō* are with *zākar* "remember" (Qal: Jer 3:16, 20:9, 23:36; Hiph: Josh 23:7, Amos 6:10, Isa 19:17, 26:13). In this usage, *zākar* (or *hizkîr*) has the sense "call to mind" (i.e., "mention"), and thus displays a marked semantic difference from the idiom(s) for "giving a name." The source of this latter usage would appear to be cultic; cf. Josh 23:7, "do not mention [i.e., "call on"] the name of the gods."

[354]Cf. also other "names" for Jerusalem in BH: "city of God" (Ps 46:5, 48:2, 87:3), "city of *YHWH*" (Isa 60:14, Ps 48:9), "holy city" (Isa 48:2, 52:1, Sir 49:6), and etc. Cf. also Isa 62:4, Jer 3:17, and Bar 2:15.

[355]Bar 4:31, 32; Hos 7:13; Nah 3:7; and Ezek 5:15.

[356]In its only other occurrence with a Hebrew equivalent, *deilaios* represents *gedûpāh* "taunt" (Exod 5:15) and thus has there a different connotation. The equivalents of Sy (a verbal form of *deḥel* "dread, be fearful") and Syh (a participle from

dᵉwāʾ "be wretched, miserable") interestingly serve to underscore the two prominent aspects of the Greek term *deilaios*, the former of which approximates its original sense and the latter the extended.

357 If vs. 31 were to be treated as an independent bicolon instead of as one colon of a tricolon with vs. 32, metrical imbalance might suggest consideration of the possibility of the copula.

358 It occurs for the Piel stem of *ʿānāh* III fifteen times, for the Hiphil stem of *rāʿaʿ* nineteen times, and for eight other verbs eight times. See HR II, 711. In addition, an example of each equivalence is found in Sirach: for *ʿānāh* III (Piel) in Sir 49:7, and for *rāʿaʿ* (Hiph) in Sir 7:20. In Baruch the verb appears only here.

359 See Mandelkern II, 1100.

360 The LXX translation here is too free to be helpful.

361 See HR II, 711. Cf. also below, 5:1, where the equivalency *kakōsis* = *ʿonî* is to be found.

362 See HR II, 1239.

363 Ibid., 1135-37.

364 Not *kîd* as with Kneucker, 339, 360.

365 Once (Job 18:12) the related *ptōma* is used to translate *ʾêd*, but that is the extent of any such support. Nevertheless, this represents the rendering of Kahana (360).

366 See HR II, 1239. Cf. also *mappālāh* applied to a city in Isa 17:1, and *mappēlāh* applied to a city in Isa 23:13, 25:2.

367 Cf. Exod 1:13, Gen 47:21, Ezek 29:18, Jer 15:14, 17:4.

368 Cf. the similar reconstruction of Kneucker, 339, 360. The rendering of Kahana (360-61) also follows the tradition of Sy.

369 See HR I, 345-46.

370 Ibid., 294-95.

371 Ibid., II, 1384-1404.

372 Ibid., 1340-42.

373 See Mandelkern I, 446, 486.

374 This has been pointed as a Niphal infinitive construct as in Prov 24:17. The form *bᵉhikkāšᵉlēk* as in Dan 11:34 is also possible here. The Qal infinitive construct, **bᵉkošlēk*, is perhaps a possibility though it is unattested in BH.

[375]See HR II, 1452.

[376]Cf. the discussion above at 3:34, and see HR I, 581-82.

[377]Ps 16:9, 2:2, 48:12, 96:11, 97:8, 149:2, 1 Chr 16:31 in this sequence; and Ps 14:7, 31:8, 53:7, 97:1, 118:24 in the reverse sequence.

[378]In two other passages exemplifying this Hebrew pairing (Isa 9:2, Prov 23:24), though the LXX lacks an equivalent for *gîl*, *śāmaḥ* is in both instances represented by *euphrainō*.

[379]*Ptōma* also occurs twice in the LXX for Hebrew *šeber* "shattering, disaster." Even though *šeber* is more commonly paired in MT with such terms as *rāʿāh* "evil," *makkāh* "defeat," and *milḥāmāh* "battle," its verbal root does appear once (Jer 51:8) paired with *nāpal*. But there is no correspondence between the Greek of this and that of Bar 4:33.

[380]See HR II, 1239.

[381]See Jackson, 100, and Boling, 79-80.

[382]As in vs. 8 above, Syh again uses the verb *ʿâq* and Sy the verb *kedāʾ*, but the conflate Sy text features the Syh reading in addition.

[383]See HR I, 545.

[384]Ibid., II, 1121.

[385]Kneucker, 340.

[386]Cf., e.g., the four LXX occurrences of this equivalency: 1 Chr 21:8, Ps 119:39, Jonah 3:6, 2 Sam 3:10, and such passages as Esth 8:3 and Zech 3:4.

[387]Similarly, cf. with *šābat*, Ezek 30:13 (of Memphis), and with *kārat* "cut off," Ezek 30:15 (of Sais).

[388]See HR II, 1121.

[389]An additional five are with other stems of the same verb. The next most common in frequency are *pārar* "break" (six times, all in Numbers 30) and *ʿābar* (four times). Six other verbs add eleven occurrences.

[390]Other Hebrew verbs used in this same figure of removing from a city its noisy population or its merriment (i.e., the chief signs of its vitality, security, and capability for endurance) are *lāqaḥ* (Ezek 30:4, *welāqeḥû hamônāh*; 24:25), *nāśāʾ* (Ezek 29:19, *wenāśāʾ hamōnāh*), and *gālāh* (Isa 24:11, *gālāh meśôś hāʾāreṣ*; cf. Jer 52:15), none of which are ever translated by *periaireō* in the LXX.

[391]The denominative verb *polyochleō* has the meaning "be crowded with people, be numerous" and is commonly applied to cities as being densely populated. Cf. Strabo, *Geography*, trans. H. L. Jones (LCL, IV; London: W. Heinemann, 1927) viii, 6,2, pp. 190-91. The related adjective, *polyochlos*, similarly means "populous."

[392]Cf. further Isa 32:4, *hᵃmôn ʿîr ʿuzzāb*, "the populous city deserted"; 2 Kgs 7:13; Ezek 32:32; Isa 5:13-14; 31:4; 33:3; as well as the passages cited above for the verb.

[393]See HR I, 4; e.g., four times for *śāśôn*, four times for *śimḥāh*, twice for *gîl*, and once each for *rinnāh* and *māśôś*.

[394]Note that Sy presents here a conflate text, "idols and exultation," which reflects the apparently inadvertently erroneous G^A variant *agalma* "idol," which that tradition has instead of *agalliama*.

[395]Kahana, 361.

[396]Here *egeneto* is the equivalent of *estai*.

[397]Here the LXX employs *apobainō* in the sense of "turn out, eventuate, issue in" in order to convey the Hebrew idiom, *hāyāh l-*. It is also perhaps possible that *estai* is a facilitation, but the Versional witness is widespread and in its favor.

[398]Cf. in addition *gaurotēs* "exultation," *agauros* "stately, proud," and the denominative verb, *gauriaō* "bear oneself proudly." For this verb, cf. Jdt 9:7. See also LSJ, 6, 339-40, and Frisk, *Wörterbuch* I, 1, p. 292.

[399]See BDB, 240, no. 5.

[400]Cf. also Jer 51:41 (of Babylon), *tᵉhillāh kol-hāʾāreṣ = to kauchēma* ["boast"] *pasēs tēs gēs*, "the pride of the whole earth"; Jer 49:25 (of Damascus), *ʾêk lōʾ-ʿuzzᵉbāh ʿîr tᵉhillāh qiryat mᵉśôśî*, "How forsaken is the famed city, the exuberant town"; and further for Jerusalem, Isa 60:18, Jer 33:9, Zeph 3:19; and in general, Jer 13:11 and Deut 26:19.

[401]See HR II, 1242-44.

[402]See BDB, 98, no. 2b. Parallels for the former construction may be found in such passages as Ezek 32:11, *ḥereb melek-bābel tᵉbôʾekā = rhomphaia basileōs babylōnos hēxei soi*; Prov 10:24; Job 20:22; 15:21; et al. Parallels for the latter include: Isa 47:9, *bāʾû ʿālayik = hēxei . . . epi se*; Josh 23:15, *bāʾ ʿᵃlêkem = hēkei pros hēmas*; Gen 34:27; et al.

[403]For fire as a figure of *YHWH*'s anger, cf. Isa 66:15, Jer 23:29, Ps 89:47, Lam 2:4, Ezek 21:36, 22:31, 38:19, Jer 23:29, and Ezek 36:5. For fire in the general imagery of city-destruction, cf. Neh 1:3; 2:3, 13, 17; Josh 6:24; Judg 18:27; Isa 1:7.

[404]See HR II, 893.

[405]Cf. Gen 21:34, 37:34, Deut 1:46, 2:1, et al.

[406]Cf. also Deut 30:20; Ps 21:5; 23:6; 91:16; 93:5; Prov 3:2, 16; Lam 5:20.

[407]See HR II, 751-55.

[408]See BDB, 514, no. 5e.

[409]See HR I, 283.

[410]For further examples of this topos, cf. Jer 50:39-40, 51:37, Zeph 2:14-15, Isa 32:14, Tob 8:3, and Luke 11:24.

[411]See HR II, 1122.

[412]Also enlightening for the reconstruction of this bicolon is Isa 43:5 (et seq.), particularly the phrase *mimmizrāḥ 'abî' zar'ekā = apo anatolōn axō to sperma sou*. Cf. further Bar 4:37, 5:5, and see HR I, 83-84.

[413]Ryle and James, *Psalmoi Solomontos*, 100-03. For substantiation of the priority of the Baruch material over that of Psalms of Solomon 11, see Pesch, "Die Abhängigkeit," 251-63.

[414]Cf. further Isa 43:9, 34:15, 56:8. See also Margolis, "The Greek Preverb," 53ff.

[415]See HR II, 1249-51.

[416]See Mandelkern I, 129.

[417]See HR II, 880-81.

[418]Cf. also the Hebrew *kᵉbôd 'ᵉlōhê yiśrā'ēl* in Ezek 8:4, 9:3, 43:2 and its LXX equivalents. Note also that Kahana (361), apparently in the light of the poetic imbalance of vs. 37c, has proposed (without textual support) the restoration of a supposedly lost verbal parallelism in this final bicolon between *yiśmᵉḥû* and [*ya'ᵃlōzû*].

[419]Although no LXX mss. follow *penthous* with the possessive pronoun *sou*, the readings of Sy, Syh, Eth, La^{C}, and Bo would support such. Cf. Ziegler, 466.

[420]The Sy conflation *wadbîšᵉteky wadḥaššeky* "and your evil and your suffering" may well thus represent both the Greek and Hebrew terms.

[421]See *GKC*, §135m, p. 439. Similarly, cf. Eth, La^{C}, Bo.

[422]See HR I, 576.

[423]In Ps 93:1 *euprepeia* (+ *endyō*) represents Hebrew *gē'ût* "majesty, pride." This term is properly applied to God alone, but in Isa 28:1, 3 it is used with reference to Samaria. Thus it remains a remote possibility with regard to Jerusalem in Bar 5:1. The individual constituent elements of the final colon have been dealt with in previous verses. For *k^ebôd-'ēl*, cf. immediately above, 4:37 (and 5:2, 4:24, for the construction); for *l^e'ôlām*, cf. 4:1, 5:4.

[424]See HR I, 337, and II, 1471.

[425]The other examples of this equivalency are: Isa 59:17, *wayya'aṭ kam'îl qin'āh*; Ps 71:13; Cant 1:7; Lev 13:45. See HR II, 1121-22.

[426]The combination *ṣedeq YHWH* does appear in BH in Lev 19:36, Ezek 45:10, and Deut 25:15.

[427]See HR I, 535-37.

[428]Cf. also Gen 41:42; Exod 12:7; 25:12; 1 Kgs 12:4, 9; 18:23; Jer 27:2; 28:14; Ezek 16:11; et al.

[429]Cf. other examples of this construction, *śîm + 'al-*, in Num 21:8-9, 1QH 1:28, 6:26, and Isa 59:17. The LXX passages cited with *epitithēmi* often appear to have *kai* whether there is a Hebrew equivalent or not. There is slight support for *kai epithou* in Bar 5:2 from La^{L,V}, Sy^{W}, Eth, and Tht. Cf. Ziegler, 466.

[430]See K. Elliger and W. Rudolph, eds., *Biblia Hebraica Stuttgartensia* (Stuttgart: Deutsche Bibelstiftung, 1967/77) 771 for Isa 61:10c; and Claus Westermann, *Das Buch Jesaja* (ATD 19; Göttingen: Vandenhoeck und Ruprecht, 1966) 293, who translates this, "Wie den Bräutigam, der den Turban 'knüpft.'"

[431]See HR II, 931.

[432]See BDB, 857.

[433]Ibid., 802.

[434]In 1QM 7:10 is a parallel, *wpry mnb'wt br'syhm*, "turbaned headdresses on their heads." This is the plural of *p^e'ēr*, *pa'^arê* (construct form), as in Ezek 39:28, 44:18, but lacking the *aleph*. See the discussion in Yadin, *The Scroll of the War*, 292-93. Cf. also Zech 3:5 and Exod 29:6, quoted above. Curiously, Sy has in Bar 5:2 *sannurtā'* "helmet," while Syh has *maṣnaptā'* "turban."

[435]See HR II, 760-62.

[436]See Mandelkern I, 529.

[437]Note that the reverse of this verse's action occurs in *Pss. Sol.* 2:21-22, where Jerusalem in her humiliation removes the *mitran doxēs* which God had put on her. The Syriac equivalent

of that phrase is *zîwā' d^e tešbuḥtā'*, "the brightness of glory" (i.e., "glorious brightness"). See Ryle and James, *Psalmoi Solomontos*, 18-19; and J. Rendel Harris, *The Odes and Psalms of Solomon: Now First Published from the Syriac Version* (Cambridge: Cambridge University, 1909) 140, 34.

[438] See HR I, 286.

[439] Cf. also *mittaḥat haššāmayim* in Exod 17:14 and Deut 25:19. Some parallels from the Apocrypha and Pseudepigrapha obtain also: Add Esth 3:3, *pan thaumazomenon en tē hyp' ouranon*, "every wondrous thing under the heavens." For the text, see Otto Fritzsche, *Libri Apocryphi Veteris Testamenti Graece* (Leipzig: F. A. Brockhaus, 1871) 46-47 (hereafter cited as *LAVTG*). Cf. also *Pss. Sol.* 2:36, *tēn hyp' ouranon* = (Sy) *l^e daltaḥt men kullāh š^e mayyā'*, "what is under the whole heaven" (i.e., "everything under heaven"). See *LAVTG*, 572, and Harris, *The Odes and Psalms*, 141, 35. The Latin text of 4 Ezra 11:6, *omnia sub caelo* (*LAVTG*, 626) is substantially the same as the Latin for Bar 5:3, *omni quae sub caelo est* (La^V), "everything under heaven."

[440] See HR II, 712-15.

[441] For *soi*, cf. the Marchalianic Minuscule 26 (and Arm). For a reading suggesting transposition of *sou* and *to onoma* in the Greek, cf. Syh, *š^e mā' dîleky*, LXX Minuscule 106, $La^{L,S}$, and Irenaeus. For a combination reflecting both of those, cf. La^V, *nominabitur enim tibi nomen tuum*. See Ziegler, 466.

[442] See HR II, 995-99. In the Baruch prose section it is found in 2:11, 14, 15, 26, 32; 3:5, 7.

[443] The rendition of Kahana (361), *šēm 'ôlām*, is thus quite unlikely in this light.

[444] For *eirēnē* = *šālôm*, see HR I, 401-03, and cf. Bar 3:13, 14 and 4:20; for *dikaiosynē* = *ṣedeq/ṣ^e dāqāh*, see HR I, 332-34, and cf. Bar 4:13, 5:2 and 9; and for the use of the two in combination, cf. Ps 85:11, Isa 32:17, and Jas 3:18. *Doxa* is the normal LXX equivalent for *kābôd* (see HR I, 341-43, and cf. Bar 4:3, 24, 37; 5:1, 2, 6, 7, 9). For the pairing of *šālôm* and *kābôd*, cf. 1QH 7:15, 11:27; for *eirēnē* and *doxa*, cf. Luke 2:14.

[445] See HR I, 648.

[446] Barthélemy and Milik, DJD I, 127.

[447] It appears there fourteen times. See Mandelkern I, 505-06. For the idea of the verse as a whole, cf. Isa 32:17, and for other names of the new Jerusalem, cf. Isa 1:26, Jer 33:16, and Ezek 48:35.

[448] See Pesch, "Die Abhängigkeit," 261-62.

[449] See HR I, 102-04. Cf. also Bar 3:19.

[450] Ibid., 689-92.

[451]Kneucker, 360, has *ʿal-gābōᵃh*.

[452]Statistically the most common Hebrew equivalent for *hypsēlos* is *bāmāh* "high place," occurring in abundance especially in the historical narratives of MT. But *bāmāh* is hardly likely here because of its particularized cultic connotation and narrow contextual limitations.

[453]Eccl 12:5 and Job 41:26 are the only examples of such.

[454]Sy appears to have been influenced expansively here by the Deutero-Isaianic source-texts to the extent even of including the repeated imperative, "awake, awake!," of Isa 52:1. Sy includes *wᵉqūmy ʿal yāʿîtē'*, "ascend the battlements," a curiously militaristic expression which may well be corrupt. See Whitehouse, "1 Baruch," 595. Kneucker (133) speculates a haplography. Further expansions in the text of Sy suggest the possibility at least of its use of a more replete LXX variant text-tradition that adhered much more closely to the Deutero-Isaianic sources.

[455]Kneucker, 346, 361. Cf. the same in Kahana, 361.

[456]See BDB, 99-100.

[457]See also Ziegler, 466.

[458]Or perhaps *ʿad-mᵉbōʾô* or *ûmimmaʿᵃrābāh*. Cf. the BH citations below.

[459]For *mizrāḥ* (A) - *maʿᵃrāb* (B), cf. Ps 103:12, 107:3, 1 Chr 7:28, 12:16, Isa 43:5, 45:6. For the reverse, cf. Isa 59:19. For *mizrāḥ* (A) - *mābôʾ (haššemeš)* (B), cf. Zech 8:7, Judg 11:18, Ps 50:1, 113:3. For *mizrāḥ* (A) - *yāmmāh* (B), cf. Josh 11:3, 1 Chr 9:24. The same sequence holds in the extra-canonical parallel in *Pss. Sol.* 11:3, and in Bar 4:37 above.

[460]See HR I, 491-95.

[461]Ibid., II, 1114.

[462]Ibid., I, 9-10. G^A has *agō* in Bar 4:16 instead of *apagō* "lead away" as in G^B, et al.

[463]Ibid., 407-08.

[464]Ibid., 34-36; and cf. Bar 4:26, where it has the connotation "carry off."

[465]Cf. Kahana, 361.

[466]The reading of Sy, "raised up in glory on a royal throne," perhaps suggests a more spiritualized interpretation of this event.

[467]Fritzsche, *Kurzgefasstes exegetisches Handbuch* I, 201. Cf. also that of De Wette, quoted without reference in Kneucker (347): "erhöhet gleich einem Königsthrone."

[468]Kneucker, 347-48. See also Whitehouse, "1 Baruch," 595; and Thackeray, "Baruch," 111.

[469]See *GKC*, §118s-w for a discussion of this with examples.

[470]Cf. also Judg 20:39 where the LXX translates *kammilḥāmāh* "as in the battle" with *hōs hē parataxis* (G[A], *kathōs ho polemos*). H. Preserved Smith (*The Books of Samuel* [ICC, VIII; New York: C. Scribner's Sons, 1909] 138) notes that in 1 Sam 15:22 *kšm'* stands "where the comparison would be fully expressed by *kbšm'*. Such an ellipsis needs no justification, . . ." See also George Buchanan Gray, *Isaiah, I-XXXIX* (ICC, X; Edinburgh: T. and T. Clark, 1912) 35, for Isa 1:25.

[471]There is little question of the equivalency here. The correspondence between *thronos* and *kissē'* in the LXX is extremely regular. See HR I, 655.

[472]See Whitehouse, "1 Baruch," 595. George B. Gray ("The Psalms of Solomon," *APOT* II, 628), observes that the LXX translation for Bar 5:6 "seems to be due to a thoughtless disregard of a well-known use of the Hebrew particle *k* (BDB 458a): the sense requires 'borne as on a throne'; this the Hebrew *kks'* would admit, but the Greek yields only the unsuitable meaning 'borne as a throne.'" See also the editorial remarks of R. H. Charles in *APOT* (I, 573), to the effect that this Greek phrase is a mistranslation from the Hebrew and that one familiar with Greek (i.e., if original authorship in Greek were to be presumed) would not likely have written *hōs thronon* if he had meant *hōs epi thronon*. For the association of *kissē'* with *kābôd*, cf. 1 Sam 2:8, Isa 22:23, Jer 14:21, 17:12, Sir 47:11, 4QpIs[a],D,3.

[473]See Ziegler, 466.

[474]See HR I, 192-94.

[475]See Kuhn, *Konkordanz*, 123-25.

[476]See HR II, 1318.

[477]The infinitive construct of *šāpēl* appears similarly in Eccl 12:4.

[478]See also HR II, 1334-35.

[479]Ibid., 1014-17, for the extreme regularity of this equivalency.

[480]Ibid., 1419, and cf. Bar 3:25 and 5:5 above.

[481]Cf. Gen 7:19, Isa 10:33, 30:25, 40:9, 57:7, Ezek 17:22, 40:2, Ps 104:18, Jer 3:6, Job 41:26.

[482]See HR I, 652. Curiously, Syh has *rāṣinē'* "brooks" for the plural of LXX *this*, just as it does in Gen 49:26.

[483]See HR I, 28; and G. Bertram, "Der Sprachschatz der Septuaginta und der des hebräischen Alten Testaments," *ZAW* 16 (1939) 88f.

[484]HR II, 1424, reveals that *pharagx* almost twice as frequently in the LXX renders *naḥal* "wadi" as *gay'*, but the equivalency in the source-text makes the latter certain. Cf. the cognate *naḥlē'* in both Sy and Syh.

[485]See HR II, 1147-48. Cf. also the cognate forms in Sy (*netmallūn*) and Syh (*l^emetmallāyū*).

[486]See HR II, 990. Further, in Ps 5:9 Symmachus uses *homalizō* to render the Hebrew *hôsar* (K) / *haysar* (Q). Cf. also Sir 21:10 and *Pss. Sol.* 11:5.

[487]The combination of *homalizō* and *tēn gēn* also occurs in the classical literature in Theophrastus' *De Causis Plantarum: Theophrasti Opera*, ed. F. Wimmer (Paris: Didot Libraire, 1931) 5.9.8, p. 277.

[488]See HR I, 188.

[489]Ibid., 174.

[490]The same natural phenomena of mountains lowering and valleys leveling are found in an interesting parallel in Ovid, *Amores*, trans. and ed. Franco Munari (Firenze: La Nuova Italia, 1955) ii,16,51-52, p. 65:

At vos, qua veniet, tumidi, subsidite, montes,
Et faciles curvis vallibus este, viae,

But you, towering mountains, subside wherever she comes,
And you paths, be easily approachable in the winding valleys.

This parallel was first noted by Fritzsche, *Kurzgefasstes Handbuch* (201).

[491]Cf. Job 40:22, *y^esukkūhû ṣe'^elîm ṣillô*, "The lotus trees screen him for his shade" (= LXX, *skiazontai de en autō dendra megala syn rhadamnois*, "And the great trees shade him with branches").

[492]Both Sy and Syh here use forms of the cognate verb *ṭal* "shade." But Syriac lacks a verb cognate to Hebrew *sākak*

[493]Kahana, 361.

[494]In this use of the past tense in Hebrew to delineate future action, the writer or speaker is generally assumed to be so firmly convinced of the ultimate eventuation of a yet future event that he thus describes that future action with a perfect

verb form as though already accomplished and done. See *GKC*, §106n, pp. 312-13; and S. R. Driver, *Hebrew Tenses*, 2nd rev. ed. (Oxford: Clarendon, 1881) §14, pp. 21-25.

[495]See HR I, 349.

[496]Ibid., II, 958-59.

[497]Ibid., I, 584-85.

[498]Ibid., II, 1018-19.

[499]See Charles, *The Book of Enoch*, 301.

[500]There is also very slight support (C') for a LXX variant, *euōdes* "sweet" (cf. Ziegler, 467), which is used elsewhere in the LXX only in Exod 30:23 for Hebrew *bōśem*.

[501]See HR II, 1219-20. Cf. also Bar 4:37; Gen 24:50; Deut 15:1; 19:4; Josh 8:27; Dan 9:2, 12, et passim.

[502]See Pesch, "Die Abhängigkeit," 251-63.

[503]Ryle and James, *Psalmoi Solomontos*, 102-03. An allusive expansion on this same theme of the majestic return appears in the *Carmen Apologeticum* (ll. 963-68) of the third century African bishop, Commodian (p. 177):

Omnia virescunt ante illos, omnia gaudent,
Excipere sanctos ipsa creatura laetatur:
Omni loco fontes exsurgunt e se parati,
. . . .
Umbraculum [illis] faciunt nubes, ne vexentur a sole,
Et ne fatigentur, substernunt se montes et ipsi;

All things are green before them, all things rejoice,
Creation itself delights to welcome the saints:
In every place fountains spring up spontaneously,
. . . .
The clouds provide shade [for them] that they be unmolested by the sun,
And lest they become weary, the very mountains prostrate themselves.

[504]See HR I, 602-03.

[505]See BDB, 231b, and cf. especially such BH passages as Exod 13:21, 23:23, 32:34, Num 14:14, Isa 52:12, and 58:8.

[506]See HR II, 1450.

[507]See HR I, 450 and 332-34; and cf. Bar 4:13, 5:2 and 4.

[508]Cf. Ps 36:11, 103:17, Prov 21:21, et al., for further examples of this pairing.

[509]This matter of the equivalencies of *eleēmosynē* is discussed in considerable detail above at 4:22, as is the equivalency between *mē'ēt* and *para* + gen. Support for *para tou theou* in lieu of *par' auton* in Bar 5:9 is found most particularly in G^A, Sy, La^L, and Ar. See Ziegler, 467.

CHAPTER VI

AN ANALYSIS OF THE BARUCH POETRY

The Evidence of Hebraisms, Mistranslations, and other Indications of a Hebrew Original in the Texts of the Primary Versions

The Septuagint Text

The most significant evidence of Hebraisms, mistranslations, and other indications of dependency on Hebrew rather than Greek source-texts in the Septuagint text of Bar 3:9-5:9 is here itemized according to chapter and verse.

3:9 The Hebrew phrase *ḥuqqôt ḥahayyîm* "the commandments of life," has its source in MT Ezek 33:15. The LXX translation of that phrase in Ezek 33:15, *prostagmasin zōēs* (and not *entolas zōēs* as in LXX Bar 3:9), indicates that the borrowing in Bar 3:9 was from the original Hebrew source and not its Greek equivalent in the LXX. In addition, the syntax of the verse is markedly Hebraic even in Greek dress (note especially the use of the infinitive).

3:10 The LXX phrase *en gē tōn echthrōn* "in enemy territory" is the literal equivalent of the common Hebrew idiom *bᵉʼereṣ ʼôyēb*. Such use of a substantive in the genitive in lieu of an adjective (just as in the Hebrew) typically marks Greek works that are translations from Hebrew originals.

3:11 The Sy reading, "those descending into Sheol," makes clear that the Greek equivalent, *meta tōn eis hadou*, is a Hebraism that somewhat less than adequately represents the common Hebrew idiom, *ʻim yôrᵉdê šᵉʼôl* "with those going down to Sheol." See further, Chapter III, ad loc.

3:12 The canonical source for *mᵉqôr ḥokmāh* "the source of wisdom" is MT Prov 18:4. The LXX in that passage has *pēgē zōēs* "source of life" instead of *pēgēn tēs sophias* as in Bar 3:12, strongly indicating again that the borrowing was from the original Hebrew source and not its LXX translation.

3:13 The metaphorical representation of a personal or collective lifestyle as "walking in the way of X" is decidedly Hebraistic.

3:14 The source-text for *'ê-zeh m^{e}qôm bînāh* "where is the place of understanding" is Job 28:12, 20, and the verbal correspondence that obtains is with the Hebrew text and not that of its LXX translation. Further, two Hebraisms are apparent in this verse. The Greek expressions *makrobiōsis* and *phōs ophthalmōn* quite literally reproduce the Hebrew idioms *'ōrek-yāmîm* "length of days" and *'ôr 'ênayim* "light for the eyes."

3:15 The conception of "treasuries" as applied to such personifications as Wisdom is particularly Semitic. See Chapter III, ad loc.

3:16 The LXX rendering of "wild animals" as *tōn thēriōn tōn epi tēs gēs* is an overly literal reproduction of the common Hebrew means of expressing that concept, *ḥaytô 'ereṣ* (or *ḥayyat hā'āreṣ*). Similarly, the Greek phrase *orneois tou ouranou* "birds of the air" is patently the literal rendition of the common Hebrew idiom *ṣippôr šāmayim* (or *'ôp šāmayim*).

3:17 The ambiguity of the Hebrew verbless clause explains the Greek mistranslation in this verse. The LXX employs a present tense verb in the phrase *ouk esti telos*, thus yielding the meaning "there is no end" instead of the expected "there was no end." This phrase, *ouk esti telos*, may thus be considered a slightly miscast attempt to approximate the Hebrew conception of continuance commonly expressed in the idiom *'ên qēṣeh l-* "there was/is no end to X."

3:18 The Greek phrase *ouk estin exeuresis* literally represents the Hebrew idiom for indiscoverability, *'ên ḥēqer l-* "there was/is no discovering X." The confusion regarding the tense of the verb is the same as that in the above verse.

3:19 See above, 3:11.

3:20-21 The source-text for *derek bînāh* "the way of knowledge" is MT Prov 9:6 and not its LXX translation. See Chapter III, ad loc. In addition, the use of "sons" here and frequently throughout the poetry is reflective of Hebrew thought.

3:23 *Huioi Agar* "the sons of Hagar" constitutes a literal rendering of the Hebrew *bᵉnê Hāgār*. The otherwise unidentifiable geographic noun *Merran* in the LXX text most probably reflects the territory known in BH as Medan/Midian, and has resulted from the familiar *d/r* confusion in Hebrew.[1] *Mythologoi* is a hapax legomenon in the LXX and must reflect Hebrew *môšᵉlîm* "balladeers, minstrels."[2]

3:26 The direct source for the first bicolon of this verse is clearly MT Gen 6:4, and not its LXX counterpart. See Chapter III, ad loc. The distinctly Hebrew idiom for "famous," *ʼanšê haššēm* "men of name," is reflected in the LXX rendering *hoi onomastoi* in Bar 3:26. In the Gen 6:4 source-text, the LXX more literally translates *ʼanšê haššēm* with *hoi anthrōpoi hoi onomastoi*. The expression *epistamenoi polemon/mᵉlummᵉdê milḥāmāh* "knowledgable of battle" is equally idiomatic in both Greek and Hebrew and thus ambiguous for the question of originality.

3:27 The Greek phrase *hodon epistēmēs* reflects an important conception in the Hebrew Wisdom genre, *derek bînāh* "the way of knowledge." See above, 3:21.

3:28 Here the cumbersome Greek phrase *para to mē echein phronēsin* "from not having sense" rather literally reflects the Hebrew idiom *biblî-daʻat* "by lack of sense."

3:29-30 Examination of the source-text, Deut 30:12-13, suggests that here also the borrowing occurred at the level of the Hebrew texts rather than the Greek. Close BH parallels for *ḥārûṣ nibḥār* "fine gold," for example, indicate that the dependency is on the Hebrew sources and not the Greek. See further, Chapter III, ad loc.[3]

3:31 The imagery of "ways" and "paths" is clearly Hebraic, and the Greek syntax with its participial phrases mirrors precisely that of the Hebrew.

3:32 In the combination *ktēnōn tetrapodōn* (literally, "animals, quadrupeds") the LXX text joins two essentially synonymous terms in a context where one would appear to suffice. This suggests that the combination represents an attempt to approximate the picturesque Hebrew idiom *hôl^e^kê 'al-'arba'* (literally, "those that go about on all fours").

3:34 The application of military metaphor to the stars is common in Hebrew literature. See Chapter III, ad loc.[4] The Greek verb form *paresmen* "we are nigh" is an approximation of the Hebrew quasi-verbal (+ suffix) *hinnēnû* (literally, "behold us," but with the sense "here we are"). In BH, *hinnēh* + suffix constitutes the idiomatic response that is made to a call or address, and in the LXX its regular, if not exact, translational equivalent is the verb *pareimi*, appropriately inflected. In this instance, the equivalency and the originality of the Hebrew is confirmed beyond doubt by the Sy equivalent *hā' ḥ^e^nan* "behold us."

3:36 See above, 3:27.

4:1 The use in the Greek of the preposition + noun, *eis zōēn* (literally, "to life"), to express the verbal idea "will live," is the literal and exact equivalent of the nonverbal Hebrew idiom for the same idea, *l^e^ḥayyim* (literally, "to life").

4:5 Imperative forms of the Greek verb *tharseō* "be confident" are consistently used in the LXX to represent the consoling Hebrew idiom *'al-tirā'* "fear not." The appearance of the imperative of *tharseō* here (and throughout this poem) in a context of consolation and encouragement strongly suggests that it is once again serving as the positive translational counterpart to the Hebrew idiom *'al-tirā'*.[5]

4:6-8 Much of the material in this section has been directly appropriated from Deut 32:15-30 (Esth 7:4 is also a significant source). Comparison of this Baruch passage with the source-text in both its MT and LXX forms reveals that the borrowing occurred already on the Hebrew level (see Kneucker, 318, and above, Chapter V n. 7). The asyndetic character of the MT Deuteronomy 32 source and, no doubt, of these excerpted portions in Baruch, is to some degree recognizable from the LXX syntax. This is especially true in verse 7 where the unconnected participle (cf. the causal coordinators used in the Syriac texts) probably reflects Hebrew asyndeton. See Chapter V, ad loc.

The Greek phrase *kai ou theō* "and not to God" in 4:7 is a mistranslation of the Hebrew *lō' 'ᵉlōᵃh* "non-deity," both here and already in the Deut 32:17 source-text (see Chapter V, ad loc., and especially n. 29). This fact could suggest that the borrowing occurred on the level of the LXX text, but the similar Sy reading, together with the obliqueness of the source-text's reference to child sacrifice, suggests that this is an easily made interpretative mistake. Finally, the syntax of verse 8 in the Greek text reflects precisely that which would be expected in Hebrew. The disposition of the post-verbal modifiers after the verb in initial position and the placing of the direct object in final position are particularly characteristic of Hebrew syntax (see Chapter V, ad loc., and especially n. 41).

4:10 The conjunctive pairing of "sons and daughters" is an obvious Hebraic feature, and there is good reason to believe that the epithet *ho aiōnios* "the Eternal," used here and throughout this poem, represents a circumlocutory attempt to render the Hebrew Tetragrammaton (see Chapter V, ad loc., and n. 60).

4:11 The object of the verb "let go" in the second colon is lacking in the major Greek Uncials, but is preserved in Sy. It is very likely that the Hebrew would not have elided this element and the Greek is awkward without it.

4:12 The theme of rejoicing over the disaster of one's enemies is common in Hebrew literature and, in general, the Semitic literature of the Ancient Near East. Also, the interpretative Sy reading, "left desolate by many people," underscores the possibility that the technical connotation possessed in late Hebrew by the term *rabbîm* ("community," "public") was simply missed by the translator who used the literal equivalent, *polys* "many." See Chapter V, ad loc.

4:12d-13a Here the close affinity of the LXX text of Baruch to the Greek Version of the source-text, Job 34:27, appears to indicate borrowing on that level, but see Chapter V, ad loc., for an alternate possibility. Of most significance in this passage are two pointed examples of the tendency to represent in Greek translation the Hebrew *status constructus* by the absence of the definite article before the *nomen regens*. In the phrases *ek nomou theou* "from the law of God" and *hodois entolōn theou* "the ways of God's commandments" the noticeable absence of the definite article before *nomou* and *entolōn* points to a Hebrew original that syntactically employed the familiar *status constructus*.[6]

4:13 The imagery of "walking in the way" and "treading the path" is markedly Hebraic (see Chapter V, n. 104). Further, there is good reason to believe that the Greek preposition *en* is only a translational facilitator (see Chapter V, ad loc., and nn. 109, 110).

4:14 See above, 4:10.

4:15 Once again the borrowing can be seen to have been done on the basis of the Hebrew Version of the source-text, which in this instance is Deut 28:49-50. A comparison of Bar 4:15 with the source-text in both its Hebrew and Greek forms shows a stronger affinity with the Hebrew source than with its Greek translation. For example, the Hebrew idiom *'imqê śāpāh* "unintelligible language" (literally, "deep of speech") in the Deut 28:49-50 source-text is there rendered literally in the LXX by *bathyphōnos* "incomprehensible speech" (literally, "deep of speech"), but here in Bar 4:15 by *alloglōssos* "of a foreign tongue," a freer (and weaker) approximation of the Hebrew. Further, the fact that *YHWH* is the subject of the action in the Hebrew source-text tends to confirm the conclusion that *ho aiōnios*, the subject here in LXX Bar 4:15, does indeed represent *YHWH* in the Greek translation (see Kneucker, 325).

4:16 See above, 4:10.

4:17 The kind of rhetorical question implying a negative answer that is exemplified in this verse is a common Hebrew literary device. In addition, the Greek construction, *dynatos/dynamai* + infinitive, is very regular in the LXX as the translational equivalent of the idiomatic Hebrew, *yākôl* + infinitive for the meaning "be able to (do something)."

4:18 Several features in this verse may be noted as being particularly Hebraic. The conception of God "bringing evil upon" is Hebraic, as is the absolute (and often collective) use of the term "evil" (with only one exception the singular *rā'āh* "evil" is always rendered by the plural *ta kaka* in the LXX; see Chapter V, ad loc.).

The most significant feature of this verse is the appearance of the expression *ek cheiros* "from the hand of," for this is a certain Hebraism. The idiomatic use of the term "hand" with the extended or abstract sense of "power" is indisputably Semitic. Indeed, the entire second colon of 4:18 is thoroughly and inescapably Hebraic--"deliver . . . from the hand of . . . enemies" (*nāṣal + miyyad 'ôyēb*).

4:20 The phrase "in all my days" is idiomatic in Hebrew for "the rest of my life."

4:21 See above, 4:18, for the Hebraism *ek cheiros*, and the Greek text's representation of the common Hebrew idiom for rescue from the hand of enemies. An example of mistranslation also appears here. The use of the politically neutral term *dynasteia* "dominion" in the Greek text cannot be supported either on the basis of sense or parallels. It appears rather that the translator mistakenly intended it to carry the force of the properly opprobrious term *katadynasteia* "oppression." See Chapter V, ad loc.

4:22 The combination *elpizō + epi* constitutes typical LXX or translation Greek, in this case reflecting the common Hebrew idiom *bāṭaḥ + l-* "trust in, entrust to" (see further, Chapter V, ad loc.). Also, abundant BH parallels combining *bāṭaḥ* and *môšî*^{a}' "Savior" strongly support the conclusion that *ho aiōnios* does represent the Hebrew Tetragrammaton (see Chapter V, ad loc.). Finally, the absolute use of *tou hagiou/qādôš* "Holy One" as a divine title is particularly Isaianic.

4:24 Parallels indicate that the Greek construction *para* + gen., here in the phrase *tēn para tou theou hymōn sōtērian* "the salvation of our God," usually represents the Hebrew *status constructus* in the LXX. Cf. 4:9 (*tēn orgēn para tou theou* "the wrath of God"); 5:1, 2; and see Chapter V, ad loc.

4:25 The transitive use of *makrothymeō* "be patient, bear patiently," with the object following in the accusative, constitutes unusual Greek syntax (see Chapter V, ad loc.). The implication that such a construction is based on Hebrew syntax (e.g., on *śᵉʼû ʼap-ʼēl* "bear the wrath of God") is compelling, even though there is admittedly no precedent for a LXX equivalency between *makrothymeō* and *nāśāʼ* "bear."

The symbolic gesture, so familiar throughout the literature of the Ancient Near East, of the victor placing his foot on the neck of the vanquished is also indicative of Semitic character. Here, however, the LXX text of Baruch corresponds more closely with the LXX Version of the primary source-text, Deut 33:29, in that it agrees on "necks" as the anatomical feature abused by the conquerer vis-à-vis the "backs" of MT Deut 33:29. It is nevertheless likely that other Hebrew source-texts (cf. Josh 10:24, and see Chapter V, ad loc.), featuring the placing of the victor's foot on the "necks" of subdued enemies were influentially involved in the composition process followed by the Hebrew author.

4:26 It may be noted here in support of the general Semitic character of the poetry that the imagery involved in the expression "seized like a flock" is particularly representative of Ancient Near Eastern literature and life (see Chapter V, ad loc.).[7]

4:27 See above, 4:18.

4:28 Despite the claims of some early scholars[8] that the hapax legomenon *dekaplasiazō* "multiply by ten" is demonstrative of the originality of the Greek text for this section, the truth would appear rather to be the opposite. This is an extremely rare verb in Greek literature and even as used here is hardly graceful. In the words of Harwell (55), it is also "impossible Greek!" This rare verb probably represents in this instance a contrived, and thus overly wooden, rendering of the common BH idiom for repeated action, "doing something ten times" (*ʻeśer pᵉʻāmîm*).[9] That the conception set forth by such a rare Greek word is one that is common and idiomatic in BH for the idea of "continually doing something" is particularly supportive of the case for the Hebrew original (see further, Chapter V, ad loc.).

4:29 See above, 4:18.

4:30 The Greek verb *parakaleō*, meaning "summon, invoke" in classical Greek, here appears with the singular connotation ("comfort, console") that it has throughout the LXX as a result of strong semantic influence from its regular Hebrew counterpart, *nāḥam* "comfort." Such use of *parakaleō* to mean "comfort" is thus Hebraistic, but whether it constitutes a specific translational Hebraism or merely more widely represents the conventional (albeit Hebrew-influenced) Greek usage of the last centuries B.C.E. cannot be satisfactorily determined from the available evidence. It may be observed also with significance that the Greek syntax in this bicolon is precisely what would be expected in Hebrew (see Chapter V, ad loc.).

4:31-32 Here again the canonical sources used (viz., Hos 7:13, Isa 60:14, and Zeph 3:19) manifest a closer affinity to these Baruch verses on the Hebrew level than on that of the LXX texts (see Chapter V, ad loc.). For the theme of "rejoicing over an enemy's fall," see above, 4:12.

4:33 See above, 4:12.

4:34 The appearance of *estai* "it will be" in all of the Greek witnesses except G^B indicates that it may well have been a translational facilitator for the Hebrew idiom *hāyāh l-*. In this very context the Greek phrase *eis penthos* "into mourning," according to clear parallels, is a Hebraism for *l*^{e}*'ēbel* "into mourning" (see Chapter V, ad loc., and Harwell, 55).

4:36 The clearly established source-texts (Isa 49:18, 60:4) for these cola reveal that the rare Greek verb *periblepō* "look round about" was pressed into service by the translator in order to approximate the peculiar Isaianic inclusion of *sābîb* "round about" within the familiar Hebrew idiom *śā' 'ênèkā* "lift up your eyes" (i.e., "look"). The Hebrew text of the Isaiah sources was clearly the basis of the borrowing that occurred here, for the LXX Version of Isaiah does not employ *periblepō* (see Chapter V, ad loc.).

5:1-2 See above, 4:24.

5:2 The first colon, with only slight variation, is borrowed directly from the Hebrew text of Isa 61:10. The LXX

Version at Isa 61:10 is quite at variance with the MT and could hardly have been the source of the borrowing of this clause.

5:4 The appointing of such special names is especially Hebraic.

5:5 See above, 4:36.

5:6 The Greek construction *hōs thronon* "as a throne" can only be an awkward mistranslation by a translator who missed the slight but significant nuance of the Hebrew comparative particle *k*-, which allows the sense that both logic and context demand, "as *on* a throne." The clarificatory nature of the G^{A} text serves to confirm this. See Chapter V, ad loc., for further details.

5:7 See above, 3:13.

5:8 Of particular significance here is the fact that the Hebrew phrase *y^eʿārôt w^ekol-ʿēṣ* "the woods and every tree" (= LXX, *hoi drymoi kai pan xylon*) is idiomatic in Hebrew.

The Syriac (Sy) Text

Seven of the most significant examples of Sy dependence on the Hebrew original have already been assembled in the introductory chapter in connection with the discussion of the Sy text.[10] In addition, a few others may be noted.

3:10 The Sy use of *b^elāʾ* "grow old, wear out," cognate to the Hebrew *bālāh* "grow old, wear out" (most frequently the equivalent of the LXX's *palaiaō* "become old, worn out"), would be expected if the Sy translator did indeed have access to the Hebrew original. It is also of some significance that the text of the later Syh, dependent wholly on the Greek, employs a different verb, *ʾ^etēq* (Aphel) "become old, obsolete."

3:26 Sy here supports the G^{B} reading, *egennēthēsan* "they were born" (= Hebrew, *yull^edû*; cf. Gen 6:1, 4) vis-à-vis considerable textual support for the variant, *egenēthēsan* "there were" (cf. $G^{A,Q}$, O, La, Sa, some Lucianic mss, et al.), suggesting awareness of the original Hebrew. See Chapter III, ad loc., n. 82, and Ziegler, 461.

3:33 It has already been noted (see Chapter III, ad 3:33) that the *'ar'ā'* "the earth" of Sy^W may possibly reflect the original reading of the Hebrew of the verse. Without this element, the metre of the verse is difficult; with it a well-balanced 3 + 3 + 3 tricolon results (see Chapter III, ad loc.). Also, logically and semantically it would make far better sense if "the earth responded with trembling" when the lightning was sent forth, than for the lightning itself to "obey and respond with fear."

3:35 The Sy reading here approximates more closely the Deutero-Isaianic source-texts than does the LXX reading, and restores balance to a bicolon clearly deficient in its first colon as it stands according to the Greek text.

4:18 The Sy text preserves the indirect object of the verb "bring" (*'alaykūn bîšātā'* "the evil upon you") where parallel passages show that it is to be expected (see Chapter V, ad loc.). Although this element ("upon you") is lacking in G^B, O, et al., its inclusion is amply supported by G^A, L', Sy, La^V, and Syh^{mg} (see Chapter V, ad loc., and Ziegler, 463-64). The presence of this element in the original Hebrew text may also be observed to be a metrical desideratum.

4:26 Here Sy appears to reflect an attempt to reconcile this passage in more precise detail with the Hebrew of the Isa 40:4 source-text (see Chapter V, ad loc.).

4:27 The Sy text includes here the (metrically desirable) direct and indirect objects of the verb "bring" that are wanting in the Greek text, but in view of other Sy expansions in the the immediate context, the originality of these is suspect. The elision of these two elements is awkward in the Greek, and a metrical difficulty for the Hebrew reconstruction, but such is not impossible or unprecedented for BH. In the light of similar passages in 4:18 and 29, it may be best to assume that *hārā'āh 'ᵃlêkem/hymin ta kaka* was lost in this verse and that the Sy reading is a more or less neutral attempt to smooth over the felt loss. See Chapter V, ad loc.

4:37 Sy preserves the indirect object ("coming *to you*") that is lacking in the Greek text of this verse, but not in that of its repetition in 5:6.

5:4 The Sy *d^e^deḥl^e^tēh d(')allāhā'* "fear of God" is a much more literal and natural equivalent of the Hebrew *yir'at-'ēl* "fear of God" than is the Greek *theosebia* "godliness."

5:5 Sy, along with Syh, La, et al. (vis-à-vis G^B and the major LXX Uncials), preserves what must, according to canonical and extra-canonical parallels, have been the original sequence of the phrase "from East to West" (see Chapter V, ad loc., and cf. Isa 45:6, 43:5, Bar 4:37, and *Pss. Sol.* 11:3). It appears that the two directions suffered a reversal of sequence at some point in the LXX transmission process, but only after they had already been preserved in their usual canonical sequence in Sy and other secondary Versions.

5:6 With regard to the controversial phrase "as on a royal throne," Sy lacks the comparative particle but specifically employs the preposition *'al* "on." This confirms the suspicion that the Greek reading "as a royal throne" resulted from the misreading of a "pregnant" Hebrew construction featuring the comparative particle *k-*. The Sy reading, lacking the comparative particle, may well represent a facilitative effort to make more obvious the easily misread Hebrew construction.

The Evidence of the Employment of Basic Syntactic and Semantic Features of Classical Hebrew Poetry

Examples of Conjunctive Fixed Pairs Appearing in Expected Canonical Sequence

3:17 The conjunctive pairing *kesep w^e^zāhāb* "silver and gold" appears here in the expected canonical sequence that is well-established and familiar in BH.

4:10 The common conjunctive pairing *bānay ûb^e^nôtay* "my sons and daughters" is found here in the expected canonical sequence.

4:11 Here the conjunctive pairing *ûbibkî w^e^'ebel*, "and with weeping and mourning," appears. There is, however, no established canonical sequence for this pairing (cf. 4:23, below). The antithetical parallelism of this bicolon also features *b^{e}śāśôn* "with joy" as the opposite counterpart in the first colon to the above conjunctive pairing that appears in the second colon. The use of a ballast variant may be noted in the second colon.

4:14 See above, 4:10.

4:23 The sequence *śāśôn w^{e}śimḥāh* "joy and gladness" is the usual or canonical sequence for this conjunctive pairing. The other conjunctive pairing in this tricolon, *'ēbel ûb^{e}kî* "mourning and weeping," appears in the reverse of its previous appearance above in 4:11. No sequence preference is established in BH, however, for this pairing.

5:5 Whenever "east" and "west" are paired in BH, whether in parallel, conjunctively, or otherwise, the sequence preference is (with but one exception in thirteen examples) for "east" as the initial word and "west" as the latter. Prepositionally linked in this verse, *mimmizraḥ šemeš 'ad-ma'^{a}rāb* "from east to west," this fixed pair (according to O, Sy, La^{V}, et al., vis-à-vis LXX) follows the expected canonical sequence (see Chapter V, ad loc., and n. 459). The expected canonical sequence for the conjunctive pairing of these two directions appears in 4:37, *mimmizrāḥ ûmimma'^{a}rāb* "from east and west."

Examples of *Parallelismus Membrorum*, Common BH Patterns of Parallelism, and the Appearance of Fixed Parallel Pairs in Expected Canonical Sequence

3:9 The parallel pairing, *š^{e}ma'* "hear" (A) // *ha'^{a}zînû* "pay attention" (B), appears here in the expected canonical sequence for the two verbs in parallel.

3:10 A significant parallel here is *b^{e}'ereṣ 'ôyēb* "in enemy territory" (A) // *b^{e}'ereṣ nokriyyāh* "in a foreign land" (B).

3:11 The parallelism between *'im mētîm* "with the dead" (A) and *w^{e}'îm yôr^{e}dê š^{e}'ôl* "and with those in Sheol" (B) is notable. Also, the use of a ballast variant may be seen in the second colon.

3:14 While there is no semantic correspondence between the members of the parallel cola *'ôrek-yāmîm wᵉḥayyîm* "length of days and life" (A) // *'ôr 'ênayik wᵉšālôm* "light for the eyes and peace" (B), the formal or structural parallelism that obtains is both striking and precise.

3:15 Parallelism of members is a prominent feature of this bicolon: *mî māṣā' mᵉqômāh* "who has found her place?" (A) // *ûmî bāh 'el-'ôṣᵉrôtèhā* "and who has entered her treasure-houses?" (B). The pattern may be analyzed as abc:ab'c'.

3:16 The parallel between *ḥaytô 'ereṣ* "beasts" (A) and *ṣippôr šāmayim* "birds" (B) in the second and third cola of this tricolon is notable. The relationship between these two cola in their entirety may be analyzed thusly: abc:a'b'c'.

3:20c-21a In this bicolon two parallel pairings appear in their expected canonical sequences: *derek* "way" (A) // *nᵉtîbôt* "paths" (B) and *yāda'* "know" (A) // *bîn* "perceive" (B). The overall pattern of this bicolon is abc:c'a'.

3:22 In this bicolon the parallelism of members is precise, both semantically and formally: *lō' nišmᵉ'āh bikna'an* "she has not been heard of in Canaan" (A) // *wᵉlō' nir'ᵃtāh bᵉtêmān* "nor seen in Teman" (B). The pattern may be analyazed as abc:ab'c'.

3:23d,e The parallelism of this bicolon is very similar to that of 3:20c-21a: *derek ḥokmāh lō'-yādᵉ'û* "they have not known the way of Wisdom" (A) // *wᵉlō' zākᵉrû nᵉtîbôtèhā* "nor remembered her paths" (B). Both these bicola feature ellipsis of the subject (Wisdom) in the second colon and follow the pattern abc:c'a'. The pairing *derek* (A) // *nᵉtîbôt* (B) again appears in the expected canonical sequence.

3:25 In this bicolon a well-conceived parallelism pairs *gādôl* "great" (A) // *gābōᵃh* "high" (B) and *'ên-qēṣ* "boundless" (A) // *'ên middāh* "immeasurable" (B). The parallelism may be analyzed as abc:a'c'.

3:28 The pairing in parallel of *da'at* "knowledge" (A) // *'iwwelet* "folly" (B) conforms to the normal canonical sequence.[11]

3:29 Significant parallel pairings here are: *ʿālāh* "ascend" (A) // *yārad* "descend" (B) and *šāmayim* "heavens" (A) // *šeḥāqîm* "clouds" (B). The sequence of the latter pairing is the regular canonical sequence for these two words used in parallel.

3:31 The parallelism of this bicolon is very similar to that of 3:20c-21a and 3:23d,e as described above. In this instance, however, there is no ellipsis and each member of the first colon is carefully matched by one in the second (abc:ab'c'). Both parallel pairings here appear in the expected canonical sequences: *yādaʿ* (A) // *bîn* (B) and *derek* (A) // *netîbāh* (B). See also above, 3:20-21, 23.

3:35 The sequence *mibbalʿadê* "except" (A) // *zûlāh* "besides" (B) is the expected canonical sequence for this pairing in parallel.

3:36b,c The familiar BH pairing, Jacob (A) // Israel (B), appears here in the normal canonical sequence.

4:1a,b The canonical sequence, *miṣwāh* "commandment" (A) // *tôrāh* "law" (B), appears in this bicolon.

4:1c,d The parallelism of this bicolon is particularly well-conceived and balanced. It features two significant parallel pairings: *ḥāzaq* "hold fast" (A) // *ʿāzab* "abandon" (B) and *leḥayyîm* "live" (A) // *mût* "die" (B).

4:6a,d Here the first and last cola manifest parallelism of members and the parallel pairing *mākar* "sell" (A) // *hisgîr* "deliver over" (B) appears in the normal canonical sequence in this verse. The other parallel pairing is *gôyīm* "nations" (A) // *ṣārîm* "enemies" (B).

4:8 This bicolon is yet another example of excellent poetic structure. The parallelism is a complete abc:a'b'c' in which each member of the first colon has its semantic and syntactic counterpart in the second.

4:11 An example of antithetical parallelism is presented in this bicolon. The use of a ballast variant in the second colon may be noted as well. The overall pattern of the parallelism is abc:b'c'. *Śāśôn* "joy" is contrasted with *ʾēbel* "mourning" several times in BH (cf. Isa 61:3 and Jer 31:13).

4:12d-13a In BH, *tôrāh* "law" is most frequently the A-word in parallel pairing to both *mišpāṭ* "ruling" or *ḥôq* "statute." This bicolon thus furnishes yet another example of a parallel pairing appearing in the expected canonical sequence. The pairing of the verbs *sûr* "swerve away" (A) // *lōʾ-yādaʿ* "disregard," is also worthy of mention.

4:13 Parallel pairs found in canonical sequence here are *derek* "way" (A) // *n^{e}tîbôt* "paths" (B) (cf. also 3:20-21, 23, 31) and *hālak* "walk" (A) // *dārak* "tread" (B) (cf. Isa 42:16). The parallelism of this bicolon is sharply delineated, with each colon featuring a three-member construct chain and a negated verb. Each member of the first colon has its precise semantic and formal counterpart in the second, with the exception of the middle elements where *miṣwôt ʾ^{e}lōhîm* "the commandments of God" is approximated in the second colon by means of a ballast variant (*mûsar ṣidqātô* "the instruction of his righteousness").

4:15 The first bicolon of this verse presents an excellent example of the "progressive" ab:b'c pattern of parallelism. In the second bicolon the sequence of *zāqēn* "elder" (A) // *naʿar* "youth" (B) follows that of the prose source-text, Deut 28:50.[12]

4:16 The parallelism here is complete. Each member of the first colon has its semantic counterpart in the second, but variation is achieved syntactically (abc:c'a'b').

4:20 The first two cola of this tricolon are intimately related by *parallelismus membrorum* (abc:a'b'c'). The third colon, however, stands only in a formal relationship to the others, as it offers a comparable rhythm but no correspondence of its members with the preceding. Also of significance in this verse is the appearance of the expected canonical sequence for the parallel pairing *pāšaṭ* "strip off" (A) // *lābaš* "put on" (B). The parallel pairing, *b^{e}gādîm* "garments" (A) // *śaq* "sackcloth" (B), may also be noted.

4:23 Within this tricolon stand several examples of antithetical parallelism. The verb *šālaḥ* "dismiss" in verse 23a is antithetically parallel to *šûb* "return" in verse 23b, as is the conjunctive pairing *ʾēbel ûb^{e}kî* "mourning and weeping" in verse 23a to the conjunctive pairing *śāśôn w^eśimḥāh* "joy and gladness" in verse 23c.

4:33 Close parallelism of members unites the three cola of this tricolon: *śāmaḥ* "rejoice" (A) // *gîl* "be glad" (B) // *'āṣab* "be grieved" (C) and *n^epōl* "fall" (A) // *hikkāšēl* "disaster" (B) // *ḥorbāh* "desolation" (C). And not only do these members correspond semantically, but also syntactically [abc: ()b'c':a'b"c"]. In the case of the verbs *śāmaḥ* and *gîl*, BH reveals a clear sequence preference for the above A-B sequence (see Chapter V, ad loc., and n. 381). Although BH does reveal a sequence preference for *kāšal* as the A-word to *nāpal* in parallel, the reverse sequence in this case appears certain from the Prov 24:17 source-text (see Chapter V, ad loc.).

5:1 See above, 4:20.

5:2 In this bicolon, close correspondence of parallel members may be observed: *'^aṭî m^e'îl ṣidqat '^elōhîm* "wrap yourself in the cloak of God's righteousness" (A) // *śîm 'al-rō'šēk p^e'ēr-k^ebôd YHWH* "put on your head the tiara of the glory of the Eternal" (B) (abcd:a'b'c'd').

5:7 The familiar BH parallelism between mountains and hills appears in 5:7b,c in the expected canonical sequence: *har* "mountain" (A) // *g^ebā'ôt* "hills" (B).

Examples of tricola within which two of the member cola are related by synonymous parallelism and the third merely by a formal parallelism may be found throughout the poetry (cf., e.g., 3:23, 3:36, and 4:20). Examples of both bicola and tricola whose metre and balance are clear but whose cola are related to one another only by a formal parallelism, may be found throughout the poetry (cf., e.g., 3:13, 3:19, 5:6, 4:14, 4:17-18, 5:8, 5:9, etc.).

Examples of Repetition

The device of repetition is employed variously. For example, the same word or phrase may be repeated within a limited context for emphatic effect. Cf. 3:9-10 (Israel); 3:14 (where); 3:28 (perish); 3:31 (none); 4:19 (go); and 4:31-32 (wretched).

There is also some repetition on a larger scale; a substantial portion of the content of 5:1-9, for example, is repeated or reworked from the preceding material in Baruch 4. A prominent feature of the second poem (4:5-5:9) is yet another kind of repetition, the patterned repetition of an imperative + vocative that occurs eleven times throughout the poem (in some instances manifesting lexical continuity). This striking introductory effect thus clearly delineates each successive stanzaic subdivision. Beginning at 4:5, the pattern repeats at 4:9, 4:14 (cf. 4:9), 4:19, 4:21 (cf. 4:5), 4:25 (cf. 4:19, 21), 4:27 (cf. 4:5, 21, 27, etc.), 4:30 (cf. 4:5, etc.), 4:36, 5:1, and 5:5.

The Auditory Evidence

The Metrical Scheme[13] for the Wisdom Poem

	Accentual Unit Pattern	Syllable Count Pattern	
3:9	2 + 2 + 3	5/5/7	(or 4 + 3, 10/7)
3:10-12	3 + 3 + 3	6/8/9	
	3 + 3 + 3	6/7/7	
3:13	3 + 3	9/9	
3:14	2 + 2	4/4	(or 4 + 4, 8/10)
	2 + 2	5/5	
	2 + 3 + 3	3/8/8	
3:15	3 + 3	6/9	
3:16-18	3 + 3 + 3	8/7/8	
	3 + 3 + 3	8/7/7	
	3 + 3	8/7	
3:19	3 + 3	9/7	
3:20-21	3 + 3	6/7	
	3 + 3	8/10	
	3 + 3	9/9	
3:22	3 + 3	7/8	
3:23	3 + 3 + 3	11/8/11	
	3 + 3	7/10	
3:24	3 + 3	10/7	
3:25	3 + 3	6/6	
3:26	3 + 2	8/4	

	3 + 2	9/7	
3:27	3 + 3	9/9	
3:28	2 + 2	7/7	
3:29	3 + 3	9/9	
3:30	4 + 3	11/8	
3:31	3 + 3	5/8	
3:32	3 + 3	7/8	
	3 + 3	7/9	
3:33	3 + 3	8/12	
3:34	2 + 2	10/7	
	2 + 2	4/7	(or 4 + 4 + 4,
	2 + 2	6/5	17/11/11)
3:35	2 + 2 + 3	5/6/9	(or 4 + 3, 11/9)
3:36	3 + 3 + 2	6/9/8	
3:37	3 + 3	9/10	
4:1	3 + 3	8/10	
	2 + 2	8/8	
4:2	3 + 3	8/10	
4:3	3 + 3	10/9	
4:3	2 + 2 + 2	6/9/4	

The Metrical Scheme for the Consolation Poem

	Accentual Unit Pattern	Syllable Count Pattern
4:5	2 + 2	5/4
4:6	2 + 2	6/4
	3 + 2	10/6
4:7	3 + 3	7/9
4:8	3 + 3	11/12
4:9	3 + 2	6/5
	3 + 2	7/5
	3 + 2	7/3
4:10	4 + 4	11/10
4:11	3 + 3	7/8
4:12	3 + 3 + 3	5/10/9
4:12d-13a	3 + 2	9/8
4:13	3 + 2	8/4
	3 + 2	9/4

4:14	3(4?) + 4 + 4	7/9/10	
4:15	4 + 4	10/9	
	2 + 2 + 3	4/4/6	(or 4 + 3, 8/6)
4:16	3 + 3	12/12	
4:17-18	3 + 3 + 3	9/10/10	
4:19	3 + 3	6/8	
4:20	3 + 3 + 3	7/8/9	
4:21	2 + 2	6/6	(or 4 + 4, 12/12)
	3 + 2	8/4	
4:22	2 + 2	6/7	
	3 + 3 + 3	10/10/9	
4:23	3 + 3 + 3	9/9/8	
4:24	3 + 3	7/8	
	3 + 2	6/7	
	3 + 2	9/6	
4:25	3 + 2	6/5	
	2 + 3 + 3	7/8/8	
4:26	2 + 2	6/6	(or 4 + 4, 12/11)
	2 + 2	5/6	
4:27	2 + 2	6/7	(or 4 + 4, 13/14)
	3 + 2	8/6	
4:28	3 + 3	9/8	
	3 + 2	5/7	
4:29	4 + 4	10/12	
4:30	3 + 3	8/8	
4:31-32	4 + 4 + 3	12/12/8	
4:33	3 + 2 + 3	9/7/9	
4:34	2 + 2 + 3	6/4/9	(or 4 + 3, 10/9)
4:35	2 + 2 + 2	7/5/5	
	2 + 2	6/5	
4:36	2 + 2	6/7	(or 4 + 4, 13/15)
	3 + 2	10/5	
4:37	3 + 2	8/5	
	2 + 2	6/7	(or 4 + 4 + 4, 13/13/10)
	2 + 2	4/6	
5:1	2 + 2	6/7	(or 4 + 4, 13/11)
	2 + 2	5/6	
5:2	4 + 4	9/11	

5:3	3 + 3	6/6	
5:4	3 + 3	5/6	(or 4 + 4, 11/11)
	2 + 2	5/6	
5:5	2 + 2 + 3	6/7/10	(or 4 + 3, 13/10)
	3 + 3	8/7	
	2 + 2	4/6	
5:6	3 + 3	9/7	
	2 + 2 + 2	5/6/5	
5:7	3 + 3 + 2	6/6/5	
	2 + 2	8/5	
	3 + 3	7/7	
5:8	2 + 2 + 3	5/4/9	(or 4 + 3, 9/9)
5:9	4 + 3 + 3	11/8/9	

A Brief Summary of the Metrical Data

The Wisdom Poem

As might well be expected in a poem of this genre, a 3 + 3 pattern characterizes the metre of this poem, but it is by no means so rigidly uniform a pattern as that envisaged by R. R. Harwell (2, 56-58). Harwell contended that the metre consisted entirely of 3 + 3 bicola. In actual fact, however, twenty-one of thirty-one bicola are 3 + 3, and the remainder 3 + 2, 2 + 2, or 4 + 3. There are also ten tricola of which five are 3 + 3 + 3 (other patterns represented are: 2 + 2 + 3, 2 + 2 + 2, 3 + 3 + 2, and 2 + 3 + 3).

Analysis by syllable count yields the following statistics for the Wisdom poem:

Total syllables	482
Total bicola	31
Average length of bicolon	15.5[14]
Longest bicolon	20
Shortest bicolon	8

The Consolation Poem

Harwell (2, 58-59) similarly conceived this consolation and lament poem to have consisted entirely of a rigidly uniform series of 3 + 2 bicola. But as should be expected from any degree of familiarity with canonical lament and consolation poetry (e.g., that of Second Isaiah, the major source and inspiration of this Baruch poem, or Lamentations 1-4) the so-called *Qinah* or lament metre (3 + 2) is hardly any more uniform or regular in this Baruch poem than it is elsewhere in the Hebrew Scriptures. In fact, of a total of forty-eight bicola, approximately a third (fifteen) are 3 + 2, another third (sixteen) are 2 + 2, and yet another third (thirteen) are 3 + 3. The seventeen tricola reveal an even greater variety. The most common patterns are 3 + 3 + 3 (five) and 2 + 2 + 3 (four).

Analysis by syllable count yields the following statistics for the Consolation poem:

Total syllables	669
Total bicola	48
Average length of bicolon	13.9[15]
Longest bicolon	24
Shortest bicolon	9

Rhyme

The presence of rhyme, or correspondence of terminal syllables in parallel cola, is noticeable throughout the poetry. In twenty-one instances, two (or three) consecutive cola, related to each other either by parallelism of members or merely a formal parallelism, reveal rhyming sounds in their final syllables. The followed passages may be consulted: 3:10-11; 3:14a,b; 3:22; 3:29; 3:31; 3:34a,b; 3:37; 4:2; 4:6c,d; 4:11; 4:12d-13a; 4:13; 4:15c,d; 4:17-18; 4:20a,b; 4:27a,b; 4:29; 4:30; 4:31-32; 4:33a,b; 4:35d,e.

Conclusion

The considerable cumulative evidence of Hebraisms, mistranslations, etc., in the texts of the primary Versions presents a very convincing case for the original Hebrew text of the Baruch poetry. This case is strengthened by the numerous examples of basic semantic and syntactic features of classical Hebrew poetry that manifest themselves in the Hebrew (as assembled above) even though the Hebrew text is a reconstruction. Similarly, the fact that the text of this poetry is only a reconstruction and yet still exhibits impressive examples of common Hebrew metrical patterns and a not inconsiderable amount of metrical regularity (vis-à-vis the LXX text which is not metrical) is compelling.[16]

Thus, even though a reconstruction can be accurate only to a degree of probability, and nothing short of an actual copy of the Baruch poetry will ever really suffice, there would appear to be, in the light of all the lines of evidence gathered together in this study, little excuse for any lingering doubts about the originality of the Hebrew text of the poetry of Baruch.

NOTES TO CHAPTER VI

[1]See Harwell, 54; *HNTT*, 420; Heinisch, "Zur Entstehung des Buches Baruch," 708; and Kneucker, 293-95.

[2]See Graetz, "Abfassungszeit," 393.

[3]The anomalous appearance of the verb "bring" in the future tense (*oisei*) in LXX Bar 3:30 is a puzzle. Curiously, the problem can be most pointedly highlighted in English--where the context and parallels demand "bought," the Greek text has "brought" (or rather, more accurately, "bring"). It may perhaps be speculated that this difficulty is the result of a mistranslation. Could the Greek translator perhaps have misread a form of the Hebrew verb *qānāh* "buy" as a form of such a verb as *qābaṣ* "collect, gather," *nāśāʾ* "lift, carry," or the like, and have rendered the sense "bring"? See also *HNTT*, 421.

[4]See Graetz, "Abfassungszeit," 392.

[5]If the theory of Harwell (55) and Torrey (*The Apocryphal Literature*, 62 n. 59) that *mnēmosynon* "memorial" resulted from a misreading of *zikrû* "remember" as *zikkārôn* "memorial" be deemed likely, it would add further weight to the case for the originality of the Hebrew text.

[6]See Harwell, 54; J. W. Wevers, "Evidence of the Text of the John H. Scheide Papyri for the Translation of the *Status Constructus* in Ezekiel," *JBL* 70 (1951) 211-16.

[7]Harwell (54) suggests that in the context of the "seizing of a flock" (especially when it is done *hypo echthrōn* "by enemies" and not, for example, *en cheiri echthron* "by the hand of enemies"), the Greek *echthrōn* may point to a confusion occurring already in the original Hebrew between *ʾybym* "enemies" and *zʾbym* "wolves."

[8]See, e.g., Whitehouse, "1 Baruch," 573) who says that this "phraseology is such as Hebrew could hardly employ."

[9]That the unusual Greek form *dekaplasiasate* "increase tenfold" was an attempt in translation to represent the Hebrew idiom *ʿeśer pᵉʿāmîm* "ten times" was apparently first suggested by H. Graetz in "Abfassungszeit" (393).

[10]See above, Chapter I, pp. 13-14.

[11]The sequence for this pairing in parallel is the same in four of five occurrences in BH (Prov 12:23; 13:16; 15:2, 19). It is the reverse in Prov 14:18.

[12]In conjunctive pairing, the sequence for this pair is most often (seven of nine times) the reverse, "youth and elder" (cf. Exod 10:9, Isa 3:5, 20:4, Gen 19:4, Josh 6:21, Lam 2:21, Esth 3:13, and the opposite order in Jer 51:22, and Psa 148:12).

[13]On the one hand, the Baruch poetry has been analyzed according to the traditional system of defining Hebrew metre in terms of the number of stressed syllables or accentual units that appear, line by line, in a number of regular and repeated patterns (e.g., 3 + 3, 3 + 2, 2 + 2 + 3, etc.). But, on the other hand, since no one of the metrical systems adopted by scholars has ever proven wholly adequate to the task of fully defining the auditory organization of Hebrew poetry, these poems have also been analyzed in terms of the "syllable count" system advocated by David Noel Freedman (elaborated, for example, in his Prolegomenon to G. Buchanan Gray's *Forms of Hebrew Poetry*, xxxiiff.). This system operates on the principle that "unstressed syllables played a role in Hebrew poetry along with stressed syllables, and that counting the total number of syllables in lines and larger units produces a more reliable picture of the metrical structure than any other procedure now in use" (ibid., xxxii).

In achieving the syllable count statistics according to the Freedman system, one count has been attributed to all segholates and to all examples of the dual termination (*-ayim*), the *ḥaṭef* resolution (e.g., *waʿ^a-*, *heḥ^e-*, etc.), and the pronominal suffix, *-ayik*.

[14]This compares favorably with the figure obtained by Freedman for the average bicolon length in Lamentations 5, another poem in which the 3 + 3 pattern is dominant; that figure is 16.5 (Prolegomenon to G. Gray, *Forms of Hebrew Poetry*, xxxviii).

[15]This compares favorably with the figures obtained by Freedman (ibid., xxxix) for the average bicolon length in Lamentations 1-4, where the 3 + 2 pattern is most characteristic. The average bicolon in Lamentations 1 has 12.9 syllables, in Lamentations 2, 12.9, in Lamentations 3, 13.2, and in Lamentations 4, 13.8.

[16]It is also a matter of interest that throughout the reconstruction process there has been a noticeable absence of any necessity for assuming Ugaritic features, archaisms, etc.--a possible mark of the post-exilic date of the poems.

BIBLIOGRAPHY

Ackroyd, Peter R. "Some Notes on the Psalms." *JTS* 17 (1966) 392-99.

Aeschylus. *Persae*. Edited by H. D. Broadhead. Cambridge: Cambridge University, 1960.

Andersen, Francis I. "Studies in Hebrew Syntax." 2 vols. Ph.D. dissertation, Johns Hopkins University, 1960.

André, L. E. T. *Les Apocryphes de l'Ancien Testament*. Florence: Osvald Paggi, 1903.

Arndt, William F., and Gingrich, F. Wilbur. *A Greek-English Lexicon of the New Testament and Other Early Christian Literature*. Translated and adapted from Walter Bauer's *Griechisch-deutsches Wörterbuch zu den Schriften des Neuen Testaments*, 4th ed. (Berlin, 1949-52). Chicago/ Cambridge: University of Chicago, 1957.

Baillet, Maurice. "Un Recueil liturgíque de Qumrân, Grotte 4: 'Les Paroles de Luminaires.'" *RB* 58 (1961) 195-250.

________, Milik, J. T., and de Vaux, Roland. *Les 'Petites Grottes' de Qumrân*. DJD III. Oxford: Clarendon, 1962.

Barthélemy, D., and Milik, J. T. *Qumran Cave 1*. DJD I. Oxford: Clarendon, 1955.

Battistone, J. J. "An Examination of the Literary and Theological Background of the Wisdom Passage in the Book of Baruch." Ph.D. dissertation, Duke University, 1968.

Bauer, H., and Leander, P. *Historische Grammatik der hebräischen Sprache des Alten Testaments*. Hildesheim: Georg Olms, 1962 (orig., 1922).

Bentzen, Aage. *Introduction to the Old Testament*. 2 vols. Copenhagen: G. E. C. Gad, 1948-49.

Bertholdt, Leonhard. *Historisch-kritische Einleitung in sämmtliche kanonische und apokryphische Schriften des Alten und Neuen Testaments*. 4 vols. Erlangen: J. J. Palm, 1812-19.

Bertram, Georg. "Der Sprachschatz der Septuaginta und der des hebräischen Alten Testaments." *ZAW* 16 (1939) 85-101.

Bevan, A. A. "Book of Baruch." *Encyclopaedia Biblica* (1889) I, cols. 492-94.

Bewer, J. "The River Sud in the Book of Baruch." *JBL* 43 (1924) 226-27.

"Bible, Ancient Versions: Egyptian (Coptic)." *Encyclopaedia Judaica* (1971) IV, col. 861.

"Bible, Ancient Versions: Ethiopic." *Encyclopaedia Judaica* (1971) IV, cols. 860-61.

Bickerman, Elias J. "The Septuagint as a Translation." *PAAJR* 28 (1959) 1-39.

Bietenhard, Hans. "*onoma, onomazō*." *TWNT* V, 242-83.

Birdsall, J. N. "Apocrypha." *The New Bible Dictionary*. Edited by J. D. Douglas, et al. London: The Inter-Varsity Fellowship, 1962 (pp. 44-47).

Bissell, Edwin Cone. *The Apocrypha of the Old Testament*. Vol. XV of *A Commentary on the Holy Scriptures*. Edited by John P. Lange. New York: Scribner's Sons, 1890.

Blank, S. H. "The Septuagint Renderings of Old Testament Terms for Law." *HUCA* VII (1930) 259-83.

Blass, F., and Debrunner, A. *A Greek Grammar of the New Testament and Other Early Christian Literature*. Translated and revised from the 9th-10th German edition by Robert W. Funk. Chicago/Cambridge: University of Chicago, 1961.

Boling, Robert G. "'Synonymous' Parallelism in the Psalms." Ph.D. dissertation, Johns Hopkins University, 1959.

________. "'Synonymous' Parallelism in the Psalms." *JSS* 5 (1960) 221-55.

Brockelmann, Carl. *Syrische Grammatik*. Leipzig: Verlag Enzyklopädie, 1960.

Brockington, L. H. "Septuagint and Targum." *ZAW* 66 (1954) 80-86.

________. *A Critical Introduction to the Apocrypha*. London: G. Duckworth, 1961.

Brown, Francis; Driver, S. R.; and Briggs, Charles A. *A Hebrew and English Lexicon of the Old Testament*. Corrected impression of the 1st edition. Oxford: Clarendon, 1952.

Brownlee, William H. *The Dead Sea Manual of Discipline*. *ASOR* Supplement, nos. 10-12. New Haven: American Schools of Oriental Research, 1951.

Brugsch, H. "Das Buch Baruch, koptisch." *ZÄS* X (1872) 134-36; XI (1873) 18-21; XII (1874) 46-49.

Bultmann, Rudolf. "*eleos, eleeō, eleēmōn, eleēmosynē*." *TWNT* II, 474-83.

________. "*elpis, elpizō*." *TWNT* II, 515-20.

Burrows, Millar. *The Dead Sea Scrolls.* New York: Viking, 1956.

________. *More Light on the Dead Sea Scrolls.* New York: Viking, 1958.

Buttrick, G. A., ed. *Interpreter's Dictionary of the Bible.* 4 vols. and suppl. Nashville: Abingdon, 1963.

Ceriani, A. M. *Monumenta Sacra et Profana: Baruch, Threni, et Epistola Jeremiae Versionis Syriacae Pauli Telensis.* Tomus I, fascicle 1. Milan: Biblioteca Ambrosianae, 1861.

Charles, R. H. *The Apocalypse of Baruch: translated from the Syriac.* London: Adam and Charles Black, 1896.

________. *The Ethiopic Version of the Book of Enoch. Anecdota Oxoniensia* XI. Oxford: Clarendon, 1906.

________. *The Book of Enoch.* Oxford: Clarendon, 1912.

________, ed. *The Apocrypha and Pseudepigrapha of the Old Testament.* 2 vols. Oxford: Clarendon, 1913.

________. *Religious Developments Between the Old and New Testaments.* New York: Henry Holt, n.d.

________. "Baruch." *Encyclopaedia Britannica.* 11th ed. (1910) III, 453-54.

________. "II Baruch." *APOT* II, 470-526.

________. "The Book of Enoch." *APOT* II, 163-281.

Cheyne, T. K. "Baruch." *Encyclopaedia Biblica* (1889) I, cols. 491-92.

Clermont-Ganneau, Ch. S. "Deux inscriptions israélites archaïques de Gezer." *Recueil d'Archéologie Orientale.* Vol. VIII. Paris: Ernest Leroux, 1924 (pp. 103-12).

Commodian. *Carmen Apologeticum. Corpus Scriptorum Ecclesiasticorum Latinorum* XV. Vindobonae: C. Geroldi Filium Bibliopolam Academiae, 1887 (pp. 113-188).

Conzelmann, Hans. "*syniēmi, synesis.*" *TWNT* VII, 886-94.

Cornill, Carl H. *Einleitung in das Alte Testament mit Einschluss der Apokryphen und Pseudepigraphen.* 4th ed., completely revised. Freiburg/Leipzig: J. C. B. Mohr, 1896.

Cross, Frank M., Jr. "Notes on a Canaanite Psalm in the Old Testament." *BASOR* 117 (1950) 19-21.

________. "A New Qumran Biblical Fragment related to the original Hebrew underlying the Septuagint." *BASOR* 132 (1953) 15-26.

________. *The Ancient Library of Qumrân.* London: Gerald Duckworth, 1958.

Cross, Frank M., Jr. *Canaanite Myth and Hebrew Epic: Essays in the History of the Religion of Israel.* Cambridge: Harvard University, 1973.

Crum, Walter E. *A Coptic Dictionary.* Oxford: Clarendon, 1939.

Dahood, Mitchell J. *Psalms* I, II, III. AB 16, 17, 17A. Garden City: Doubleday, 1966-70.

Dalman, G. H. *Aramäisch-Neuhebräisches Handwörterbuch zu Targum, Talmud und Midrasch.* Hildesheim: Georg Olms, 1967 (orig., 1901).

Dancy, J. C. "Baruch." *The Cambridge Bible Commentary: The Shorter Books of the Apocrypha.* Edited by P. R. Ackroyd, et al. Cambridge: Cambridge University, 1972 (pp. 169-96).

Daniel, Suzanne. "Bible, Ancient Versions; Greek: The Septuagint." *Encyclopaedia Judaica* (1971) IV, cols. 851-56.

Davidson, Samuel. *An Introduction to the Old Testament.* Vol. III. Covent Garden/Edinburgh: Williams and Norgate, 1863.

Deissmann, Adolf. *The Philology of the Greek Bible.* London: Hodder and Stoughton, 1908.

Delling, Gerhard. *Jüdische Lehre und Frömmigkeit in den Paralipomena Jeremiae.* BZAW 100. Berlin: Alfred Töpelmann, 1967.

Denis, Albert-Marie. *Introduction aux pseudépigraphes grecs d'ancien Testament.* Leiden: E. J. Brill, 1970.

Dillmann, August. *Biblia Veteris Testamenti Aethiopici: Veteris Testamenti Aethiopici Tomus Quintus, quo continentur Libri Apocryphi.* Berlin: A. Asher et Socios, 1894.

________. *Ethiopic Grammar.* 2nd ed. enlarged and improved (1899) by Carl Bezold. Translated by James A. Crichton. London: Williams and Norgate, 1907.

Driver, G. R. *The Judean Scrolls.* New York: Schocken, 1965.

Driver, S. R. *Hebrew Tenses.* 2nd rev. ed. Oxford: Clarendon, 1881.

________. *Deuteronomy.* ICC, V. Edinburgh: T. & T. Clark, 1965 (orig., 1895).

Dupont-Sommer, A. *The Essene Writings from Qumran.* Translated by Geza Vermes. Cleveland/New York: World, 1962.

Eben-Shoshan, A. *Millôn Ḥādaš.* Jerusalem: Kiryat Sepher, 1964.

Edgar, Campbell Cowan, ed. *Zenon Papyri*. Vol. III. *Catalogue général des antiquités égyptiennes du Musée du Caire*, no. 85. Le Caire: Imprimerie de l'Institut français d'archéologie orientale, 1928.

Ehlen, Arlis J. "The Poetic Structure of a Hodayah from Qumran: An Analysis of Grammatical, Semantic, and Auditory Correspondence in 1QH 3:19-36." Ph.D. dissertation, Harvard University, 1970.

Eissfeldt, Otto. *The Old Testament, An Introduction: The History of the Formation of the Old Testament*. Translated by P. R. Ackroyd. New York/Evanston: Harper and Row, 1965.

Elliger, K., and Rudolph, W., eds. *Biblia Hebraica Stuttgartensia*. Stuttgart: Deutsche Bibelstiftung, 1967/77.

Epstein, I., ed. *The Babylonian Talmud, Seder Moʿed*. Vol. 8, Part 2: *Megillah*. Translated by Maurice Simon. London: Soncino, 1938.

Ewald, Heinrich. *Die Geschichte des Volkes Israel*. Vol. IV. Göttingen: Dieter, 1864.

________. *Die Propheten des Alten Bundes*. Band III: *Die Jüngsten Propheten des Alten Bundes mit den Büchern Barukh und Daniel*. 2nd ed. Göttingen: Vandenhoeck u. Ruprecht, 1868.

Ferrar, W. J. *The Uncanonical Jewish Books: A Short Introduction to the Apocrypha and the Jewish Writings*. London: SPCK, 1918.

Fitzgerald, Aloysius. "Baruch." *The Jerome Biblical Commentary*. Edited by Raymond E. Brown, Joseph E. Fitzmyer, and Roland E. Murphy. Englewood Cliffs, NJ: Prentice Hall, 1968 (pp. 614-18).

Flashar, Martin. "Exegetische Studien zum Septuagintapsalter." *ZAW* 32 (1912) 81-116, 161-89, 241-68.

Foerster, Werner. "*eirēnē*." *TWNT* II, 398-400, 405-18.

________. "*Kyrios*." *TWNT* III, 1081-98.

Fohrer, Georg. "*sōzō, sōtēria*." *TWNT* VII, 970-81.

________. "Baruch." *Calwer Bibellexicon*. Stuttgart: Calwer, 1959 (p. 127).

Freedman, David Noel. "The Prayer of Nabonidus." *BASOR* 145 (1957) 31-32.

________. Prolegomenon to G. Buchanan Gray, *The Forms of Hebrew Poetry: Considered with Special Reference to the Criticism and Interpretation of the Old Testament*. New York: Ktav, 1972 (orig., 1915) (pp. vii-lvi).

Freedman, H., and Simon, Maurice, eds. *Midrash Rabbah*, VI: *Song of Songs*. Translated by Maurice Simon. London: Soncino, 1939.

Frisk, Hjalmar. *Griechisches Etymologisches Wörterbuch*. 3 vols. Heidelberg: Carl Winter, 1960-72.

Fritzsche, Otto F. *Kurzgefasstes exegetisches Handbuch zu den Apokryphen des Alten Testaments*. Band I. Leipzig: Weidmann, 1851.

________. *Libri Apocryphi Veteris Testamenti Graece*. Leipzig: F. A. Brockhaus, 1871.

Geffcken, Johannes. *Die Oracula Sibyllina*. Leipzig: J. C. Hinrichs, 1967 (orig., 1902).

Gehman, H. S. "The Hebraic Character of Septuagint Greek." *VT* 1 (1951) 81-90.

________. "Some Types of Errors of Transmission in the Septuagint." *VT* 3 (1953) 397-400.

________. "*Hagios* in the Septuagint, and its Relation to the Hebrew Original." *VT* 4 (1954) 337-48.

________. *The New Westminster Dictionary of the Bible*. Philadelphia: Westminster, 1970.

Geiger, P. Eduard Ephraim. *Der Psalter Salomos*. Augsburg: J. Wolff, 1871.

Gelin, Albert. *Jérémie, Les Lamentations, Le Livre de Baruch*. *SBJ* XX. 2nd rev. ed. Paris: Cerf, 1959.

Gerleman, Gillis. "Studies in the Septuagint Book of Job." *Lunds Universitets Årsskrift*. N.F. Avd. 1, 43, 2. Lund: C. W. K. Gleerup, 1946 (pp. 1-86).

________. "Studies in the Septuagint, II: Chronicles." *Lunds Universitets Årsskrift*. N.F. Avd. 1, 43, 3. Lund: C. W. K. Gleerup, 1946 (pp. 1-46).

________. "Studies in the Septuagint, III: Proverbs." *Lunds Universitets Årsskrift*. N.F. Avd. 1, 52, 3. Lund: C. W. K. Gleerup, 1956 (pp. 1-63).

________. "The Septuagint Proverbs as a Hellenistic Document." *OTS* 8 (1950) 15-27.

________. "Altgriechische Bibelübersetzungen." *RGG*. 3rd ed. (1957) I, 1193-95.

Gevirtz, Stanley. *Patterns in the Early Poetry of Israel*. Studies in Ancient Oriental Civilization 32. Chicago: University of Chicago, 1963.

Gifford, E. H. "Baruch." *The Speaker's Commentary on the Holy Bible, The Apocrypha: with an Explanatory and Critical Commentary and Revision of the Translation.* Vol. II. Edited by Henry Wace. London: John Murray, 1888.

Ginzberg, Louis. "Baruch in Rabbinical Literature." *The Jewish Encyclopedia* (1902) II, 548-49.

________. "Jeremiah in Rabbinical Literature." *The Jewish Encyclopedia* (1904) VII, 100-02.

Goettsberger, Johann. *Einleitung in das Alte Testament.* Freiburg im Breisgau: Herder, 1928.

Goodspeed, E. J. *The Story of the Apocrypha.* Chicago: University of Chicago, 1939.

Gordis, Robert. Review of *The Forms of Hebrew Poetry: Considered with Special Reference to the Criticism and Interpretation of the Old Testament*, by G. Buchanan Gray. With prolegomenon by David Noel Freedman. New York: Ktav, 1972 (orig., 1915). *CBQ* 35 (1973) 241-44.

Gordon, Cyrus H. *Ugaritic Textbook.* Analecta Orientalia 38. Rome: Pontificum Institutum Biblicum, 1965.

Goshen-Gottstein, M. H. "Theory and Practice of Textual Criticism: the Text-critical use of the Septuagint." *Textus* III (1963) 130-58.

________. "Prolegomena to a Critical Edition of the Peshitta." *Text and Language in Bible and Qumran.* Edited by M. H. Goshen-Gottstein. Tel Aviv: Orient, 1960 (pp. 163-204). [= *Scripta Hierosolymitana* 8 (1960) 26ff.]

Graetz, H. "Abfassungszeit und Bedeutung des Buches Baruch." *MGWJ* 36 (1887) 385-401.

Gray, G. Buchanan. *Isaiah, I-XXXIX.* ICC, Xa. Edinburgh: T. & T. Clark, 1912.

________. "The Psalms of Solomon." *APOT* II, 625-52.

Greenfield, Jonas C. "Ugaritic *mdl* and Its Cognates." *Biblica* 45 (1964) 527-34.

Greeven, Heinrich. "*deomai, deēsis.*" *TWNT* II, 39-42.

Grossfeld, Bernard. "Bible, Ancient Versions: Syriac." *Encyclopaedia Judaica* (1971) IV, cols. 858-60.

Haenchen, Ernst. "Das Buch Baruch." *Gott und Mensch.* Edited by Ernst Haenchen. Tübingen: J. C. B. Mohr (Paul Siebeck), 1965 (pp. 299-334).

Hävernick, H. A. C. *De libro Baruchi apocrypho, commentatio critica.* Königsberg: Boruss, 1843.

Halkin, A. S. "Bible, Ancient Versions: Arabic." *Encyclopaedia Judaica* (1971) IV, cols. 863-64.

Harris, J. Rendel. *The Rest of the Words of Baruch: A Christian Apocalypse of the Year 136 A.D.* London: C. J. Clay and Sons, 1889.

________. *The Odes and Psalms of Solomon: From the Syriac Version.* Cambridge: Cambridge University, 1909.

Harrison, R. K. *An Introduction to the Old Testament.* Grand Rapids: William B. Eerdmans, 1969.

Harwell, R. R. *The Principal Versions of Baruch.* New Haven: Yale University, 1915.

Hastings, James, ed. *A Dictionary of the Bible.* Vols. 1-4. New York: Scribner's Sons, 1905.

Hatch, Edwin, and Redpath, Henry A. *A Concordance to the Septuagint and the other Greek Versions of the Old Testament (including the Apocryphal Books).* 2 vols. and 2 supplements. Oxford: Clarendon, 1897-1906.

Heinisch, Paul. "Zur Entstehung des Buches Baruch." *Theologie und Glaube* 20 (1928) 704-10.

Herodotus. *Historiae.* Vol. VII. Translated by A. D. Godley. LCL, III. London: William Heinemann, 1928.

Hieronymus. *Commentariorum In Esaiam, Libri I-XI.* Corpus Christianorum Series Latina, LXXIII, pars 2. Turnholti: Typographi Brepols Editores Pontificii, 1963.

Hillers, Delbert R. "Ugaritic *snpt* 'wave-offering.'" *BASOR* 198 (1970) 42.

________. *Lamentations.* AB 7A. Garden City: Doubleday, 1972.

Hilgenfeld, Adolf. "Das Buch Baruch." *ZWT* 5 (1862) 199-204.

________. "Das Buch Baruch und seine neueste Bearbeitungen." *ZWT* 22 (1879) 437-54.

________. "Baruch." *ZWT* 23 (1880) 412-22.

Hitzig, Ferdinand." "Zur Kritik der apokryphischen Bücher des Alten Testaments: (3) einige Bemerkungen über das Buch Baruch." *ZWT* 3 (1860) 262-73.

Holm-Nielsen, Svend. *Hodayot, Psalms from Qumran. Acta Theologica Danica* II. Aarhus: Universitetsforlaget, 1960.

Holmes, R., and Parsons, J. *Vetus Testamentum Graecum cum variis lectionibus.* Oxford: Clarendon, 1798-1827.

Horst, Johannes. "*makrothymia, makrothymeō, makrothymos, makrothymōs.*" *TWNT* IV, 377-90.

Hunzinger, Claus-Hunno. "Fragmente einer älteren Fassung des Buches *Milḥamā* aus Höhle 4 von Qumran." *ZAW* 69 (1957) 131-51.

"Introduction to the Prophets: Baruch." *The Jerusalem Bible.* Edited by Alexander Jones, et al. Garden City: Doubleday, 1966 (p. 1128).

Iranyi, L. A. "Book of Baruch." *New Catholic Encyclopedia* (1967) II, 138-39.

Jackson, Thomas A. "Words in Parallelism in Old Testament Poetry." Ph.D. dissertation, Johns Hopkins University, 1970.

James, Montague R. "Apocrypha." *Encyclopaedia Biblica* (1889) I, cols. 249-61.

________. *Apocrypha, Anecdota.* Second Series, Texts and Studies V/1. Cambridge: Cambridge University, 1897.

Jastrow, Marcus. *A Dictionary of the Targumim, the Talmud Babli and Yerushalmi, and the Midrashic Literature.* 2 vols. New York/Berlin: Choreb, 1926 (orig., 1903).

Jellicoe, Sidney. *The Septuagint and Modern Study.* Oxford: Clarendon, 1968.

Jeremias, Joachim. "*polloi.*" *TWNT* VI, 536-45.

Jirku, Anton. "Zur magischen Bedeutung der Kleidung in Israel." *ZAW* 37 (1917-18) 109-25.

Josephus. *The Antiquities of the Jews.* Vol. X. Translated by Ralph Marcus. LCL, VI. London: William Heinemann, 1937.

________. *The Jewish War.* Translated by H. St. John Thackeray. LCL, II-III. Cambridge: Harvard University, 1956-57.

Kahana, Abraham. *Hassefārîm Haḥîṣônîm.* 2 vols. Tel Aviv: Masada, 1936-37.

Kalt, Edmund. *Das Buch Baruch.* HSAT VII, 3/4. Bonn: Peter Hanstein, 1932.

Kasser, Rodolphe. *Papyrus Bodmer XXII: Jérémie XL,3-LII,34; Lamentations; Epître de Jérémie; Baruch I,1-V,5; en sahidique.* Genève: Bibliotheca Bodmeriana, 1964.

Kautzsch, Emil, ed. *Die Apokryphen und Pseudepigraphen des Alten Testaments.* 2 vols. Tübingen: J. C. B. Mohr, 1900.

________, ed. *Gesenius' Hebrew Grammar.* 2nd Eng. ed., translated and revised in accord with the 28th German edition by A. E. Cowley. Oxford: Clarendon, 1960 (orig., 1910).

Kedar, Benjamin. "Bible, Ancient Versions: Latin." *Encyclopaedia Judaica* (1971) IV, cols. 856-58.

Keil, Carl F. *Lehrbuch der historisch-kritischen Einleitung in die kanonischen und apokryphischen Schriften des Alten Testaments.* 3rd ed. Frankfurt: Heyder u. Zimmer, 1873.

Kenyon, Frederic G. *Our Bible and the Ancient Manuscripts.* New York: Harper and Brothers, 1958.

Kittel, Gerhard. "*dokeō, doxa.*" *TWNT* II, 235-40, 245-58.

________, and Friedrich, G., eds. *Theologisches Wörterbuch zum Neuen Testament.* 10 vols. Stuttgart, 1932-78.

Kittel, Rudolf, ed. *Biblia Hebraica.* 3rd ed. Stuttgart: Privilegierte Württembergische Bibelanstalt, 1936 (9th rev. ed., 1954).

________. "Die Psalmen Salomos." *Die Apokryphen und Pseudepigraphen des Alten Testaments.* Vol. II. Edited by Emil Kautzsch. Tübingen: J. C. B. Mohr, 1900 (pp. 127-48).

Kneucker, J. J. *Das Buch Baruch: Geschichte und Kritik, Übersetzung und Erklärung auf Grund des wiederhergestellten hebräischen Urtextes.* Leipzig: F. A. Brockhaus, 1879.

Koehler, Ludwig, and Baumgartner, Walter. *Lexicon in Veteris Testamenti Libros.* 2nd ed. Leiden: E. J. Brill, 1958. (3rd ed.; Band 1, 1967; Band 2, 1974.)

König, Eduard. *Einleitung in das Alte Testament.* Bonn: Eduard Weber, 1893.

Kraft, C. F. *The Strophic Structure of Hebrew Poetry: as Illustrated in the First Book of the Psalter.* Chicago: University of Chicago, 1938.

Kraus, Hans-Joachim. *Psalmen 1.* BKAT 15/1. Wageningen/Niederlande: Neukirken Kreis Moers, 1960.

________. *Psalmen 2.* BKAT 15/2. Neukirchen: Neukirchener, 1961.

Kuhl, Curt. *Die Entstehung des Alten Testaments.* 2nd rev. ed. Sammlung Dalp, Band 26. Bern/München: Francke, 1960.

Kuhn, Karl G. *Konkordanz zu den Qumrantexten.* Göttingen: Vandenhoeck u. Ruprecht, 1960.

de Lagarde, Paul. *Libri Veteris Testamenti: Apocryphi Syriacae.* Leipzig: F. A. Brockhaus, 1861 (pp. 93-104).

________. *Le Targum de Job.* (*Hagiographa Chaldaicae Paulus de Lagarde edidit.*) Leipzig: B. G. Teubner, 1873.

Lagrange, Marie-Joseph. *Le Judaîsme avant Jésus-Christ.* Paris: J. Gabalda, 1931.

Lambert, W. G. *Babylonian Wisdom Literature.* Oxford: Clarendon, 1960.

Lefèvre, A. "Baruch." *Introduction à la Bible*. Vol. I. Edited by A. Robert and A. Feuillet. Tournai: Desclée, 1959 (pp. 733-39).

Levy, Jacob. *Neuhebräisches und Chaldäisches Wörterbuch über die Talmudim und Midraschim*. 4 vols. Leipzig: F. A. Brockhaus, 1876.

Liddell, H. G., and Scott, Robert. *A Greek-English Lexicon*. 9th ed., revised and augmented by Henry S. Jones. Oxford: Clarendon, 1940.

McKenzie, John L. "Baruch." *Dictionary of the Bible*. Milwaukee: Bruce Publishing, 1965 (pp. 81-82).

Mandelkern, Solomon. *Veteris Testamenti Concordantiae Hebraicae atque Chaldaicae*. 2 vols. Graz: Akademische Druck und Verlaganstalt, 1955.

Margolis, M. L. "The Greek Preverb and its Hebrew-Aramaic Equivalent." *AJSL* 26 (1909-10) 33-61.

________. "Complete Induction for the Identification of the Vocabulary in the Greek Versions of the Old Testament with its Semitic Equivalents. Its Necessity and the Means of Obtaining it." *JAOS* 30 (1910) 301-12.

Marshall, J. T. "Book of Baruch." *A Dictionary of the Bible*. Vol. I. Edited by James Hastings, et al. New York: Scribner's Sons, 1905 (pp. 251-54).

May, Herbert G. "(Introductory Notes to) Baruch." *The Oxford Annotated Apocrypha: The Apocrypha of the Old Testament, RSV*. Edited by Bruce M. Metzger. New York: Oxford University, 1965 (p. 198).

Mayer, Rudolf. *Einleitung in das Alte Testament*. München: Max Hueber, 1967.

Metzger, Bruce M. *An Introduction to the Apocrypha*. New York: Oxford University, 1957.

________, ed. *The Oxford Annotated Apocrypha: The Apocrypha of the Old Testament, RSV*. New York: Oxford University, 1965.

Meyer, Rudolf. "Das Qumranfragment 'Gebet des Nabonid.'" *TLZ* 85 (1960) cols. 831-34.

Milik, J. T. *Ten Years of Discovery in the Wilderness of Judea*. London: SCM, 1959.

Moore, George Foot. *Judaism in the First Centuries of the Christian Era*. 3 vols. Cambridge: Harvard University, 1927.

Mowinckel, Sigmund. "Note XXXVIII (Hebrew Metrics)." *The Psalms in Israel's Worship*. Vol. II. Translated from the Norwegian by D. R. Ap-Thomas. New York/Nashville: Abingdon, 1967 (pp. 261-66) (orig., 1962).

Nestle, Eberhard. "Septuagint." *A Dictionary of the Bible.* Vol. IV. Edited by James Hastings, et al. New York: Scribner's Sons, 1905 (pp. 437-54).

Nöldeke, Theodor. *Die alttestamentliche Literatur in einer Reihe von Aufsätzen dargestellt.* Leipzig: Quandt u. Händel, 1868.

________. *Compendious Syriac Grammar.* Translated from the 2nd rev. German edition by James A. Crichton. London: Williams and Norgate, 1904.

Oesterley, W. O. E. *The Books of the Apocrypha: Their Origin, Teaching and Contents.* New York/Chicago: Fleming H. Revell, 1914.

________. *The Jews and Judaism During the Greek Period.* London: SPCK, 1941.

________. *An Introduction to the Books of the Apocrypha.* London: SPCK, 1953.

Orlinsky, Harry N. "The Septuagint--its use in Textual Criticism." *BA* 9 (1946) 23-34.

Ottley, R. R. *A Handbook to the Septuagint.* London: Methuen, 1920.

Ovid. *Amores.* Translated and edited by Franco Munari. Firenze: La Nuova Italia, 1955.

Payne Smith, J. *A Compendious Syriac Dictionary.* Oxford: Clarendon, 1957.

Payne Smith, Robert, ed. *Thesaurus Syriacus.* Tomes I-IV. Oxford: Clarendon, 1879-97.

Penna, Angelo. *Baruch. La Sacra Bibbia* 11. Torino/Rome: Marietti Editori, 1952.

Pesch, Wilhelm. "Die Abhängigkeit des 11 Salomonischen Psalms vom letzten Kapital des Buches Baruch." *ZAW* 26 (1955) 251-63.

Pfeiffer, Robert H. *A History of New Testament Times: with an Introduction to the Apocrypha.* New York: Harper and Brothers, 1949.

________. "Edomitic Wisdom." *ZAW* 3 (1926) 13-25.

Philo Judaeus. *De Opificio Mundi.* Translated by F. H. Colson and G. H. Whitaker. LCL, I. London: William Heinemann, 1929.

________. *De Cherubim.* Translated by F. H. Colson and G. H. Whitaker. LCL, II. London: William Heinemann, 1929.

Philo Judaeus. *De Plantatione*. Translated by F. H. Colson and G. H. Whitaker. LCL, III. London: William Heinemann, 1930.

________. *De Migratione Abrahami*. Translated by F. H. Colson and G. H. Whitaker. LCL, IV. London: William Heinemann, 1932.

________. *De Aeternitate Mundi*. Translated by F. H. Colson. LCL, IX. Cambridge: Harvard University, 1941.

Plato. *Laws*. Translated by R. G. Bury. LCL, II. London: William Heinemann, 1926.

van der Ploeg, J. P. M., and van der Woude, A. S. *Le Targum de Job de la Grotte XI de Qumrân*. Leiden: E. J. Brill, 1971.

Plöger, Otto. "Baruchschriften." *RGG*. 3rd ed. (1957) cols. 900-03.

Polybius. *The Histories*. Vol. IV. Translated by W. R. Paton. LCL, II. London: William Heinemann, 1960.

Pope, Marvin H. *Job*. AB 15. 3rd ed. Garden City: Doubleday, 1973.

Procksch, Otto. "*hagios*." *TWNT* I, 87-97.

Rabin, Chaim. *The Zadokite Documents*. 2nd rev. ed. Oxford: Clarendon, 1958.

________. "The Translation Process and the Character of the Septuagint." *Textus* 6 (1968) 1-26.

Rahlfs, Alfred, ed. *Septuaginta*. 2 vols. 5th ed. Stuttgart: Privilegierte Württembergische Bibelanstalt, 1952.

Ratner, B. *Seder ʿolam Rabba: Die grosse Weltchronik*. Wilna: Buchdruckerei v. W-we und Gebr. Romm., 1897.

Reider, Joseph. "The Dead Sea Scrolls." *JQR* 41 (1950) 59-70.

Reusch, F. H. *Erklärung des Buches Baruch*. Freiburg: Herder, 1853.

Reuss, Eduard. *Die Geschichte der Heiligen Schriften Alten Testaments*. Braunschweig: C. A. Schwetschke u. Sohn, 1881.

________. *Das Alte Testament*, VI: *Religions und Moral-philosophie der Hebräer*. Braunschweig: C. A. Schwetschke und Sohn, 1894.

Rife, J. M. "The Mechanics of Translation Greek." *JBL* 52 (1933) 244-52.

Ringgren, Helmer. *Word and Wisdom: Studies in the Hypostatization of Divine Qualities and Functions in the Ancient Near East*. Lund: H. Ohlssons, 1947.

Roberts, B. J. *The Old Testament Text and Versions*. Cardiff: University of Wales, 1951.

Robins, H. T. "The Complexity of the Book of Baruch. *International Journal of the Apocrypha* 20 (Jan., 1910) 4-7.

Robinson, T. H. *The Poetry of the Old Testament*. London: Gerald Duckworth, 1960.

Rosenthal, Franz. "Sedaka, Charity." *HUCA* 23/1 (1952) 411-30.

Rost, Leonhard. *Einleitung in die alttestamentlichen Apokryphen und Pseudepigraphen einschliesslich der grossen Qumran-Handschriften*. Heidelberg: Quelle und Meyer, 1971.

Rothstein, Johann Wilhelm. "Das Buch Baruch." *Die Apokryphen und Pseudepigraphen des Alten Testaments*. Vol. I. Edited by Emil Kautzsch. Tübingen: J. C. B. Mohr, 1900 (pp. 213-25).

Russell, D. S. *The Jews from Alexander to Herod*. Oxford: Oxford University, 1967.

Ryle, Herbert E. *The Canon of the Old Testament*. London: Macmillan, 1892.

________, and James, Montague R. *Psalmoi Solomontos: Psalms of the Pharisees, Commonly called the Psalms of Solomon*. Cambridge: Cambridge University, 1891.

Sanders, J. A. *The Psalms Scroll of Qumrân Cave 11 (11QPs^{a})*. DJD IV. Oxford: Clarendon, 1965.

Sasse, Hermann. "*aiōn, aiōnios*." *TWNT* I, 197-209.

Schmitz, Otto, and Stählin, Gustav. "*parakaleō*." *TWNT* V, 771-98.

Schürer, Emil. *A History of the Jewish People in the Time of Jesus Christ*. Vol. II/iii. Translated by S. Taylor and Peter Christie. New York: Scribner's Sons, 1891.

________. "Apocrypha." *The New Schaff-Herzog Encyclopedia of Religious Knowledge* (1908) I, 212-25.

Segal, M. H. *A Grammar of Mishnaic Hebrew*. Oxford: Clarendon, 1958.

Sellin, Ernst. *Introduction to the Old Testament*. Translated by W. Montgomery. New York: George H. Doran, 1923.

Simpson, D. C. "Tobit." *APOT* I, 625-52.

Smend, Rudolf. *Das hebräische Fragment der Weisheit des Jesus Sirach*. Berlin: Weidmanns, 1897.

________. *Die Weisheit des Jesus Sirach, hebräisch und deutsch*. Berlin: G. Reimer, 1906.

Smend, Rudolf. *Griechisch-syrisch-hebräischer Index zur Weisheit des Jesus Sirach.* Berlin: Georg Reimer, 1907.

Smith, H. Preserved. *The Books of Samuel.* ICC, VIII. New York: Scribner's Sons, 1909.

von Soden, Wolfram. *Akkadisches Handwörterbuch* 11. Wiesbaden: Otto Harrassowitz, 1972.

Speiser, Ephraim A. *Genesis.* AB 1. Garden City: Doubleday, 1964.

Steuernagel, Carl. *Lehrbuch der Einleitung in das Alte Testament mit einem Anhang über die Apokryphen und Pseudepigraphen.* Tübingen: J. C. B. Mohr, 1912.

Stoderl, Wenzel. *Zur Echtheitsfrage von Baruch 1-3,8.* Münster: Aschendorff, 1922.

Stone, Michael E. "Book of Baruch." *Encyclopaedia Judaica* (1971) IV, cols. 272-73.

________. "Bible, Ancient Versions: Armenian." *Encyclopaedia Judaica* (1971) IV, cols. 861-62.

Strabo. *Geography.* Vol. VIII. Translated by H. L. Jones. LCL, IV. London: William Heinemann, 1927.

Strack, Hermann L. *Die Sprüche Jesus', des Sohnes Sirachs: Der jüngst gefundene hebräische Text.* Leipzig: A. Deichert, 1903.

________. *Einleitung in das Alte Testament einschliesslich Apokryphen und Pseudepigraphen mit eingehender Angabe der Literatur.* 4th ed., entirely revised. München: C. H. Beck, 1895.

Swete, Henry Barclay. *The Old Testament in Greek: According to the Septuagint.* 4th ed. Cambridge: Cambridge University, 1909-12.

________. *An Introduction to the Old Testament in Greek.* 2nd ed. revised by R. R. Ottley. Cambridge: Cambridge University, 1914.

Tedesche, Sidney S. "Book of Baruch." *IDB* (1962) I, 362-63.

Thackeray, H. St. John. "The Greek translators of Jeremiah." *JTS* 4 (1902) 245-66.

________. "The Greek Translators of the Prophetical Books." *JTS* 4 (1902-03) 578-85.

________. "The Renderings of the Infinitive Absolute in the Septuagint." *JTS* 9 (1907-08) 597-601.

________. "The Poetry of the Greek Book of Proverbs." *JTS* 13 (1912) 46-66.

Thackeray, H. St. John. *A Grammar of the Old Testament in Greek According to the Septuagint.* Vol. I (of an incomplete series). Cambridge: Cambridge University, 1909.

________. *The Septuagint and Jewish Worship.* 2nd ed. Schweich Lectures, 1920. London: British Academy, 1923.

________. *Some Aspects of the Greek Old Testament.* London: George and Allen and Unwin, 1927.

________. "Baruch." *A New Commentary on Holy Scripture.* Edited by Charles Gore, H. L. Goudge, and Alfred Guillaume. New York: Macmillan, 1929 (pp. 102-11).

The Holy Bible, Revised Standard Version: The Apocrypha. New York: Thomas Nelson and Sons, 1952.

The New English Bible: The Apocrypha. New York: Oxford University, 1970.

Theophrastus. *De Causis Plantarum. Theophrasti Opera.* Edited by Frederik Wimmer. Paris: Didot Libraire, 1931.

Thucydides. *History of the Peloponnesian War.* Vol. III. Translated by Charles F. Smith. LCL, II. London: William Heinemann, 1920.

Torrey, C. C. *The Apocryphal Literature.* New Haven: Yale University, 1945.

Ṭov, Emanuel. *The Book of Baruch.* Missoula: Scholars, 1975.

________. "Septuagint." *IDB*, Supplementary Volume. Edited by Keith Crim, et al. Nashville: Abingdon, 1976 (pp. 807-11).

Toy, Crawford H. "Book of Baruch." *The Jewish Encyclopedia* (1902) II, pp. 556-57.

Vatke, Wilhelm. *Historisch-kritische Einleitung in das Alte Testament.* Bonn: Emil Strauss, 1886.

Vattioni, Francesco. *Ecclesiastico: Testo ebraico con apparato critico e versioni greca, latina e siriaca.* Naples: Istituto Orientale di Napoli, 1968.

de Vaux, Roland. "Téman, ville ou région d'Edom." *RB* 76 (1969) 379-85.

Vincent, Albert. *Les Manuscrits Hébreux du Désert de Juda.* Paris: Arthéme Fayard, 1955.

Walters, Peter. *The Text of the Septuagint: Its Corruptions and their Emendation.* Edited by D. W. Gooding. Cambridge: Cambridge University, 1973.

Wambacq, B. N. *Jeremias, Klaagliederen, Baruch, Brief van Jeremias.* (*De Boeken Van Het Oude Testament.*) Roermond en Maaseik: J. J. Romen und Zonen, 1957.

Wambacq, B. N. "L'unité littéraire de Baruch 1,1-3,8." *Sacra Pagina Bibliotheca Ephemeridum Theologicarum Lovaniensium* XII (1959) 455-60.

________. "Les prières de Baruch (1,15-2,19) et de Daniel (9,5-19)." *Biblica* 40 (1959) 463-75.

________. "L'unité du livre de Baruch." *Biblica* 47 (1966) 574-76.

Weber, Robert, ed. *Biblia Sacra: Iuxta Vulgatam Versionem.* Tomes I, II. Stuttgart: Württembergische Bibelanstalt, 1969.

Weiser, Artur. *The Old Testament: Its Formation and Development.* Translated from the 5th rev. German edition by Herbert Hartwell. New York: Association, 1966.

Westermann, Claus. *Das Buch Jesaja.* ATD 19. Göttingen: Vandenhoeck u. Ruprecht, 1966.

de Wette, Wilhelm M. L. *Lehrbuch der Historisch-kritischen Einleitung in die Bibel Alten und Neuen Testaments.* Berlin: Georg Reimer, 1869.

Wevers, J. W. "Evidence of the Text of the John H. Scheide Papyri for the Translation of the *Status Constructus* in Ezekiel." *JBL* 70 (1951) 211-16.

Whitehouse, O. C. "1 Baruch." *APOT* I, 569-95.

Williams, Ronald J. *Hebrew Syntax: An Outline.* Toronto: University of Toronto, 1967.

Wright, William. *A Short History of Syriac Literature.* London: Adam and Charles Black, 1894.

Würthwein, Ernst. *The Text of the Old Testament.* Translated by Peter R. Ackroyd. Oxford: Basil Blackwell, 1957.

Yadin, Yigael. *The Scroll of the War of the Sons of Light Against the Sons of Darkness.* Translated by Batya and Chaim Rabin. London: Oxford University, 1962.

________. *The Ben Sira Scroll from Masada.* Jerusalem: Israel Exploration Society, 1965.

Zeitlin, Solomon. "Jewish Apocryphal Literature." *JQR* 40 (1950) 223-56.

Ziegler, Joseph, ed. *Septuaginta, Vetus Testamentum Graecum auctoritate Societatis Litterarum Gottingensis editum,* XV: *Ieremias, Baruch, Threni, Epistula Ieremiae.* Göttingen: Vandenhoeck u. Ruprecht, 1957.

Zöckler, Otto. *Die Apokryphen des Alten Testaments.* (*Kurzgefasstes Kommentar zu den Heiligen Schriften*, Series A, Abt. 9.) München: C. H. Beck, 1891.

INDEX OF AUTHORS

INDEX OF GREEK TERMS

ἀποστέλλω	apostellō	3:33
ἀποθνῄσκω	apothnēskō	4:1
ἀργύριον	argyrion	3:17, 18
ἀρεστός	arestos	4:4
ἁρπάζω	harpazō	4:26
ἀρχή	archē	3:26
ἄρχων	archōn	3:16
ἀστήρ	astēr	3:34
ἀσφαλῶς	asphalōs	5:7
αὐτός (αὐτή)	autos (autē)	3:15, 18, 19, 21, 23, 24, 27, 28, 29, 30, 31, 32, 33, 34, 36; 4:1, 10, 11, 13, 14, 15, 25, 28, 34; 5:6, 9
ἀφανίζω	aphanizō	3:19
βαδίζω	badizō	4:19, 5:7
βασιλεία	basileia	5:6
βίβλος	biblos	4:1
βοάω	boaō	4:21, 27
βοηθέω	boētheō	4:17
γάρ	gar	4:7, 9, 10, 11, 15, 18, 19, 22, 23, 27, 29, 33, 35; 5:3, 4, 6, 7, 9
γεννάω	gennaō	3:26
γῆ	gē	3:16, 20, 23, 32, 37; 5:7
γίγας	gigas	3:26
γί(γ)νομαι	gi(g)nomai	3:21, 26; 4:28
γινώσκω	ginōskō	3:9, 14, 20, 23, 31, 32; 4:13
γνωστός	gnōstos	4:4
δαιμόνιον	daimonion	4:7, 35
δέ	de	3:20, 23, 34; 4:1, 6, 8, 11, 17, 20, 23; 5:6, 8
δέησις	deēsis	4:20
δείκνυμι	deiknymi	5:3
δεκαπλασιάζω	dekaplasiazō	4:28
δείλαιος	deilaios	4:31, 32
δέχομαι	dechomai	4:32
διά	dia	3:28; 4:6, 12
διαβαίνω	diabainō	3:30
διανοία	dianoia	4:28
δίδωμι	didōmi	3:27, 36; 4:3

δικαιοσύνη	dikaiosynē	4:13; 5:2, 4, 9
δικαίωμα	dikaiōma	4:13
διοδεύω	diodeuō	4:2
διότι	dioti	4:12
διπλοῖς	diploïs	5:12
δόξα	doxa	4:3, 24, 37; 5:1, 2, 4, 6, 7, 9
δουλεύω	douleuō	4:32
δρυμός	drymos	5:8
δύναμαι	dynamai	4:17
δυναστεία	dynasteia	4:21
δυσμή	dysmē	4:37, 5:5
ἑαυτῆς	heautēs	4:33
ἐγκαταλείπω	egkataleipō	3:12
ἐγώ (μου, μοι)	egō (mou, moi)	4:5, 10, 12, 14, 17, 19, 20, 22, 23, 25
ἔθνος	ethnos	3:16; 4:3, 6, 15
εἰ	ei	3:13
εἶδον	eidon	3:20, 32; 4:9, 10, 36; 5:5
εἰμί	eimi	3:14, 16, 17, 18, 31; 4:4, 27, 34
εἶπον	eipon	3:34, 4:9
εἰρήνη	eirēnē	3:13, 14; 4:20; 5:4
εἰς	eis	3:12, 13, 15, 19, 29, 32; 4:1, 6, 23, 28, 34, 35; 5:1, 4, 7
εἰσάγω	eisagō	5:6
εἰσέρχομαι	eiserchomai	3:15
ἐκ	ek	3:29; 4:12, 18, 21
ἐκδύω	ekdyō	4:20, 5:1
ἐκεῖ	ekei	3:26
ἐκζητέω	ekzēteō	3:23
ἐκκλίνω	ekklinō	4:12
ἐκλέγομαι	eklegomai	3:27
ἐκλεκτός	eklektos	3:30
ἐκπέμπω	ekpempō	4:23
ἐκτρέφω	ektrephō	4:8
ἐλεέω	eleeō	4:15
ἐλεημοσύνη	eleēmosynē	4:22, 5:9
ἐλπίζω	elpizō	4:22
ἐμπαίζω	empaizō	3:17

ἐμπίπλημι	empiplēmi	3:32
ἐμπορεύομαι	emporeuomai	3:23
ἐν	en	3:13, 17, 22, 34, 37; 4:13, 20, 25
ενδύω	endyō	4:20, 5:1
ἐνθυμεόμαι	enthymeomai	3:31
ἐντολή	entolē	3:9, 4:13
ἐνωτίζομαι	enotizomai	3:9
ἐξαιρέω	exaireō	4:18, 21
ἐξαποστέλλω	exapostellō	4:11, 37
ἐξέρχομαι	exerchomai	5:6
ἐξεύρεσις	exeuresis	3:18
ἐξευρίσκω	exeuriskō	3:32, 36
ἐπάγω	epagō	4:9, 10, 14, 15, 18, 27, 29
ἐπέρχομαι	eperchomai	4:9, 24, 25, 35
ἐπί	epi	3:16, 20, 23, 37; 4:15, 22, 25, 33; 5:2, 5
ἐπιβαίνω	epibainō	4:13, 25
ἐπιλανθάνω	epilanthanō	4:8
ἐπιμῆκος	epimēkos	3:24
ἐπίσταμαι	epistamai	3:26
ἐπιστήμη	epistēmē	3:20, 27, 36
ἐπιστρέφω	epistrephō	4:2, 28
ἐπιτίθημι	epitithēmi	5:2
ἐπιχαίρω	epichairō	4:12, 31
ἔργον	ergon	3:18
ἐρημία	erēmia	4:33
ἐρῆμος	erēmos	4:19
ἐρημόω	erēmoō	4:12, 16
ἔρχομαι	erchomai	4:14, 22, 36, 37
ἕτερος	heteros	3:35, 4:3
εὐμεγέθης	eumegethēs	3:26
εὐπρέπεια	euprepeia	5:1
εὑρίσκω	heuriskō	3:15, 30
εὐφραίνω	euphrainō	3:34, 4:33
εὐφροσύνη	euphrosynē	3:34; 4:11, 23, 29, 36; 5:9
εὐωδία	euōdia	5:8
ἐχθρός	echthros	4:18, 21, 25, 26; 5:6
ἔχω	echō	3:25, 28

καταβαίνω	katabainō	3:12, 19
καταβιβάζω	katabibazō	3:29
καταδιώκω	katadiōko	4:25
καταλείπω	kataleipō	4:1, 12, 19
κατασκευάζω	kataskeuazō	3:32
κατέναντι	katenanti	4:2
κατοικέω	katoikeō	3:13, 20; 4:35
κεφαλή	kephalē	5:2
κλαυθμός	klauthmos	4:11, 23
κράζω	krazō	4:20
κρατέω	krateō	4:1
κτάομαι	ktaomai	3:17, 24
κτῆνος	ktēnos	3:32
κυριεύω	kyrieuō	3:16
λαμβάνω	lambanō	3:29
λαμπρότης	lamprotēs	4:24, 5:3
λάμψις	lampsis	4:2
λάμπω	lampō	3:34
λαός	laos	4:5
λογίζομαι	logizomai	3:35
λυπέω	lypeō	4:8, 33
μακάριος	makarios	4:4
μακροβίωσις	makrobiōsis	3:14
μακρόθεν	makrothen	4:15
μακροθυμέω	makrothymeō	4:25
μακρός	makros	4:35
μανθάνω	manthanō	3:14
μεγᾶς	megas	3:24, 25; 4:9, 24
μεριμνάω	merimnaō	3:18
Μερραν	Merran (GN)	3:23
μετά	meta	3:34, 37; 4:11, 23, 24, 29; 5:6, 9
μή	mē	3:28, 4:3
μηδείς	mēdeis	4:12
μιμνήσκομαι	mimnēskomai	3:23, 4:14
μίτρα	mitra	5:2
μνεία	mneia	4:27, 5:5
μνημόσυνον	mnēmosynon	4:5
μόνος	monos	4:16

πείθω	peithō	3:17
πένθος	penthos	4:9, 11, 23, 34; 5:1
πέραν	peran	3:30
περιαιρέω	periaireō	4:34
περιβάλλω	periballō	5:2
περιβλέπω	periblepō	4:36, 5:5
πηγή	pēgē	3:12
πιπράσκω	pipraskō	4:6
πλανάω	planaō	4:28
πληρόω	plēroō	5:7
ποιέω	poieo	3:34, 4:7
ποίμνιον	poimnion	4:26
πόλεμος	polemos	3:26
πόλις	polis	4:32
πολυοχλία	polyochlia	4:34
πολύς	polys	4:12, 35
πορεύομαι	poreuomai	3:13, 33; 4:13, 26
πόῤῥω	porrhō	3:21
ποῦ	pou	3:14, 16
πρεσβύτης	presbytēs	4:15
πρός	pros	3:35; 4:2, 20, 21, 27, 36; 5:5, 6
πρόσταγμα	prostagma	4:1, 5:8
πτῶμα	ptōma	4:33
πτῶσις	ptōsis	4:31, 33
πῦρ	pyr	4:35
ῥῆμα	rhēma	4:37, 5:5
σακκος	sakkos	4:20
Σιών	Siōn (GN)	4:9, 14, 24
σκιάζω	skiazō	5:8
σός (σή, σόν)	sos (sē, son)	4:3, 31, 33; 5:3
σοφία	sophia	3:12
στολή	stolē	4:20, 5:1
σύ	sy	
(σοῦ)	(sou)	4:32, 33, 37; 5:1, 2, 4, 5, 6
(σοί)	(soi)	4:36
(σέ)	(se)	4:25, 30, 31; 5:6
συμμιαίνω	symmiainō	3:11
συμφέρω	sympherō	4:3

φρόνησις	phronēsis	3:9, 14, 28
φυλακή	phylakē	3:34
φῶς	phōs	3:14, 20, 33; 4:2; 5:9
χαίρω	chairō	4:33, 37; 5:5
χαναaν	Canaan (GN)	3:22
χαρά	chara	4:22
χαρμόσυνος	charmosynos	4:23
χείρ	cheir	4:18, 21
χήρα	chēra	4:12, 16
χρόνος	chronos	3:13, 32; 4:35
χρυσίον	chrysion	3:17, 30
ὥς	hōs	3:24, 4:26, 5:6
ὥσπερ	hōsper	4:24, 28, 33

INDEX OF HEBREW TERMS

בֶּגֶד	beged	4:20; 5:1
בְּהֵמָה	b^{e}hēmāh	3:32n
בּוֹא	bô'	3:15; 4:9, 10, 14, 22, 24, 25, 27, 29, 35, 37; 5:6
בּוֹר	bôr	3:12n
בָּחַר	bāḥar	3:27, 30
בָּטַח	bāṭaḥ	3:17, 4:22
בֶּטַח	beṭaḥ	5:7
בִּין	bîn	3:21, 31
בִּינָה	bînāh	3:9, 14, 20, 23, 27, 36
בַּיִת	bayit	3:24
בְּכִי	b^{e}kî	4:11, 23
בָּלָה	bālāh	3:10
בְּלִי	b^{e}lî	3:28
בַּלְעַד	bal'ad	3:35
בֵּן	bēn	3:21, 23; 4:10, 12, 14, 19, 21, 25, 27, 32, 37; 5:5
בָּקַשׁ	bāqaš	3:23, 4:28
בֹּשֶׂם	bōśem	5:8n
בַּת	bat	4:10, 14, 16
גָּבֹהַּ	gābō^{a}h	3:25; 5:5, 7
גְּבוּרָה	g^{e}bûrāh	3:14
גִּבְעָה	gib'āh	5:7
גָּדוֹל	gādôl	3:24, 25; 4:9, 24
גָּדַל	gādal	4:11
גּוֹי	gôy	4:3, 6, 15
גָּזַל	gāzal	4:26
גַּיא	gay'	5:7
גִּיל	gîl	4:33
דָּאַג	dā'ag	3:18
דָּבָר	dābār	4:37; 5:5, 8
דַּעַת	da'at	3:28
דָּרַךְ	dārak	4:13, 25
דֶּרֶךְ	derek	3:13, 20, 21, 23, 27, 31, 36; 4:13, 26
דָּרַשׁ	dāraš	3:22
הָגָר	Hagar (PN)	3:23
הָדָר	hādār	4:24; 5:3
הוּא	hû'	3:25, 31, 32, 35, 36; 4:18

טוֹבָה	ṭôbāh	4:3
טָמֵא	ṭāmē'	3:10
יַד	yad	3:25; 4:18, 21, 26; 5:6
יָדִיד	yādîd	3:36, 4:16
יָדַע	yāda'	3:9, 14, 20, 23, 31, 32; 4:4, 13
יהוה	YHWH (PN)	4:10, 14, 20, 22, 24, 36; 5:2
יוֹם	yôm	3:14; 4:20, 35
יַחַד	yaḥad	3:14
יְחִידָה	y^{e}ḥîdāh	4:16
יָכֹל	yākol	4:17
יָלַד	yālad	3:26, 4:8
יָם	yām	3:30
יַעֲקֹב	ya'^{a}kōb	3:36, 4:2
יַעַן	ya'an	4:6, 12
יַעַר	ya'ar	5:8
יָצָא	yāṣā'	5:6
יָרֵא	yārē'	4:5, 21, 27, 30
יִרְאָה	yir'āh	5:4
יָרַד	yārad	3:12, 19
יְרוּשָׁלַיִם	y^{e}rûšālayim (GN)	4:8, 30, 36; 5:1, 5
יִשְׂרָאֵל	yiśrā'ēl (PN)	3:9, 10, 24, 36; 4:4, 5; 5:7, 8, 9
יָשַׁב	yāšab	3:13, 20, 35
יָשַׁע	yāša'	4:22
יְשׁוּעָה	y^{e}šû'āh	4:22, 24, 29
יָשָׁר	yāšār	4:4n
יִתְרוֹן	yitrôn	4:3n
כָּבוֹד	kābôd	4:3, 24, 37; 5:1, 2, 4, 6, 7, 9
כּוֹכָב	kôkāb	3:34
כּוּן	kûn	3:32
כִּי	kî	3:10; 4:4, 6, 7, 9, 10, 11, 15, 18, 19, 23, 27, 29, 33, 35; 5:3, 6, 7, 9
כֹּל	kōl	3:31, 32, 36; 4:1; 5:3, 7, 8
כֵּן	kēn	4:24, 28, 33
כְּנַעַן	k^{e}na'an (GN)	3:22
כִּסֵּא	kissē'	5:6
כֶּסֶף	kesep	3:17, 18
כַּעַס	ka'as	4:6
כָּשַׁל	kāšal	4:33

נֹגַהּ	nōgah	4:2
נָהַג	nāhag	5:6
נָחַם	nāḥam	4:30
נָכְרִי	nokrî	4:3
נָכְרִיָּה	nokriyyāh	3:10
נַעַר	na'ar	4:15
נָפַל	nāpal	4:31, 33
נָפִיל	nāpîl	3:26
נֶצַח	neṣaḥ	4:35
נָצַל	nāṣal	4:18, 21
נָשָׂא	nāśā'	4:15, 25, 26, 36; 5:5, 6, 7
נְתִיבָה	n^e^tîbāh	3:21, 23, 31; 4:13
נָתַן	nātan	3:27, 36; 4:3
סָבִיב	sābîb	4:36, 5:5
סָגַר	sāgar	4:6
סָכַךְ	sākak	5:8
סֵפֶר	sēper	4:1
סוּר	sûr	3:21; 4:12, 34
עָבַד	'ābad	4:32
עֶבֶד	'ebed	3:36
עָבַר	'ābar	3:30
עֵבֶר	'ēber	3:30
עַד	'ad	3:13, 32; 5:5
עֵדֶר	'ēder	4:26
עוֹד	'ôd	3:35n
עוֹלָם	'ôlām	3:13, 26, 32; 4:1, 8, 23, 29; 5:1, 4, 7
עַז	'az	4:15
עָזַב	'āzab	3:12; 4:1, 12
עָזַר	'āzar	4:17
עָטָה	'āṭāh	5:2
עַיִן	'ayin	3:14; 4:4, 36; 5:5
עִיר	'îr	4:32
עַל	'al	3:20, 32, 37; 4:9, 10, 12, 14, 15, 18, 22, 25, 27, 29, 33, 35; 5:2, 8
עָלָה	'ālāh	3:29
עָם	'ām	3:16; 4:5
עִם	'im	3:12; 4:22, 28; 5:6
עָמַד	'āmad	4:1, 5:5

רָדָה	rādāh	3:16
רָדַף	rādap	4:25
רָחָב	rāḥāb	3:25n
רָחוֹק	rāḥôq	4:15
רָחַק	rāḥaq	3:21
רֵיחַ	rê^{a}ḥ	5:8
רָכַל	rākal	3:23
רָם (רום)	rām	3:24
רָנַן	rānan	3:34
רְעָדָה	r^{e}ʿādāh	3:33
רָעָה	rāʿāh	4:18, 27, 29
שָׂחַק	śāḥaq	3:17
שִׂים	śîm	5:2
שִׂישׂ	śîś	3:34n
שֶׂכֶל	śekel	3:23n
שָׂמַח	śāmaḥ	3:34; 4:12, 31, 33, 37; 5:5
שִׂמְחָה	śimḥāh	4:22, 23, 29, 36; 5:9
שָׂעִיר	śāʿîr	4:35
שָׂפָה	śāpāh	4:15
שַׂק	śaq	4:20
שָׂשׂוֹן	śāśôn	3:34; 4:11, 23
שְׁאוֹל	š^{e}ʾôl	3:12, 19
שָׁאַר	šāʾar	4:19
שְׁבִי	š^{e}bî	4:10, 14, 24
שֵׁד	šēd	4:7
שׁוּב	šûb	4:2, 23, 28
שׁוֹד	šôd	4:31, 32
שָׁחַר	šāḥar	3:23
שָׁכַח	šākaḥ	4:8
שָׁכֵן	šākēn	4:9, 14, 24
שָׁלַח	šālaḥ	3:33; 4:11, 23, 37
שָׁלוֹם	šālôm	3:13, 14; 4:20; 5:4
שָׁם	šām	3:26
שֵׁם	šēm	3:26; 4:30; 5:4
שָׁמַד	šāmad	4:6
שַׁמָּה	šammāh	4:19n
שָׁמַיִם	šāmayim	3:17, 29; 5:3
שָׁמַם	šāmam	4:12

INDEX OF SYRIAC TERMS

ܚܟܡܬܐ	ḥekm^{e}tā'	3:12
ܚܫܒ	ḥ^{e}šab	3:11, 35
ܛܢܦ	ṭ^{e}nep	3:11
ܛܦܣ	ṭ^{e}pas	4:14
ܠܐ	lā'	3:35; 4:6, 12
ܠܒܪ	l^{e}bar	3:35
ܠܝܬ	layt	3:35
ܡܒܘܥܐ	mabbû'ā'	3:12
ܡܕܝܢܬܐ	m^{e}dînā'	4:32
ܡܕܢܚܝܐ	madn^{e}ḥāyā'	5:5
ܡܛܠ	m^{e}ṭul	3:10; 4:6, 12
ܡܝܬܐ	mîtā'	3:11
ܡܢ	man	4:18
ܡܢ	men	3:21, 35; 4:12, 18; 5:5
ܡܢܘ	mānaw	3:10
ܡܥܪܒܐ	ma'arbā'	5:5
ܡܪܕ	m^{e}rad	3:21
ܢܘܟܪܝܬܐ	nukr^{e}yātā'	3:11
ܢܚܬ	n^{e}ḥet	3:12
ܢܦܫܐ	napšā'	3:21
ܣܓܝܐܐ	saggî'ā'	4:12
ܥܒܕ	'^{a}bad	4:32
ܥܕܡܐ	'^{a}dammā'	5:5
ܥܠ	'al	4:18
ܥܡ	'am	3:11
ܥܡܐ	'ammā'	4:6, 12
ܥܡܘܪܐ	'āmûrā'	4:9, 14
ܦܪܩ	p^{e}raq	4:18
ܨܕܐ	ṣ^{e}dā'	4:12

INDEX OF SUBJECTS

Ab, ninth/tenth of, 22, 56
Acharnenses (Aristophanes), 124
Adversative *kî*, 153
Akkadian, 126, 261, 286
Akiba, Rabbi, 9
Alexandrinus, Codex (G^A), 9, 15, 16, 17, 79, 84, 92, 97, 121, 140, 144, 167, 173, 184, 186, 193, 208, 220, 237, 252, 260, 270, 271, 276, 281, 283, 290, 294, 295, 297, 308, 309
Almsgiving, 203, 204, 279
Ambrosianus, Codex (Syriac), 11
Amores (Ovid), 296
Angelology, 33, 35, 36
Apocalyptic, 35, 190
Apocalypse of Abraham, 274
Apocrypha, 8, 9, 13, 33, 35, 37, 101, 121, 165, 203, 281, 293
Apostolic Constitutions, 56
Aquila, 12
Arabia, 55
Arabic Version (of Baruch), 16, 17, 84, 92, 110, 130, 131, 159, 168, 173, 209, 220, 270, 285, 297
Aramaic, 53, 54, 108, 122, 260
Armenian Version (of Baruch), 16, 17, 84, 91, 168, 186, 209, 249, 285, 293
Asa, 276
Assi, Rabbi, 279
Assyria, 250
Athanasius of Antioch, 11, 62

Baasha, 276
Babylon, 3, 17, 18, 20, 30, 45, 46, 47, 168, 215, 218, 236, 238, 284, 290
Babylonian Talmud, 9, 46, 130, 270, 279
Barberianus, Codex, 10
Baruch, Book of
--authorship, 17, 18, 19, 20, 21, 22, 26, 50, 53, 63
--canonicity, 23, 31
--Consolation Poem (third section), 3, 5, 6, 19, 22, 23, 24, 30, 33, 41, 53, 57, 60, 63, 135-50, 319f.
--content, 6
--date of composition, 21, 26, 28, 29
--derivative character, 18, 21, 22, 30, 38, 222, 254

Baruch, Book of
--form, 4, 6
--genre, 6, 22, 29
--Hebraisms, 24, 38, 39, 187, 193, 199, 251, 252, 299ff., 305, 307, 320
--Hebrew original, 5, 7, 8, 12, 13, 23-26, 36-39, 44, 52, 53, 54, 56, 57, 63, 106, 108, 117, 122, 133, 152, 161f., 172, 187, 191f., 194f., 200, 207, 210, 214-18, 220-22, 226, 228, 230, 233-35, 237-39, 243, 246, 248f., 255, 259, 273, 299ff., 304, 306, 308f., 320, 321, 323
--Hebrew syntactic features, 7, 38, 155, 156, 220, 263, 299, 300, 320
----asyndeton, 256, 302
----ballast variant, 311, 313, 314
----canonical sequence of pairs, 39, 111, 229, 310ff.
----conjunctive fixed pairs, 38, 39, 229, 249, 303, 310ff., 323
----ellipsis, 313
--historical inaccuracies, 20, 21, 29
--Introduction (1:1-14), 1, 6, 22, 23, 32, 55, 58, 63
--literary problems, 18, 20, 21, 22, 29
--liturgical character, 25, 55, 56
--loss of original Hebrew text, 7
--metre, metrics, 5, 39, 106, 109, 170, 177, 188, 220, 236, 315, 316-20, 321, 324
--Palestinian provenance, 25, 55, 63
--poetic features, 7, 24, 38, 39
----parallelism, 24, 38, 39, 97, 111, 167, 177, 278, 311-15, 323
----repetition, 39, 315f.
----rhyme, 167, 320
--Prayer of Confession, 1, 2, 4, 6, 21, 29, 32, 41, 51, 52, 53, 61, 63
--prose section (first section), 6, 7, 19, 22, 24, 29, 31, 33, 57, 63
--pseudepigraphic character, 18ff., 32
--purpose, 3